Human Sexuality and Social Work

❦ ❦ ❦

Human Sexuality

and

Social Work

EDITED BY

Harvey L. Gochros and LeRoy G. Schultz

Foreword by LEONTINE R. YOUNG
Epilogue by VIRGINIA M. SATIR

ASSOCIATION PRESS / NEW YORK

to

JEAN, RUTH, SUZY, and two DAVIDS

Contents

Wayne Donald Duehn, Ph.D., is Associate Professor, Graduate School of Social Work, University of Texas at Arlington, Arlington, Texas.

This chapter was prepared especially for this book and reports a study conducted at the Reproductive Biology Research Foundation, St. Louis, Missouri. The authors wish to acknowledge with appreciation the cooperation and help of Dr. William H. Masters and Mrs. Virginia E. Johnson of the Foundation. The help of Mr. Ghassan M. Rubeiz in preparation of this report is gratefully acknowledged.

Dr. Ellis is the Executive Director of the Institute for Advanced Study in Rational Psychotherapy, New York. The article is reprinted by permission of the journal and the author from *Psychological Reports* 8 (1961): 333–38.

Pamela Lee Lowry is Coordinator of the Pregnancy Counseling Service, Incorporated, Boston, Massachusetts, and a graduate of Wellesley College. She has extensive experience in family planning both in America and in Great Britain.

Joan E. Blank is a public health educator.

Miriam I. Weisberg is a caseworker at the Family Service Association, Cleveland, Ohio. Her article originally appeared in *Social Casework*, Vol. 51, No. 6, (June 1970). It is reprinted by permission of the author and the journal.

Irvin D. Yalom, M.D., is with the Henry Phipps Psychiatric Clinic, The Johns Hopkins Hospital, Baltimore, Maryland. The article is

❦ ❦ ❦

Foreword

Leontine R. Young

Among the plethora of revolutions sparked by our astonishing era of change, the sexual revolution ranks high in its impact upon individuals and families. Social workers necessarily involved in the many concerns of people under a wide variation of circumstances must consider not only that impact upon the people they serve, but also their own attitudes and values which create their own impact.

In a practice- and action-oriented field, that cannot be an academic matter. It requires, in the first place, new examination of goals and values that were previously taken for granted or, at least, were overtly unquestioned. Thus, work with a homosexual had usually as its stated objective a heterosexual adjustment for the individual. While there might be questioning of ways and means of accomplishing such an adjustment, the objective itself was pretty much taken for granted. Counseling with adolescents on sexual behavior concentrated upon the objective of postponing sexual experience until after marriage, however unrealistic that may in reality have been for many young people. Again, the emphasis was upon understanding of the personal behavior within the context of that moral standard and its prohibitions. Objectives for unmarried mothers, while in part pragmatic, still operated within that context of morality. The objective of preventing future illegitimate births was often inextricable from discouragement of further sexual experience until after marriage. I am not here discussing the validity or otherwise of those standards, but the fact that they determined objectives and for the most part unquestioned objectives.

This assumption of objectives has now become impossible. Greater sexual freedom combined with growing knowledge of contraception and its readier accessibility have called into question almost all our former objectives and by the very fact of that questioning have weakened the imperative of the standards which determined them. Research in human sexuality has added another dimension—that of scientific investigation and open discussion. The new knowledge combined with the rupture of secrecy has added tremendous impetus to the questioning and has brought into the open contradictions as well as hypocrisies that were formerly ignored if not negated. Legalized abortion has brought into focus another aspect of moral conflict which formerly could be shunted aside or, at least, confined within certain prescribed limits.

The initial result of so great a change has been predictably confusion and conflict. For social workers this raises complex and difficult, as well as immediate, demands. It is not enough to evaluate old objectives in new perspectives. The requirement is to determine what objectives are consonant with the needs of people, what directions are productive of feasible alternatives, what standards and values are enduring. By the nature and responsibility of their work, social workers must make some decisions, and these will inevitably reflect value judgments as well as pragmatic demands. Do we offer contraceptive information to adolescents? If we postulate sexual fulfillment as a positive goal, what help do we give people with the realities of future conflict, of responsibilities accepted or denied? How do we help parents find a direction and a philosophy that may enable them to understand the needs of their children without abandoning all guideposts from the past? What is our responsibility for sex education, particularly among children and youth? The questions are many, and the answers problematic.

While social workers have no greater and no lesser responsibility than that demanded by the needs of their work, this is sufficiently encompassing and confusing. As people, they are subject to the same concerns, conflicts, and contradictions that are the common lot of everyone in this changing time, and they have the same need to clarify their own convictions and philosophy. As professionals, they have an obligation to examine their convictions and philosophy in the context of the philosophies, the needs, and the directions, both of the people they serve and of the community's social requirements. Certainly a first step is open and serious consideration of the questions, their implications, and imperatives for action. This book is addressed to that consideration.

Preface

IN 1948 DR. ALFRED C. KINSEY in his historic *Sexual Behavior in the Human Male* stated, "[S]ocial workers are involved with sexual problems even more often than physicians."[1] In 1970 Dr. William H. Masters of the Reproductive Biology Research Foundation estimated that 75 percent of all sexual problems are treated by four professions other than medicine, one being social work.[2] Yet, in the 22-year interval between these statements by two authorities on human sexuality, very little of the social work literature has reflected a concern for sexual problems. Our main purpose in compiling this anthology of original and reprinted articles is to make available a set of readings that cut through the relative silence surrounding explicit sexual problems as they relate to social work practice. Social workers have too long been intimidated by sexuality. They have deferred to other professions, (hopefully more prepared than they); they have needlessly complicated sexual problems encountered by their clients by applying outmoded practice theory and often by supporting antisexual policies.

This book is prepared at a time of accelerating social change in sexual attitudes and behavior. It is our opinion that these changes will require a more aggressive role in dealing with their consequences, both intended and unanticipated. America has erected facades to hide sexuality or covered sexual realities with facades that make sexuality *seem* more humane. These facades should be dismantled or the hollowness of the facade will be demonstrated as more stress is applied. Such stress is all about us. The hypocrisies, shams, deceits, and sex role-playing charades of our asexual sexuality are being exposed by a substantial number of American youth who are refusing to have the millstone of yesterday's sexual "hangups" hung around their necks. There is a marked disregard for the artificial, plastic, and colorless sexuality of their parents. They do not share their parents' depressing "end-of-all options" mind set; instead they work toward overcoming sexual unauthenticity. Michele Clark, perhaps, expresses it best:

> Male and female, we are all recent emigrants from an arctic wilderness, a
> frigid and frightened ancestry. Parents, teachers, innumerable and un-

15

nameable adult forces told us the body was shameful dirt, a vessel of sin
and pollution . . . mustn't touch! We were small and weak and we believed them, just as they had been force-fed to believe their parents and
teachers. Now in some ways the chain is severed. . . . We learn to love
our bodies . . . or some of us do, some of the time. This freedom is hard-
won and not pervasive. It is the delicious domain of a lucky few who have
had the leisure to fight their myriad hang-ups and overcome some [the
leisured hippies, students, miscellaneous drop-outs, and the upper class
. . .]. The loving messy fleshy intimacy of whole persons, whole selves
is rarely spoken about or experienced. In this sense, while sexuality receives much public acclaim, little has changed. . . . While we are
obsessed with sex and bodies because we are just now discovering their
pleasures, we are also obsessed because there is almost nothing else we can
legally, privately enjoy. Genitals become the one wee cover of satisfaction
in a world of NO TRESPASSING signs.[3]

Our book is predicated upon the authors' values and beliefs. Some of
these values and beliefs are:

1. Sexuality is a legitimate and imperative area of concern to social
   workers and other helping professions.
2. Sexuality involves an interplay of social, behavioral, emotional, physical,
   and aesthetic factors.
3. Most sexual behavior, both functional and dysfunctional, is learned in
   social interaction.
4. Sexual fulfillment is the right of every person regardless of income,
   gender, or age, unless prohibited by publicly enforced laws.
5. There is a wide variety of functional sex life styles for both married
   and single persons.
6. Social workers and members of other helping professions have the
   responsibility to keep abreast of and contribute to the evolving knowledge and values regarding sexual behavior and the technologies for
   altering sexual dysfunction.
7. Social workers and members of other helping professions are responsible
   for assisting society in formulating a humane, rational sexual policy
   reflected in public laws.
8. Social workers and other helping professions are responsible for contributing to the development of a relevant, rational policy of sex education and information for all ages and for assistance in enabling others
   to make responsible, rewarding sexual decisions.
9. Social workers should be aware that a wide variety of sexual problems
   exist, some of which they may themselves have, and many of which will
   be presented to them, and that they will need more than personal
   experience or private opinions to help these clients.

This readings book hopefully reflects these values and is an outgrowth
of graduate courses on Human Sexuality and Social Work as well as on

Social Welfare Policy that we have been teaching at the graduate schools of social work at West Virginia University, Case Western Reserve University, and the University of Missouri, as well as at various schools of medicine and nursing. It is our hope that the book will have utility for other schools and universities teaching the problems and treatment of human sexuality in both graduate and undergraduate courses.

Because human sexuality is a broad and complex phenomenon touching on many aspects of life, we could not hope to cover all aspects, even those highly relevant to social work. Due to space limitations, we had to eliminate many important and relevant articles. Therefore, the selection of materials may appear unbalanced to some readers and perhaps our biases will be clearly evident. For example, social work practice regarding "family planning" is an area of sexuality adequately covered in recent social work literature (see Suggested Readings for Chapter 20); it was therefore not included in this book.

Each section of the book has an introduction that presents issues concerning social work in relation to Human Behavior and the Social Environment, Practice, and Social Policy—the traditional divisions in social work education—and each chapter is followed by the editors' Suggested Readings.

We owe a great deal to a number of people who have helped us in preparation of this book of readings: Dr. Leon Ginsberg, Director of the Division of Social Work, West Virginia University, whose academic leadership and administrative skill created an atmosphere conducive to this effort; Leontine Young for her Foreword, Virginia Satir for her Epilogue, and the others who contributed original articles; and Roland Burdick, Senior Editor, Association Press, who nurtured the book from conception through delivery. Finally, our thanks go to our secretaries for their patience and time: Miss Viola Smith, Mrs. Diana Stemple, Mrs. Darla Foster, and Mrs. Inge Wagner.

H. L. G.

L. G. S.

NOTES

[1] A. Kinsey, W. Pomeroy, and C. Martin, *Sexual Behavior in the Human Male* (Philadelphia: W. B. Saunders Company, 1948) p. 387.

[2] "Repairing the Conjugal Bed," *Time,* May 25, 1970, p. 49.

[3] M. Clark, *WIN,* January 1971, p. 2.

Sexual Behavior and Its Social and Psychological Determinants

Dr. Albert Kinsey was exceedingly careful in his selection of interviewers for his research projects regarding human sexuality. He selected each of the interviewers himself. On one occasion he rejected a psychologist who had wanted to be an interviewer with the comment, "You don't really want to do sex research." The psychologist was shocked and insisted that he did. "Well," said Dr. Kinsey, "look at your attitudes. You say masturbation is immature; premarital intercourse and extramarital intercourse, harmful to marriage; homosexuality, abnormal; and animal contacts, ludicrous. You already know all the answers, so why waste time on research?"[1] It is not at all uncommon for practitioners to approach sexual problems with similar views, based on their own biases and experiences, rather than operating on acquired findings of objective laboratory, clinical, and empirical explorations.

There still remains much that we do not know regarding sexuality. But significant data are beginning to emerge regarding the social and psychological determinants of sexual behavior.

In this section five articles are presented representing a range of observations concerning human sexuality and the factors that influence the sexual behavior of several diverse groups.

The first chapter, by Floyd M. Martinson, focuses on "The Sexual Knowledge of Values and Behavior Patterns of Adolescents." This chapter describes a group of American adolescents searching for help in their sexual decisions. Americans seem most concerned about the way their adolescents behave, but their guidance has been less than clear, consistent, and objective. Adolescents are, indeed, the postulants of society and their appropriate integration into society determines whether that group can survive.

A group that has often been depicted as one of the primary "failures" of that sexual assimilation is the unwed mothers—a group that is universally, to a greater or lesser extent, chastised by society. The second chapter, "Unwed Mothers and Their Sex Partners," by Hallowell Pope, provides information regarding women who become pregnant out of wedlock and are all too often depicted as cut of the same cloth while their sex partners are almost universally ignored.

"Understanding Sexuality in Another Culture—and in Our Own," by Beatrice S. Reiner, brings an international perspective to the discussion of sexuality, depicting a very different sexual pattern from our own and exploring how we can better perceive our own mores from the viewpoint of another social system.

The fourth chapter, "Human Sexual Behavior and Social Class Structure," by Marjorie Buckholz summarizes the findings of various observers regarding the impact of heterogeneous groups on changing sexual behavior and attitudes. It reveals that while there are only a few universals regarding sexual behavior, each culture develops its own code of what is "normal" and "desirable" for its members, and defends it against other modes of sexual expression.

Finally, Chapter 5, "Sex, Racism, and Social Work," by Leon F. Williams, shows how much contemporary racist attitudes are still influenced by the white majority's sexual needs, fears, fantasies; and how the sexual behavior of American black citizens is equally affected by the behavior and attitudes of the white majority.

H. L. G.

NOTE

[1] Wardell B. Pomeroy, "The Masters-Johnson Report and the Kinsey Tradition," in *An Analysis of Human Sexual Response,* ed. by Edward Bracher (Boston: Little, Brown, and Company, 1966), p. 117.

1

Sexual Knowledge, Values, and Behavior Patterns of Adolescents

FLOYD M. MARTINSON

This paper will present the findings of a recent study in Minnesota of sexual behavior patterns of a number of unmarried adolescents. During the 15-month duration of the study, we spent a month apiece in each of four communities—two rural, one suburban, and one inner-city—observing and interviewing around the general theme: What is it like to grow up in a Minnesota community? Or, more specifically: What is it like to grow up *sexually* in a Minnesota community? We were primarily interested in learning of the sources, the extent, and the quality of both sex and family life education. We also analyzed dating histories of 500 Minnesota high school students from throughout the state. These were youth in the leadership group, youth who upon graduation from high school enrolled in college. We also interviewed nearly 200 unwed mothers who received services offered by the Unwed Mother Unit of Lutheran Social Service of Minnesota.

Our study did not cover a complete cross section of the unmarried in Minnesota, but concentrated on that part of the youth population which comes within the middle class. This report does not deal to any degree with the "Gold Coast" or the slums. In some states the high rate of illegitimacy can be traced in large part to the presence in the state of large numbers of culturally deprived members of some minority group. We have no such convenient scapegoat for the incidence of illegitimacy in Minnesota.

Sexual Behavior and Values

In Minnesota the number of illegitimate births increased tenfold during the last decade and can be expected to increase tenfold in the next decade. The question being asked by Lutheran Social Service of Minnesota, sponsor of the research in question, and its board of directors is this: Are we to take care only of the results of nonmarital sexual activity—unwed

21

parents and their offspring—or do we have a responsibility for influencing, more directly than we are doing at present, the conditions leading to the ever-increasing problem of illegitimacy?

Assuming for the moment that we want to do something about the present situation, it is necessary to understand the situation in some depth. To do so, we must look at the dating practices of these young people and try to understand why they pattern their behavior in the ways they do.

Even these dating practices, however, are conditioned by certain imperatives. First, we must bear in mind that man is a sexual being, without season to his sexual desire. Sexual desire and capability are at their height during the years following pubescence. There is little evidence that a healthy adolescent boy does not need regular sexual outlet, through nocturnal emission (wet dreams), masturbation, or some other means. Sexual drive and interest are ever-present factors in the life of a healthy human being. Second, the age period of man's fertility is lengthening with earlier onset of pubescence (perhaps because of better nourishment and care) and later onset of menopause. The age at which people enter marriage is not decreasing. Hence the period calling for continence on the part of the unmarried (according to our traditional morality) is lengthened. Third, man does not live primarily by instinct, but by chosen values. Man is not born with the knowledge of how best to use his sexual powers for his own good or for the good of others. He must be taught. He can learn from responsible adults, through such agencies as the home, the church, and the school. If adults are unwilling or unable to teach, he will still learn, but he will learn from other sources, sources that do not share the reticence on this subject that has characterized home, church, and school. Some of these sources are popular magazines, the movies, and peers. A number of studies of young people show that youth prefer to get their values for important life decisions from responsible adults, primarily their parents, rather than from their peers and the mass media.[1] It is when responsible adults fail them that they turn to their peers and other sources.

Claims on Adolescence

Society to date has not provided any direct sexual outlet for the unmarried to which it unequivocally gives its blessing. Sublimation of the sex drive may be what our society ideally recommends for the unmarried, but this requires a degree of maturity that cannot be expected of adolescents. All that is left according to our mores is for the sex drive to be repressed. This is hardly a positive prescription.

Just as the period of adolescence is a time when young people are supposed to be preparing for responsible adulthood in areas of vocation and social adaptation, so is it even more fundamentally a time when sexual nature and identity become central concerns of the maturing individual. The establishment of a comfortable sense of sexual identity and of understanding about the implications of human sexuality for healthy personality development are crucial tasks of adolescence.

In their attempt to understand and relate to persons of the opposite sex youth develop patterns of their own. One of the main patterns is to band together in groups—groups of boys and groups of girls—and to relate to each other within the safety of numbers. In sixth or seventh grade or earlier, often with the assistance or at least the consent of parents, young people plan parties in their homes. They get together and eat potato chips and drink Cokes, they listen to music, they talk, and they dance. At the same time they are subject to myriad suggestions from the mass media, older youth, and publicized behavior of some adults that there is more to relating to the opposite sex than these things. So they not uncommonly play suggestive games and turn out the lights and "make out." "Making out" at this age usually refers to kissing, necking, and perhaps some degree of petting. As one girl reflects:

> Eighth grade was when I began kissing a boy with some affection. Parties used to be just "make out" parties. It all seems so silly now: the parents would take us to the party; we would go to the basement and neck; and then our parents would take us home again.

Children do not always want such sexual involvement at this early age:

> I shall never forget one Christmas party I attended when I was in seventh grade. There were only couples there. We ate and danced for a while and then everyone sat on the couch with the lights out and kissed. I was so embarrassed and confused at such activity that I left the party early, went home, and cried. I hated that boy from then on and refused to go any place with him.

If the parents are away from home when a party is held, as our subjects reported was often the case, young people may use not only the living or recreation room, but also the bedrooms for "making out." Many high school youths attested from experience that "making out" on a bed is better than "making out" in a car or on a davenport. If father has left the liquor cabinet unlocked, this can help to liven up the party. Drinking is prevalent among Minnesota high school youth. According to a student from a suburb:

> I never went to a party, school or private, where there wasn't some drinking, and usually a lot of it.

The relationship between drinking and sexual activity is indicated in the report of one girl about an outdoor party:

> Accompanied by a case of beer and sleeping bags, we proceeded on an evening canoe trip. We paddled across the lake and set up camp. We drank and proceeded to our sleeping bags. I had never felt so comfortable in a boy's arms.

Dating Patterns

Besides group parties, which continue on into senior high school, some adolescents in Minnesota begin paired dating in junior high school, with parental approval or support. Parents sometimes encourage early dating.

> In the selection of my friends my mother did let me make my own decisions. One time, though, she was quite perturbed when, in sixth grade, I turned down my first date offer because I felt I was too young to accept.

Paired dating develops into going steadily or going steady (they are not the same thing). "Going steadily" means that neither person is dating anyone else. "Going steady" commonly involves the exchange of expressions of love, promises to be faithful, and some outward ritual and symbols, such as the wearing of matching clothing or the giving or exchanging of rings or pins. Judging from our study, few Minnesota high school students "play the field" once they begin dating. They go steadily or steady. They explain that they find it difficult to "play the field." Boys find the idea of a regular date to be satisfying and convenient. Girls find that if they do not agree to go steady, no other boy may ask them out and they may end up with no dates at all.

In dealing with illegitimacy, we have learned that promiscuity is not part of the problem among the young people with whom we work. We find, rather, the problem of paired, unchaperoned dating of high school students who lack the required sophistication to handle intimate involvement.

Intimate dating is greatly facilitated by the availability of family cars. Raising the age requirement for a driver's license could in itself affect the illicit sex problem, especially in rural areas. After a date that often consists of going to a movie and having a snack, there is usually some time left before the girl's curfew, and many parents set a very late curfew or none at all. For example:

> My mother never set a curfew for me to be home; it was left up to me to be in at a decent hour. As a result we would park or sit in my

yard for an hour before going in. This made petting happen very often, whereas if we had to be in earlier, I don't think it would have happened frequently.

This parking time is "free" time. A couple may only sit and talk, but there is tremendous personal and peer pressure to use the parking period for "making out." Some of the more astute young people, and those who want to remain unattached, say that it is in this period before curfew that there are few alternatives to parking and petting. If a boy and girl are going steadily, they need not "make out," but if they are going steady, it is generally understood in the peer group that they will be together a great deal and will "make out" when they are together.

> . . . By the beginning of my junior year, we carried on an enjoyable intimate relationship. I loved our physical relationship. We would park for hours at a time and never tire of necking and petting. We petted heavily until there was nothing left but sexual intercourse. His parents went to church every Sunday night and we usually occupied the house while they were gone. He had seen me without clothes and neither of us felt especially guilty.

"Making out" among high school students is progressive. It begins on first dates with kissing and the light embrace and progresses to deep kissing, body fondling, petting to orgasm, simulated intercourse ("humping"), mutual masturbation, and in some cases sexual intercourse.

> Sex played an important part in our life, and though we never did have intercourse, we would pet to orgasm four or five times a week and maybe even more.

Nudity or seminudity is not at all uncommon among Minnesota high school daters. One reported:

> . . . we progressed rapidly from one stage to the next. . . . We were alone quite a lot of the time, either at his home or mine, and our involvement became quite serious. Many times we would be in bed with no clothes on. We got so completely caught up in this sexual exploration, however, that all other aspects of our relationship suffered.

Yet, I repeat, Minnesota young people are not promiscuous. This kind of behavior does not occur unless the two like each other very much or think that they are in love. They do not know how to cope with their feelings. They think that it is love rather than sex and that it should not be denied. The more sophisticated may feign love in order to establish grounds for sexual involvement.

I discovered that one does not simply "go steady" in high school. One *must* be in love and admit it. This was just pushing things a little too far for my comfort, but to me this "love" was just a game that brought me an abundance of attention so I played. Little did I realize what I was letting myself in for.

Love makes sexual behavior right. This teenage morality has been labeled "permissiveness with affection." If you have strong affection for the other person, you will be permissive.

Petting to sexual climax is widely utilized by couples who do not want to engage in coitus. Petting is their way of forestalling coitus, which they have been taught to avoid by the parent generation.

We neck and pet a lot and are both able to achieve orgasm without intercourse. We practice mutual masturbation most of the time. We find it to be a very workable technique for letting off tensions that are built up by extensive necking and petting.

Methods of Birth Control

Those who do have sexual intercourse are quite successful in preventing conception. Adolescents as a group are relatively sterile. They utilize the withdrawal method of conception control quite extensively; they use condoms and rhythm to some extent. Girls not uncommonly expect the boy to be responsible for contraception. But, out of ignorance and for other reasons, they do not necessarily insist. In general, it appears that they use contraceptives in a hit-or-miss fashion—sometimes yes, sometimes no.

The lack of a consistent and reliable source of supply of contraceptives to teenagers in the state, coupled with the lack of sex education, is no doubt a deterrent to their use.

We didn't use any contraceptives, as I was too bashful to buy condoms.

Condom vending machines did appear in service station restrooms in the southern part of the state within the last year. However, the attorney general ruled that they are illegal in Minnesota. The vending machine is a source of supply in many other states. In doing research in an eastern state last summer, we noted that there were as many as three brands of condoms available in vending machines in a single filling station.

These patterns of youth behavior that I have described are not carried out with confidence, with arrogance, or with much assurance that the behavior is right or proper. But youth have not found many adults, or any adults, who appear to understand or care enough about their situation to be helpful.

Available Sex Education

In evaluating the sex education they receive from childhood up until graduation from high school, the majority of Minnesota youth whom we studied are dissatisfied. Too often they feel themselves to be poorly informed and to have formed impressions about sex and sexual behavior that are negative and unwholesome. All of the institutions stand under their indictment—the home, the school, and the church, as well as other media of sex information such as peer group, dates, and the mass media. It is from the mass media and peers that they have learned that sex is fun, and that it is a proper expression of one's feeling for another person. This confuses them. Why have adults let them understand that sex is dirty, shameful, secretive, wrong, or so sacred that it is completely out of reach, while they and their peers have found much about it that is fun, exciting, enjoyable, and meaningful? And why is there this discrepancy between adult and youth experience?

In some homes parents give no sex instruction at all, and in many homes sex is regarded as a taboo subject never to be brought up.

> My parents never came out and actually told me about the facts of life. . . . But indirectly they told me plenty. They made me feel that sex was dirty and something to be ashamed of or embarrassed about. Yet they joked about it and my father always had some "girly" magazines lying around the house. At first I got a big kick out of looking at them, but later they just disgusted me and made me hate being a girl if all that men did was look at our bodies and make jokes about us.

Some Minnesota parents actually refuse to give their children information when asked for it.

> When I asked my mother where the kittens came from in the first place and why they couldn't go back again, she scolded me and said that nice girls don't ask things like this. . . . How I made it through my adolescent years I will never know. My parents, like so many parents, didn't take advantage of the opportunities to explain love and sex expression. They were neither sympathetic nor helpful to my adolescent needs.

Some parents emphasize only the negative, telling only what should not be done. Some of the confusion develops because parents teach rules of behavior without giving the factual information needed to appreciate the rules.

> My parents attempted with all their ability to hide the facts of life from me. . . . I feel that this is why I have always been afraid of sex. . . . Strict dating rules were laid down for me partly because "something" might happen. That something was always left up to my imagination. I was never told what it was. I put myself on a pedestal (as my parents directed), and inwardly scoffed at those who were teasing the boys with their flirting and suggestive ways. In a way I considered myself better because I knew something that they didn't know. Yet did I? I only knew what I wasn't supposed to do, but not why. I guess my mother never thought that a little knowledge could do more than the strictest set of rules. . . . I sought information by reading romance magazines. My feelings of horror and repulsion grew as I read of the ugly thoughts that boys had in their heads about sleeping with girls and wanting to fondle and caress them. I saw the pain caused by illegitimate babies and out-of-wedlock mothers. I also saw the filthy ways people made love in dirty motels and cabins, in back seats of cars, and lying in the weeds. I could see no beauty in sex. It was hateful and repulsive, and I wanted no part of it.

On the other hand, there are Minnesota youth who are appreciative of relationships with their parents and the sex education received in the home.

> . . . I think that I know more about sex than most of the students my age. Anything that the other students knew about sex was mostly what they had heard and learned from each other. My mother had informed me at an early age about where babies come from, etc. She always told me things about sex in advance so that I never heard anything from the other students that I didn't know or hadn't already heard. As a result . . . I never believed any of the perverted and misleading ideas about sex. I have always respected my mother a great deal for the free and honest way that she spoke to me about sex.

Sex and family life educating can be done in the home, but most parents are not doing it, and I am not hopeful that it will be well done in the home in the foreseeable future. Good sex education in the home, when it does occur, often is a part of an open and affectionate relationship between parent and child. Expecting the child to take the initiative in parent-child discussions on sex is not realistic. The child early becomes embarrassed about sex and may be as unable to bring up the subject with parents as parents are with the child. Good sex education is more than instruction in the physical aspects of love. The few Minnesota students we encountered who have been well taught show their appreciation by wholesome attitudes and values, proper etiquette, and respect for other persons, especially the person being dated.

In speaking about major sources of sex education, a minority of Minnesota high school students mention the school. Whatever Minnesota schools have offered to date in sex education seems to have made little impact on students. I have not made a systematic survey, but I have not run across a single school in Minnesota that in my estimation is doing an adequate job of sex and family life education.

As with the school, so also with the church; the majority of our group of Minnesota youth do not mention the church as a major source of sex and family life education.

> I felt that my church beat around the bush and whatever was said about it was a paraphrase of the idea that "you should keep your body pure and holy because it is a temple of God." I certainly maintain that the sex act is holy. . . . But I believe that my church should not stop with this idea, but go on [to] a more liberal and full explanation about sex, with the unabashed use of technical terms.

An occasional person will mention the sex education he has received under religious auspices with appreciation. More characteristically, however, young people appear to be critical of sex education received under religious auspices. The concept of body-soul dualism and the lower nature of the body is a common impression left by religious instructors.

A commonly mentioned source of sex information is peers. Sex is a major topic of conversation among both sexes. The person one is dating often becomes a source of sex instruction especially in those cases where responsible educational agencies in the community have not done a satisfactory job. Occasionally, a young person will look back with satisfaction to the high school boy friend or girl friend as a source of sex education.

> I know now that if I ever marry I will always consider my years with him as a healthy experience and one to be cherished and never ashamed of. I value our relationship as one that helped both of us in our attitude toward goals and ideals to try to attain. I have never experienced any other sexual partners besides him. . . . I am not condemning my relationship with him, but only wish that we had used more discretion and that it had happened when we were both more mature, for I feel that it would have brought less conflict.

But persons whose primary source of sex education has been the date often give the date a low rating as a source of information.

Conclusion

We conclude our report with the general observation that many Minnesota high school graduates look back upon going steady in high school as having been a mistake. The following case is not atypical:

> It is a pity that we had such a strong association when we were so young. Had we been older, we probably would have known much more about sex and about life in general . . . I am sure that if we had been older we would have realized the extreme seriousness of the results of sexual intercourse. To us, then, a pregnancy seemed so impossible. Now we know how very possible it was and how it could have ruined both of our lives. When I have children of my own, I do not think I will let them go steady.

These are some of the facts we learned about the sexual behavior and attitudes of the young people we studied. We believe that these behavior patterns and these confused, searching attitudes are typical of today's middle-class adolescent. It is our firm conclusion that if young people are to develop a healthy and mature sexuality, they need help.

NOTE

[1] See, for example, Jessie Bernard (special ed.), "Teen-Age Culture," *The Annals of the American Academy of Political and Social Science* vol. 338 (November 1961); Clay V. Brittain, "Adolescent Choices and Parent-Peer Cross Pressures," *American Sociological Review* 28 (1963); Ernest A. Smith, *American Youth Culture: Group Life in Teen-Age Society* (New York: The Free Press, 1962).

SUGGESTED READINGS

Ehrmann, W. *Premarital Dating Behavior.* New York: Holt, Rinehart and Winston, 1959.

Packard, V. *The Sexual Wilderness.* New York: Pocket Books, 1970.

Reiss, I. *The Social Context of Premarital Sexual Permissiveness.* New York: Holt, Rinehart and Winston, 1967.

Schofield, M. *The Sexual Behavior of Young People.* London: Longmans, Green and Co., 1965.

Unwed Mothers and Their Sex Partners

HALLOWELL POPE

In his ground-breaking book on unwed motherhood, Vincent pointed out that different theories of causation of illegitimacy have been popular at different times. For example, during the 1930's the emphasis was on "ecological" or environmental causes of illegitimacy and in the late 1930's and early 1940's on cultural causes. Then in the 1940's and early 1950's, psychological and psychiatric theories took over, and so forth.[1] All these approaches have assumed that there must be salient differences defined in terms of their theoretical perspectives—maybe even a single important difference—between those women who have illegitimate children and those who do not. These perspectives encouraged the view that it takes a very deprived, a very immoral, a very stupid, a very deviant, or perhaps a very exploited girl to make such a disastrous mistake as to have an illegitimate child. Folk wisdom put it: there's no such thing as being half-pregnant. Some obvious causal factor was looked for, because such an obviously important result—the illegitimate child—seemed necessarily the consequence of some clear-cut initial difference.

Both the folk saying and the various research perspectives may have been making erroneous assumptions. The probability of a girl having a birth out of wedlock is related to many interconnected factors, among them: the composition of her field of eligibles, the nature of her heterosexual partnerships, frequency of premarital intercourse, her fecundity, her knowledge and use of contraception, and, if she becomes premaritally pregnant, her attitudes toward and the availability of abortion as well as her possibilities of getting married before giving birth. There is no reason to believe that a "normal" person in a "normal" relationship might not become premaritally pregnant—*if we avoid the tautology* of arguing that a relationship is abnormal or deviant *because* it results in a premarital pregnancy for the girl. The premarital pregnancy may indicate a prior deviant act as defined by traditional moral standards, but it is a mistake nowadays to assume that such an act must have been committed by an abnormal person, within a deviant relationship, and in an unusual social

31

setting. We also must avoid the mistake of using single-cause theories and common-sense research categories in trying to account for illegitimacy.

In this period of ill-defined and shifting sexual standards, the criteria are blurred by which one would classify a premarital heterosexual relationship as deviant. The difference between those couples that do and do not make the decisions and perform the acts that lead to unwed motherhood may be subtle and not easily identified. For example, as the distinction between chastity and its absence diminishes in importance, the distinction between intercourse with and without appropriate contraceptive precautions has not developed apace. Linkages between social characteristics, attitudes, and patterns of behavior previously associated with illegitimacy may now be attenuated. We may be unable to comprehend these linkages in the terms we have been employing up to this time. However, we must continue to search them out. We must also search for relevant and theoretically grounded variables and develop explanatory models that allow the analysis of interaction among these variables and of the sequence of events that results in unwed parenthood.

This paper cannot hope to unravel even a portion of the complex problems mentioned above; it can only point out the likelihood of a large overlap in the nature of the prepregnancy relationship and the context within which it occurs between those girls who do and those who do not eventually become unwed mothers. This paper, then, has the following purposes: (1) the presentation of data on the nature of the prepregnancy relationship between sex partners who later had illegitimate children; (2) the presentation of data on the similarity of their social characteristics; (3) the discussion of whether the prepregnancy relationships can be considered deviant, not subject to social controls, and characterized by exploitation; and (4) the discussion of some of the racial differences that are indicated in the data.

Research Procedures

The universe sampled consisted of all those women in selected counties of North Carolina who were recorded on birth certificates as mothers of illegitimate children during 1960 and 1961—North Carolina had about 1,700 white and 8,200 nonwhite, live illegitimate births for each of these years. (The illegitimacy ratio for 1960 was 9.0 percent overall: 2.2 percent for whites and 23.8 percent for nonwhites.[2]) Counties in each of the state's major socioeconomic regions were chosen so that interviews in them might complete a sample that would be reasonably representative for the state. The goal was to contact all officially recorded white unwed mothers and a one-third sample of Negro unwed mothers in each county selected.

The completed sample included over 1,000 interviews, including 939 with women who had never before been married. The completed cases represent 32 percent of the white cases in sampled counties and 42 percent of those cases actually sought by interviewers. (Because of time limitations and other factors, we were unable to try to contact all sampled white subjects.) For Negroes, 65 percent of the cases in the sampled counties brought completed interviews or 67 percent of the respondents actually sought. In the sampled counties, the completion rates varied from a high of 70 percent in one county to a low of 24 percent in another county (where a maternity home for white unwed mothers-to-be was used as an address by its former residents). Ten percent of the white and two percent of the Negro women with whom personal contact was made refused interviews.

There are probable biases in our completed sample: in the official records from which the sample was drawn, in the counties selected, through variations in interviewer location skills, and in the type of respondents who were inaccessible or who refused interviews. The completed sample overrepresents urban cases and is limited in the number of cases from the upper socioeconomic groups, particularly for whites. However, this is the only study of unwed mothers that has employed sampling from some known universe.

Each respondent was interviewed by a female interviewer of the same race during the summer of 1962—a time period of from 6 months to 2½ years after the woman had borne her illegitimate child. The interview schedule included a number of open- and closed-end questions. The interviews averaged 75 minutes in length and were conducted in the respondents' homes, in private.

Some characteristics of the women in the sample are: about one-half are under 21; over two-fifths have completed less than the tenth grade in school; almost one-half of the whites and three-quarters of the Negroes are daughters of semi- and unskilled workers, farm laborers, or sharecroppers; 19 percent of the whites and 54 percent of the Negroes had borne more than one illegitimate child; and, finally, two-thirds live in urban areas (U.S. Census definition), even though North Carolina has no large metropolitan areas.

This paper will deal only with the 552 Negro and 387 white nevermarried primiparas—that is, those unwed mothers each of whom at the time of the birth of her first child in 1960 or 1961 had never yet been married. For the most part the generalizations for the primiparas also hold for the multiparas.

Results

THE SOCIAL CONTEXT: What was the social context within which the fathers and these primiparous unwed mothers associated? Two-thirds of the white and over four-fifths of the Negro unwed mothers had sex partners who were living in the same localities as they did (same town or "place"—see Table 1 for question used). In addition, in Table 2 over

Table 1. *Comparison of the Place where the Father and Unwed Mother lived when she met him, by Race*

Race	Place Where the Father Lived*		Total
	Same as Unwed Mother	Different from Unwed Mother	
White	68% (212)	32% (101)	100% (313)
Negro	85% (216)	15% (38)	100% (254)

$X^2 = 22.8$; df = 1; P < .001; ϕ = .20.

* The question used: "Where was he living when you met him—in the same town or place you were, or did he usually live in (come from) a different place?"

Table 2. *Degree to which the Unwed Mother's Family knew the Father at the time she became pregnant, by Race*

Race	Degree to Which the Unwed Mother's Family Knew the Father*			Total
	Knew him and had seen him a lot	Knew him but had seen him no more than now and then	Did not know him	
White	55% (172)	27% (83)	18% (57)	100% (312)
Negro	77% (193)	15% (37)	9% (22)	101% (252)

$X^2 = 28.2$; df = 2; P < .001; ϕ = .22.

* The question used: "Did your family know him?" (If yes) "How well did they know him—had they seen him very much?"

one-half of the white and three-quarters of the Negro unwed mothers' families knew the alleged father well; on the other hand, one-fifth of the white and one-tenth of the Negro families of the unwed mothers did not know the father at the time the woman became pregnant. Among the younger girls (aged 16-20) of both races, the proportion of parents who did not know the father before the pregnancy was even less. Parents of both races apparently had an opportunity to become acquainted with their daughters' sex partners, and, consequently, it may be assumed that they had an opportunity to exercise control over the relationship.

Table 3. *Number and Strength of Mutual Friendships held by the Father and Unwed Mother at the time she became Pregnant, by Race*

| Race | Mutual Friendships of Unwed Mother and Father* | | | Total |
	Knew many of the same people very well	Knew many of the same people, but knew them no more than pretty well	Did not know many of the same people	
White	28% (88)	44% (137)	28% (86)	100% (311)
Negro	39% (96)	47% (114)	15% (36)	101% (246)

$X^2 = 15.6$; df $= 2$; P $< .001$; $\phi = .17$.

* The question used: "At the time you became pregnant, did you know many of the same people?" (If knew many of the same people) "Would you say you both knew these people a little bit, or would you say you both knew them very well?"

As Table 3 indicates, many of the unwed mothers and their sex partners were in a group of mutual associates; seven-tenths of the white and four-fifths of the Negro unwed mothers knew many of the same people that their sex partners did and knew them at least "pretty well." However, over one-quarter of the white and just under one-fifth of the Negro women did not have many mutual friends with their sex partners at the time the women became pregnant. From the evidence it appears that the Negro more often than the white woman is bound into a network of relationships that includes her family, friends, and the friends of her sex partner. In addition, these findings indicate that only a minority of women have a liaison that results in unwed motherhood while they are in isolation from their normal social ties. Most of these unwed mothers had partners who were from their home towns and were known by their families and members of their peer groups.

THE PREPREGNANCY RELATIONSHIP BETWEEN THE FATHER AND THE UNWED MOTHER: There is inevitable distortion in the following data, because they deal with the prepregnancy relationship between the father and the unwed mother as subsequently reported by the woman in an interview situation. But after checking the internal consistency of the interviews, we believe it is largely reliable and valid.

We tapped the extent of promiscuity on the part of the unwed mothers and their sex partners in several different ways. By all these measures the amount of promiscuity—both concurrent and serial—was limited.

1. Most of the women had "gone with" their sex partners *exclusively* for at least six months *before* becoming pregnant; few had never gone with their sex partners exclusively (Table 4).

Table 4. *Length of time Unwed Mother had "gone with" the Father exclusively before she became Pregnant, by Race*

Race	Time Gone with the Father Exclusively*				Total
	More than 2 years	6 months– 2 years	Less than 6 months	Never	
White	21% (64)	39% (119)	23% (70)	18% (54)	101% (307)
Negro	32% (78)	46% (112)	9% (21)	14% (34)	101% (245)

$X^2 = 25.9$; df $= 3$; P $< .001$; $\phi = .22$.

* The questions used: (a) "Had you ever gone with the father of your child—I mean gone with him fairly regularly—even if you saw other men at the same time, too?" (b) "Before you got pregnant, for how long had you gone with him fairly regularly?" (c) "During this time did you go out with other men also?" (d) "Did you ever go out with just the father of your child and no one else?"

2. Most of the women were, at the time of their pregnancies, either planning to marry their sex partners or were going with them regularly (Table 5). Less than 15 percent of women of both races were only seeing their sex partners "now and then."
3. Our respondents were asked how they had felt about the father before becoming pregnant, that is, were they in love with him, did they like him a lot, were they friendly toward him, didn't they care very much for him, etc. Over four-fifths of the white and three-quarters of the Negro unwed mothers reported they either were or thought they were in love with their sex partners (Table 6). Almost

Table 5. *Commitment between the Father and Unwed Mother before her Pregnancy, by Race*

Race	Commitment Between the Father and Unwed Mother Before Her Pregnancy*			Total
	Seeing each other no more than now and then	Going together regularly	Planning to be married	
White	14% (44)	45% (139)	41% (125)	100% (308)
Negro	12% (29)	57% (142)	32% (80)	101% (251)

$X^2 = 7.3$; df = 2; P < .05; ϕ = .11.

* The question used: "Just before you became pregnant, were you and he (the father of your child) seeing one another now and then, going together regularly, planning to get married, or what?"

none of the women in our entire sample expressed any hatred toward the father in answering this question.

4. Over seven-tenths of the whites and over two-fifths of the Negroes reported that they had had intercourse with *one man only* (the alleged father); less than 5 percent of the whites and less than 15 percent of the Negroes had had intercourse with four or more men.

Table 6. *Unwed Mother's involvement with the Father before her Pregnancy, by Race*

Race	Involvement with the Father*					Total
	In love	Thought was in love	Liked him a lot	Friendly toward him	Neutral	
White	49% (153)	35% (110)	10% (32)	3% (8)	3% (8)	100% (311)
Negro	50% (127)	24% (60)	23% (58)	2% (4)	1% (3)	100% (252)

$X^2 = 22.8$; df = 3; P < .001; ϕ = .20. (The "Friendly" and "Neutral" columns were combined in computing X^2.)

* The question used: "Thinking back to before you became pregnant, how did you used to feel about the father of your child—were you in love with him; like him a lot; friendly toward him; not care very much for him; or what?"

Because the sample is predominantly young women (over one-half of them under 21), these facts might lead one to characterize them as "loose." However, this is true only in the sense that they began sex relations while young and eventually had illegitimate children; most of them were not serially or concurrently promiscuous.[3] By all of the four indicators presented above, the amount of concurrent as well as serial promiscuity was limited among our sample; the relationship between the unwed mothers and the fathers was much more often close than not.

COMPARATIVE SOCIAL STATUS OF THE FATHER AND UNWED MOTHER: Thus far, we have characterized the unmarried mother's relationship to the father of the child from two perspectives: first, the degree to which

Table 7. *Age difference between Unwed Mother and the Father, by Race*

Race	Age Difference Between Unwed Mother and the Father				
	Male no more than 1 year older than female	Male 2–3 years older than female	Male 4–5 years older than female	Male 6 or more years older than female	Total
White	30% (92)	23% (71)	19% (60)	28% (86)	100% (309)
Negro	31% (77)	36% (89)	20% (50)	12% (30)	99% (146)

$X^2 = 25.7$; df $= 3$; P $< .001$; $\phi = .21$.

both partners were members of the same social setting; and second, the amount of the unmarried mother's involvement with and commitment to her sex partner. We will now compare the partners' social statuses using age, socioeconomic status, education, and marital status. These comparisons determine the extent to which the sex partners came from similar social backgrounds.

As Table 7 shows, a high proportion of the unwed mothers had partners no more than three years their senior—53 percent for white, 67 percent for Negroes. Among the white unwed mothers, 28 percent had sex partners who were six or more years older; the comparable figure for Negroes was only 12 percent. The older more often than the younger unwed mothers, particularly among the Negroes, had partners who were close in age or even younger than themselves. For example, among the Negroes who were over 20, almost one-half had sex partners no more than one year their senior.

Table 8. *Comparison of the Education of Unwed Mother and the Father,*

Education of Unwed Mother	Education of the Father			Total
	Eighth grade or less	Some high school	High-school graduate	
White				
Eighth grade or less	56% (33)	25% (15)	19% (11)	100% (59)
Some high school	26% (37)	38% (53)	36% (51)	100% (141)
High-school graduate or beyond	6% (7)	24% (26)	70% (77)	100% (110)
Negro				
Eighth grade or less	49% (31)	38% (24)	13% (8)	100% (63)
Some high school	19% (23)	39% (47)	43% (52)	101% (122)
High-school graduate or beyond	7% (5)	26% (18)	67% (46)	100% (69)

	Education of the Father in Comparison to That of the Unwed Mother			Total
	Father More	Same	Father less	
White	25% (77)	53% (163)	23% (70)	101% (310)
Negro	33% (84)	49% (124)	18% (46)	100% (254)

X^2 (for lower portion of table) $= 5.1$; df $= 2$; P $> .05$; $\phi = .09$.

Considering education (Table 8), we find that about one-half of the unwed mothers of both races have the same general level of education as their sex partners (when educational levels are grouped into no high school, some high school, and high school or beyond). One-quarter of the white and one-third of the Negro women had less education than their sex partners, whereas one-quarter of the whites and one-fifth of the Negroes had more education than did their partners. In our data there is a tendency for the younger women to have sex partners who had had more education than themselves. For example, among the whites, 31 percent of the 16–20-year-old women, as contrasted with 16 percent of the 21-year-old and older women, had sex partners with at least the next higher level of education.

Another check on the degree of social–status similarity of the unmarried mothers and their sex partners is the comparison of their respective socioeconomic statuses. Only two stratum levels were distinguished—

Table 9. *Comparison of the Socioeconomic Status of the Father and Unwed Mother, by Race**

Race	Socioeconomic Status of the Father in Comparison to That of the Unwed Mother			Total
	Father Higher	Same	Father Lower	
White	31% (60)	55% (105)	14% (26)	100% (191)
Negro	24% (39)	61% (98)	14% (23)	99% (160)

$X^2 = 2.1$; df $= 2$; P $> .05$; $\phi = .03$.

* In computing figures for this table, we cross-classified the cases by socioeconomic class of the unwed mother and of the child's father. The occupational statuses of their respective fathers were used as the best measure of their statuses. We used two status levels for our computations: white-collar and upper blue-collar vs. lower blue-collar.

There is a large number of not ascertained cases. This is because many of the unwed mothers did not know the occupation of the sex partner's father.

white-collar and upper blue-collar versus lower blue-collar. One-half of the whites and three-fifths of the Negroes were in the same stratum as their sex partners (Table 9). About one-third of the white and one-quarter of the Negro unwed mothers had sex partners from the higher of the two strata, and only 14 percent of the unwed mothers of each race were from a higher stratum that their sex partners. As is the case with married pairs, the women more often "chose" upward in social stratum, the men downward. Admittedly, the measurement here is crude—partly because many of the respondents did not know enough about their sex partners' parents to allow reliable coding of status.

One aspect of the social location of the fathers in relation to the unwed mothers remains to be examined: the father's marital status at the time of the woman's pregnancy, as reported by the women. As Table 10 indicates, nine-tenths of the Negro unwed mothers had sex partners whom they believed had never been married; only 2 percent of them had sex partners whom they knew were married and living with their wives. The situation was distinctly different among the white unwed mothers. Only 61 percent of them were impregnated by men who had never before been married, 10 percent by previously married men who were divorced or widowed, 16 percent by men who were married but separated, and, finally, 13 percent by men who were married and living with their wives. This

Table 10. *Marital Status of the Father at time Unwed Mother became Pregnant, by Race of Unwed Mother*

Race	Marital Status of the Father				Total
	Never married	Ever married, but divorced or widowed	Married, but separated	Married and living with his wife	
White	61% (189)	10% (31)	16% (51)	13% (40)	100% (311)
Negro	91% (230)	4% (9)	4% (9)	2% (6)	101% (254)

$X^2 = 50.4$; df $= 2$; P $< .001$; $\phi = .30$. (The "ever-married" columns were combined in computing X^2.)

last figure—13 percent of white unwed mothers impregnated by men they knew to be married and still living with their wives—does not vary between the younger and older unwed mothers; but the women over 20 years of age more often than those 20 or younger associated with men who were formerly married but now separated, widowed, or divorced (38 percent versus 18 percent). For the Negroes a comparable difference for the younger and older women exists, but the differences are smaller (14 percent versus 4 percent).

Table 11 tabulates the marital history of the father as well as his age in comparison to the unwed mother to further check the social similarity of the sex partners, particularly among the whites. Over one-quarter of the white women had a sex partner who had both been previously married and was four or more years older; on the other hand, two-fifths had sex partners close to their own ages who had never been married. Those few

Negroes who had never-married partners about equally divided themselves between those partners who were near their ages and those who were four or more years older.

Table 11. *Marital History of the Father and Age differences between him and Unwed Mother, by Race*

Race	Marital History of the Father and Age Difference Between Him and Unwed Mother				Total
	Ever Married*		Never Married		
	Male 4 or more years older	Male less than 4 years older	Male 4 or more years older	Male less than 4 years older	
White	28% (85)	12% (37)	20% (61)	40% (124)	100% (307)
Negro	5% (12)	4% (10)	28% (68)	63% (155)	100% (245)

* Now married or has been married at some time in the past.

Discussion

The data have been presented, and we turn to their implications. We wish to ask whether the heterosexual relationships experienced by our sample can be considered deviant, not subject to social control, and characterized by exploitation. Is the deviant outcome—an illegitimate birth and unwed motherhood—the consequence of an atypical and deviant relationship? Our data cannot directly answer this question because: (1) we have no comparable sample of women who were dating or courting and whose relationship resulted in marriage or was terminated without childbirth; (2) we do not have results directly bearing on all the questions we seek to answer—for example, we lack first-hand information from the fathers—and (3) we were unable to gain an unbiased sample from our universe of women who were officially recorded as unwed mothers. The reader is reminded that the sample on which our data is based is not representative of all officially recorded illegitimacies. It underrepresents those middle- and upper-status women, particularly the whites, who were not interviewed because they had moved, did not give home addresses on birth certificates, etc. It may be that these very women, those who most carefully guarded against public acknowledgment of their illegitimacies, were the same women who were not included in our sample. They may be among those most deviant, most exploited or exploitative, and most subject to certain forms of social control, for example, pressures to maintain family honor. If this is true, our data overestimate the extent of similarity between courtship for our sample and courting couples in general. However, even if this is so, the data from the cases that were obtained would heavily weight the final results in the direction herein reported, particularly for the Negroes, for whom almost two-thirds of the sampled cases resulted in completed interviews. The probable sample deficiencies, because they are more pronounced for the whites, cause our data to understate Negro-white differences. In sum: the deficiencies of the sample cause overestimation of the similarity between courtship practices in the sample and the general population, but cause underestimation of Negro–white differences.

Do our data indicate that these relationships between the women in our sample and their sex partners were deviant? Deviancy must be considered relative to some set of normative standards. Our sample was composed mostly of lower-class Negroes and whites, and we can consider the question of deviancy from both lower-class and dominant middle-class standards.[4] Also, the differences that exist between Negroes and whites with regard to sexual standards and standards governing family life must be recognized.[5] An integral part of deviancy is the social control mechanisms utilized to reorient deviant behavior and tendencies toward it. If deviant tendencies did exist among our sample of women, we must investigate whether they were isolated from those agents of social control who could have applied the appropriate sanctions.

Tables 4-6, which give data on the duration and levels of involvement and commitment between the unwed mother and her sex partner, strongly indicate that even according to middle-class normative standards only a small proportion of these women could be considered promiscuous. This is true of both racial groups, with the Negroes showing a higher proportion with a long-term (six months or more) exclusive relationship with the alleged father before pregnancy. Having sex relations with a man whom one has been dating exclusively for six months, for whom one feels deep affection, and with whom one may have discussed marriage does not severely violate sexual standards of the present youthful generation. There is reason to believe that one of the dominant standards of the future will be permissiveness-with-affection.[6] Of course, the crux of the societal reaction expressed through parents, schools, the mass media, and other channels, is not premarital intercourse but premarital pregnancy and illegitimate childbirth.[7] For some time a large proportion of men of diverse social categories have engaged in premarital intercourse, as have a significant proportion of women.[8] This behavior is becoming increasingly tolerated normatively if it occurs within the context of a "close" relationship. However, the continuing public clamor about the rise in illegitimacy rates indicates that, although illicit coitus is being more openly discussed, illegitimacy is still condemned by the "official" morality. In addition, it is not an acceptable state of affairs in any group.[9] The women in our sample were deviant mainly by becoming unwed mothers, not by the nature of their relationships with the fathers of their children.

Now we may consider the degree to which the women in our sample were subject to the normal mechanisms of social control. Because sexual intercourse can be accomplished briefly and secretly, the most effective controls are internalized ones. Short of these, persons of close acquaintance—family, friends, neighbors—are the most likely effective agents of control. Were the women in our sample subject to surveillance and possible sanctioning by such persons? The evidence indicates that by and large they probably were. Parents and peer groups were acquainted with the sex partners and could have applied sanctions if they had wished to do so and if they had the necessary knowledge. However, it is doubtful if members of peer groups would desire to sanction negatively these women and their sex partners; most of the relationships involved were of fairly long duration and of a high level of commitment. (Whether intercourse preceded or followed the development of commitment was not ascertained in this study.) Consequently, they conformed to the standard of permissiveness-with-affection. Parents may suspect what their children are doing heterosexually, but they usually do not have proof and may find it difficult to control sexual behavior in the face of possible support from their children's peer group for the more liberal standards. However, most parents of both races apparently had an opportunity to become acquainted with their daughters' sex partners and, in all probability, often had an opportunity to attempt to exercise control over the relationship. That they did not may reflect a lack of intense moral concern on their part as well as the feeling that no effective action could be taken. But note that a significant proportion of the couples, particularly among the whites, were not subject to controls from those persons most likely to administer them.

We may now shift perspective slightly and ask how likely it is that exploitation characterized the relationships between the sex partners. One exploits when he attempts to get more than he gives; he forgoes reciprocity. In an exploitative relationship there is no identification of ends, and the exploiting partner intrinsically values neither the relation nor the other person. The exploiting partner uses some lever of interpersonal influence—such as a "line," sophistication, or status—to manipulate his partner into acts that the person does not wish to commit. For example, an older male may give promise of affection and security to a younger woman through his "line" and his worldliness; he bargains with these for sexual favors, but returns no real lasting affection and breaks off the liaison after the girl becomes pregnant.

Because we have no direct evidence concerning exploitation, a subtle determination at best, we will compare the partners' social status using marital status, age, education, and socioeconomic status. This comparison will determine the extent to which the sex partners came from similar social backgrounds and indicate their comparative bargaining power in the heterosexual relationsip. If their backgrounds are similar (at least to the same extent as normally married couples), this supports the conclusion that the relationship might best be considered as courtships punctuated by an atypical event—the pregnancy. If, on the other hand, there is a marked dissimilarity in social background between the sex partners (for example, the men are much older than the women), we might conclude from this indirect evidence that these relationships were extraordinary and characterized by potential exploitation.[10]

As Table 7 shows, most of the unwed mothers had partners no more than three years their senior.[11] These data indicate that exploitation due to age differences was minimal, particularly among the Negroes. However, fully one-quarter of the white women (31 percent for women 20 years old or younger) were involved with males six or more years their senior; these women were potentially subject to exploitation.

When considering the social-status similarity of the sex partners on education and social class, our data show that the younger women (under 21) quite frequently had partners with the next highest level of education (31 percent for whites and 38 percent for the Negroes). However, this pattern of women going with older and more-schooled men is not uncommon in the United States. Of course, the intent of such women at the time may be to finish their schooling (e.g., graduate from high school) and thereby catch up to the men who have already finished their education, but such plans may be interrupted by pregnancy and/or marriage. Even so, there is a tendency on the part of the younger women to have associated with better-educated men; perhaps some exploitation based on the male's greater sophistication took place in this minority of cases. Before reaching this conclusion, however, two questions must be answered: (1) Is there more educational differential among these couples than among other courting couples? If not, the relationships under consideration may have produced no more exploitation than is usual. (2) Does the greater education and age of one partner increase the potential of exploitation when the male is the older and more-schooled partner? It is commonly assumed that women attain social sophistication at a faster pace during the teenage years than do men. If this is the case, the age and schooling of the men may be counter-balanced by the greater social sophistication of the women.

A majority of the women had partners homogamous with them on socio-economic status. And even though our measurement of status was relatively crude, it indicates that the proportion of women who were dating "up" is not high (less than one-third for the whites and less than one-quarter for the Negroes) when one notes that in courting and married pairs the woman is the one that more often chooses "up" than the man. The evidence presented thus far indicates that the heterosexual associations that result in illegitimate children are usually between partners who are similar in social status and that there is no clear-cut evidence of more status discrepancy between the partners in these couples than between the members of those couples who marry before having children—although the data necessary to make this comparison properly are unavailable.

A married man who is living with his wife and who has an illegitimate child with a single girl as mother is likely to represent an exploitative or, at least, a reckless relationship; the girl has little chance to escape unwed motherhood through marriage, and the man may be exposed as an adulterer. Table 10 shows that this was an infrequent occurrence among Negroes, but not uncommon among whites. Coupled with evidence in Table 11 showing that white, prior-married men who were four or more years older than their female partners was an even more frequent occurrence, this leads us to surmise that exploitation of some of our sample of white women was a distinct possibility. However, it may be that the women involved understood the risks they were taking and accepted them.

Because the deficiencies of the completed sample tend to minimize rather than maximize the Negro-white differences manifest in the data, they are worth discussion. We shall now consider whether the white or Negro prepregnancy relationship would be more likely to lead to marriage. Presumably, the more the alleged father is part of the unwed mother's social network, the closer the relationship between them; and the greater their status equivalence, the more likely that a marriage would follow a premarital pregnancy. Although none of the Negro-white differences are pronounced, the Negro more often than the white alleged father was integrated into the unwed mother's social life (Tables 1-3). As mentioned above in the discussion of exploitative relationships, the Negro alleged father was less frequently much older than the unwed mother (six or more years). He was also more frequently legally available to marry: 95 percent versus 71 percent for the whites. Given these differences coupled with the higher proportion of the Negro couples that had been going together six months or more, we might expect the Negroes to be more frequently highly involved and committed than the whites. However, the whites were more often involved or committed in a way that would lead to marriage. Over two-fifths of the white couples were planning to be married (before the pregnancy), whereas this was true for less than one-third of the Negro couples. Also, five-sixths of the white women were (or, in retrospect, thought they were) in love with the alleged fathers; this was true for three-quarters of the Negro women.

We must try to account for this relative lack of marital plans and involvement on the part of the Negroes, even though, in comparison to the whites, they were more frequently in a long-term courting relationship of which their families and friends were aware. Two related reasons have been advanced in the literature: (1) Negroes have a lesser commitment to the norm of legitimacy than do whites; (2) Negro women have less reason and desire than white women to form a stable marriage, pregnant or not. The explanation of these two facts is based on the social and cultural situation of the Negro in the United States, both presently and historically.

Goode argues that populations such as the American Negro that were denuded of their culture and then "kept from either being integrated into the Western cultural and social systems *or* establishing independent, *internally* integrated cultural and social systems of their own" manifest a low commitment to the norm of legitimacy.[12] The dominant white (or Iberian) society maintained caste barriers and so did not provide the rewards necessary for effective acculturation, nor did it allow Negroes to develop cohesive communities with the accompanying control over sanctions to enforce their own norms. Although the Negro is now being integrated into the national culture, this process has not proceeded far enough to foster development of a high commitment to the norm of legitimacy among Negroes or to arm the Negro with the sanctions necessary to enforce conformity to this norm.

Along with Goode's conclusions, we may place the analysis of why the Negro less often than the white female has the desire to get married (even though pregnant). Such a practice, of course, frequently results in a matrifocal family in which the female head of household is the dominant member.[13] Some account for the matrifocal family pattern among Negroes mainly as a result of historical factors, treating it as a holdover from the past by noting that the woman was the center of the slave family. They also note that the Negro was unlikely to institutionalize a stable male-dominated family during the social disruption brought about by Reconstruction and Negro rural-urban migration. However, certain current conditions of Negro life may be considered as either supplementary factors or even sufficient in themselves to produce the matrifocal family pattern. We suggest that, in strata living under the following conditions, the woman has lessened motivation to marry and that a relatively high proportion of matrifocal families is the result.

1. It holds a class position at the lowest rank of the society.
2. It has limited chance for upward vertical social mobility.
3. Its members have a high degree of job insecurity.
4. However, opportunity exists for women to engage in money-making activities (in low-paying jobs—for example as domestics, farm or factory laborers).
5. The male is expected (by the dominant cultural ethos) to be the family's main money-earner.[14]

In strata faced with this social situation, the female has lessened economic motivation for seeking marriage and lessened respect for men as marital partners; if sanctions are not forthcoming to support legitimacy, pressures to marry even after premarital pregnancy are limited. The combination of these two factors—lessened stress on the norm of legitimacy and the lessened motivation for the woman to marry—may account for the Negro-white differences shown in our data.

Summary

The data on this sample of unwed mothers indicate that the prepregnancy relationship with the alleged father was in most cases like that of courting couples in general. Though these courtships produced illegitimate children, they cannot be described as deviant, exploitative, or lacking exposure to the normal social controls. The firmness of this conclusion is reduced because of the low completion rate for the sample of white unwed mothers. The Negro-white differences, probably underestimated in our data, are consistent with the interpretations that Negroes in comparison to whites have more permissive premarital sexual attitudes, are less committed to legitimate childbirth, and that the Negro female is less desirous of getting married than the white female. These factors help explain the findings that the Negro in comparison to the white unwed mother was more often in a long-term relationship, but yet less often planning marriage.

That some courtships produce illegitimate births is not surprising in a period in which American youth exercise much control over their courtship activity, given a culture that emphasizes the importance of sexual attractiveness. Many couples engage in premarital sexual relations, and yet some unknown proportion of these avoid having children—either through contraception or abortion or because they are not fertile. Others get married after a premarital pregnancy but before a premarital birth. Why some couples have illegitimate children and others do not awaits an investigation in which couples are followed through time to see which couples have illicit sexual relations and, among those who do, which have illegitimate births and which do not. By conducting rigorous longitudinal studies, we can more adequately unravel the factors associated with illegitimate childbirth.

NOTES

[1] Clark E. Vincent, *Unmarried Mothers* (New York: The Free Press of Glencoe, 1961), pp. 17–21.

[2] Among the 34 states reporting in 1960 North Carolina ranked seventeenth from the highest in white illegitimacy ratio (2.2 percent) and thirteenth from the highest in nonwhite illegitimacy ratio (23.8 percent). The eleven former Confederate states ranked from fifth (Tennessee and Florida, 2.7 percent) to thirty-second (Mississippi, 1.4 percent) in white illegitimacy ratios and from second (Tennessee, 29.5 percent) to eighteenth (Louisiana, 20.4 percent) in nonwhite illegitimacy ratios. See *Vital Statistics of the United States: 1960,* Vol. 1 (Washington, D.C.: Government Printing Office, 1962), Table 1-U, pp. 1–31.

[3] The linkage of sex to purposes other than gratification of sexual drives is basic to the institution of marriage. Therefore, the factor that characterizes a promiscuous woman is not her exchange of sexual favors for economic security and other rewards (received as well by married women) or her emotional indifference to the sexual act (an attitude found among many wives). Rather, it is indifference to her partner and the consequent lack of selectivity and exclusivity that characterize the "loose" woman. In the promiscuous sexual relationship, sexual intercourse is divorced from any stable or affectional social relationship; it is made contingent neither on genuine affection nor on the possibility of marriage. See Kingsley Davis, "Sexual Behavior," in *Contemporary Social Problems,* 2nd ed., edited by R. K. Merton and R. A. Nisbet (New York: Harcourt, Brace & World, 1966), pp. 322–72.

Many of the white women were well aware of traditional chastity standards and professed belief in them. Eighty-three percent among the whites answered that premarital sexual relations were never all right (even with a man whom one planned to marry soon). The comparable figure for Negroes was 28 percent. Thus, a majority of the white women now held personal sexual codes that they, in the past, had violated. (We, of course, have no data on what standards they held before they became pregnant.) We will not stress data on self-reported standards for behavior, because they are subject to more bias in reporting than the data presented in the body of the paper.

[4] See Vincent, *op. cit.,* pp. 1–30, for a discussion of social attitudes toward illegitimacy in the United States as well as some of the shifts that have occurred in these attitudes. For a convenient collection of articles on unwed motherhood, see Robert W. Roberts, ed., *The Unwed Mother* (New York: Harper & Row, 1966).

[5] See Jessie Bernard, *Marriage and Family Among Negroes* (Englewood Cliffs, N.J.: Prentice-Hall, 1966), for a recent summary of literature on the Negro. Bernard warns against oversimplification about Negro subculture. Note especially her discussion in Chapter 2 of the "acculturated" and "externally adapted" cultures and, within this context, her section on Negro attitudes toward out-of-wedlock births. Also see the work on sexual standards cited in footnote 6 below.

[6] In this recent work, Ira L. Reiss has provided data on the sexual *standards* of American adults and youth. His general findings may be summarized as follows: men are more permissive than women (permissiveness being characteristic of

those who accept premarital coitus); Negroes are more permissive than whites; youth (high-school and college age) are more permissive than adults; and there is no relationship between permissiveness and social class. His analysis suggests, however, that in a liberal attitudinal setting the social class and permissiveness relation is positive, whereas in a conservative setting it is negative. See his following articles for further interesting analysis of the above zero-order relationships: "The Scaling of Premarital Sexual Permissiveness," *Journal of Marriage and the Family* 26 (May 1964): 188–98; "Premarital Sexual Permissiveness Among Negroes and Whites," *American Sociological Review* 29 (October 1964): 688–98; and "Social Class and Premarital Sexual Permissiveness: A Re-examination," *American Sociological Review* 30 (October 1965): 747–56. Also see his "Sexual Codes in Teen-age Culture," *Annals* 338 (November 1961): 53–62.

In an earlier work Reiss has discussed the various sexual standards in the United States. For a discussion of the emergence of the permissiveness-with-affection standard, see I. L. Reiss, *Premarital Sexual Standards in America* (New York: The Free Press, 1960), especially Chapter 10. For a cautionary view on the past and likely future rates of change in American sexual standards, see Hallowell Pope and Dean D. Knudsen, "Premarital Sexual Norms, the Family, and Social Change," *Journal of Marriage and the Family* 37 (August, 1965): 314–23. See Winston Ehrmann, *Premarital Dating Behavior*, Bantam ed., (New York: Henry Holt, 1960), for a detailed study of the sexual standards and behavior of college students. In *Journal of Social Issues* 22 (April 1966), Reiss has served as editor for articles on "The Sexual Renaissance in America." See especially the article by Lee Rainwater, "Some Aspects of Lower Class Sexual Behavior," pp. 96–108.

[7] See William J. Goode, *The Family*, (Englewood Cliffs, N.J.: Prentice-Hall, 1964), pp. 19–30; and Pope and Knudsen, *op. cit.*

[8] See Ehrmann, *op. cit.*, pp. 39–44, for a summary of the incidence of premarital intercourse among college and high-school sample populations as reported by various investigators. Clifford Kirkpatrick, *The Family as Process and Institution*, 2nd ed. (New York: The Ronald Press Company, 1963), Table 28, pp. 351–3, presents the "evidence of sexual nonconformity" from the Kinsey findings for both males and females.

The use of contraceptive techniques may be the only significant difference between the courting behavior of the women in our sample and courtships in which premarital intercourse takes place but in which no pregnancy occurs. We collected limited data on the contraceptive practices of our sample (but have no comparative data on the contraceptive practice of "typical" courtships). That 64 percent of the Negro and only 39 percent of the white women reported use of some contraceptive technique again indicates that our white sample was particularly biased toward those women who had the least concern about unwed motherhood. Of those women who reported use of a contraceptive technique, almost all (92 percent for Negroes and 84 percent for whites) said that their sex partners only employed the technique (exclusively the condom in over seven-tenths of the cases). Only 28 percent of the white and 14 percent of the Negro women who reported use of some technique said that it was used "every time" they had sex relations. It is clear that the women in our sample reduced the risk of pregnancy only minimally through contraception. And it is striking that, even when contraception was used, the female partner so often relied exclusively on the male. Although the woman might be expected to insist on the use of contraception or to employ some technique herself, her inabilities here are linked to her cultural position. She is expected to be subordinate to the male and not obviously aggressive in sexual matters. However, taking responsibility for contraceptive techniques violates both of these norms. Thus, though the majority of women in our sample reported concern about having an illegitimate child as a result of premarital sex relations, very few employed contraceptive techniques of their own—only 6 percent among the whites and 5 percent among the Negroes.

[9] See William J. Goode, "Illegitimacy in the Caribbean Social Structure," *American Sociological Review* 25 (February 1960): 21–30.

[10] Cf. Vincent's discussion, *op. cit.,* Chapter 4.

[11] Comparable figures for white married couples are very closely similar. Vincent, using data from the 1950 U.S. Census on 1,763,000 white wives between the ages of 14 and 22 who had been married less than three years, found that 53 percent of these wives were within three years of the same age as their husbands. *Op. cit.,* p. 76.

[12] See William J. Goode, "Illegitimacy, Anomie, and Cultural Penetration," *American Sociological Review* 26 (December 1961): 910–25 at p. 918. Reiss, "Premarital Sexual Permissiveness Among Whites and Negroes," *op. cit.,* gives data showing that Negroes are more often permissive than whites in their attitudes toward premarital sexual behavior.

[13] The matrifocal family also includes an emphasis on kin relations in the female line and perhaps the assumption by the maternal grandmother of the head of household. The father of the children may be totally absent, or there might be a succession of temporary fathers. A "weak" but stable father might even be present, but then his importance and authority are marginal to the primary sphere of mother-child relationships.

The U.S. Census provides figures giving some indication of the proportion of matrifocal families. For North Carolina in 1960, 21 percent of the Negro and 8 percent of the white families had female heads. U.S. Bureau of the Census, *U.S. Census of Population: 1960,* Vol. I, *Characteristics of the Population,* Part 35, North Carolina, Table 109, p. 381. For a brief comparison of the Negro and white family structure in the United States as a whole, see U.S. Department of Labor, *The Negro Family: The Case for National Action* (the "Moynihan Report") (Washington, D.C.: Government Printing Office, 1965).

[14] The most influential discussion of the historical factors generating the matrifocal family from among Negroes is E. Franklin Frazier, *The Negro Family in the United States,* (Chicago: University of Chicago Press, 1939). For more recent discussions, see Bernard, *op. cit.;* and Andrew and Amy Tate Billingsley, "Illegitimacy and Patterns of Negro Family Life," in Roberts, ed., *op. cit.,* pp. 133–157. For insightful analyses of the forces that create the matrifocal family, see Raymond T. Smith, *The Negro Family in British Guiana* (London: Routledge and Kegan Paul, 1956); and Helen M. Icken, *From Shanty Town to Public Housing: A Comparison of Family Structure in Two Urban Neighborhoods in Puerto Rico* (Ph.D. diss., Columbia University, 1962). Also relevant are the data and discussion in Robert O. Blood, Jr., and Donald M. Wolfe, *Husbands and Wives* (New York:The Free Press, 1960), pp. 11–46.

SUGGESTED READINGS

Chaskel, R. "Illegitimacy—the Dimensions of Prevention." *Social Casework,* February 1969, pp. 95–101.

N. C. I. *Double Jeopardy, Triple Crises and Illegitimacy Today.* New York: National Council on Illegitimacy, 1969.

Pierce, R. *Single and Pregnant.* Boston: Beacon Press, 1970.

Roberts, R., ed. *The Unwed Mother.* New York: Harper & Row, 1966.

3

Understanding Sexuality in Another Culture—and in Our Own

BEATRICE SIMCOX REINER

Teaching Human Growth in another culture may result in more learning for the teacher than for the students, at least in the beginning. This learning includes recognition that: (1) we Americans have cultural hangups and shibboleths of our own, (2) sex mores are related to economic and political conditions as well as to religious and philosophical ideologies, (3) we can neither learn nor teach adequately until we are able to enter the other cultural framework, and (4) students have stereotypes of us that interfere with their learning from us. These factors are present in relation to any other culture or subculture, whether foreign or within our own borders, but for me the experience of working in a developing country helped to clarify them. (From 1966 to 1969 I was on the staff of the School of Social Work of Haile Selassie I University, Addis Ababa, Ethiopia.)

In Ethiopia one is spared any false sense of "knowing all the facts," because in a developing country facts may not be easy to get. There may be no accurate census, and valid estimates may be suppressed or padded by the government for reasons of external or internal security or for foreign loans. But even in the United States, where elaborate demographic statistics are available, it is sometimes difficult to obtain local figures about deaths, illness, or unemployment in minority groups.

I found a serious gap in information about family relationships, child care, and sexuality in Ethiopia. Everyone took for granted the prevalence of strict patriarchal family discipline, the importance of the extended family, and widespread prostitution, but little had been written about the family as such. The most comprehensive book, based entirely on the dominant ethnic group, contained valuable information but made some generalizations that were open to question. There was one good study on prostitutes, but most of the other sociological or anthropological studies were concerned with rituals or magic beliefs of small, remote tribes. A qualified European mental health team was making useful studies of mental illness on an epidemiological basis, but there was still no material on the dynamics of family life and sexuality.

Obviously, then, this material had to come from the social work students and it was they alone who could breathe some life into the United Nations statistics: a literacy rate of 7 percent, a life expectancy of 26 years, and an average yearly income of less than $50. Here one was faced with the same problem that the middle-class white American has in feeling the impact of statistics about our Black ghettoes. It is only recently that books about Black America have begun to contain explicitly sexual material from the Black man's point of view or family material that illustrates feelings.

To get useful information from Ethiopian students meant that (1) they had to be experienced enough to know what was important, and (2) they had to have some confidence that it would be understood by the teacher. Here the stereotypes about Western (and especially American) social workers come into play. Under the polite but reserved friendliness of Ethiopians there is some resentment of our affluence and our tendency to feel that our way is right. The more sophisticated students watch for signs of neocolonialism and are quick to suspect that one is in the pay of the CIA. Rarely was Viet Nam mentioned, though the facts are well known in the Third World.

In working within another culture, stereotypes about the worker (which often may have some basis) cannot be ignored. In spite of our training in "the use of the self," which simply means understanding the whole situation and acting appropriately within it, white American social workers seem limited in applying it. We just cannot believe that anyone would think these things about us! Our ability to relate to people with different values even in the United States leaves something to be desired.[1]

Another barrier to understanding seems to lie in the concept of "self-determination," which is regarded by European and African social workers as purely American. Personally, this came as a surprise to me, perhaps because I have always regarded self-determination (like freedom of the will) as an entirely relative matter. However, it is true that in the United States most clients do have some choice of alternatives open to them; they are not faced, as Ethiopians often are, with only a choice between life and death. Subsistence farming does not mean that the farmer necessarily subsists, and for many people death is never very far away. This is one meaning of a life expectancy of 26 years and of the frequent funeral processions winding slowly toward the Coptic church.

The figure of 300 physicians for a population of 22 million people means that a person in the countryside faced with a serious illness may sell his ox and go to Addis Ababa to look for treatment. Unless he locates relatives or friends who take him into their crowded one-room house, he is in a strange city, sick, without money, and perhaps encumbered with hungry children. Until the teacher learns this, he is horrified by frequent student cases in which clients, with gestures of profound humility, beg the student to tell them what to do. The new foreign teacher is shocked by this "dependency" and the client's statements about relying on "God's will." Later the teacher comes to understand that "Tell me what to do" may be a cry of despair. Everything the client has tried has failed and he feels he is an unlucky person who is doomed. After some material help, this same client may show considerable resourcefulness and initiative. The problem is not "dependency" but "crisis."

As the economic and political background comes more clearly into focus, its relationship to sexual and family mores becomes more apparent. A short excursion into psychohistory may be helpful, revealing that Ethiopia is in a postfeudal stage of history. This country of nearly 400,000 square miles was ruled by warring regional overlords until consolidated as a nation under Emperor Menelik II in 1895. The process of national unification was continued and intensified by Emperor Haile Selassie I both before and after the Italian Occupation (1935–45).

Originally the overlord gave the peasant protection in return for crops and services. He was regarded as a father and endowed with grandiose and omnipotent powers. The negative part of the peasant's ambivalent relationship to the lord was discharged by acting like his lord in relation to his own wife and children. The wife, in turn, expressed her resentment in devious ways and often fostered rebellion in her sons.[2] With the coming of national unity, the overlord became a local landlord with certain enforceable powers (especially to confiscate up to 80 percent of the crops) but few, if any, responsibilities. His godlike attributes were transferred to the Emperor, whose descent from King Solomon was promulgated.

As the lord became less of a father and more of a local tyrant, the peasant continued to carry on his authoritarian family pattern but adopted some of the female methods of expressing devious resentment under a cloak of submission. Graphic examples of such postfeudal behavior are familiar in Molière's plays where the servant outwits the "Big Man" and makes fun of him while appearing to follow his orders. There is an Amharic phrase that means "bowing low while emitting gas."[3]

In this connection the client's "Tell me what to do" may have another meaning. It can be the conventional response of a lower-class person to someone in a higher position. Here the outward appearance of submission and humility masks negative or ambivalent feelings that ultimately will find indirect expression, perhaps in saying one thing and doing another, or sabotaging the worker's plan in insidious ways, or pursuing it so half-heartedly that it is bound to fail, or punishing others by making them uncomfortable. The foreign teacher must be aware of this pattern operating at times between his students and himself—and only as he begins to be able to cut through to the real feeling will he also be able to show the students that this pattern operates between their clients and them. The student who has recently come from a distant village may not be aware that to an illiterate client a University student is a "Big Man."

In the postfeudal peasant world where there is little or no social structure, the only source of help in emergencies is from relatives. The result is close ties to the kinship group, with some ritualizing of obligations and respect for elders. Perhaps the first discipline the child encounters is related to visits from relatives. At these times the children must stand quietly at one end of the room until all the adults have finished eating. At other times small children are indulged, loved, and enjoyed.

One of the surprises for the American social worker is the discovery that toilet training is no problem to Ethiopian families. Students are amused by the space devoted to it in American books. An occasional child may present a mild problem with bedwetting, but since otherwise most of life goes on out of doors, urination and defecation can be done anywhere. At about the same time that the American child may be coping with active toilet training, the Ethiopian child is being trained to avoid dirt and to show unfailing respect for older people. However, among the new urban elite who live in European-style "villas" with flush toilets one begins to see the inevitable signs of early and severe toilet training.

A change comes at the age of five or six for the rural child (especially the boy) when he ceases to be a baby and is expected to herd the family cattle. From this time on, the father's expectations of the child are paramount. He has little interest in the child's personal needs or problems and there is quick punishment for transgressions.

The fact that only 7 percent of Ethiopian children are in school means that most rural children are on the hillsides with the cattle. Many children do go to "priest school" where (for a fee) they sit under a tree and drone in sing-song the complicated characters of the Amharic language. If a family is both fortunate and ambitious for the children, they may attend a primary school and then be sent to relatives in a town or city for intermediate and high school education. Some children leave their own homes at the age of six or seven. When you add the children who are living with relatives for the sake of education to those who are there because of the death or divorce of parents, the importance of the extended family is further appreciated. However, this may take time to comprehend. A team of European psychosocial experts, wanting to assess the impact of parental loss on Ethiopian children, undertook a survey of two rural schools, with the extraordinary finding that the children from "broken homes" did better than the others! Ethiopian social workers pointed out that the children who were not living with their families but were attending these schools (which were not free) were an especially favored group—either their own parents were paying for their care or their relatives were giving them an unusual privilege, possibly because they had shown unusual aptitude.

The Ethiopian social work student is somewhat mystified by our emphasis on adolescence. He is not acquainted with the behavior that we describe. The American social worker begins to realize, perhaps for the first time, that in agricultural communities where the succession of generations works naturally, there are fewer adolescent problems. Bettelheim points out that only the youth who is kept dependent on his parents, economically and emotionally, suffers problems related to revival of the Oedipus in adolescence.[4] Consequently, adolescent difficulties, per se, arise chiefly in upper-class families. However, Ethiopia has increasing identity problems among the late adolescents and postadolescents who are students in high schools and the University, and who tend to be several years older than American students. The intense pressure for education has often cut them off from community life, postponed marriage, and perhaps forced them into fields of study for which they have little aptitude. Emotional problems among University students and suicides among high school students are not uncommon.

In rural areas subsistence farming influences the marriage pattern. A marriage is arranged for the girl by the time she is 13 or 14 or even earlier to a man who may be 19 or 20. By this time the girl, who has been in the company of her mother since she was 7 or 8, is skilled in cooking or household tasks. Her marriage means for the family: one less mouth to feed, further extension of the family, and eventually grandchildren. In a country where farming requires physical strength, children are an asset as well as a form of old-age insurance. A rural couple knows that they must have seven or eight children in order to be sure that any will survive to support them in their old age. Failure to have children is one common reason for divorcing a woman.

Although arranged marriages are still the rule in rural areas, among educated city people there are many variations. A girl who has met an acceptable man may encourage him to approach her parents in the traditional way, while she tries to induce them to consent. In this way she feels she has the best of both systems. Or to avoid the overwhelming burden of wedding costs, a traditional "kidnapping" may be staged, with the agreement of all concerned. In general, the female role is conceived as passive, with aggression expressed subtly rather than directly. In a culture where there is still a kind of Victorian secrecy about sex, with resulting fear of men and of losing one's reputation as a "good girl," the American pattern of dating and playing the field is too fear-provoking to be acceptable to many girls. This seems hard for some foreign teachers to imagine. As a result, they tend to blame the men for wanting to keep the women in bondage. The students are aware of teachers' biases in this respect.

The conspiracy of silence about sex means that the young bride enters her arranged marriage with little or no sex information. She has left her own family and is perhaps living in a distant village. The typical history of a prostitute begins in this way. She tells of being beaten by her husband and weeping beside her cooking fire. After a year or so she ran away, perhaps encouraged by a visiting friend or relative who operated a drinking house in the city and promised her nice clothes. In the city she eked out a meager existence in one drinking house after another, moving to "better herself" or because she quarreled with the owner. There was no other work available; factories are few and far between, and pay only seventy–five cents a day. Social workers encounter many prostitutes after they have contracted a venereal disease or tuberculosis or become pregnant. Many have been forced to turn to begging for a living. Prostitutes are estimated at 17 percent of women in towns and cities.

Lack of preparation for marriage not only produces prostitutes but also helps to increase the demand for their services. Among the prostitute's customers are husbands of women who have adjusted to marriage with a kind of joyless resignation. Undoubtedly, lack of preparation is also one factor in the high divorce rate. It will take a new generation of women who have been exposed to sound biological and psychological knowledge of sex to change this. The mothers of this generation of girls not only were inhibited but lacked information. For instance, there is almost no understanding of menstruation. Since Ethiopian girls do not usually begin to menstruate until they are at least 15 or 16, they have traditionally been married before the onset. Consequently, menstruation is believed to be the result of sexual intercourse, and this belief causes great confusion for girls in orphanages or boarding schools. Actually, some women seldom menstruate, because they are pregnant or lactating during much of their fertile years.

It may take the foreign newcomer a little time to discover the custom of performing clitorectomies on girl babies a few days after birth, presumably to prevent promiscuity by making sex less pleasurable. This operation is not talked about readily, though it is responsible for some related problems: (1) it is said to increase the dangers of childbirth through extensive scar-tissue that does not stretch, (2) it raises questions for educated girls about orgasms, and (3) it is a source of conflict between educated women and their mothers at the birth of a female child.

This drastic operation expresses not only the sinfulness of sexual enjoyment for women and men's lack of belief in women's trustworthiness, but also a basic mistrust of the human body. Unlike the Mexicans, who tend to oppose operations as interference with the "natural balance" of the body,[5] Ethiopians resort to cutting or burning the body to relieve stubborn physical symptoms. Children with swollen glands have their necks burned with fire and infants with digestive troubles may have the uvula cut, as if the body were at fault.

Students who have already had some public health indoctrination from foreign teachers brand these measures as "superstition" and may be extremely impatient when clients turn to local healing practitioners, who not only perform these services but also prescribe herb remedies and invoke spirits. It seems to help the students to know that medical specialists in many developing countries have begun to take more seriously the magical beliefs of peasants and have had some success in incorporating "witch doctors" into the scientific healing process.[6] They have found that these practitioners are able to adapt their methods and to incorporate new ones that seem more effective. Such information comes as a relief to the student, offering him a bridge between the magical beliefs of his own childhood and the scientific truths he has now adopted. It may be one small step in unifying an identity that is threatened in so many ways by the values of Westerners.

One cultural area about which the American teacher must exercise great caution is that of the position of women. There is probably no issue about which we are more militant; yet the position of women in Ethiopia is not easy for a foreigner to grasp. In spite of the child marriages and the clitorectomies and in spite of the fact that the Ethiopian woman may walk a pace or two behind her husband on the road and leave major decisions to him, she is by no means a chattel. Women, as well as men, can and do terminate marriages, and after a divorce any property is divided equally. There is no opposition to education for women, though it may be considered less essential for a girl. Women have often been rulers in Ethiopia, and in recent times aristocratic women have shown leadership in educational and philanthropic projects. Among lower classes, even though the woman may show outward signs of submission, she is a person in her own right and quite capable of maneuvering the men in her family. It takes time for a foreigner to discover this, and students who have not been taught to observe are not always aware of it, either.

The process of helping the student to observe his own culture makes special demands on the foreign teacher in appreciating the values and satisfactions inherent in the culture. There is a game, "But this is the culture," which is played by students and foreign teachers. It usually starts with a comment by the teacher that meets with resistance. After a student says,

"But this is the culture," the game can go in one of two ways. One teacher, believing that the culture must never be questioned, drops the subject and the students have scored a point. Another teacher, who has missionary zeal, endeavors to point out how the culture is wrong. Lively discussion ensues with no one convinced; the students' conviction of the teacher's lack of understanding may have been reinforced, or else their identifications have been further confused.

One Ethiopian marital case always evoked heated class discussion. A young, educated couple asked advice from a young Ethiopian social worker in a hospital. The wife had left the husband's home, refusing to share it with his sister. Since the wife and husband came from different ethnic groups, the students always began by insisting that this was a "cultural problem" because the wife "refused to accept responsibility for relatives." Presumably it was untreatable. Supreme effort was always required to get the students to look at other factors in the disagreement. For six years prior to the recent marriage the husband's younger sister had lived with him and managed his home, so that it was the wife who was the intruder. The wife, who had been pregnant at the time of the marriage, was made extremely uneasy by her mother-in-law, who came for the wedding and stayed in the home for a month. Because the two women spoke different languages, they could communicate only through the husband, who made little attempt to interpret and left his wife suspicious about what her mother-in-law was saying about her. The sister, feeling the wife's hostility, accused her of not wanting to give the mother food for her journey home. The husband, with the kind of assured complacency that is the despair of marriage counselors in any culture, assumed a self-righteous attitude and regarded his wife as totally unreasonable for not wanting to live with his sister. The social worker, accepting the situation at face value, tried to reason kindly with the wife and met with pleasant but firm resistance. Even when the sister and the man's mother begged the husband to make another arrangement for the sister (money was not a problem), he refused, saying that it was his duty to take care of her. It finally took the intercession of elders of his own ethnic group to convince him to give in. (After the reconciliation the social worker was invited to lunch.)

The students' expectation that the foreign teacher would side with the wife against the husband (in line with the principle of self-determination) was always an initial obstacle to their understanding the case. Before they could move on to discussion of the individuals it was necessary to convince them that the teacher understood the social value of family responsibility. This issue also came up in cases referred to social work students in schools because children were unhappy or mistreated in the homes of relatives. Family responsibility provides almost the only care available for orphans, widows, and the sick, as well as reciprocal services of other kinds within the extended family. When the system works well, it is far better than institutional services. Many of the students are still benefiting from the system, although they are beginning to look ahead to the burden of repayment in kind. Their own conflicting feelings contribute to their vigorous defense of the system against an anticipated attack by the foreigner. Only when the immense importance of the system is appreciated mutually can its variations and defects be recognized.

In the United States we have similar reluctance to question anything that has been accepted as "cultural" behavior. For instance, social workers are apt to assume that the Black mother's care of her teenage daughter's baby completely solves the problem. Acceptance of the baby within the family group is important, but we may overlook its negative aspects: unequal competition between mother and daughter for the love of the baby, postponement of motherhood on the part of the girl until major responsibility for the child is required of her (often too late), confusion in the child about whose child he is, and his feeling of lack of worth because his mother "gave him" to the grandmother.[7] We need perhaps to learn to distinguish among: behavior that is part of a unified, balanced culture; that which a minority group is forced to assume because of lacks in the host culture; and traditional mores that are in process of change because of the impact of outside influences. A cultural solution that amounts to making the best of a bad situation may be improved by appropriate auxiliary service.

The ambivalence of a people about their own changing culture must also be understood. It is like one's feeling about one's own family. I may criticize my family severely but I am, after all, part of it so that criticism by outsiders is also criticism of me. Another problem for the foreigner is the coexistence of apparently contradictory or paradoxical attitudes, especially in the area of sex. An American teacher of English in Thailand referred to his students as seeming at the same time immaculately innocent and astoundingly knowing. "In one's teaching one would proceed with greatest caution, as if addressing a band of particularly young and delicate nuns, only to be greeted with a ripple of curious laughter, alerting one to some accidental innuendo in one's discourse."[8] This sounded familiar to me. Such experiences always served as a reminder that where expression of feelings is subject to cultural controls and restrictions, there are much more awareness and intuitive feeling than appear on the surface. It is the job of the social work teacher to make the intuitive feeling more accessible to the student, not only for his own benefit and that of individual clients, but also for his society.

In a developing country the relation of the individual to the society seems more apparent than it does in Western fragmented, industrialized societies. One becomes aware in Ethiopia that the client in question represents thousands of other people in similar situations. No case discussion is ever complete until there has been discussion of the kinds of resources that should be available and of desirable preventive measures. However, perhaps we Westerners are too pat in thinking of setting up services, rather than of integrating them into community life. Ultimately, the test of any system is what happens to the individual, whether the system is a social agency, a factory, or a nation. Until the system is geared to the needs of all people, it is not functioning properly.

For instance, in Ethiopia the interrelated problems of prostitution, early marriage, and secrecy about sex, as well as population control, cannot be solved solely by education and enlightenment, important as these are. Until the economic problems of land ownership, farming methods, and transportation of farm products are met, perhaps in conjunction with industrialized food packing and marketing and adequate employment for urban workers, there will be no appreciable change. We will see only a growing separation in life styles between the educated elite and the mass of the population. In the United States we have had our own experience with "gradualism" and we have seen the violence it can breed.

The future of civilization depends on the ability of men to integrate knowledge of human development and human needs with technological, political, and social planning. In spite of tremendous economic and political handicaps, the developing countries are in a better position to do this than the industrialized countries because they have less to undo. They have not spent the last two hundred years since the Industrial Revolution trying to turn man into a machine. With our help, they may not have to repeat all the mistakes we have made, and out of their new experience there could be lessons for us.

We now have the means to help developing countries to achieve integrated planning. In the last few years we have incorporated into our knowledge of human growth and development the influences of social, cultural, and economic forces; now we have come full circle so that we should be able to feed back this integrated knowledge into our critiques of social systems and into future planning. Whether or not we can do this on any appreciable scale depends on two things: (1) whether we recognize the value of the human knowledge we now have, and (2) whether we can acquire a more detached view of our own culture in relation to other cultures.

NOTES

[1] Phyllis Southwick and Milton Thackeray, "The Concept of Culture in the Neighborhood Center," *Social Casework* 50, no. 7 (July 1969).

[2] Seymour Rubenfeld, *Family of Outcasts* (New York: Free Press, 1965).

[3] Donald Levine, *Wax and Gold: Tradition and Innovation in Ethiopian Culture* (Chicago: University of Chicago Press, 1965).

[4] Bruno Bettelheim, "Problems of Generations," in Erik Erikson, ed., *Youth: Change and Challenge* (New York: Basic Books, 1963).

[5] William Madser, "Value Conflicts and Folk Psycho-therapy in South Texas," in Ari Kiev, ed., *Magic Faith and Healing,* (New York: The Free Press, 1964).

[6] H. T. Adeoye Lambo, "Patterns of Psychiatric Care in Developing African Countries," in Ari Kiev, ed., *op. cit.*

[7] Beatrice S. Reiner, "The Real World of the Teenage Negro Mother," Child Welfare 47, no. 7, (July 1968).

[8] D. J. Enright, "Poetry Makes You Nice and Neat," *Transition* magazine no. 37 (Kampala, Uganda).

SUGGESTED READINGS

Gochros, H. "Sex and Marriage in Rural Appalachia," *Social Welfare in Appalachia* 2 (1970): 33–39.

Khaing, M. *Burmese Family*. Bombay, India: Orient Longmans, Ltd., 1946.

Mace, D. and V. *Marriage East and West*. Garden City, N.Y.: Doubleday & Company, 1960.

Pommerenke, M. *Asian Women and Eros*. New York: Vantage Press, 1958.

Ryan, B. *Sinhalese Village*. Miami, Fla.: University of Miami Press, 1958.

Human Sexual Behavior and Social Class Structure

MARJORIE H. BUCKHOLZ

All human behavior is determined primarily by the social environment in which the individual lives. Human sexual behavior is no exception. Strong as the sex drive is, like that of hunger, it is satisfied or denied according to the controls and ideology of the group in which the person lives. Early rearing and the peer group relationships of the young are the most important determinants of behavior.

Groups Within American Social Structure

Our society is made up of a variety of groups or social structures and each one has a somewhat different set of values. Also, some people are more closely associated with the groups about them and therefore they are more influenced by the norms. All of these differences contribute to a great variation in sexual behavior. There are social class groups, ethnic, religious, foreign-born, and color caste groups. Social class or status is measured in different ways, but economic level and occupation have been considered significant criteria. However, even within these measures, there are differences in levels of education and this factor is more closely associated with style of life, part of which is sexual behavior. Within most ethnic, religious, and color groups there also exist statuses and different life styles.

Having attempted to outline the types of groups in which human beings live their lives, we will endeavor to list differences in human sexual behavior and summarize some of the research that has been done to establish an association between the life style of a group and the most prevalent behavior by which they express or suppress sexuality.

Sexual Behavior in Children and Adolescents

Some parents believe that sexual impulses are dormant in infants and that any erotic stimulation is harmful. The Italian peasant is known to stimulate the genitalia to put the child to sleep. In Bali, on the other hand, it has been observed that, judged by the mother's evident enjoyment of both the baby's responsiveness and the temper tantrum which often follows, the purpose of the masturbation is to wake the baby up.[1]

In American and English culture among adults even the notion of infantile sexuality is strongly resisted. It therefore follows that the latency period may be culturally induced rather than due to a hypothetical endocrine change.[2] Freud's description of the latency period is as follows:

> For a period of years, roughly between the ages of five, when the Oedipus complex is repressed by fear of castration, and twelve, when the energy of the sexual instinct is greatly augmented by physiological changes in the reproductive system, the sexual and aggressive impulses of the child are in a subdued state. This is called the *latency period*. With the onset of puberty, the impulses are revived and occasion the typical stresses and strains of adolescence. New adaptations and transformations take place during these adolescent years which culminate finally in the stabilizing of the personality.[3]

Erik Erikson interprets the latency period as those years in which the child develops the skills important to his culture, including formal education and athletic skills. This has been described as a time in which the child develops skills and companionship with peers of his own sex.[4]

This is the style of rearing provided for the middle-class American child as well as the British and European. The social structure in which the child is living restricts his activities with the opposite sex and emphasizes accomplishment. Parents from the shtetl of Eastern Europe interviewed in New York indicated that:

> Parents discourage opposite–sex siblings from playing together by reminding them of their sex differences, and attaching to these implications of prestige. Thus, a boy attending *cheder*, Hebrew school, is told it is beneath him to play girls' games, if he is found playing with his sister.[5]

Ethnographic reports on cultural behavior in different primitive societies describe different attitutes toward sexual activities of children. Mead[6] and Malinowski[7] have described sexual experimentation carried out by children in the latency years and by adolescents, without the condemnation that this behavior would receive in middle-class culture in western countries.

Summarizing learning about sexual activity for four cultures of poverty in Mexico, Puerto Rico, England, and the United States, including white and black people, Rainwater concluded that the close living together of children and adults without privacy between members of families or even from one family to the other introduces children to sexual activity at an early age both through direct observations of sexual intercourse and through conversations of adults. However, Rainwater in writing about the Tepoztlan, the Puerto Rican, and the English working class and the lower class in the United States differs from Ladner and Hammond, who conducted research in a housing project in St. Louis occupied by poor blacks, with regard to the extent that the early sexual knowledge is acted out or suppressed during the latency years and the effect upon the adolescent, particularly the female. Rainwater reports:

> The sexual stimulation that comes in all of these cultures from the close living together of children and adults is apparently systematically repressed as the child grows older. The sexual interests stimulated by these and other experiences are deflected for the boys onto objects defined as legitimate marks (loose women, careless girls, prostitutes, etc.) and for the girls are simply pushed out of awareness with a kind of hysterical defense (hysterical because of the fact that, later, women seem to protest their ignorance too much).[8]

Ladner and Hammond report quite the opposite for blacks, quoting one mother: "These kids grow up fast in this project. The five and six year old heifers (girls) know as much about screwing as I do!"[9] The asexual childhood is almost inconceivable among this group. Instead, the child is held to be very sexual in his interests and capacities and it is expected that he will become aware of the sexual area as soon as he is able to do so. Some parents will boast of the early sexual conquests of their children. There is more reservation expressed with girls because of the grave consequences of pregnancy resulting from promiscuity. However, since promiscuity is more common in the ghetto and the father is usually not a part of the family group, there are not the extreme sanctions for illegitimacy that exist in the middle-class group, and the black female has an early awareness of as well as interest and involvement in sexual activities. In the housing project, sex is openly discussed among all age groups of both sexes.

> This gross lack of privacy forces into public and semi–public areas behaviors which would normally be conducted in privacy. Areas such as

stairways, halls, corridors, elevators, washrooms, parking lots, lobbys, etc., which are used to gain access to apartments, work areas, and recreational spaces, are also the favorite and main locations in which sexual activities of all variety take place.[10]

There is less of age barrier between the sexes in the black ghetto. When a boy or girl makes sexual advances they are accepted. There is little promise of the possibility of the family life pattern of the middle-class. The black male has been limited in his ability to support a family and the girl learns early that she will have to make it herself. For both boys and girls sex provides a sense of togetherness, identity, utility, and enjoyment. In the later adolescent years, sex frequently takes on the important function of being a form of exchange for material goods and services. Thus sexual intercourse will be an exchange for a movie date or a car ride. For the teenager it is also an escape from the dull life with its many deprivations. "The shy female is considered the troublemaker in the slums. Open aggressiveness on the part of the woman is considered honesty."[11]

In spite of the frequency of pregnancy and its limitations for the girl's future, there is seldom consideration of protection. However, the interviewers in the Ladner-Hammond study found that one-fourth of the girls had a sophisticated knowledge of the contraceptives listed on their schedule.

Eula M. Masingale, in discussing social class and socialization, has stated:

> In our society, an individual is born into a family which is a member of a particular socially ranked group. His family's social and sexual participation is largely limited to its own class group.

> His opportunities for social learning are limited by the pressure which he receives from groups above and below him to restrict his social participation, that is to "keep him in his social place."

> The effect of such pressure is usually to prevent him from learning new habits, and thus from increasing his social and economic privileges.

> Social class patterning of child's learning as exerted through the family, extends from control of the types of food he eats and of the way he eats it to kinds of sexual, aggressive educational training he receives.[12]

The black in the ghetto has been limited in his social contacts and in his opportunities for gratification. This contributes to the pattern of sexual gratification as an escape from the reality of his deprivations, and without the hope of a different future there is little reason for delayed gratification. The middle-class black has a very different record with very strong and lasting marital relationships, according to most writers.

Adult Sexual Behavior by Social Class

Adult sexual behavior varies widely in many aspects: sexual activities are looked upon as expressions of mutual love and satisfaction; as an evil expression of human nature; as acceptable only for the purpose of reproduction; or as an obligation that a woman has for a husband. There are variations in the norms for premarital and extramarital relations. These differ for the sexes as well as between social groups. The age at which sexual activities are discontinued varies as well as the age at which it is first experienced. Sex for the male may mean an important manifestation of his masculinity, the fulfillment of his obligation to produce children, or a romantic love affair based on a substantial agreement with his partner. Other variations exist in attitudes toward and participation in homosexuality, masturbation, foreplay, and the sex act.

Having identified the variations, we will look at the research findings which relate these differences in sexual practices to social or economic classes. Theodore N. Ferdinand in "Sex Behavior and the American Class Structure: A Mosaic" has examined the ethos of each of six broad strata of American social class structure, which he defines as "a series of discrete social classes each with its own distinctive life style and its own solution of the problem of sexual behavior."

In describing the basic values and attitudes of most upper-upper-class members in this country, he identifies quality, rather than ability or dedication, as the quintessence of virtue.

> Quality in this context refers to a capacity to excel by virtue of one's inherent excellence rather than by an accelerated effort or an extra desire to excel, and it is readily discernible in the natural ease with which the typical upper-upper-class person discharges the most difficult of tasks.[13]

The upper-upper-class considers its members superior to those of the other classes and therefore their sanctioned sexual relations are limited to their own class. They have disdain and contempt for the compulsive industriousness of the lower-upper and upper-middle classes, the moralistic conservatism of the lower-middle classes, and the unbridled impulsiveness of the lower classes. The striving of the upper-class male for an individualism of excellence imparts an intensity and self-consciousness to his relationships with the opposite sex. He strives to awaken a similar response in his feminine partner. It is therefore possible that he would be less motivated to be exploitative or inconsiderate. The quality of the sexual relationship is dependent upon the mutual satisfactions of the two partners and not upon the conventional standards of morality.

Drawing upon the Kinsey material,[14] Ferdinand reports that due to the separation of the sexes during the years of secondary education the members have resorted to masturbation to an unusually high degree. There is also homosexuality relatively frequently among women, both married and spinsters.

The lower-upper and upper-middle classes are characterized as aggressively ambitious, having arrived in their positions by intensive competition, especially the lower-upper class who also tend to be well-known within the community and high participators in civic and business associations.

> The view that these classes hold toward sexual behavior is powerfully shaped by the fact that nearly everyone has been exposed to a large university in which Greek-letter societies closely govern relationships between the sexes.[15]

Within the fraternity and sorority setting, consideration of sex is very pervasive: "It becomes the ultimate of human values."[16] This class encounters the sharpest ambivalence toward sexual behavior. Its young adults are exposed with equal intensity to sex expression as all-important and to traditional moral standards as all-controlling. An examination of the empirical findings for this group disclosed a large amount of premarital sexual relations among the younger members of this class who were in college.[17] Their interest in the physical aspect of sex falls off rather rapidly in middle age, and extramarital affairs are seldom part of the behavior. Masturbation is universal among both sexes; homosexuality is not common. Rather, for males value is attached to an assertive masculine manner.

The lower-middle class, which includes the white-collar worker who performs the routine tasks with little recognition, prefers predictability and stability to uncertainty, and security to opportunity. More than any other class it gives support to the conventions of society and is most puritanical with regard to sexual behavior.

> For them, sex is an ugly aspect of the human situation, and they do their best to ignore it. They try to suppress it in their teen-agers, and they take a detached, utilitarian attitude toward it in marriage. Extramarital affairs occur infrequently, and the members of this class masturbate relatively little.[18]

If they attend college they are usually on the social fringe and are not affected by the Greek-letter societies. They have most of the moral reservations of the orthodox community and fewer erotic stimulants than the higher classes. They approach sex gingerly, and they attempt to keep it at arm's length.

Ferdinand refers to the upper-lower class as the typical working class, whose members respect their own feelings but do not trust others because they have been deprived of the material goods available to those whom they see as less deserving than themselves. The sexes are competitive with little common understanding between them. An impersonal tone pervades the relationships between the sexes. Sex relationships, even among marriage partners, tend to fall into a matter-of-fact routine in which little effort is made to heighten or prolong enjoyment. He reports a great amount of premarital intercourse for both sexes and extramarital relations as a common occurrence, with the utilization of prostitutes. Homosexuality seems to be a common experience among the men of this class.

Rainwater's studies of lower-class Americans add another component to our understanding of the relationships or lack of feelings of mutuality between the sexes in the lower classes.[19] (In comparing studies of social classes, there is always the possibility that the classification schemes are not based on the same criteria or the same cutoff points. However, it seems likely that the two authors identified the same phenomena that Rainwater studied more extensively.) It is in the conjugal role that the lower-class-mates are "highly segregated" in their activities and their companionships in contrast to those in the upper classes who are "jointly organized."

> Very few working or lower class couples show that jointly organized pattern, but there is variation in the intermediate to the highly segregated range. When the influence of this variable on sexual enjoyment and interest is examined, we find a very strong relationship.
>
> . . . it is primarily among couples in highly segregated conjugal role relationships that we find wives who reject or are somewhat negative towards sexual relations. Similarly, it is primarily among couples in less segregated conjugal role relationships that we find husbands and wives who express great interest and enjoyment in sexual relations.
>
> These results suggest that the lower value placed on sexual relations by lower class wives, and to a lesser extent by lower class husbands, can be seen as an extension of the high degree of segregation in their conjugal role relationship more generally.[20]

In the lower-class white group, close and satisfying sexual relationships are difficult to achieve because there is little communication between the man and wife and little effort on the part of the husband to assist the wife in gaining gratification. Men attach little importance to mutual gratification. Another factor contributing to the low degree of satisfaction is the limited preparation that the girl has for the sexual role in marriage. In many slum groups, there is a double standard for sex conduct for boys and for girls. The boy is free to experiment at will. But the girl who is promiscuous is of lower value than the virgin or one-man girl.[21] The mothers do little to talk with their daughters about sex and many enter marriage, romanticizing it with fear of sex and thinking that sex is evil. Rainwater, Ferdinand, and Kinsey indicate that the higher-class and more highly educated woman finds greater satisfaction in sexual relationships in marriage than the girl of lower class and less education.

In Rainwater's study of marital sexuality in four cultures—Mexican, Puerto Rican, English, and American—he found the same conjugal role pattern prevailing among the lower class, involving a high degree of segregation of male from female and low sexual satisfaction for the wife.[22]

The same pattern of segregated roles for married couples that Rainwater identified among the urban poor, Weller describes for the poor of Appalachia.[23] The boy joins a peer group early in life, from whom he learns hunting and fishing as well as information about sex. After adolescence, sex appears to be minimized. The girl remains in the home with the older women in her kinship group. After marriage the same pattern continues with the husband spending his free time with the "boys." Parents sleep with infants and small children in the home partly to protect them. They sleep in clothing and members of families avoid dressing before one another.

The black girl in the lower class has had greater freedom for sexual experience earlier in life and there is not the double standard of the good and loose girl. But the competition among the sexes and the inability of the black male to provide for his family leave the lower-class black woman with many frustrations in sexual relationships.

Sex Revolution or Evolution

Let us take a brief look at the popular notion of a sex revolution in America. Ferdinand assumes that there is one;[24] Ira L. Reiss calls the notion a "myth";[25] and John Corry calls it mostly talk.[26] Ferdinand attributes a large part of the change in sexual behavior from traditional to more liberal, especially in relation to premarital relationships, to the extraordinary growth in the relative size of the middle class in America. With this increase in the size of the middle class and the trend for a larger segment of the middle- and upper-class youth to attend the large university, more youth come under the influence of an atmosphere in which sexual experience has become a pre-eminent aim of virtually all of its members. Reiss states that:

. . . today's more permissive sexual standards represent not revolution but evolution, not anomie but normality.[27]

His conclusions are based on research involving a representative sample of about 1,500 people, 21 and older, from all over the country; and about 1,200 high-school and college students, 16 to 22 years old, from three different states. Unlike the common belief that the difference between blacks and whites is one of class difference, Reiss found a large variation in the way whites and Negroes of *precisely the same class* view premarital sexual permissiveness. In his data on the lower-class, those approving of intercourse before marriage under some circumstances were 32 percent for white males, 70 percent for black men; 5 percent for white women and 33 percent for black women. Lower-class students were more permissive than the adults: white men, 56 percent, black men, 86 percent; white women, 17 percent, and black women, 42 percent.

Change in behavior occurs even though there have been guilt feelings about the conduct. Eighty-seven percent of the women and 58 percent of the men said that they had eventually come to accept sexual activities that had once made them feel guilty. The factor most decisive in motivating women to engage in coitus was the belief that they were in love. Almost two-thirds of the students thought that their sexual standards were close to those of their parents. Parents' values and commitments appear to influence the child's behavior indirectly as well as directly. Young people who rank high on church attendance rank low on premarital coitus. A larger percent of students felt that their sex standards were closer to those of their friends than to those of their parents. However, parents may indirectly affect their children's choice of friends.

Older people are more conservative, but the difference is not marked. What is significant is that parents are less permissive in their attitudes toward premarital sex than childless couples. The more permissive group of students were those with fathers who were professional men. This finding shows that within the upper segments of society, like the lower, there is a highly permissive group.

Reiss concludes that the differences in degree of permissiveness between men and women and between white and black may be attributed to the higher stock in the institution of marriage that whites possess compared to blacks and that white women have had. In the past, permissiveness was accompanied by a lower commitment to marriage.

The sources of the new American permissiveness are different. They include access to contraception; ways to combat venereal infection; and—quite as important—an intellectualized philosophy about the desirability of sex accompanying affection. "Respectable," college-educated people have integrated this new philosophy with their generally liberal attitudes about family, politics, and religion. And this represents a new and more lasting support for sexual permissiveness, since it is based on a positive philosophy rather than hedonism, despair, or depression.[28]

John Corry in his article, "A U.S. Sex Revolt? It's Mostly Talk,"[29] agrees with Reiss that American society is moving toward an acceptance of permissiveness with affection, meaning that sex among unmarried partners is respectable when there is mutual affection. Both writers see sex behavior and attitudes moving closer together with open discussion of both becoming one of the changes in all levels of society. The college students' sexual behavior changes within a continuum with the parents' attitudes at one side and the fellow students on the more permissive end.

The greatest change in sexual behavior is occurring in the middle range of the American social structure, particularly among university students. The student from the more liberal, intellectual background is the most permissive, and the girl who is a church-goer or from a family that is most conservative is experiencing the greatest amount of change in the behavior she learns to accept, influenced primarily by being in love.

The fact that sexual behavior and attitudes toward this behavior are culturally induced and not an absolute solution to man's sexual needs is evident in a study of the differences in societies. George P. Murdock studied the regulations of sex conduct in 118 societies, using the cross-cultural method. The sample included North America (mainly Indian tribes), Africa, Oceania, Eurasia, and South America. The only non-preliterate people were a group of Chinese and a group of New England whites. Only three societies in the sample of 118 seemed to have a general taboo against all sexual intercourse outside of marriage. These were the Connecticut Yankees and the Ashanti and Timne of West Africa. The other societies did not regulate sexual intercourse per se, but other social phenomena were connected with it. "To few people is sex an evil, albeit a necessary one, and thus to be confined exclusively within the limits of the one social relationship vested with the responsibility for reproduction."[30]

With these evidences that men solve their needs for sexual experience in different ways according to their social group, it is not surprising that, in a heterogeneous social organization such as the United States, we find a wide variation in sexual behavior and the sanctions that control it, and that we are encountering change. The rapid communication between groups and the mobility of the working class into the university culture of the upper classes has made change more rapid, more visible, and more verbal.

NOTES

[1] Gregory Bateson, "Sex and Culture," in Douglas G. Haring, Ed., *Personal Character and Cultural Milieu* (Syracuse, N.Y.: Syracuse University Press, 1956), p. 150.

[2] *Ibid*

[3] Calvin S. Hall, *A Primer of Freudian Psychology* (New York: World Publishing Company, 1954), pp. 110–11.

[4] Erik Erikson, *Childhood and Society,* 2nd ed. (New York: W. W. Norton & Company, Inc.), pp. 247–74.

[5] Ruth Landes and Mark Zborowski, "Hypotheses Concerning the Eastern European Jewish Family," in Herman D. Stein and Richard A. Cloward, eds., *Social Perspectives on Behavior* (New York: The Free Press, 1958), p. 61.

[6] Margaret Mead, *Coming of Age in Samoa* (New York: William Morrow, 1929).

[7] Bronislaw Malinowski, *Sex and Repression in Savage Society* (New York: Harcourt, 1927). (Carlfred B. Broderick, "Sexual Behavior Among Pre-adolescents," *Journal of Social Issues* 22, no. 2 (April, 1966), pp. 6–22, also discusses latency as a culturally induced period of asexual behavior.)

[8] Lee Rainwater, "Marital Sexuality in Four Cultures of Poverty," *Journal of Marriage and the Family* 26, no. 4 (November 1964), p. 458.

[9] Joyce Ladner and Boone Hammond, "Socialization into Sexual Behavior," a paper prepared for Society for the Study of Social Problems annual meeting, August, 1967; p. 4.

[10] *Ibid.,* p. 6.

[11] W. Allison David and Robert J. Havighurst, *Father of the Man* (Boston: Houghton Mifflin Company, 1947), p. 10.

[12] Eula M. Masingale, "Social Class, Socialization and Child Rearing Practices as They Influence Learning," *Journal of Social and Behavioral Sciences,* 13, no. 3 (Fall 1968), p. 36.

[13] Theodore N. Ferdinand, "Sex Behavior and the American Class Structure: A Mosaic," *Annals of the American Academy,* Vol. 376 (1968), p. 79.

[14] Alfred C. Kinsey et al., *Sexual Behavior in the Human Female,* (Philadelphia: W. B. Saunders Company, 1953), Table 25, p. 180, and Table 127, p. 490. Alfred C. Kinsey et al., *Sexual Behavior in the Human Male* (Philadelphia: W. B. Saunders Company, 1948). Table 82, p. 340.

[15] Ferdinand, *op. cit.,* p. 81.

[16] *Ibid.*

[17] *Ibid.*

[18] *Ibid.*

[19] Lee Rainwater, "Some Aspects of Lower Class Sexual Behavior," *Journal of Social Issues,* 22, no. 2 (April 1966), pp. 96–108.

[20] *Ibid.,* p. 100.

[21] William Foote Whyte, "A Slum Sex Code," in Herman D. Stein and R. A. Cloward, eds., *Social Perspectives on Behavior* (New York: Free Press, 1958), pp. 441–8.

[22] Lee Rainwater, "Marital Sexuality in Four Cultures of Poverty," *Journal of Marriage and the Family,* 26, no. 4 (November 1964), pp. 457–66.

[23] Jack E. Weller, *Yesterday's People: Life in Contemporary Appalachia* (Lexington, Ky.: University of Kentucky Press, 1965); Claudia Lewis, *Children of the Cumberland* (New York: Columbia University Press, 1946).

[24] Ferdinand, *op. cit.*

[25] Ira L. Reiss, "How and Why America's Sex Standards Are Changing," *Trans-Action*, 5, no. 4 (March 1968), pp. 26–32.

[26] John Corry, "A U.S. Sex Revolt? It's Mostly Talk," *New York Times, Social Profile: USA Today,* (New York: Van Nostrand-Reinhold Company, 1970) pp. 130–37.

[27] Reiss, *op. cit.*, p. 26.

[28] *Ibid.*, p. 29.

[29] Corry, *op. cit.*

[30] George P. Murdock, *Social Structure* (New York: Macmillan Company, 1949).

SUGGESTED READINGS

Ladner, J. *Deviance in the Lower Class Adolescent Sub-Culture,* Pruitt-Igoe Project Occasional Paper 3. St. Louis, Mo: Washington University, 1966.

Rainwater, L. "Marital Sexuality in Four Cultures of Poverty." *Journal of Marriage and the Family* 26 (1964): 457–66.

Reiss, I., "America's Sex Standards—How and Why They Are Changing." *Trans-Action* 5 (1968): 26–32.

Rosenberg, B., and Bensman, J. "Sexual Patterns in Three Ethnic Subcultures of an American Underclass." *Annals,* March 1968, pp. 61–75.

Simon, W., and Gagnon, J. "Psychosexual Development." *Trans-Action* 6 (March 1969): 9–17.

5

Sex, Racism, and Social Work

LEON F. WILLIAMS

> Through it all I discern one clear and certain truth:
> in the core of the heart of the American race prob-
> lem the sex factor is rooted, rooted so deeply that
> it is not always recognized when it shows at the sur-
> face. Other factors are obvious and are the ones we
> dare to deal with; but regardless of how we deal
> with these, the race situation will continue to be
> acute as long as the sex factor persists . . . . It may
> be innate; I do not know. But I do know it's strong
> and bitter. . . .
>
> James Weldon Johnson in
> *Along This Way*

Somehow, we've always known it, though it was spoken of in half-truths
and evasions wrested from fleeting insights into an ugly truth. . . . Still,
it must be said that the old palliative of race relations may well have been
a misnomer since, to a frightening degree, physical (sexual) distance
between blacks and whites in this country has contributed as much
to the making of modern "racist" America as color difference. . . .
"There is sexual involvement, at once real and vicarious, connecting white
and black people in America that spans the history of this country from
the era of slavery to the present . . . , that all race relations tend to be,
however subtle, *sex* relations."[1]

Social work has had to pay dearly with losses in client confidence for
some of its practice "oversights," especially in its failure to anticipate the
full consequences of racism as practiced in our society. Too, it has failed
to prepare, with few exceptions, competent professionals who could handle
the plethora of practice issues raised by the social consequences of human
sexuality. These two powerful forces combined, make up the true com-
plexion of racism which has come to be viewed as a "norm" in American
society; and it comes as no new discovery that social workers, like everyone else, are *racists* and that social welfare services are delivered within

institutions which systematically exclude blacks and the black perspective from their decisions because they were built with white middle-class values and aims in mind.[2]

The middle-class social worker is both victim of and heir to the "collective" conception of blacks in our society and as such is profoundly immersed in the whole of a racist orientation. Racism like sexuality is learned behavior, and on a given plane, such as America's peculiar history of slavery, "Jim Crowism" and Victorian morality, that initial, fleeting insight into the sexuality of racism, strikes us with greater clarity.

Herndon conceptualized this relationship best by calling the tangled myths of sexuality and racism the "sexualization of racism," a uniquely American phenomenon. He saw racism and sex in tandem, concluding that the two were inextricably connected.[3]

If this, then, is the case, we must explore racism and its sexual dimension as an additional factor which may serve as a powerful constraint on the worker's judgment and skill as he attempts to practice across racial lines. The extent to which this is significant may deserve greater scientific perusal but, for the moment, let's look closely at some of the myths and stereotypes which color the racist/sex configuration of American society.

One of the most profoundly distorted and emotionally laden aspects of American racial mythology (including the concept of white supremacy) has to do with the "supersexuality" of the black man. He is imagined to have endless virility, including an enormous phallus, and, in addition, some woman-enslaving, mystical powers.[4] A point in fact can be found in the old superstition, which has its roots in the south, that states, "once a white woman mates with a black man she will never again be satisfied with a white man." As this superstition suggests, that contact between the white woman and black man has become hateful to the white man and can lead and has led to explosive confrontation between the white and the black man.

Much of the violence over school desegregation, and most of the racist "hate literature," is couched in terms of the danger to the purity of white womanhood, the dangers of miscegenation, and the like.[5] Political demagogues, both north and south, have seized upon the "issue" often to ride into political office on white male fears related to the protection of the white female vagina.

The concern over sexual relations between white women and nonwhite men (especially black men) is apparently the primary emotional basis for the persistence, in many states, of statutes forbidding racial intermarriage, often inaccurately labeled as antimiscegenation laws. "Mongrelization" or miscegenation is apparently perceived as a danger only when white women are involved. In several western states it is possible to consider this in cross-cultural terms involving both blacks and Indians. Some Indian blood is considered an honor and politicians offer boasts of having some Indian blood. Some blacks try to "pass" as Indians; a white woman marries an Indian without a thought to the antimiscegenation law. Despite the historical fact that for more than 250 years the whites were often raped, enslaved and slain by Indians while the black man was the white man's helper, it is still the black man who appears in the western white woman's dream as the brutal rapist, and the sight of a black boy dancing with a white girl moves many westerners to feelings and act of violence. The Indian was never enslaved, and thus persists the myth of the "noble red man" (dark brown though he may be); while the former slave—whose black feelings every nonslave secretly understands—is feared for his vengeance. In one version did not Oedipus, when his father whipped him aside on the road, slay him and rape his mother on his father's corpse?[6]

The sometimes pathological response to the black male phallus has its roots in more practical considerations. Prior to 1692 slaves in the colonies were free to consort with whites and to intermarry with them. A study of the slavery laws following this date suggests that the concern for intermarriage was a practical and economic one. The proliferation of mulattoes from the liaison of black and white men and women served as a serious threat to the one means of accounting for the slave population— visibility! The varied hues of the slaves and the possibility that after successive mixed marriages, the slave would approximate the coloring of the slave owner, may well have been the impetus for restricting cohabitation. In reality, the slave could literally disappear into the dominant population! Despite the economic roots of these statutes, attitudes regarding intermarriage are now thoroughly institutionalized, with most of their properties buried deeply in the unconscious of the American white male. The extension of the economic-based prohibition against intermarriage during slavery finds its ultimate absurdity in the modern question, "Would you want your daughter to marry one?" That question speaks eloquently to the fear of the white man of the black man as a sexual competitor.

Nor has the black man been free of this unconscious dimension of institutionalized racism. As Grier and Cobbs point out,

> The mythology and folklore of black people was filled with tales of sexually prodigious men. Most boys grow up on a steady diet of folk heroes who have distinquished themselves by sexual feats. It is significant that few, if any, of these folk heroes are directing armies or commanding empires. Dreams must in some way reflect reality, and in this country the black man, until quite recently, had not been in positions of power. His wielding of power had been in the privacy of the boudoir. To be

sure, black men have sexual problems. They may have impotence, pre-mature ejaculation, and the entire range of pathology which limits and distorts sexual life. Such ailments have the same dynamic origins in men of all races. But where sex is employed as an armament and used as a cautious and deliberate means of defense, it is the black man who chooses this weapon. If he cannot fight the white man openly, he can and does battle him secretly. But currently the pattern evolves of black men using sex as a dagger to be symbolically thrust into the white man.[7]

Why, then, is the black man such a special sexual threat? Why does the black man respond to his mythical sexual heroes? There are no data to support the contention that the size of the erect phallus signifies sexual virility, and thereby masculine superiority. Suppose, then, that the average black penis were larger than that of the white? The clinical experience of psychiatrists and marriage counselors has clearly revealed that a large penis does not correlate at all with virility or the ability to give special pleasure in coitus, and it is now evident in studies of sexual physiology, such as those as Masters and Johnson,[8] that a small penis is not necessarily a reason for sexual incompatibility. In fact, a "too large" penis is much more a common complaint of the allegedly maladjusted woman. Yet the male in our society continues his allusions to physi-cal size in reference to sexual virility by the use of terms such as "stud," "bull," "well-hung," whereas, often, the favorite prescription for the maiden lady who seems flighty and nervous is to give her a "horse fucking."

The concern with penis size is a masculine character trait often growing out of a boy's initial envy of the father's penis size. Small boys of every culture have had to wrestle with the impossible problem of emulating his father's mighty "tool." As a point of fact, the black male shares many of the same sexual concerns of his white counterpart, and fears him equally as a sexual competitor, with a greater basis in historical reality. For exam-ple, it has been suggested that the genesis of the word "mother-fucker" finds its root in the nightly visits of "Mr. Charley" to the slave cabins. The term represents a kind of racial "in" joke which helps relieve tension in the face of a horrible reality.

Since the fear of a black man as a sexual threat is irrational, this re-sponse is probably best understood through the study of the psychody-namics involved in the phenomena. Interviews with many clients can help us in understanding how myths may often become self-fulfilling prophecies. We are all influenced by society's general attitudes about sexuality. "Sexual activity unrelated to reproduction is still considered sinful, especially for poor people (and blacks), a necessary evil to be performed in secrecy, a biological necessity. It is something to be talked about in whispers, snickers, and boasts by men—but women, good women, do not even think about it. (And many social workers are good women.)"[9] Dr. West postulates that many whites apparently deny their own "black" sexual and associated violent, instinctual strivings, and project them onto the black. Would the southern white boy wish to overthrow paternal authority, grow a penis larger than his father's, possess his mother, and even have her prefer him? Such unacceptable wishes and powers, denied in oneself, are easily attributed to the nearby numerous black men.

However, with the projection of these feelings and attributes, there also tends to develop an unconscious identification with the black. Put into him these parts of yourself, and you become a part of him as you now imagine him to be. Thus arises the secret erotic wish that black men will actually be successful in transgressions against white women, and from this derives the necessity for a violent conscious denial. The greater a man's insecurity regarding his own masculinity (i.e., conscious, passive strivings or latent homosexuality), the more strenuously these mechanisms must be called into play.

When ego defenses break down in psychiatric illness the repressed wish may be acted out, with the psychotic or pathologically intoxicated white husband dragging home a black man to set upon his wife. Within "liberal" circles in the north more subtle examples are not infrequent, wherein the black friend is literally maneuvered and unconsciously invited to cuckold his white liberal friend—who might truly be termed a liberal under these circumstances.[10]

The social worker is also a victim of the kinds of cultural "screens" which create in him a sex-tinged, racial paranoia which drains much of his energies and creates blockages in his attempt to understand the blacks with whom he works. Social workers are middle-class and middle-class people have very definite standards for sex behavior. These standards are often spelled out in their choice of symbols and their use of semantic language; black is bad, white is good. To quote Jonathan Edwards, "Since holiness comprehends all the other virtues, it is typified by white, which also represents purity because it signifies mother's milk and childish innocence . . . while sin, sorrow, and death are all represented in Scripture by darkness or the color black . . ." and thus the myth is continuously reinforced throughout all aspects of our living and acculturation and can, as a result, stultify human transactions through the simple process of perpetuating a non-negotiable stance based on interracial mythology. How much easier to attack the veracity of a Martin L. King by intimating that he had a vigorous sex life, apart from his wife, which "clearly" shows his deviancy from the white, middle-class ideal. It also addresses, at the visceral level the sexual paranoia of the white male; after all, he "knows" the sexual excesses of the black man: they may well be an intimation of his own rich inner life.

Does one not wonder at the unconscious conflict created in the white social worker when confronted by the white woman who has a black child out of wedlock? Further, and more typical, the worker may experience unconscious conflict in the instance of the black woman who continues to have children out of wedlock, whose behavior may contribute subtly to the unconscious, phobic aspect of racial/sexual feelings inherent in the worker as a product of his culture and social class. Is it any wonder that the manifestations of the "white man's burden" ideology found in social work's "paternalism," and "clinicalism,"[11] all seem to be noble but dysfunctional approaches to the problems of ethnicity and poverty? These stances toward those we would help can be seen as ego defenses guarding against destructive impulses which would reject that which is foreign to and/or threatening to us. The phenomenon of racism, as it is defined through sexual and caste taboos, is worthy of complete study as one of the knowledge objectives for any student who is to enter a field of practice. The student should be helped to understand how and why a society attempts to control sexual behavior, why sexual behavior is such an intimate part of the institution of racism. Further, social work should begin examining those aspects of racial/sexual mythology which have an effect on the institutional arrangements of social welfare services. Housing discrimination and the AFDC program immediately come to mind.

It is clear that the social worker must become free of the sociocultural constraints of a racist/sexist society in order to pursue, fully, social justice and system change. Major emphasis should be placed upon becoming aware of and analyzing misconceptions, stereotypes, and myths about minorities . . . social work has managed to join with other social sciences in promoting stereotypes and myths regarding minority groups.[12] Because attitudes about race and sex are learned, having been conditioned and reinforced by a society which has something to gain by maintaining the prevailing order, then social work, to be truly effective, must seek and root out those myths and bigotries which often cast the client in the role of enemy rather than victim.

Because racism and its sexualization have not been openly dealt with, because we have avoided acknowledging them, we rarely find content on either of the concepts in the social work curriculum, especially as they converge as constraints to practice. Treating the two notions together is virtually unheard of, suggesting that powerful emotions and deeply unconscious factors have come into play to "cool out" our efforts to look critically and objectively at a subject which appears to lie at the root of social reality in America.

The Kerner Commission Report on Civil Disorders was unequivocally clear about the extent of racism in our society. The violence which was fueled by racist practices in the 1960s should be adequate evidence of the festering sore called American racism and its concomitants of sexual paranoia and sexual persecution . . . and if we are preparing students to participate in the struggle for human justice and understanding, they must examine racism in our society and in themselves.[13]

NOTES

[1] Calvin C. Herndon, *Sex and Racism in America* (New York: Grove Press, Inc., 1965) p. 7.

[2] Andrew Billingsley, "Black Students in a Graduate School of Social Welfare," *Social Work Education Reporter* 17, no. 2 (June 1969), pp. 41–42.

[3] Herndon, *loc. cit.*, pp. 3–8.

[4] Louis J. West, "Psychobiology of Racial Violence," *Archives of General Psychiatry* 16 (June 1967), p. 647.

[5] *Ibid.*

[6] *Ibid.*, p. 648.

[7] W. H. Grier and P. M. Cobbs, *Black Rage* (New York: Basic Books, Inc., 1968), p. 58.

[8] W. H. Masters and V. Johnson. *Human Sexual Response* (Boston: Little, Brown, and Company, 1966).

[9] Harvey Gochros, "Introducing Human Sexuality into the Graduate Social Work Curriculum," *Social Work Education Reporter* 18, no. 3 (September-October 1970), 48.

[10] West, *loc. cit.*, pp. 648–49.

[11] Henry Miller, "Social Work in the Black Ghetto: The New Colonialism," *Social Work* 14, no. 3 (July 1969), pp. 69–70.

[12] E. Herzog, and C. Sudia, "Family Structure and Composition Considerations for Research Toward Improving Race Relations," (Paper delivered at Institute on Research Toward Improving Race Relations of the National Association of Social Workers, Airlie House, Warrenton, Virginia, August 13–16, 1967), p. 1.

[13] Mary E. Robertson, "Inclusion of Content on Ethnic and Racial Minorities in the Social Work Curriculum," *Ethnic Minorities in Social Work Education,* ed. Carl Scott, New York, Council on Social Work Education, 1970, p. 75.

SUGGESTED READINGS

Billingsley, A. *Black Families in White America.* Englewood, N. J.: Prentice-Hall, 1968.

Grier, W., and Cobbs, P. *Black Rage.* New York: Basic Books, 1968.

Herndon, C. *Sex and Racism in America.* New York: Grove Press, 1965.

Sager, C., et al. *The Black Ghetto Family in Therapy.* New York: Grove Press, 1970.

Sexual Problems in Social Work Practice

Whether or not we are going through a sexual revolution is, perhaps, a senseless debate. It is certain, however, that there is a growing openness about sexuality, a recognition and acceptance of the nonreproductive functions of sex, and a tolerance for differences in sexual expression.

Examples of these changes abound: anti-abortion laws have been eliminated in several states; reports of scientific investigations of the physiology of sex and sexual manuals remain on the top of best-seller lists for months; unorthodox models for conjugal living arrangements are gaining popular attention; motion pictures and television display greater sexual openness; women's liberation movements, and pressures for civil, religious, and vocational rights for homosexuals are showing success; coed dorms are becoming more common on college campuses; and, despite heated criticisms, relevant sex education seems here to stay. An emphasis on individual freedom, along with the availability of effective birth control is leading to greater sexual freedom and increased opportunities for sexual fulfillment. There is, indeed, an emerging conviction among many segments of our society that what adults voluntarily do with their genitalia in private should be of no concern to the state or society as a whole.

But even if these changes are perceived as desirable, they are not without their problems. Sexual changes, like all major social changes, can be expected to have significant unforeseen consequences. These consequences compound the already existing problems associated with sexuality. Indeed, probably no other aspect of human life remains as complex and subject to stress. But despite these problems and the fact that sex is clearly a social phenomenon, social workers have often seemed reluctant to provide help to those experiencing explicit sexual difficulties. Some of the reasons for this reluctance are discussed in "Social Work's Sexual Blinders." This article sets the stage for this section, arguing that sexual problems can and should be approached directly by social workers, and that in doing so we should avoid the trap of becoming preoccupied with inferred underlying disease processes or common, basic "personality inadequacies," as is a frequent approach of the limited social work material dealing explicitly with sexual material. Rather, this section generally approaches sexual problems as specific sexual behavior, to be treated as discrete behavior.

The social worker's hesitancy to deal aggressively with sexual problems is often related to the difficulties in discussing sex with his clients. "Talking about Sex," by Jean Schaar Gochros, reviews approaches to a sensitive area of professional communication. An attempt to investigate the significant effects of the expectations of both therapists and clients on their communication is reported in the chapter "Expectations of Sexual Treatment" by Rosen, Connaway, and Duehn.

Sexuality incorporates three aspects of human life: Reproduction, genital stimulation, and the feelings and expressions of love, intimacy, and identity. These three components of sex often coincide, but each can create its own joys, as well as problems. The social worker finds himself today confronting significant changes in all three areas, and each is reflected in the content of this section.

REPRODUCTION: The availability and effectiveness of contraceptive devices, along with the possibility of legal abortion in several states make it possible for couples to have control over the number and spacing of their children, and for unmarried individuals to divorce reproduction from sexual activity. Thus, for the first time in human history, married and unmarried people can make their sexual decisions relatively free from the concern over pregnancy. This does not mean that mistakes do not happen or that problems are not associated with birth control and, particularly, abortion. The chapter on "Abortion Counseling" by Pamela Lee Lowry and Joan E. Blank discusses social work help for the diverse problems experienced by women who go through legal and illegal abortions, as well as for their sexual partners.

GENITAL STIMULATION: Social workers are beginning to reflect the cultural attitude that there are many socially and emotionally appropriate avenues for sexual fulfillment. There is increasing permission, if not pressure, for social workers to assist people to focus on their explicit sexual needs, concerns, and problems, and to achieve sexual fulfillment in their marriage or even without marriage. Albert Ellis's chapter, "A Rational Approach to Premarital Counseling," offers some suggestions on how a professional helper can prepare couples for a less traumatic sexual entry into marriage. Some of the sources of sexual problems in marriage along with application of new approaches to resolving them are discussed in the chapter on "Treatment of Common Marital Sexual Problems."

One of the ramifications of dysfunctional sexual problems in marriage, as well as a reflection often of the emotional problems in a marriage (see next section), is the not uncommon incidence of extramarital activities. Miriam I. Weisberg discusses an approach to these problems in her chapter, "Early Treatment of Infidelity in the Neurotic Man."

There are also many obstacles to the realization of sexual rights and opportunities for many individuals, such as the aged, the imprisoned, the unmarried, and the homosexual. The chapter entitled "The Silent Sexual Problems" discusses some of these often-overlooked problems regarding sexuality encountered by a variety of groups, along with some practice suggestions.

For the first time a validated technology for helping people experiencing diverse sexual problems is appearing and being adapted to various settings and needs. A comprehensive review of these techniques and approaches is provided in the chapter on "Behavior Modification of Sexual Problems" by Ernest Vargas. There is also a range of unorthodox experiments with new approaches to enhancement of sexual functioning, such as that described by Paul Bindrim in his "Report on a Nude Marathon."

Finally, there is an increasing attempt both to understand and to intervene with the problems not only of sexual offenders but of their victims as well. The two chapters, "Group Therapy of Incarcerated Sexual Deviants" by Irvin D. Yalom, and "The Social Worker and the Treatment of Sexual Victims," by LeRoy G. Schultz attempt to explore some basic principles for working with these groups.

LOVE, INTIMACY, AND IDENTITY: Often overlooked in a world concerned with sexual fulfillment is the longing for intimacy which many experience. All too often this yearning as well as the quest for confirmation of one's sexual identity can only be expressed through genital sexuality. Paradoxically, we live in a time in which the need for sex is begrudgingly accepted and the need for intimacy is ignored. Our industrialized, urbanized, depersonalized, and transient way of life can limit the development of really close emotional ties, certainly with neighbors, friends, and relatives and often even with the members of one's immediate family. We cannot embrace our friends, kiss our growing children, or even stand too close or shake hands too long—but we can engage in silent impersonal sex! How much is our fascination with sensitivity and encounter group experiences and the appeal of commune living (often nonsexual in orientation) a thirst for the intimacy and love which we have lost from our daily lives and which genital sexuality alone cannot replace?

These concerns must be the core of any attempt to encourage social work practice in the area of sexuality (see Chapter 18, "The Education of Graduate Social Work Students for Practice with Sexual Problems"). Social workers, with their "informed hearts" must not lose sight of the greatest gift they can help people attain, singly and collectively: love.

H. L. G.

6

Social Work's Sexual Blinders

Harvey L. Gochros

Much of social work practice has a sexual blind spot. It is true that social workers have long taken leadership with the problems of unmarried mothers and have begun to show concern for the field of family planning. Although in the past, social work was identified with some of the more shabby, antisexual public welfare policies, more recently it has had a role in abolishing them. But these activities have tended to be concerned largely with the periphery of sexual behavior, rather than the behavior itself. Despite the plethora of explicit contemporary sexual problems, there is little evidence to suggest that any significant number of social workers have had the interest or the ability to provide skilled help with these problems.

It could be argued that the profession has long "recognized" sex. For about forty years, much of its practice theory has been influenced by psychoanalytic theory and its derivatives which have their basis in psychosexual development. But generally this framework has provided only inferential interpretation of intrapsychic phenomena, has been of minimal utility, and has provided little incentive to approach directly and aggressively those areas of overt sexuality which should be of concern to social work.

Indeed, psychoanalytic theory has led social workers to adopt a "disease" orientation in which unorthodox, dysfunctional, and problematic behaviors are perceived as only "symptoms" of underlying pathology. Perhaps this orientation is one of the reasons that the profession has had only token participation—at best—in national organizations concerned with education and practice directly related to problems of enhancing sexuality. Further, neither social work writers nor practitioners, with a few notable recent exceptions,[1] have provided practitioners with substantial guidance for practice in this area.

What are some illustrations of the explicit problems social workers might more aggressively address themselves to?

—distribution of birth control information to all income groups and to single as well as married women, yet preservation of the right of the individual to choose the number and spacing of children.

—attention to the array of problems of women, married and unmarried, who are about to or already have had an abortion, along with the problems of their male partners.

—the difficulties encountered by "average" married couples of all ages whose attempts to achieve sexual fulfillment and mutual satisfaction, by their definition, have been hindered not necessarily by broad interpersonal conflict but by lack of specific sexual knowledge and/or problems in communication regarding sexuality.

—the need for sex education for all age groups not limited to reproductive and disease information but appropriate to the age and needs of the consumer, emphasizing sex as a responsible interpersonal activity only occasionally related to reproduction and more often to interpersonal communion and physical pleasure.

—the channeling of the behavior of adolescents too young to marry but with strong biological and emotional needs, creating problems which are compounded by a society which unfortunately identifies all intimacy with genital sexuality.

—the blocks to sexual fulfillment and the resulting problems of the aged, the unmarried, the handicapped, the imprisoned, and the deviate from sexual norms.

—the readjustment of a sexual offender's victim.

It has been possible for the profession in the past, operating in and, indeed, often representing a sexually repressive society, to avoid working with some of these problems, using such rationalizations as "sexual problems are merely symptoms of underlying intrapsychic dysfunctioning or interpersonal problems," or "sex is properly in the domain of the physician or family and not within the competence of social work." Social workers are increasingly challenging both of these premises: (1) that complex mental processes explaining human behavior and specifically sexuality are sacred and not open to question,[2] and (2) that the medical profession is superordinate in dealing with sexual problems. Medical education is only beginning to equip future doctors with knowledge and skills for dealing with human sexuality.[3] Only a small number of medical schools at this point offer any comprehensive education regarding sexuality. Furthermore, human sexuality involves discrete behavior; it is not only a physical act but clearly a learned social act—shaped, altered, and limited by the interaction of the individual with his interpersonal environment. As such, it can be perceived as an area of legitimate social work knowledge and concern and subject to social work intervention. As intermediaries between society and individuals, we have the opportunity to seek sanctions, interpret, implement, and work with emerging patterns of acceptable sexual behavior and their consequences.

But despite these opportunities for service, there still remain resistances, on the part of both practitioners and consumers of social work services, to a concerted approach to many sexual problems. The sources of these resistances are diverse and complicated but some can be described.

CONSUMER RESISTANCES: Most Americans, with the exception of the most sophisticated and educated, do not find it easy to speak openly and seriously of their own or anybody else's sexual behavior. They are taught that sexual pleasure is a private matter, shameful, and possibly somewhat evil. Admitting and discussing problems regarding sex is even more forbidden. Sexual inadequacies, failures, deviations from implicit norms, or even certain wishes are considered unpardonable and are perceived as likely to bring about ridicule, disgust, and resentment. Little hope is held out for objectivity or concern from others.

Social workers and other potentially helpful people are seen as representatives of a sexually inconsistent but generally repressive society, with the assumption that there might be danger in revealing sexual problems in view of the strong social sanctions regarding sexuality. Indeed the social worker—often a young, unmarried woman—may be viewed as a "moralistic," sexually pure or asexual individual whose response to sexual material might well reflect common societal responses of disgust or shock and might even lead to social retribution.

Even in situations where fears are less severe, there might still be reluctance to seek help because of concern over how to express the problem verbally. When it comes to sex, many potential clients are literally speechless. A fear of demonstrating ignorance by an inadequate vocabulary for describing sexual problems in explicit socially acceptable language and by even the knowledge of correct pronunciation may be handicaps to seeking help. In an as yet unpublished research project by the Institute of Sex Research, Indiana University, a large number of subjects, principally young women, gave misleading responses to certain questions because of their misunderstanding of the word "masturbation."[4]

Finally, the client may not seek social work help with sexual problems because he does not perceive social workers as interested or competent in dealing with these problems. This is understandable. Certainly there is rarely explicit reference in the occasional advertisements for social work services to indicate social work readiness to offer help in these areas. This leads to a discussion of the social workers' resistances to dealing with sexual problems.

PRACTITIONER RESISTANCES: Social workers are people first, then professionals. They, too, have been brought up in a society where it is permissible to talk around sex, joke about it or be self-righteous about it but not to discuss it comfortably, calmly, and objectively.[5] They, too, have been affected by strong social and moral attitudes about sexual activities. While the acceptability and comfort of such discussions vary from rural to urban areas and among various cultural groups and regions, it is still difficult for many practitioners to discuss sexual problems directly and explicitly. Some must indeed work through the conviction that sex is a completely private matter, where even the social worker does not have the right of access to pertinent information.

Further, to initiate or pursue such discussions very often calls into question the practitioner's motivation. He may well be concerned how other people, including the client, may interpret his interest: seduction? voyeurism? curiosity? working through his own problem? or seeking vicarious satisfaction? To probe such areas and indeed to set onself in the position of helper calls into question and makes vulnerable the practitioner's *own* sexual adaptation, an area of functioning in which few practitioners—or people in general—feel complete confidence. "Let him who is without problems cast the first advice." This problem is even more sensitive for many young unmarried men and women dealing with sexual problems early in their career, and, perhaps, insecure in their own sexual identity.

However, more significant than personal risks by the worker are his perceived professional risks. The treatment or prevention of sexual problems brings him into one of the most sensitive of human areas. Nowhere else in our society do we find as much hypocrisy, inconsistency, confused legality, ignorance, and emotionalism. In an effort to be effective, the social worker might well find his professional values and commitments in conflict with social values or with his own personal values. Indeed, the most desirable course of professional action might well brush the edge of "morality," or even legality. Unfortunately, laws often lag behind the uneven changes in society's attitudes. The result may be that the practitioner hesitates or avoids asserting himself in these hazy areas. He may know what is socially desirable or effective for individual clients or groups but draws back when he fears social sanctions and more particularly professional or agency retribution.

What would happen, for example, to a school social worker who encouraged teaching birth control in high school? To the child guidance worker who sanctioned or even encouraged adolescent masturbation? To the family agency worker who approached a homosexual community to provide counseling services to those who are having interpersonal problems within the context of their chosen life styles? To the child welfare worker who contacts a physician willing to do a safe abortion in a state which still has laws against abortion? To the social worker in a prison setting who actively lobbies for overnight visits for wives and girl friends of prisoners? To the community organizer who appears at a city council meeting to fight for reevaluation of sexual censorship? Or to the marriage counselor who suggests that a woman learn to stimulate herself before she can hope for improvement in her marital sexual adjustment? What would happen to the funding of an agency if it were to engage in controversial sexually oriented services?

Obviously, often *nothing* happens to the social worker or the agency and the fears prove to be unrealistic. Even when they are realistic, they have not necessarily inhibited appropriate practice. There is a story, perhaps apocryphal, that Gordon Hamilton, while practicing casework in the early 1930s kept a desk drawer full of wedding rings to give to unmarried girls who wanted to receive birth control service from the Margaret Sanger clinic, which was then restricted to married women. More recently, a young social worker found that the only way he could involve husbands who were opposed to their wives' interest in family planning was to run after-hour beer parties to break down communication barriers. An undergraduate social work major at a state university chose to assist the beleaguered local homosexuals to organize and press for their social and civil rights. But fears of professional and personal risk remain a major barrier for many to actively providing needed services.

What Can Social Workers Do?

In few areas of practice is it so obvious that a comprehensive social work approach is necessary. Effective sex education, for instance, requires that the social worker be able not only to work effectively with groups but to deal with individual problems within the group and to base the program on a sound foundation of organization and planning with the parents and school administration involved.

With their broad orientation social workers clearly have much to offer in such preventive work as sex education in various settings—from schools to prisons to homes for the aged.

As in other areas of practice, the goal of social work activities in the area of human sexuality should be optimizing the choices of their clients and minimizing those limitations of sexual expression which result from dysfunctional taboos, ignorance, or irrationality. No one, including a social worker, can specify what should give happiness to another human being. The sexual rights of individuals and groups must be preserved, regardless of the income or circumstances of an individual, as long as they do not impinge on the rights of others.

Unfortunately, the liberal sexual rights espoused here are unevenly accepted by communities,[6] agencies, social workers, and even client groups. Changes in sexual laws do not necessarily guarantee a parallel change in the attitudes and behavior of the people we work with. The worker must therefore assert himself, guided by his awareness of a particular situation and his interpretation of professional values, and accept but not exaggerate the risks associated with valid social work practice. At the same time he accepts responsibility for promoting a change in just those attitudes which inhibit not only his own practice but the needs of his constituency.

We must increase our knowledge of the range of both functional and dysfunctional sexual behavior and the technology of successful intervention and communicate this to the field, both in the formal education of social workers[7] and in-service agency training. Such researchers as Masters and Johnson and the Indiana Institute staff have begun to develop information on what people do as well as say about sexual behavior.[8] Much more must be accumulated. The National Council on Family Relations, the Sex Information and Education Council of the United States, and the American Association of Sex Educators and Counselors have attempted to acquire and distribute information regarding sexuality. (They would welcome more social work involvement.) Social workers can also make a contribution to the development of this knowledge, especially relating cultural and economic variables to sexual behavior.

Although a beginning has been made in quantitative analysis of specific sexual acts, there has been little attention to broader questions of sexuality:[9] What do people want from sex? How do they make their sexual decisions? What hinders their sexual fulfillment and how does this vary according to ethnic affiliation, income, gender, and age? What interventions are most successful for affecting specific sexual problems? Without such data, the worker is all too likely to fall back on his own sexual experiences and private opinions as a guide for helping his clients. These are idiosyncratic to his own learning experiences, class, and ethnic group, and are influenced by his own emotions, traditional taboos, and prejudices. There are many functional sexual life styles; the worker can rarely use his own as a model for others.[10]

Social workers must learn to accept their own sexuality and be comfortable with it. Only then can they feel really free to discuss and relate to sexuality in their practice. This comfort is also necessary for the worker to express warmth and sensitivity and even physical contact to clients without being caught up in fears of the connotations of this intimacy.

Finally, as preoccupation with right and wrong and normalcy of sexual behavior diminishes, social work can join the search for a new meaning to sexuality. What is it besides a physical act? How does it relate to man's desire for intimacy and meaning in life? What *is* a man and what *is* a woman? What is our responsibility to bear or not to bear children? What is to be the function of marriage and the family? Can society do without sex?

Sexuality is one of the most powerful experiences of man. It can provide the most spiritually and emotionally satisfying and pleasurable experiences known, or it can lead to loneliness, fear, and misery. Social workers could do much to enhance the former and minimize the latter.

NOTES

[1] See Suggested Readings.

[2] "To speak in terms of complex inner states is to gain a sense of understanding of the mysterious while at the same time preserving the dignity of the mystery." Robert D. Carter and Richard B. Stuart, "Behavior Modification Theory and Practice:A Reply," *Social Work* 15, 1 (January 1970), p. 50.

[3] Edward Tyler, M. D., "Introducing a Sex Education Course into the Medical Curriculum," unpublished manuscript, (Bloomington, Ind.: Indiana University Medical Center, 1970).

[4] James E. Elias, Ph.D., Institute for Sex Research at Indiana University, personal communication, April 9, 1970.

[5] The initial suggestion to schedule the first regional NASW conference on social work and sexuality (Fort Lauderdale, Fla., June 1970) was originally proposed as a joke!

[6] Howard S. Becker and Irving Horowitz, "The Culture of Civility," *Trans-Action* 7, 6 (April 1970).

[7] Harvey L. Gochros, "Introducing Human Sexuality into Graduate Social Work Education," *Social Work Education Reporter,* September-October 1970.

[8] See Edward M. Brecher, *The Sex Researchers* (Boston: Little, Brown and Company, 1969).

[9] See, for instance, Lester A. Kirkendall, "Characteristics of Sexual Decision Making," *Journal of Sex Research* 3, 3, (August 1967), pp. 201–211.

[10] As an illustration, a worker coming from the upper classes may be well aware of the taboos against premarital relations, but be baffled by the general discomfort about nudity and masturbation in many lower-income groups.

SUGGESTED READINGS

Green, B., ed. *The Psychotherapies of Marital Disharmony.* New York: The Free Press, 1965.

Greenbank, R. "Patients Who Talk Without Words." *Psychosomatics* 6 (1965): 210–14.

Klemer, R., ed. *Counseling in Marital and Sexual Problems.* Baltimore: The Williams & Wilkins Company, 1965.

Satir, V. *Conjoint Family Therapy.* Palo Alto, Calif.: Science and Behavior Books, 1967, pp. 63–90.

7

Talking About Sex

JEAN SCHAAR GOCHROS

We are living in an "enlightened age," in which sex blares out at us from billboards and TV commercials, and youngsters receive more explicit sexual information than ever before. Theoretically, social workers not only share in this enlightenment but promulgate it, talking freely with clients about sexual problems with honesty and understanding.

Yet there are many such suppositions in social work that, when tested, turn out to be more myth than reality. Unfortunately—perhaps significantly—there is little, if any, social work research in this area. But even an instant do-it-yourself research project of reading records and talking to workers, if not altogether reliable, reveals startling gaps and errors in both recording and actual handling of sexual material with clients.

Gaps and Errors

In adoption studies, for instance, one often finds a single sentence: "Mr. and Mrs. Jones have a normal sexual adjustment." What *that* means is anybody's guess. One worker, asked to define terms, could not do so. Asked to account, then, for her statement, she said merely, "I asked them." But what did she ask? "Do you have a normal sexual adjustment, Mr. and Mrs. Jones?" It sounds incredibly naive, yet unfortunately, only the extent of this phenomenon remains an unknown; that it occurs is indeed a fact.

It is possible, of course, that such discussion is an unnecessary invasion of privacy in an adoption study. But presuming it relevant, for the purposes of this paper, it seems pointless to ask intimate questions unless they are in enough detail and appropriately enough presented to render the answers reasonably valid.

In marital counseling, the need for direct discussion may be less debatable, hence conversations should be more visible. And so they are. But so are the gaps. A record, for instance, will give ample material about finances, employment, fighting, housekeeping—everything, in fact, but sex. Sometimes clients are asked if sex is a problem, but no matter what the answer, the subject is never again mentioned. Often a worker thinks he or she has dealt with the subject by giving a long summary of psychodynamics, unresolved dependency needs, and role reversals, conjecturing about the client's unconscious feelings. But information about actual behavior is almost totally absent. There may be recitation of complaints like "all he wants is sex" or "he calls me dirty names and asks me to perform 'unnatural' acts." One worker, when asked, had not even tried for clarification, and another, when told by the client, "It's too obscene to repeat," had dropped the subject entirely. Treatment plans often state, "Sex will not be treated per se, but will be dealt with by treating causes, such as poor communication throughout the marriage." This may or may not be useful in individual cases; but since there is usually not enough known to determine even what the sexual problems are, much less the causes and solutions, any success in this approach is sheer chance.

In counseling with single adults, teenagers, or adults contemplating divorce, sexual behavior is often not brought up unless the client has named it as a specific problem. Dating may be discussed, but not sexual intercourse; and if single adults or adolescents do not date, they are seldom asked how they meet their sexual needs.

Errors not only of omission but of commission are found. These range from bits of misinformation to extremely harmful practices. Two examples are pertinent here. In one case, a worker told an adolescent girl that while she was not "bad" for masturbating occasionally, there were "healthier" ways to handle sexual needs—for instance, "tennis." One doubts that feeling "sick" instead of "bad" was particularly reassuring to the girl, or that the "cure" was as "healthy" as the original behavior. In the other example, a Welfare Department was ready to remove a small child permanently from his mother's custody because his masturbating was considered proof of emotional neglect.

Causes

There are various reasons for gaps, of course, and not all of them are bad. One, for instance, is wise restraint in dealing in sensitive areas, based on accurate perception of clients' needs. Another is the very real need to summarize in recording in order to avoid long, unnecessary detail. Also, both the gaps and errors often occur with students or new workers, and it can be hoped that experience and supervision will correct many mistakes.

But this can hardly be the whole answer, for gaps and errors occur with experienced workers who deal appropriately with other sensitive areas, and the lack of written material in this one area often stands in direct contrast to excessive detail in other areas.

LACK OF KNOWLEDGE: Lack of knowledge is another cause. It is one thing to have general knowledge, but quite another to know specifics in the broad range of sexual behaviors.

But adequate knowledge on the part of a worker is essential. One needs not just a casual, but a fairly thorough, reading acquaintance with such authors as Kinsey, Masters and Johnson, and Pomeroy. Moreover, one needs constantly to keep up with the current literature, for, in the light of new research, old beliefs about behavior are continually changing.

One must know the vocabulary and terminology (to be discussed later) with an awareness of differences based on client ignorance, socioeconomic status, generation, or locale. Also, cultural and religious differences may dictate not only what words are used and understood, but what behavior is acceptable to the client and what is permissible discussion material. While this chapter does not purport to deal with cultural differences, it behooves workers to be alert to such factors. It should be noted that differences based on generation can change with enough rapidity to challenge even the youngest worker, and these are important enough so that, if one rests on one's laurels, an entire treatment plan may be thrown off. Similarly, a term may mean different things in different places.

No worker can be a walking encyclopedia, however, and—given common sense—there are times when "I don't know, let's find out" is acceptable and even useful to a client.

COMMUNICATION PROBLEMS: Often communication itself is a problem. Our society has so many sexual taboos that our patterns of communication concerning sex provide a fascinating study in contradictions. They are so complex as to seem designed for confusion, yet so precise that it is possible to communicate sexual implications even in TV commercials, using no "dirty" words at all, and have them immediately understood by most viewers. On one hand we insist on proper terminology, while on the other hand we use any word, vulgar or euphemistic, to avoid proper terminology. And no matter which words we choose, they somehow manage to come out sounding "obscene." Moreover, words are given caste and class status, often become erotic stimuli in themselves, and vary considerably between groups. In such a confusing milieu, it is no wonder that even willing parents find it difficult to talk with their children, and that workers will find it difficult to talk with clients.

These, then, are some of the problems involved in talking about sex. The remainder of this paper will concentrate on suggestions for more effective communication.

Creating a Comfortable Climate

PERSONAL COMFORT: It is impossible to talk about techniques, however, without first recognizing that they are useless unless they are used in a relaxed climate, created by a comfortable worker. And here we face several problems. Fear of being considered obscene or overly curious by one's client, peers, or supervisors is an inhibiting factor both in interviews and in recording interviews. Conflict about one's own values or behaviors increases such fear: if one is uncomfortable about himself, he may hesitate to chance "exposing" his own problems, and if he is indeed in conflict about the morality of certain behaviors, he will have trouble evaluating or even feeling free to discuss the behavior of a client. It almost goes without saying that such problems must be faced and overcome.

While it may be debatable that a client will not be embarrassed unless the worker is, the worker's attitude can create, reduce, or even eliminate client embarrassment: he can be either a poor or a good role model. It is important that he have the conviction that sex *is* a legitimate area of exploration. He must also be aware that people are usually willing to discuss any area considered appropriate by the counsellor, are often looking for all the information they can get "and then some," and because of the wealth of popular literature, almost expect the worker not only to be interested in their sexual experience but also to initiate the discussion.[1]

Personal comfort is not enough: the worker must be sensitive to expressions of client discomfort, whether verbal or nonverbal (such as blushing, squirming, avoidance of eye contact), and be able to deal with embarrassment both verbally and nonverbally. This is an elemental part of all casework. It is worth noting, however, that nonverbal communication may be unusually important. In no other area is a client so fearful that he will shock or disgust his worker; a lack of shocked behavior at a client's revelations helps to reduce anxiety within the interview, or to modify behavior that occurs outside the interview. This is so important that if a worker cannot prevent himself from feeling shocked, he must make every effort not to convey his feelings to the client.

Unfortunately, practically all literature—from magazine articles for parents to professional journals and books—admonishes people to be comfortable, to at least pretend comfort, and to be "honest." But what happens if one *is* embarrassed and cannot hide it? Obviously, it is impossible to "pretend" and to be honest at the same time. Again, communication itself poses a real problem. The struggle of finding the right words, of forcing oneself to use alien words, or of gauging when and how to talk about what may be sensitive areas for a particular client, is an uncomfortable business.

A worker may be actually physically unable to hide his discomfort.

For example, a worker recently told the writer that he was embarrassed when a client asked about sex, and he was afraid he had given himself away. One hardly had to ask why he feared this for, at that moment, the worker had turned bright red. Dictums to "be comfortable," with threats of dire consequences if one cannot make his "comfort button" work, increase, rather than allay, anxiety.

There are two possibilities that workers can fall back on:

1. Despite our admonishments, people are seldom as fragile as we make them out to be, and are often too wrapped up in their own struggles to be aware of ours. Rather than worrying about their own embarrassment, workers need only be sensitive to the client's reactions and deal directly with the client's increased anxiety.
2. *Workers need to become comfortable about discomfort;* they need to recognize that discomfort can come from neither the client's nor the worker's "sickness," but from the interview situation itself. Honesty may be quite feasible in direct discussion of the situation, and humor can be quite useful in reducing tension for all concerned. Furthermore, such discussion demonstrates that uncomfortable aspects of life can be alleviated by dealing with rather than avoiding them, and the worker's patterns of communication become an effective role model for communication outside of the interview.

There are other aspects of creating a climate of ease apart from what a worker thinks, knows, or does. Attention must be paid to the atmosphere engendered by the interview office itself, and who participates in the interview. Often interviews are more easily conducted at home, and often, in family counseling, children may participate. (Some writers, in fact, insist that they do, on the grounds that children know far more than their parents realize, and can both contribute to and benefit from honest discussion. However, it is this writer's opinion that participation by children should be individually determined.)

The sex of the therapist should also be considered. Masters and Johnson suggest such strategies as having both a male and a female counselor for a marital couple, with each dealing alternately with the client of the same and opposite sex, partly to enhance comfort and partly because only a member of the same sex can understand some experiences. They also suggest such strategies as having four-way interviews, with a worker often acting as advocate for his or her particular client.[2] But caseworkers in small agencies may not have the staff and resources to acquire the ideal situation that Masters and Johnson create, and will need to make their own modifications. In doing so, it is well to keep in mind that there are practically no "absolutes"; the type of material brought out and the degree of attendant anxiety will be affected by the sex of the therapist, but it does not always hold that a client will be more embarrassed with a worker of the opposite sex, or that he will be helped better by a worker of the same sex.

TIMING: Ease of discussion can often depend upon timing. Workers sometimes shy away from questions about sex in intake interviews for fear that it will be too threatening. But introduced casually, as merely one aspect of inquiry into the client's life in general, and given neither more nor less emphasis than any other aspect, it sets a climate that may be less threatening than if introduced later as a "problem" area.

Often, faced with a communication that holds both oblique references to sex and more direct questions in less sensitive areas, a worker deliberately chooses the more direct questions, hoping that he can deal with hidden ones when they are brought up more directly in the future. He may be right, but often it is the more sensitive area that must be tackled first; if this is not done, the client may feel that his caution was justified, will not bring it up again, and the worker will be trapped in a "conspiracy of silence." It may be far better to make a contract that this is a legitimate area to be discussed, leaving both the client and the worker free to reintroduce the subject.

Workers may also attempt vainly to find the "right time" to ask whether a client "had to" get married or a husband did "fool around," trying to find tactful ways to make the client announce the facts himself. Neither such timidity nor the use of euphemisms should be mistaken for tact; usually the client is aware of the hidden message and builds up far more anger and fright than an early, more direct question would have created. This is not to say that workers need not be sensitive to a client's ability to deal with a certain issue, but merely that over-caution and "talking about sex by not talking about it" are as poor in timing as under-caution.

THE ART OF ASKING QUESTIONS: What one says and how one says it, of course, is important in itself. As in any other area, tone, facial expression, and other phases of behavior tell a lot to a client. As in interviewing on any subject, open-ended questions are most useful, and words must be chosen with care. To ask "Do you masturbate?" for instance, suggests a right or wrong answer, produces anxiety, and makes the answer both unreliable and relatively useless, for it cuts off spontaneity. To ask "how often" immediately suggests that the worker considers such activity acceptable; asking "Do you have problems with sex relations?" "Are you able to have sex relations?" and "What kinds of problems do you have?" are similar questions, but convey just enough difference in worker assumptions to make a difference in the kind and validity of answer given.

One must be sensitive, then, to the anticipated needs and reactions of the individual client, and to the attitude that one wants to impart.

The need for knowledge was discussed earlier. Some of this knowledge, however, does not come from any book, but can be obtained only from the client himself in clarification of his own particular situation.

How much detail should be obtained? How far should a worker go and how specific should he get? There is only one practical answer: as far as necessary to get the information required by the situation. With the wide variance in terminology, for example, "making out" can mean anything from sexual intercourse to casual kissing. One worker threw out an entire diagnosis and treatment plan when she suddenly realized that she had ascribed the wrong meaning to such a term. One client thought her husband unreasonable in objecting to "playful biting" during lovemaking; the worker agreed, until after considerable prodding by male colleagues, she asked enough detail to learn that the "biting" was not on the ear, as she had supposed, and that it was anything but "playful." At least enough detail, then, must be asked to ensure that the therapist and the clients are talking about the same thing. Sometimes the worker will need to be creative in helping an embarrassed client explain a particular behavior, but one cannot even know the reality of the situation, much less help a client deal with it, if specifics are avoided.

Sometimes even more is necessary. Social workers have long insisted that, because they do not attempt to change basic personality structure, they should not probe into dream or fantasy material. But a competent assessment and treatment plan may depend on such probing. For example, in approaching problems related to masturbation, it is often not the behavior itself that arouses guilt but the accompanying fantasies. A worker who fails to explore this may become embroiled in a hopeless task; worse yet, he may unwittingly create intolerable guilt and anxiety by encouraging what the client regards as horrible thoughts. A particular client may be far better off if helped to deal with his fantasies or, on the other hand, the worker *may* learn that this really is an area where intervention may harm rather than help.

USE OF WORDS: In discussing sexual activity, what terms should one use? Are "vulgar" words ever useful? There is considerable conflict here, both in counselling and in ordinary life. Some writers suggest that it is important to use whatever terminology the client is apt to understand and feel at ease with, and that inability to do so suggests a worker's inability to come to terms with sex itself. Klemer, on the other hand, points out that one can "call a spade a spade without calling it a damned old shovel";

he further notes that people expect correct terminology from professionals (for example, the competence of a mechanic who talked about a "gizmo" rather than a carburetor would be open to question). He suggests a danger in adding to the emotional charge of words at a time when one wishes to tone them down.[3]

Any worker venturing into the realm of the four-letter words should keep these dangers in mind. No technique is equally appropriate for every worker, client, or situation, and must depend on the worker's competent appraisal of what he is trying to achieve and how best he can achieve it. To jump into such words with a client who will be so shocked that the relationship will be destroyed is obviously senseless. But used with a good measure of comon sense, there are times when only the "vulgar" will do. To avoid misunderstanding or anxiety because a client has no knowledge of scientific terminology, such a vocabulary is essential (although it is important also to guard against "talking down" to a client). Further, the use of multisyllable technical or medical vocabulary often connotes an antiseptic, medical disease orientation to sexual activities and creates unnecessary distance between worker and client. To cut through overintellectualization, or for use as a role model for freer expression, the impact of one four-letter word can accomplish more than ten hours of abstract conceptualizing about "releasing inhibitions."

Moreover, there are behaviors in our society that have no adequate name other than the four-letter variety, and many words carry subtle but important different shades of meaning. It is important to know the words well enough to hear the delicate nuances of client vocabulary, to have at one's disposal and to use the exact word that will convey to the client what is wanted. This is especially true because so many of our sexual terms carry hidden messages of anger or of confusion with excretory function, and because so much problematic sexual behavior becomes tangled up in expressions of anger.

USE OF HUMOR AND DRAMA: Humor deserves more attention than it is usually given. Too often counsellors (and parents) treat sex with such formality that no matter what the words used, the hidden message is imparted that this is a frightening area. Sex has its humorous aspects as well as any other part of life, and a sense of humor should not be eliminated from the interview. Not only can it be useful in reducing anxiety, but as long as one is sensitive to the potential of a particular situation, it can become an extremely effective tool in treatment.

Drama is another neglected device that often goes along with humor (although, again, it must be used with sensitivity to the client's feelings). With a client who has just struggled through a painful confession of a piece of behavior and who is awaiting the worker's reaction with terror, a dramatic "Whew! Am I relieved! I thought for a minute you were going to say you'd shot the President!" may be far more useful than a long, sober, and neutral discussion of how he "felt" about it. Provided that the worker will then quickly address himself to the very real concerns of the client, both assurance of the worker's acceptance and a better perspective have been immediately given, paving the way for a more serious and realistic evaluation.

Role-playing of potentially stressful discussions can also be useful to many immobilized clients. This is especially true since most people are ill-prepared for direct, purposeful discussions related to their own sexuality.

Summary

Although our profession has long dealt, to some extent, with sexual problems in various situations, it has not developed the skill in interviewing about sexual problems that it has in other areas. Partly this is due to lack of knowledge about sexual behavior in a changing world; partly it is due to fear of one's own image; partly the cause may be personal conflict about sexuality; and partly the many complex problems in communication itself, stemming from both society's embarrassment at talking about sex and the widely different backgrounds and experience of our clients.

Workers need convictions about the validity of discussing an important area of a client's life, and to feel comfort in doing so. This requires knowledge, an ability to separate one's own conflicts from those of his clients, and sensitivity to client needs and reactions. Furthermore, in view of the fact that embarrassment in talking about sex is not easily eliminated in today's society, it requires honesty and comfort about embarrassment itself, with the courage to tackle new areas and new approaches.

Despite the many special problems that sexual discussions involve, interviewing in this area requires the same basic approach as interviewing in any other area: setting up a comfortable climate; choosing words that are direct, understood, acceptable, and useful to the client; handling feelings and directing questions that will enhance spontaneity and honesty; showing acceptance of the client and his value system; and obtaining adequate clarification of the situation. As in any other situation, both the worker's ease and his ability to handle functional sexual discussions can make him an effective role model for his client.

It is essential never to underestimate the importance of sex in people's lives, especially in today's changing world. Perhaps a client expressed it best when in discussing an impending unwanted divorce, and various crises in child-rearing, employment, and finances, she suddenly broke into sobs, wailing, "But, what am I going to do about SEX?"

NOTES

[1] Richard H. Klemer, "Talking with Patients about Sexual Problems," in *Counseling in Marital and Sexual Problems,* ed. Richard Klemer (Baltimore: The Williams & Wilkins Company, 1965), pp. 119–20.

[2] Masters, W. H. and Johnson, V. J., *Human Sexual Inadequacy* (Boston: Little, Brown and Company, 1970), Chapter 13.

[3] Klemer, *op. cit.,* pp. 120–21.

SUGGESTED READINGS

Beigel, Hugo G. *Sex from A to Z.* New York: Frederick Ungar Publishing Co., 1961.

Hamilton, Eleanor. "Encouraging Sexual Communication," in *Counseling in Marital and Sexual Problems,* ed. Richard Klemer. Baltimore: The Williams & Wilkins Company, 1965, Chapter 18.

Kinsey, A. C., Pomeroy, W. B., and Martin, C. E. *Sexual Behavior and the Human Male.* Philadelphia: W. B. Saunders, 1948, pp. 52–61.

Kirkendall, L., "Semantics in Sexual Communication," *The Coordinator* (1959), 7: 63–65.

Klemer, Richard. "Talking with Patients about Sexual Problems," in *Counseling in Marital and Sexual Problems,* ed. Richard Klemer. Baltimore: The Williams & Wilkins Company, 1965, Chapter 12.

Lief, H. *How to Take a Sex History.* Topeka, Kans.: Group for the Advancement of Psychiatry, 1971.

Masters, W. H. and Johnson, V. J. "Counseling with Sexually Incompatible Marriage Partners," in *Counseling in Marital and Sexual Problems,* ed. Richard Klemer. Baltimore: The Williams & Wilkins Company, 1965, Chapter 13.

Masters, W. H., and Johnson, V. J. *Human Sexual Inadequacy.* Boston: Little, Brown and Company, 1970, pp. 1–90.

The Patterning of Pre-Treatment Expectancies and Their Relation to Interview Content in Treatment of Sexual Adjustment Problems

AARON ROSEN, RONDA S. CONNAWAY, AND WAYNE D. DUEHN

Introduction

The expectations that clients and workers have of treatment and its process have been mentioned repeatedly as important factors determining the course of treatment and its outcome. Clients' initial conceptualizations of the therapeutic encounter were viewed by Kelly[1] as major determinants of their initial behavior in treatment. In their detailed analysis of psychotherapy and the conditions conducive to behavior change, Goldstein, Heller, and Sechrest[2] regarded the accuracy of clients'' content expectancies, their organization and extent of differentiation as critical facilitating factors for the progress of psychotherapy. In a more specific sense, Rosen[3] suggested that clients' expectancies regarding the subject matter to be discussed in the treatment relationship, and the extent to which these expectations are met in the actual treatment process, are related directly to the satisfaction they may experience in treatment, and should, therefore, relate to their likelihood of continuing in that relationship. Supporting such contentions, a number of studies[4,5] tend to indicate that the extent to which content expectancies are fulfilled is related to the likelihood that the relationship will continue.

Most studies of treatment and its outcomes, however, address the question of client expectancies only indirectly. Expectancies have been implicated in studies concerned with the identification of characteristics of clients and workers that were related to outcomes of treatment. They seem consistent in suggesting that premature discontinuance and lack of improvement in treatment are associated with differences in clients' and workers' social backgrounds and personalities and with specific constellations of these.[6-13] While of interest, these studies did not investigate the actual forms and manifestations of personality and background characteristics as they occur within the treatment process. The refocusing of attention from the discrete charactristics of clients and workers onto their manifestations in differential role expectations, and more specifically, expectations about the content of treatment responses, may serve to generate knowledge of more practical usefulness to workers and counselors engaged in psychological treatment.

If knowledge of clients' expectations of treatment and of their expectancies of content to be discussed in treatment interviews is important for the successful management of therapy processes in general, an understanding of clients' content expectancies may become critical when the therapeutic encounter is concerned primarily with problems of sexual adjustment. It has long been recognized that discussion of sexual content in treatment can be problematic. Acknowledging the unique nature of counseling for sexual problems, Klemer[14] places responsibility on the worker for recognizing and facilitating clients' eagerness and inclinations for discussion of sexual material. Similarly, Masters and Johnson[15] attribute the notion that sexually distressed couples will not discuss sex history willingly and in adequate detail to workers' misconceptions. They further suggest that these misconceptions may contribute to difficulties in sexual counseling. Such contentions raise the question as to whether workers engaged in sexual counseling assess accurately clients' readiness for divulging intimate sexual material, or whether the observed reluctance of workers to discuss specific sexual content results from an inaccurate assessment of clients' expectancies for discussing such content in treatment.

The issue of clients' content expectancies in counseling for sexual problems and the extent to which sexual subject matter may be handled directly and explicitly in the treatment process is further confounded by questions regarding the appropriate client-worker sex pairing for treatment of sexual adjustment problems. The findings of Binder, McConnell, and Sjoholm[16] and of Cieutat[17] support the contention that the nature of sex pairing of clients and workers affects the subject matter and the form of responses in treatment. Benney, Riesman, and Star[18] found that sex pairing influenced the rate of output in addition to the content discussed in treatment.

The relevance of the issue of worker–client sex pairing in treatment of sexual adjustment problems is emphatically underscored in the procedures devised by Masters and Johnson to insure adequate content coverage in the counseling process.[19] Their treatment process is designed specifically to provide for the variety of circumstances and conditions where differential sex pairing might be advisable; thus, sex pairing is so manipulated as to facilitate maximally the progress of treatment. These considerations are evident in the structure of the initial intake phase of

the treatment process where client–worker sex pairings are alternated for
each member of the marital unit seeking counseling. In this manner, by
having each spouse interviewed separately by a worker of his own and
of the opposite sex, the difficulties related to sex pairing and thought to
occur in the process of history taking and assessment of sexual problems
may be overcome.

Although these and other therapeutic procedures for facilitating discussions of sexual subject matter have been devised, seldom were they systematically evaluated. In addition, the question of the differential readiness
of clients to discuss sexual subject matter depending upon the composition
of client–worker sex pairing has not been studied.

The Study: Questions and Procedures

The preceding discussion highlighted a number of issues related to
clients' content expectancies of treatment for sexual adjustment problems
in which both theoretical arguments abound and actual methods of practice
vary. It was noted, however, that very little systematically collected information is available to suggest guides for professional practice. The study
and the findings reported here are part of a larger research project investigating the content, interactional patterns, and outcomes of counseling for
sexual adjustment in marriage. The following questions were posed for
investigation in the present study:

1. What is the pattern of clients' pre-treatment expectancies regarding
   the relative emphases that workers will place on different subject
   matter categories in counseling interviews for sexual adjustment
   problems? More specifically, this question was considered in terms
   of:
   (a) Clients' pre-treatment expectancies for subject matter to be
       discussed by a worker whose sex is unspecified, referred to as
       generalized counselor.
   (b) Client's pre-treatment expectancies for subject matter to be
       discussed by a male worker.
   (c) Clients' pre-treatment expectancies for subject matter to be
       discussed by a female worker.
2. Do the pre-treatment content emphases expected of workers differ
   for male and female clients?
3. What are the relationships between clients' expected content emphases and the actual emphases workers place on content during
   the treatment interviews, and how do these vary by client-worker
   sex pairings?

4. What are the relationships between clients' expectations of content emphases and the actual emphases that clients placed on content during their treatment interviews, and how do these vary by sex pairing?

5. What is the relationship between the actual content emphases that workers manifest during treatment interviews and the actual content emphases that clients show during these interviews?

PROCEDURES: Subjects were 48 clients who comprised 24 married couples in treatment for problems of sexual adjustment. The sample of workers was four—two male and two female workers. For purposes of this study, two types of data were obtained.

First, information regarding clients' pre-treatment expectancies for the content to be discussed in treatment was obtained by a questionnaire mailed to their homes one week prior to their first treatment interview. Each member of the marital unit received a separate questionnaire in a separate mailing and was asked to respond to it independently of his spouse. Among other information clients were asked to rate the extent of emphasis that they expected their worker to give to 14 different content areas. Each content category was rated by clients on a four-point scale depicting the extent of emphasis they expected the worker to devote to that category, ranging from (1) Not at all, (2) Little, and (3) Moderate, to (4) Very much.*

The 14 content categories that clients rated were derived and defined on the basis of a preliminary content analysis of the treatment interaction of a large number of clients in treatment for sexual adjustment. This preliminary analysis indicated not only the occurrence of these 14 different categories, but also that within some types of content, the subject matter was discussed both in a most general way as well as quite specifically. Thus, categories were derived that reflect both general and specific consideration of content in the treatment process.[20] The 14 content categories, and their defining criteria as presented to clients in the questionnaire are given below. In parentheses are the abbreviated category names used throughout the discussion.

1. Social history, including family and educational background, occupational activities, your relationships with your children, and history of courtships with other than your present spouse. (Social History)

---

* These pre-treatment questionnaires were devised and the data collected prior to Masters and Johnson's publication (1970) describing their treatment process. Therefore, contamination of clients' pre-treatment expectancies by their prior awareness of the treatment process and its emphases must be ruled out.

2. Marital relationship, that is, discussion of your past and current relationship to your spouse, other than sexual subject matter. (Marital History)

3. Medical and physical history, such as past history of illness, operations, and general health record of self and spouse. (Medical–Physical)

4. Orientation to and familiarization with the Foundation, its purposes, and procedures; and orientation to your stay in St. Louis. (Orientation)

5. Practices of and attitudes and feelings about sexual self-stimulation. (Autosexual–General)

6. Specific sexual self-stimulation practices. (Autosexual–Specific)

7. General premarital sexual history, such as premarital sexual experiences and attitudes about premarital sex. (Premarital–General)

8. Specific premarital sexual behaviors and practices. (Premarital–Specific)

9. General sexual history, such as background, extent, and manner of sex education, sex attitudes of the family during childhood, general features of present marital sexual relations, and feelings and attitudes towards sex. (Marital Sex–General)

10. Specific sexual behavior and practices with your spouse. (Marital Sex–Specific)

11. Extramarital sexual relations, referring to general features of and feelings and attitudes about sex relationships with other than your spouse. (Extramarital–General)

12. Specific extramarital sexual behaviors and practices. (Extramarital–Specific)

13. Practices of and attitudes and feelings about sexual relations with members of your own sex. (Homosexual–General)

14. Specific sexual practices with members of your own sex. (Homosexual-Specific)

On indicating their expected emphasis for each of these content categories, clients responded to each category three times. First, they indicated the emphasis they expected to be placed on the subject matter by a worker whose sex was unspecified; second, they were asked to respond to the same subject matter category in terms of the emphasis expected by a male worker; and last, they were asked to respond in terms of the emphasis expected by a female worker. The following is a sample question with the response modes and alternatives indicated.

In the following sections you are asked to share with us your ideas about what you think will be the subject matter covered in counseling sessions at the Foundation. The following are a number of topics which sometimes are discussed in counseling situations. You are being asked to indicate the degree of emphasis, if any, that you think may be placed on these topics in *your counseling sessions* at the Foundation.

1. Social history, including family and educational background, occupational activities, your relationships with your children, and history of courtships with other than your present spouse.
   a. What degree of overall emphasis do you expect to be given to this topic in discussions? (Please circle the appropriate response.)

Very		Not at
much	Moderate	Little	all

   b. The emphasis placed on the topic being discussed may be different, depending on whether the counselor is a man or a woman. What emphasis do you expect would be placed on this topic if counselor is:

Very		Not at
much	Moderate	Little	all
Man:			
Woman:			

The second type of data obtained consisted of the actual proportion of interview responses for both clients and workers that fell into each of the content categories. These data were collected from two interviews of each client that comprised the intake and assessment portion of his treatment. The interviews for each spouse were conducted on alternate days. The first day's interview was with a worker of the same sex and the second interview, on the following day, was with a worker of the opposite sex. In this manner, actual frequencies of content occurring during the interviews for clients and for workers were obtained from client–worker sex pairings that included both the same and cross–sex pairings. The actual response frequencies for each client and for each worker within an interview were coded into the 14 content categories from tape recordings of the 96 separate interviews conducted with the total sample of 48 individuals.

Results

THE PATTERNINGS OF CLIENTS' EXPECTED CONTENT EMPHASIS: The first question concerned the pattern of clients' pre-treatment expectancies regarding the relative emphasis that workers would place on the different content categories during the interviews. To answer this question an index was evolved to express the comparative emphasis clients expected to be placed across and on each of the 14 content categories. Because the data regarding clients' expected emphases were obtained for each category rated separately on a four–point scale, a method for comparing the relative ranking of expected emphases for all categories was devised. This consisted of computation of an Average Expected Emphasis Score (AEE) for each category. These scores were obtained for each content category through multiplying each scale value by the number of clients checking it, summing these products for all clients, and dividing by the number of clients (AEE = $\Sigma(fx)/n$, where x = the content category's expected emphasis on a 1—4 point scale, f = the number of clients checking this scale point for that content category, and n is the total sample of clients for which the AEE score is computed). AEE scores were computed for all content categories and separately for the male and female client sample. The AEE scores ranged from 1.00 to 4.00 and corresponded in meaning to the emphasis scale originally rated by the client.

Table 1 presents the expected emphasis scores for each of the 14 categories, the relative rank ordering of the scores for male and female clients and according to worker's sex.

One of the most outstanding features regarding the distribution of content expectancies reflected in Table 1 is the high similarity in the rank orderings of the expected emphasis for the different categories across different sex of worker, and the similarity, as well, between the distribution of AEE scores for the male and the female client samples. To further investigate the extent of the relationship between the expected emphasis in the different content categories across sex of worker and sex of client, AEE scores were subjected to correlational analysis across all categories. As is suggested by the similarity in the rank orderings, the intercorrelations obtained were exceptionally high. The range of correlations was from a low of .935 for male clients—female workers correlated with female clients—female workers to a high correlation of .998 for male clients where sex of worker was unspecified correlated with male clients—male workers. These high correlations indicate that regardless of the sex of clients, they have similar expectations across content categories when considered either with respect to a worker whose sex is unspecified or with respect to workers of either sex.

In view of this finding, the pattern of clients' content expectancies across content categories as portrayed in Table 1 may be best considered by reference to the summary column of the mean AEE scores for male and female clients and their rank ordering. As noted in these columns, the highest expected emphasis was for subject matter falling into the marital–sexual categories, both general and specific. These two categories rank the highest for both client sexes with absolute values characterizing

Table 1. *Expected Emphasis Scores for Content Categories, Their Rank Order for Male and Female Clients by Sex of Worker*

Content Category	Male Clients								Female Clients							
	G	Rank	M	Rank	F	Rank	$\bar{x}$	Rank	G	Rank	M	Rank	F	Rank	$\bar{x}$	Rank
Social History	3.25	4	3.25	4	3.29	4	3.26	4	3.00	4	2.87	4	2.92	4	2.93	4
Marital History	3.46	3	3.50	3	3.54	3	3.50	3	3.62	3	3.50	2	3.67	3	3.59	3
Medical-Physical	2.42	11	2.38	11	2.42	11	2.41	11	2.29	10	2.42	10	2.67	6	2.46	9
Orientation	2.92	6	2.88	6	2.83	6	2.87	6	2.71	7	2.71	8	2.75	5	2.72	7
Autosexual General	2.71	8	2.75	8	2.54	9	2.66	8	2.58	8	2.50	9	2.79	9	2.62	8
Autosexual Specific	2.58	10	2.58	10	2.46	10	2.54	10	2.42	9	2.46	6	2.33	10	2.40	10
Premarital General	2.96	5	2.96	5	2.88	5	2.93	5	2.92	5	2.72	5	2.72	7	2.78	5
Premarital Specific	2.88	7	2.87	7	2.71	7	2.82	7	2.79	6	2.75	3	2.71	8	2.75	6
Mari.-Sex. General	3.91	1	3.91	1	3.79	1	3.87	1	3.71	2	3.38	3	3.68	2	3.60	2
Mari.-Sex. Specific	3.83	2	3.83	2	3.66	2	3.77	2	4.00	1	3.83	1	3.83	1	3.88	1
Extra-Mari. General	2.59	9	2.59	9	2.58	8	2.59	9	2.25	11	2.21	11	2.25	11	2.23	11
Extra-Mari. Specific	2.25	12	2.29	12	2.29	12	2.27	12	1.79	12	1.79	12	1.79	12	1.79	12
Homosexual General	2.12	13	2.16	13	2.04	13	2.10	13	1.67	13	1.78	13	1.78	13	1.74	13
Homosexual Specific	1.75	14	1.75	14	1.71	14	1.73	14	1.25	14	1.25	14	1.33	14	1.27	14

* G = Worker, sex unspecified; M = Male worker; F = Female worker

109

"very much" emphasis. While the values are quite similar, the ranks are reversed for the male and the female clients with general marital sexual content given priority by males and specific sexual marital content given priority by females.

The next highest categories in expected emphasis are marital history and social history, in that order for both sexes. Whereas the extent of expected emphasis for marital history for clients of both sexes is midway between "moderate" and "very much" emphasis, the expected emphasis for social history is above the "moderate" level for male clients and just below the "moderate" level for female clients. The category of premarital–general is next in extent of emphasis for both sexes (with a rank of 5) and absolute values just below the "moderate" emphasis. The category of premarital sex–specific received similar absolute emphasis for both sexes just below "moderate" level, although the rank is higher for male than female clients. The content category of orientation received similar emphasis from male and female clients, although it was ranked a bit higher for females (6) than for males (7).

In the less than "moderate" emphasis range are also the categories of autosexual–general; autosexual–specific; and the category of extramarital sex–general. The first two were ranked equally by male and female clients while the latter received the rank of 9 for males and was ranked 11 by females with absolute content emphasis value just above "little." Alternately, the category of medical–physical content received the rank of 9 for females, with absolute value about midway between "little" and "moderate"; this category was ranked 11 for male clients with a similar absolute emphasis value to that of females.

The content categories that clients of both sexes least expected to be emphasized were those of extramarital–specific; homosexual–general; and homosexual–specific, in that order for both sexes. However, for all these categories male clients expected somewhat more emphasis than did females. The absolute values for the first two categories for males was above the "little" emphasis and the third just below. For females all three categories were accorded emphasis between "not at all" and "little." The first two were just below "little" and the last, that of homosexual–specific for female clients, was just above the "not at all" rating.

RELATION OF CONTENT EXPECTANCIES TO ACTUAL INTERVIEW CONTENT: The last series of questions of this study concerned the relationships between clients' expected content emphases and the actual emphasis placed on the different content categories during the treatment interviews by the workers and by the clients, and the variations in these relationships for different combinations of client–worker sex pairings. In addition, the question of the relative frequency of occurrence of content from the various subject matter categories was considered. The data utilized for the investigation of these questions consisted of, in addition to AEE scores, actual frequencies of workers' and of clients' interview response content. To make the actual response content frequencies comparable across all content categories, response frequencies were converted into proportions based on the ratio of responses falling into each category to the total number of responses within a given interview.

Table 2 presents the proportions of workers' and of clients' actual response content during the interviews in terms of client–worker sex pairing, the rank ordering of the different content categories for each client–worker pair, and the averages of workers' and of clients' content. A general examination of the table reveals that, unlike the distribution of expected content emphasis, the distributions of the actual content discussed during the interviews across the different sex pairings are not as similar. Obviously, client–worker sex pairing does make a difference in the relative frequency of occurrence of different content categories as well as in their relative rank orderings.

Although dissimilar across the different sex pairings, the distribution of actual content discussed in the interviews by clients and by workers is highly similar for the same sex pairing; that is, there is a high degree of correspondence between workers' content and clients' content discussed during any one interview. This high correspondence is demonstrated through the unusually high correlation coefficients, ranging between .983 and .997, that pertain to the relationships between the proportion of client content and the proportion of worker content within interviews. Table 2 portrays this close relationship in the highly similar rank order of the average proportion of interview content of workers and of clients, where only three content categories are not ranked in exactly the same manner. In two of the three instances the difference is in only one rank; in the third the difference is in two rank positions. Apparently there is a high degree of reciprocity in content of interview responses between workers and client pairings irrespective of whether the worker–client combination is same or cross–sex. The high reciprocity found between worker and client interview content may be better understood if one acknowledges the role of the worker in initiating interview content and the client's likelihood of following in responding to it. These findings about worker–client reciprocity further corroborate those of Duehn,[21] who, in another part of this research project, found the same relationships through a different method of analysis. In view of this reciprocity, and assuming workers' central role in initiating content, a decision was made to restrict all further analysis to a discussion of workers' interview response content.

A close examination of the distribution of workers' response content

Table 2. *Proportions of Workers' and Clients' Content, and their Rank Order in Same and Cross-Sex Interviews**

Content Category	Workers' Content										Clients' Content									
	MW/MC	Rank	MW/FC	Rank	FW/MC	Rank	FW/FC	Rank	x̄	Rank	MC/MW	Rank	MC/FW	Rank	FC/MW	Rank	FC/FW	Rank	x̄	Rank
Social History	.348	1	.180	2	.390	1	.440	1	.340	1	.427	1	.402	1	.195	2	.481	1	.376	1
Marital History	.070	4	.106	4	.210	2	.090	4	.119	3	.084	3	.223	2	.105	4	.075	5	.122	3
Medical-Physical	.026	10	.036	8	.011	9	.021	8	.023	9	.028	9	.017	9	.051	6	.021	8	.029	9
Orientation	.050	7	.090	5	.080	5	.040	7	.065	5	.029	8	.050	5	.046	7	.018	9	.035	7
Autosexual General	.016	12	.018	11	.009	11	.018	10	.015	11	.019	11	.007	12	.014	12	.015	11	.014	11
Autosexual Specific	.030	9	.016	12	.006	12	.017	11	.017	10	.025	10	.008	11	.015	11	.017	10	.016	10
Premarital General	.064	5	.046	7	.040	6	.060	6	.052	6	.056	5	.034	6	.034	8	.056	6	.045	5
Premarital Specific	.056	6	.019	10	.023	8	.080	5	.044	7	.051	6	.022	8	.021	10	.081	4	.044	6
Mari.-Sex. General	.080	3	.146	3	.090	4	.071	3	.102	4	.078	4	.076	4	.131	3	.087	3	.093	4
Mari.-Sex. Specific	.150	2	.259	1	.100	3	.100	2	.152	2	.136	2	.122	2	.254	1	.112	2	.156	2
Extra-Marital General	.040	8	.060	6	.026	7	.019	9	.036	8	.034	7	.024	7	.053	5	.026	7	.034	8
Extra-Marital Specific	.013	13	.031	9	.005	13	.002	14	.012	12	.012	13	.002	14	.033	9	.004	14	.013	12
Homosexual General	.012	14	.010	13	.010	10	.007	12	.010	13	.009	14	.012	10	.011	13	.006	12	.009	13
Homosexual Specific	.017	11	.001	14	.004	14	.005	13	.007	14	.016	12	.004	13	.001	14	.005	13	.007	14
Total**	0.972		1.018		1.004		0.990		0.994		1.004		1.003		0.964		1.004		0.993	

* M = Male worker or client; F = Female worker or client; C = Client; W = Worker.
** Totals should add to 1.000; deviations are attributable to rounding error.

across the different content categories and for the different sex pairings reveals the following: The most frequently occurring content category in three of the four sex pairings is that of social history which accounts for between 34 percent to 44 percent of the total content discussed during the interviews. For the sex pair of male worker–female client, social history is the second most frequent category, but with a frequency of only 18 percent as compared with the average of 34 percent for all client–worker sex pairings.

The second most frequent content category is that of specific marital sexual content which has an average frequency of 15 percent. Here too, the male worker–female client sex pair is conspicuously different from the rest and accounts for almost 26 percent of the total content as compared with the average of 15 percent for the category. The third and fourth most frequently occurring content categories are marital history and general marital sexual content which accounts for 12 percent and 10 percent, respectively, of the total responses. The pattern of content frequencies for each of these categories across the different sex pairings also is variable; the female worker–male client sex pair accounts for 21 percent of the content of the former and the male worker–female client sex pair accounts for almost 15 percent of the latter.

It is interesting to note, however, that these four content categories—social history, marital–sexual specific content, marital history, and marital–sexual general content—account for over 71 percent of the total responses, which leaves under 29 percent of the total content to be distributed among the remaining ten content categories. In comparison, the five content categories least frequently discussed during the interviews, averaging under 2 percent each, account for only 6 percent of the total responses.

In terms of the differential patterning of response content for the different sex pairings, one could conclude from Table 2 that the male worker–female client sex pair seems to manifest a different distribution of actual content emphasis discussed during the interview than any of the other sex pairings. In this pair none of the content categories seem as heavily emphasized as in the other three. Furthermore, the content categories that are emphasized are, on the whole, different than the pattern evidenced by the other three worker–client sex pairings.

The last issue for analysis pertains to the relationships between clients' expected content emphases and the actual content emphasized during the treatment interviews. As indicated above, actual content frequencies of clients may be a function of workers' interview content. Therefore, the relationship between clients' expected content emphases in the interviews was analyzed only with respect to workers' interview content. This relationship was investigated through intercorrelations of clients' content expectancies across all content categories with workers' actual content proportions across all content categories for the four different client–worker sex pairings. These intercorrelations were: male clients' content expectancies with male worker actual interview content; male clients' content expectancies with female worker actual interview content; female clients' content expectancies with male worker actual interview content; and female clients' content expectancies with female worker actual interview content. The correlations obtained between clients' expectancies and workers' actual content for each of the above sex pairings were .552, .613, .782, 355, respectively. With an n of 14 categories the correlations for both cross–sex pairings were significant at the .01 level, the correlation for male client–male worker pair was significant at .05, and the correlation for female client–female worker did not reach the predetermined level of significance of .05. The definite trend of these relationships indicates that clients' content expectancies are better met in treatment through cross–sex pairings and, in particular, for the female client–male worker sex pair. Apparently, if the meeting of clients' content expectancies by workers is a desirable feature of treatment interviewing, this is best accomplished when clients and workers are of the opposite sex.

Discussion

Investigation of the patterning and nature of clients' content expectancies in treatment for sexual adjustment problems was a central concern of the study. Questions of the readiness of clients in sexual counseling to discuss sensitive subject matter relating to their sex life and to their specific sexual practices have been argued in various ways with minimal amount of systematic study or resolution. The present study addressed these questions directly by investigating, in addition, the extent to which clients' readiness to discuss sexual content is influenced by the sex of workers or particular client–worker sex pairings.

An argument may be advanced that clients' pre-treatment expectations regarding the relative emphasis that workers place on different categories of content can be viewed as an index of clients' readiness to engage with workers in detailed discussions and explorations of such content. This argument is based on the assumption that clients for whom pre-treatment content expectancies do not coincide with their actual readiness to discuss such content with workers will most likely not engage in or will avoid treatment. Since all the clients responding to the study's pre-treatment questionnaire regarding their content expectancies did engage in treatment, the assumption that clients' expectations of workers' content emphasis reflected their readiness to discuss such content in treatment seems amply warranted.

When viewed in this manner, the findings regarding clients' content expectancies of treatment did not confirm the widespread notion that the sensitivity of the subject matter requires a particularly cautious approach on the part of workers. To the contrary, clients of both sexes expressed a high degree of readiness to discuss sensitive and specific sexual content, and moreover, their expectations did not evidence the often mentioned differentiation according to the sex of worker. Clients expected equal emphasis in discussion of sexual subject matter when the sex of worker was unspecified, when they responded in terms of male worker, or in their responses to female workers. These findings corroborate Klemer's observation that workers' hesitancy in discussing sexually sensitive content may be an indication of their own uneasiness rather than a true reflection of clients' readiness to engage in this type of discussion during treatment.

Two other findings relate directly to this issue. Clients expected as much emphasis to be placed on discussion of specific sexual behaviors and practices as on discussions of sexual content of a more general nature. In addition, the content categories of social history and of orientation to treatment and its setting, the areas traditionally most emphasized during initial stages of marital counseling and counseling in general, were expected to be emphasized noticeably less than sexual subject matter. Social history content ranked uniformly fourth in order of expected emphasis, somewhat above "moderate" levels, and orientation to treatment ranked sixth or seventh with expected emphasis being below the "moderate" level. To the extent that these findings are representative of clients' expectations for sexual counseling, they may have important implications for the planning and conduct of treatment interviews. The often mentioned need for and practice of extreme caution in moving directly into detailed discussions of sexual problems and of specific sexual practices between marital partners may be obviated completely. The findings seem to indicate that workers can be much more directive and move relatively more quickly into the problem areas that are of main concern to the client.

Social workers have always been aware of and very conscientious about starting treatment "where the client is." Unfortunately, however, social workers' conceptions of where clients are may not be very accurate. They are usually based on conceptual formulations regarding the psychological makeup of clients and on pronouncements regarding the high likelihood of meeting severe client resistance when discussion turns into the focal problem areas. However, they fail to consider the lack of empirical verification of these conceptions and claims, nor do they acknowledge the possibility that clients' readiness to move directly into and discuss their problems may vary according to the problem area itself or to other characteristics of clients. In fact, it is likely that the undue reluctance of workers to address themselves directly to clients' problems and to the content areas clients view as most relevant to treatment are in large measure responsible for clients' disenchantment with treatment and the high rate of clients' premature discontinuance (Rosen, 1970a). The present findings regarding clients' content expectancies may be useful to workers, in that in addition to their factual value, they may relieve workers from the need and tendency to engage in contorted attempts to indirectly elicit discussion of specific sexual content.

The findings of the study also may serve to clarify another of our cultural and professional myths—namely, the lesser readiness attributed to females than to males for discussion of sensitive sexual material. Not only do the findings show that female clients expect as much emphasis to be placed on sexual subject matter as do male clients, but also they expect greater emphasis on specific sexual content, and rank it higher than do male clients. Similarly, although female clients' ranking of expected emphasis on social history is the same as that of male clients (ranked fourth in emphasis), their expected emphasis score for this content category is below the "moderate" level, whereas it is above the "moderate" level for male clients. Apparently, then, female clients conform even less than male clients to the traditional view regarding readiness to discuss sensitive content.

The relation between clients' expected content emphasis and the relative frequency of content actually discussed in the treatment interview was the second concern of the study. The findings regarding the actual frequencies of workers' and clients' content revealed an extremely high correspondence between them. This was interpreted as indicating a high degree of reciprocity in clients' responding to content introduced into the treatment interviews by workers' initiative.

If one were to assume that meeting of clients' content expectancies bears a relation to the outcomes of treatment, as is generally suggested in the literature, then it would seem from the findings that the most facilitative condition for achieving this end is the utilization of cross–sex, client–worker pairings in treatment of sexual adjustment problems. The results further suggest that cross–sex pairing is more crucial for meeting the expectations of female than of male clients. It seems that since clients' content expectancies are better met by workers of the opposite sex, and since expectations of treatment do not vary according to the sex of worker, the practice of cross–sex pairing of clients and workers in treatment of sexual problems may be recommended.

In view of the findings that female clients' expectancies were most highly met with workers of the opposite sex and not met with workers of the same sex, it might be interesting to conjecture that for purposes of continuation in treatment, the predominance of female workers in marital couseling might be dysfunctional for the female client. This conjecture becomes even more tenable when considering the high rate of clients' premature discontinuance in psychologically oriented family and marital counseling agencies,[22] and the greater likelihood for women to be the members of the marital unit who engage in the counseling situation. Future studies concerned with premature discontinuance in family and marital counseling agencies might well provide for the systematic testing of such hypothesis.

Probably the most important conclusion that should be drawn from the findings of the present study does not concern their immediate practice implications, but rather the urgent need for additional studies of this nature, utilizing larger client populations and worker samples, as well as extending over different types and models of treatment. The lack of systematically collected data is particularly noticeable in the area of treatment for sexual problems. Undoubtedly, the sensitivity of the subject matter and the high degree of confidentiality that research in this area requires are among the factors making extensive studies difficult. Nonetheless, agency administrators, practitioners, and researchers alike should make provisions for carefully designed studies of the processes and outcomes of sexual counseling.

NOTES

[1] A. G. Kelly, *The Psychology of Personal Constructs* (New York: W. W. Norton & Company, Inc., 1955).

[2] A. P. Goldstein, K. Heller, and L. B. Sechrest, *Psychotherapy and the Psychology of Behavior Change* (New York: Wiley, 1966).

[3] A. Rosen "The Treatment Relationship: A Conceptualization," *Journal of Consulting and Clinical Psychology,* in press.

[4] A. Rosen "Social-Psychological Factors in Outcomes of Psychotherapy: A Conceptualization and Preliminary Findings" (Paper presented at the Third International Congress of Social Psychiatry, Zagreb, Jugoslavia, September 1970).

[5] D. A. Taylor, I. Altman, and R. Sorrenito, "Interpersonal Exchange as a Function of Reward/Cost and Situation Factors: Expectancy, Confirmation-Disconfirmation" (Paper presented at the Annual Convention, American Psychological Association, San Francisco, September 1968).

[6] M. A. Bailey, L. Warshaw, and R. M. Eichler, "A Study of Factors Related to the Stay in Psychotherapy," *Journal of Clinical Psychology* 15 (1959): 442–44.

[7] S. L. Garfield, and D. C. Affleck, "Therapists' Judgments Concerning Patients Considered for Psychotherapy," *Journal of Consulting Psychology* 25 (1961): 505–9.

[8] E. W. Hiler, "An Analysis of Patient-Therapist Compatibility," *Journal of Consulting Psychology* 22 (1958), 341–7.

[9] A. B. Hollingshead, and F. C. Redlich, *Social Class and Mental Illness* (New York: Wiley, 1958).

[10] M. Lorr, M. M. Katz, and E. A. Rubenstein, "The Prediction of Length of Stay in Psychotherapy," *Journal of Consulting Psychology* 22 (1958): 321–7.

[11] B. Overall, and H. Aronson, "Expectations of Psychotherapy in Patients of Lower Socioeconomic Class," *American Journal of Orthopsychiatry* 33 (1963), 421–30.

[12] J. Rosenfeld, "Strangeness Between Helper and Client," *Social Service Review* 38 (1964): 1, 17–25.

[13] A. E. Winder, and M. Hersko, "The Effect of Social Class on the Length and Type of Psychotherapy in a Veterans Administration Mental Hygiene Clinic," *Journal of Clinical Psychology* 11 (1955): 77–9.

[14] R. H. Klemer, "Talking with Patients about Sexual Problems," in R. H. Klemer, ed., *Counseling in Marital and Sexual Problems* (Baltimore: The Williams & Wilkins Company, 1965), pp. 118–25.

[15] W. H. Masters and V. Johnson, "Counseling with Sexually Incompatible Marital Partners," in R. H. Klemer, ed., *Counseling in Marital and Sexual Problems* (Baltimore: The Williams & Wilkins Company, 1965), pp. 126–37.

[16] A. Binder, D. McConnell, and N. A. Sjoholm, "Verbal Conditioning as a Function of Experimenter Characteristics," *Journal of Abnormal and Social Psychology* 55 (1957): 309–14.

[17] V. J. Cieutat, "Sex Difference and Reinforcement in the Conditioning and Extinction of Conversational Behavior," Psychological Reports 10 (1962): 467–74.

[18] M. Benney, D. Riesman, and S. A. Star, "Age and Sex in the Interview," *American Journal of Sociology* 62 (1956): 143–52.

[19] W. H. Masters, and V. E. Johnson, *Human Sexual Inadequacy* (Boston: Little, Brown and Company, 1970).

[20] A. Rosen, R. S. Connaway, and W. A. Duehn, "Methodological Considerations for Content Analysis in Process Studies of Sexual Counseling" (St. Louis, Mo.: Washington University, 1970). To be mimeographed.

[21] W. D. Duehn, "The Patterning of Stimulus-Response Congruence and Content Relevance: A Study of Client-Worker Interaction in the Diagnostic Phase of

[22] S. Briar, "Family Services," in H. Maas, ed., *Five Fields of Social Service: Reviews of Research* (New York: National Association of Social Workers, Inc., 1966), 9–50.

SUGGESTED READINGS

Brecher, E. *The Sex Researchers.* Boston: Little, Brown and Company, 1969.

Klemer, R., ed. *Counseling in Marital & Sexual Problems.* Baltimore: The Williams and Wilkins Company, 1965, pp. 118–25.

Masters, W., and Johnson, V. *Human Sexual Inadequacy.* Boston: Little, Brown and Company, 1970, pp. 24–92.

9

A Rational Approach to Premarital Counseling*

ALBERT ELLIS

People come for premarital counseling obviously because they have problems; and people with problems, as has been recently stressed by Ellis,[1] Harper,[2,3] Laidlaw,[4] and Lawton,[5] can often best be helped by some form of marriage counseling which not only presents a solution to their present circumstances but also goes to the root of their basic problem-creating disturbances. They need, in other words, some type of psychotherapy.

Although I see a few clients for premarital counseling who have simple questions to be answered, which can sometimes be resolved in one or two sessions, the majority come for deeper and more complicated reasons. Their typical presenting questions are: "Is my fiancée the right person for me?" "Should I be having premarital sex relations?" "How can I find a suitable mate?" and "How can I overcome my sexual incompetence or my homosexual leanings before I marry?" These and similar questions usually involve deep-seated personality characteristics or long-standing emotional problems of the counselees.

When put in more dynamic terms, the real questions most individuals who come for premarital counseling are asking themselves are "Wouldn't it be terrible if I were sexually or amatively rejected? or made a mistake in my sex-love choice? or acted wrongly or wickedly in my premarital affairs?" And: "Isn't it horribly unfair that the girl or fellow in whom I am interested is unkind? or ununderstanding? or overly demanding? or too selfish?"

Stated differently, the vast majority of premarital counselees are needlessly anxious and/or angry. They are woefully afraid of rejection, incompetence, or wrongdoing during courtship or marriage; and they are exceptionally angry or hostile because general or specific members of the other sex do not behave exactly as they would like them to behave. Since, according to the principles of rational psychotherapy which I and Dr. Robert A. Harper have been developing for the past several years, feelings of

---

* Paper delivered at the International Conference on the Family at Teachers College, Columbia University, August 26, 1960.

anxiety and resentment are almost needlessly self-created and inevitably do the individual who experiences them more harm than good, my psychotherapeutic approach to most premarital counselees is to show them, as quickly as possible, how to rid themselves of their fear and hostility and thereby to solve their present and future courtship and marital difficulties.

The main theoretical construct and counseling technique which I employ in extirpating a client's shame and anger is the A-B-C theory of personality, which has recently been outlined in several articles and books.[6-11] This theory holds that it is rarely the stimulus, A, which gives rise to a human emotional reaction, C; rather, it is almost always B—the individual's system of beliefs regarding, attitudes toward, or interpretations of A—which actually leads to his reaction, C.

Take, for example, premarital anxiety—which is usually the main presenting symptom of young people who come for counseling before marriage. I have recently been seeing a girl of 25 who, in spite of her keen desire to marry and have a family, has never been out on a date with a boy. She is reasonably good-looking and very well educated and has had a good many opportunities to go with boys because her entire family is concerned about her being dateless and will arrange dates for her on a moment's notice. But she always has found some excuse not to make appointments with boys; or else has made dates and then cancelled them at the last minute. At the very few social affairs she has attended, she has latched on to her mother or some girl friend and has literally never left her side and never allowed herself to be alone with a male.

Although it is easy to give the girl's problem an impressive "psychodynamic" classification and to say that she is pregenitally fixated or has a severe dependency attachment to her mother, such labels, even if partially accurate, are incredibly unhelpful in getting her over her problem. Instead, she was simply helped to understand that her phobic reaction to males, at point C, could not possibly be caused by some noxious event or stimulus at point A (such as her once being rejected by a boy in whom she was interested); but that her own catastrophizing sentences at point B must be the real, current cause of her extreme fear of dating boys.

"What," I asked this client, "are you telling yourself at point B that makes you react so fearfully at point C?" At first, as is the case with many of my clients, she insisted that she wasn't telling herself anything at point B; or that if she was, she couldn't say what she was telling herself. In my now distant past as a psychoanalyst, I used to take this kind of denial seriously, tell myself some of my *own* nonsense at point B to the effect that the patient was not yet ready for deep interpretation, and spend the next several months helping her avoid the main issue by demonstrating to her that she had some kind of an Electra complex which she was repressing and that she now, by long-winded processes of free association and dream analysis, had to dig up and face. Being at the present stage in the game, a less naive and wiser psychotherapist, I now refuse to take a simple no for an answer and keep insisting that the client must on theoretical grounds, be telling herself *something* at point B. Now what, and let's have no nonsense about this, is it?

My persistent questioning soon paid off. The client, on urging, found that she was telling herself that it would be perfectly awful if she went with boys and, like her two older sisters before her, was seduced sexually before marriage but (unlike these sisters) didn't actually marry her seducer. These internalized sentences, in their turn, were subheadings under her general philosophy, which held that marriage rather than sex was the only real good in life and that any girl who failed to achieve the marital state was thoroughly incompetent and worthless. Perversely enough, as happens in so many instances of neurosis, by overemphasizing the necessity of her marrying, my client literally drove herself into a state of panic which effectively prevented her from achieving the goal she most desired.

What was to be done to help this client? In my psychoanalytic days I would have encouraged her to transfer her love and marital needs toward me and then, interspersed with a great deal more free associational and dream analysis evocation and interpretation, I would have tried to show her that because I accepted her, she could fully accept herself and then presumably feel free to go off and marry some other male. Maybe, after a few thousand hours of analysis, this would have worked. Or maybe she would have become just as parasitically attached to me as she now was to her mother and would have finally, at the age of 65, realized that I was not going to marry her and been pensioned off to a home for ex-analysands which I sometimes fondly think of organizing.

Not being willing any longer to risk this dubiously fortuitous outcome of therapy, I very directly took this girl's major and minor irrational philosophies of life and directly challenged them until, after three months of counseling, she decided to give them up. More specifically, I vigorously attacked her notions that premarital sex relations are wicked and shameful; that marriage is the only good state of female existence; and that anyone who fails in a major goal, such as the goal of having a good relationship with a member of the other sex, is completely inept and valueless as a human being. I induced this client to believe, instead, that sex-love relations can be worthwhile in themselves, quite apart from marriage; that marrying may be a highly *preferable* but hardly a *necessary* goal for a female; and that failing in a given purpose is a normal part of human living and proves nothing whatever about one's essential worth.

In miracles or any other supernatural influences I passionately disbelieve. But the changes that took place in this patient concomitant with her reorganizing her sex-love and general philosophies of life were almost miraculous. It needed relatively little urging on my part to get her to make several dates with young males; she thoroughly enjoyed petting to orgasm with some of these partners; a few months later she entered into a full sex-love relationship with one of them; and she is now engaged to be married to her lover. Moreover, although we rarely talked about some of the other important aspects of her life, she has also gone back to college, which she had left in despair because of her poor social life there, and is intent on becoming a nursery school teacher. Quite a constructive change, all told!

Let us consider another case of premarital counseling along rational psychotherapeutic lines. A 28-year-old male came for counseling because he kept becoming angry at his fiancée, ostensibly because she continually "unmanned" him by criticizing him in public. On questioning, he also admitted that he had never been fully potent with a female and had acute fears of whether he would succeed sexually with his fiancée after they were married. According to psychoanalytic interpretation, he was really not afraid of his fiancée unmanning him in public, but of unmanning himself when he finally got into bed with his bride; and her so-called attacks on him were actually a projection of his own castration fears.

So I would have interpreted in my psychoanalytic youth. Fortunately, however, I had the good sense to call in this client's fiancée; and I quickly found that she was a querulous, negativistic woman and that she did, figuratively speaking, often castrate my client in public. Whereupon I quickly set about doing two nonpsychoanalytic and highly directive things. First, I talked the fiancée herself into becoming a counselee, even though she at first contended that there was nothing wrong with her, and that the entire problem was the result of her boy friend's inconsiderateness and ineptitude. When I saw her for psychotherapy (in all, 48 sessions of individual and a year of group therapy, since she proved to be a rather difficult patient) I set about showing her that her anger, at point C, stemmed not from her boy friend's inept behavior, at point A, but from her prejudiced and grandiose interpretations of this behavior at point B.

I showed this woman, in other words, that she kept saying to herself: (a) "John is doing these inept and inconsiderate things to me" and (b) "He *shouldn't* be acting that way and is a no-good sonofagun for doing so." Instead, I insisted, she would do much better by saying to herself: (a) "John is doing these things, which I consider to be inept and inconsiderate to me," and (b) "If I am correct (which I may or may not be), then *it would be much nicer* if he could be induced to stop acting this way; and I should be doing everything in my power to help him see what he is doing, without blaming him for his behavior, so that he changes his actions for the better."

When I convinced this client that, as I contended at an American Psychological Association symposium last year,[12] no one is logically ever to blame for anything, and that people's errors and mistakes are to be accepted and condoned rather than excoriated if we are truly to be of help to them, she not only stopped berating her boy friend in public but became a generally kinder and less disturbed individual in her own right.

Meanwhile, to flashback to my original client in this pair, whom we left gnashing his teeth at his fiancée and shivering in his pajamas about the spectre of his sexual impotence, he proved to be a relatively easy convert to the cause of rational thinking. After 16 sessions of highly directive counseling he was able to see that, whatever the verbal harshness of his intended bride, her words—at point A—could only hurt and anger him—at point C—if he kept telling himself sufficient nonsense about these words at point B.

Instead of what he had been telling himself at point B—namely, "That bitch is castrating me by her horrible public criticism and she has no right to do that to poor weakly me"—he was induced to question the rationality of these internal verbalizations. After actively challenging his own unthinking assumptions—particularly, the assumptions (a) that his fiancée's critical words *were* necessarily horribly hurtful; (b) that she *should not* keep repeating her criticism of him; and (c) that he *was* too weak to hear this criticism and not be able to take it in his stride—this client began to believe in and tell himself a radically different philosophy of sex-love relationships, namely: "There goes my poor darling again, making cracks at me because of her own disturbance. Now let me see if any of her points about me are correct; and if so, let me try to change myself in those respects. But let me also try, in so far as she is mistaken about her estimates of me, to help her with her own problems, so that she doesn't need to keep being nasty to me in public." When this change in his internalized sentences was made, my client improved remarkably in his ability to take his fiancée's criticism; and his hostility toward her largely vanished.

He was then also able to face the matter of his own impotence—which proved to be, as it so often does, a result of his worrying so greatly over the possibility of his failing that he actually tended to fail. When he was able to acquire a new sexual and general philosophy about failing, he became more than adequately potent.

In his new philosophy, instead of saying to himself: "If I fail sexually, it will be terrible and I will be totally unmanned," he began to say: "It is highly desirable, though not necessary, that I succeed in being potent; and in the event that I am impotent for the present, there are various extravaginal ways of satisfying my partner; so what's the great hassle?" Losing his acute fear of sex failure, he easily succeeded; and losing his terrible fear of his fiancée's publicly criticizing him, he helped her to be much less critical.

The main aspects of rational therapy which are usually applied to premarital counseling, then, include the counselee's being taught that it is *not* horrible for him to fail in his sex-love ventures; that there is no reason why his love partner should act the way he would like her to act; and that any intense unhappiness that he may experience in his premarital (or, later, marital) affairs almost invariably stems from his own self-repeated nonsense rather than his partner's attitudes or actions. Rational therapy, in these respects, directly forces the patient to accept reality, particularly in his relations with his sex-love partner.

Summary

The theory and practice of rational psychotherapy are applied to two cases of individuals who were seen for premarital counseling. In both cases, the clients were significantly helped when they were induced to accept the fact that it was not the behavior of their prospective mates which upset them, but their irrational, unrealistic expectations about and reactions to this behavior. When these premarital counseling clients were shown how to question and challenge their own self-defeating internalized sentences, their problems with themselves and their prospective mates were appreciably ameliorated.

NOTES

[1] A. Ellis, A critical evaluation of marriage counseling. *Marriage and Family Living,* 18 (1956): 65–71.

[2] R. A. Harper, "Should marriage counseling become a full-fledged specialty?" *Marriage and Family Living* 15 (1953): 338–40.

[3] R. A. Harper, "Failure in marriage counseling," *Marriage and Family Living* 17 (1955): 359–62.

[4] R. W. Laidlaw, "The psychiatrist as marriage counselor," *American Journal of Psychiatry* 106 (1950): 732–36.

[5] G. Lawton, "Neurotic interaction between counselor and counselee," *Journal of Counseling Psychology* 5 (1958): 28–33.

[6] A. Ellis, "Outcome of employing three techniques of psychotherapy," *Journal of Clinical Psychology* 13 (1957): 24–8.

[7] A. Ellis, "Neurotic interaction between marital partners," *Journal of Counseling Psychology* 5 (1968): 24–8.

[8] A. Ellis, "Marriage counseling with demasculinizing wives and demasculinized husbands," *Marriage and Family Living* 22 (1960): 13–21.

[9] A. Ellis and R. A. Harper, *Creative Marriage* (New York: Lyle Stuart, 1961).

[10] A. Ellis and R. A. Harper, *A Guide to Rational Living* (Englewood Cliffs, N.J.: Prentice-Hall, 1961).

[11] R. A. Harper, "A rational process-orientated approach to marriage counseling," *Journal of Family Welfare* 6 (1960): 1–10.

[12] A. Ellis, "There is no place for the concept of sin in psychotherapy," *Journal of Counseling Psychology* 7 (1960): 188–92.

SUGGESTED READINGS

Freedmen, L. *Virgin Wives*. London: Tavistock, 1962.

Gangsei, L. *Manual for Group Premarital Counseling*. New York: Association Press, 1971.

Peterson, J. *Marriage and Family Counseling: Perspective and Prospect*. New York: Association Press, 1968.

Rutledge, A. *Premarital Counseling*. New York: Schenkman, 1966.

10

Treatment of Common Marital
Sexual Problems

HARVEY L. GOCHROS

Over twenty years ago Margaret Mead said of American marriage: "It
is one of the most difficult marriage forms that the human race has ever
attempted."[1] It has not become any simpler. Greater premarital sexual
freedom, more tolerance of difference, changing attitudes toward sexual
expression, and improved birth control methods have added both greater
complexity and potential for sexual satisfaction in marriage.

Women are succeeding in their revolution, leading not only to economic
and social justice, but also to equal sexual rights and pleasure.[2] At the
same time, men are increasingly under social and personal pressure to become sexperts, achieving a combination of romantic, choreographic, and
athletic competence in bed, in order to maintain their own self-esteem and
the acceptance and respect of others—especially their spouses. These pressures seem to be leading to a preoccupation with the skilled accomplishment of the sex act with an unending quest for the perfect orgasm. Such
pressure has led to the development as well as uncovering of a high incidence of sexual problems in marriage. "A conservative estimate," according to Masters and Johnson,[3] who have revolutionized both the understanding and the treatment of sexual problems, "would indicate half the
marriages in America as either presently sexually dysfunctional or im-
minently so in the future." Much contemporary laboratory and clinical
sexual research is oriented toward helping to reduce these problems. Social
workers, who have long considered marriage counseling an important area
of their practice, are aware of the frequency with which sexual problems
are at the core of marital conflict. Indeed, Masters has estimated that social
work is one of the four professions, excluding medicine, which treat 75
percent of the problems in sexual inadequacy.[4]

It would seem likely, therefore, that in an age of concern, if not preoccupation, with sexual fulfillment, the number of people seeking social
work help for explicit sexual problems in their marriage will continue to

126

increase. This paper will concentrate on some of the basic sources of these problems and some approaches to them.

A major determinant of the type of sexual adjustment developed in the marriage is the learning each partner has had regarding expectations for their sexual performance. There are two currently common models of sexual expression which in their extreme form often contribute to marital sexual dysfunctioning. One is the romantic ideal and the other is the model of the sexual athlete.

Romantic Love

The sexual component of American marriage has been greatly influenced by the concept of romantic love.[5] Indeed, while love itself may be defined as an intense emotional attraction to and a feeling of interdependence with another human being, our concept of love has been greatly influenced by the tradition of *romantic* love. "Real" romantic love implies a state of intense passion toward a perfect partner and the probability of a permanent state of bliss in the relationship. This tradition leads one to perceive a potential spouse in an unrealistically idealized, highly esthetic, worshipful way. It presumes that there is the possibility of true love with only one object, who is "meant" to be the only one for the lover. If there is a sexual component in romance, it is usually perceived as being idyllic and almost nonphysical. Yet, only in romantic love, so the myth goes, is sexuality legitimate and fully realized. Without it, sex is reduced to an animalistic level and becomes worthy only of contempt.

It is this view of love and sex which is still widely portrayed in fictionalized accounts of marriage in books, magazines, on television, and even in teenage romance comic books. As such, it provides the role model and ideal for many marital relationships and has taken its toll in sexual dysfunctioning in marriage. Few couples can maintain a romantic fiction for any extended period without devastating interpersonal results. The facts of life, marriage, and intimacy preclude maintaining such an unrealistic perception of the marital relationship. Indeed, a sound marriage is based on honest benevolent acceptance of each other and not on attempts to maintain an idealized fantasy.

Because romantic love is frequently dissipated by the facts of life, the ideal of romance often pulls people out of potentially rewarding, honest interpersonal relationships to seek new romantic experiences outside of the marriage.

Clearly the role of a social worker, in relation to romantic love, is to help couples enunciate and evaluate their mutual expectations, accept each other and themselves as "just" human beings, find joy and pleasure with each other as they are, and accept the honest give-and-take satisfactions of their sexual relationship.

The Ideal of the Sexual Athlete

Whereas the romantic ideal relegates sex to an idealized spiritual experience and intellectual fantasy, the other common model is epitomized by marriage manual technocracy which portrays sex as a purely physical activity. The sexual manual, generally written by people who are (1) men, (2) past 40, and (3) physicians, antiseptically emphasizes the technical skills related to sexuality and general physiological reactions. While they provide needed information and often endorse sexual flexibility,[6] they also emphasize skill, dexterity, and orgasmic competence.

Preoccupation with the mechanical aspects of sexuality as depicted in many manuals can be threatening and do more harm than good. The athletic approach glorifies the perfectly functioning body. It is noteworthy that those books which are illustrated almost always use models who are young, well endowed, and attractive, while many of their readers are not, further encouraging feelings of inadequacy. They tend to be preoccupied with techniques, positions, and orgasms rather than general tactile and emotional satisfactions. They encourage modeling of the sexual behavior described in the book, with promised exquisite results rather than encouraging spontaneity in the sexual act as determined by the unique personalities, needs, capacities, and desires of a particular couple at a particular time.

The sex athlete model contributes to one of the main inhibitions of sexual satisfaction: the quest for normalcy. This preoccupation encourages what Masters and Johnson have described as the "spectator role" in sexual behavior. That is, an individual finds that he cannot totally immerse himself in sexual behavior, but looks upon himself as an actor in a performance with his partner, preoccupied with how well he is doing as a lover, how long it will last, and how well it will end.

Here again, the social worker can help by encouraging the couple to develop its own sexual contract, devoid of excessive performance expectations.

The presence of these two diverse models of sexual behavior and the relative absence of other more functional models for the sex relation create many of the common problems in sexual adaptation in marriage seen by social workers. Indeed, most of the problems in sexuality are bioemotional consequences of inadequate or faulty learning regarding sexuality maintained by the sexual attitudes of peers, sexual partners, and the social environment. The social worker's function is to help correct this learning.

Approach to Treatment

The social worker who treats marital sexual problems must first come to terms with his own sexuality and own marriage (or nonmarriage) style. Obviously, the worker need not be a paragon of marital and sexual success . . . whatever that is . . . in order to qualify as a competent sexual counselor. But he cannot let his own needs, biases, and anxieties interfere with his role as sexual counselor without potential harmful effects on his clients.

The next task in the process is to determine the place of the sexual problem in a client's total marital relationship. The sexual problem may well be a direct result of other basic problems that the couple is facing: an unemployed man, whose efforts to find employment have been thwarted, may seek reaffirmation of his masculinity through activities such as extramarital affairs or aggressive sexual attacks on his wife. These problems could conceivably change or be eradicated once the man's employment and masculine security is restored.

Sometimes the sexual problem is just one of a constellation of difficulties in a marriage—ranging from economic to in-law difficulties and may be unrelated to these other problems but coexistent with them. If this is the case, the social worker must determine and then contract his priorities for problem resolution with the client. He may conclude that treatment of the general marital relationship should come first and anticipate that improvement in the general relationship and communication will naturally lead to an improved sexual relationship. If the worker chooses this option, he should check out this hypothesis as treatment progresses. It is not unusual for sexual problems to precipitate other problems which may obscure—possibly purposefully—their sexual genesis. In any event, the social worker must put the sexual problem in each marriage into perspective. He should acknowledge the need and, to the extent possible, help his clients achieve adequate sexual functioning and satisfaction, but recognize, as does much sexual research, the interdependence of sexual behavior and interpersonal marital complementarity in achieving physical and consequent emotional satisfaction from the sexual relationship.

Whether the worker feels that a sexual problem is coexistent with other problems in the marriage or is a repercussion of them, he must still be prepared to deal directly with it and not minimize its importance as a result of his own discomfort in working with sexual problems and, as often happens, react by referral to another disinterested or incompetent professional. Conversely, the worker's sexual interests and curiosity should not lead him to choose sex as the focus for intervention out of his own needs, when the sexual conflict is not a logical priority.

Masters and Johnson have largely sidestepped the issue of the relation of sexual problems to general marital interaction in their work and have approached sexual problems as a learned phenomenon which can be isolated from other elements of the marital relation but can have a profound effect on the rest of the marriage. "If you can't communicate in bed," says Dr. Masters, "you probably can't communicate in a marriage." With this orientation, the Masters-Johnson team have had more than a 75 percent success rate with the problems with which they deal.[7]

Sexual problems are as diverse as the people who experience them—ranging from primary impotence to conflict over extramarital relations. Their origins often lie in the past experiences and self-image of each partner as well as in the couple's current reciprocally contingent marital relationship. Attempts to resolve marital sexual problems through increased "self-awareness" and insight into past experiences have had uninspiring results and will not be explored in this paper. Rather, the effects of current attitudes and behaviors on the sexual relationship and their modification will be reviewed.

The majority of sexual problems in marriage presented to social workers can be attributed to four sources: lack of adequate sexual knowledge; lack of clear, explicit communication and expectations between spouses regarding sexual matters; lack of consensus on sexual activities; and the lack of sexual ability. While these problems are often interrelated and stem from similar causes, they will be treated separately here.

Lack of Sexual Knowledge

Perhaps the greatest component of what many consider a copulation explosion is the recent increase in the presentation of explicit sexual material in everyday life. "Sex pervades this world of ours, dominating advertisements, fashion, plays, novels, poetry. Never have painting and literature been more outspoken. Couples copulate across the canvas; homosexuals woo each other before the footlights; lesbians hammer each other through 400 pages of prose. Sadism is almost old hat, and fetishism scarcely raises an eyebrow. Pornography is printed by the ton or shot on miles of film. Everyone knows we are in the middle of a sexual revolution. . . . Ignorance is sin and sexual instruction begins in the cradle."[8] It is this seeming saturation of sexual material—often even in our daily conversation—which leads practitioners to the mistaken idea that everyone knows everything he needs to know about sexuality. Yet, despite recent advances, there still remains much that not even our sex researchers know, and lay knowledge of sexuality is distorted by biases, personal needs, and firmly entrenched attitudes. Indeed, it is disturbing to perceive the same misconceptions and lack of knowledge in our helping professions, such as medicine, psychology, and even social work. In 1959 a study of Philadelphia area medical students from five medical schools revealed that half of the students, after three or four years of medical education, thought that masturbation is a frequent cause of mental illness. Still more frightening was the finding that one-fifth of their faculty agreed![9]

The lack of sexual knowledge in marriage (or even worse, distorted knowledge) is compounded by the inordinate need of many people to perform "normally" in sex. While most people could not care less how many slices of white bread people consume each day or what the average length of the male right index finger is, many *are* preoccupied with frequencies of sexual contact and the average length of the phallus. The fact that these vary considerably and that they tend to be irrelevant to sexual fulfillment is perhaps more significant than the knowledge of the statistics themselves.

Many marriages are blighted by false perceptions of what does or "should" go on in the marriage bed. Since sexual ideas are deeply rooted in the value system of each individual, they become harder to modify.

Sometimes sexual information given dispassionately by a social worker—ideally of the same sex as the holder of the false ideas—can make significant changes in a marital relationship. Many of our clients suffer needless problems because they do not know, for instance, that men, as well as women, have sexual anxieties and cannot always perform on command despite socially reinforced pretenses of super-masculinity, that masturbation by men does not cause "insanity" and by women is not only harmless but may enhance general sexual response, that women who enjoy clitoral as well as vaginal stimulation are not neurotic, that penis size is correlated with neither masculinity nor capacity for giving and receiving sexual satisfaction, that sexual activity need not terminate at 50, and that many mentally competent, law-abiding citizens juxtapose their mouths to their partner's genitals in sexual contacts.

An often overlooked area in which lack of knowledge can impede mutual sexual satisfaction in marriage is contraception practices.[10] It can be important for the social worker to determine whether the contraception practices in a marriage cause sexual problems or mask some more basic conflict. For example, a wife might avoid intercourse, allegedly because of fear of pregnancy but actually dislike the sex act and fear to discuss this with her husband.

Sometimes the particular birth control procedure can have a significant effect on the marital sexual adjustment. The use of withdrawal, for instance, one of the most common forms of contraception, especially among lower-income groups, is often the result of lack of knowledge of or biases regarding other contraceptive alternatives, as well as problems of access to them. This procedure not only limits sexual pleasure, but has questionable efficacy as a birth control measure. Other contraceptive methods are often avoided by couples out of the false idea that they would negatively affect sexual satisfaction, or are a threat to masculinity. It is not unusual for a woman to avoid many contraceptives because of discomfort about touching her own body or resistance to acknowledging premeditated sex activity even when she might want to limit the size of her family.

Lack of Communication

Many people of all ages find it difficult to talk directly with their marital partners about their own sexual desires, reactions, and problems. Even where communication is satisfactory in most other areas in a marriage, sexual communication can be a problem, especially for those couples who have gone through their adolescence and young adulthood before the social and sexual revolution following the Second World War. They have been conditioned to perceive discussion about sex as being so private, so embarrassing, and so revealing that they hesitate to talk about their own feelings and wishes even with the person they have been married to for years. Often this communication difficulty is a result of inability to know which words to use, or fear of revealing some inadequacy and looking ridiculous in the eyes of their spouse. They may be concerned that breaking a tacit contract of noncommunication will bring to light sexual problems or inadequacies that have been hidden by mutual consent and create a threat to the balance of a marriage. Such a void of communication prevents the establishment of reasonable mutual expectations between sexual partners and diminishes the opportunity for each partner to meet the other's needs. As the couple reaches or passes middle age, there is the additional stress of physiological and psychological changes affecting the sexual relationship. If no groundwork of communication regarding sex has been laid, then the problems of modifying the sexual relationship become even more difficult.

Such a simple problem as how to indicate explicitly the desire to have sexual intercourse is a problem for some couples. The request from one partner and an equally concise acceptance or rejection from the other partner are sometimes very difficult to get, perhaps out of sense of "nothing ventured, nothing lost!" Nonverbal cues in sex are frequently used, and can be a functional form of communication, if they are clearly understood by each partner.

Seeking help for marital and sexual problems can be the first step to enhancing communication. But it cannot be assumed that, simply because a couple has sought social work help, they have adequately discussed their sexual problems themselves. One of the major contributions of the social worker—whenever possible in a compatible two–sex team—is to have the couple explicitly discuss their sexual adjustment, first alone, and then with each other.

A useful procedure used by this writer in working with couples experiencing sexual problems is to have them stay overnight in a motel during the course of treatment, even if they have a home in the same city. Here the emphasis is easily placed on relaxation and mutual enjoyment. A similar procedure is reported by Masters and Johnson during their intensive two–week therapy program. Couples live in rented apartments for the duration of their treatment well away from family and business pressures. (It is noted that couples who came to the Masters and Johnson program from out of town had more success than those who were residents of St. Louis, and were still affected by local pressures.)

The new setting, plus the somewhat erotic atmosphere of a motel, provides stimuli which encourage new modes of communication as well as new patterns of sexual interaction. Couples can be encouarged to discuss honestly with each other what tactile experiences and sexual activities, or approaches they enjoy or don't enjoy, what wishes and reactions they have never before expressed to each other regarding sex, and then subsequently try out the results of this new communication, step-by-step. With clients who cannot afford the expense of a motel, sometimes such a simple matter as rearranging their bedroom furniture and arranging for a night away for their children will provide the stimulus for change in behavioral and communication habits.

Lack of Consensus on Sexual Activities

This problem is complicated by the ones mentioned above—the lack of knowledge and the problems in communicating sexual wishes. There is no doubt that there has been increasing acceptance and knowledge that man is capable of taking many avenues to sexual pleasure; however, this freedom is unevenly accepted by many marital couples. Religious teachings that often dwell on what limited sexual behavior falls within the range of the acceptable can exacerbate sexual confusion in a marriage, particularly when such ideas are not shared equally by the partners. The social worker can initiate and facilitate a negotiation process with the couple, perhaps assisted by a cooperative clergyman, when there is this problem. The almost trite information that what is acceptable to both partners is by definition acceptable often puts concerns about "normalcy" to rest.

Problems in Sexual Ability

Frequently, the problems of inadequate knowledge, faulty communication, and lack of consensus on sexual activity plus faulty learning combine to produce obstacles to satisfying sexual activity in the form of temporary or permanent impotence, inability to relax, or other physical sexual reactions of psychogenic origin. Many social workers hesitate to work with these problems, feeling that the body is the exclusive province of the medical profession. This is unfortunate. Generally speaking, there is no purely physical source to these problems. Further, there is nothing to prevent a social worker from having a medical consultation on clients experiencing these problems. In the work of Masters and Johnson, the vast majority of their clients were responsive to purely relearning, nonmedical, interpersonal procedures.

All sound approaches to sexual problems require the participation of both husband and wife, regardless of which partner is experiencing the specific or most obvious sexual problem. The worker should avoid the trap of seeing the marital partner with the sexual "symptom" as the sole target of intervention. In all cases of sexual dysfunction, it is the relationship of the couple which is the subject of attention and the milieu of successful treatment. "There is no such thing as an uninvolved partner in any marriage in which there is some form of sexual inadequacy," according to Masters and Johnson.

Many of the principles of the Masters and Johnson approach, a concentrated two-week (seven days a week) process of exploration and relearning of sexual behavior, may be adapted to social work practice. Already mentioned were the value of a compatible male–female therapy team—providing husband and wife with empathetic "friends in court," focus on the relationship rather than either partner, and the elimination of the spectator role in which fear of inadequate performance inhibits spontaneous behavior. The worker helps the couple to accept the naturalness of sex and assures them that once irrational obstacles are removed, sexual fulfillment becomes inevitable. As part of this philosophy, there is no pressure on performance. Rather the couple is helped to proceed step-by-step, learning to enjoy each other's bodies without a preoccupation with ultimate genital and orgasmic response.

Often anxiety over coital competence can be decreased for either spouse if the worker can convince them that there are many avenues to achieve sexual satisfaction besides genital intromission, such as oral and manual stimulation. Wolpe and Lazarus have advocated that couples experiencing problems in coital competence develop competence in those techniques which not only provide "powerful sources of sexual arousal, but also lead to distracting attention from the sufferer's genital problem through focusing on pleasures being bestowed on his partner. The primary sexual difficulty is overcome without further formal treatment when a couple learns to accept the fact that sexual satisfaction does not necessarily depend on coitus."[11]

Often, of course, adequacy can also be enhanced by encouraging sexual variation and experimentation, based on mutual exploration, compatible with mutual wishes.

In essence, the approach of the worker is to determine and then clear away the obstacles to the couple's learning the joys of each other's bodies, by "pleasuring" one another. The couple soon discovers or rediscovers the two sources of sexual satisfaction: that of giving pleasure to a partner and receiving pleasure in return.

Conclusion

Major emphasis in this paper has been placed on the common obstacles to achieving a spontaneous, natural sexual relationship. Several references have been made to the pioneering and successful work of Masters and Johnson. Their approach is in many ways novel. It may be criticized for isolating sex from other aspects of marital interaction; it has created controversy for using partner surrogates for unmarried men; so far it has been applied largely to a fairly well motivated, sophisticated client group, and has required intensive involvement by expensive, highly skilled, well qualified, and compatible practitioners. However, its substantial relevance to marital counseling provided by social workers should not be minimized. Their approach is based on generally responsible laboratory (as reported in their earlier book[12]) as well as clinical research. Its success is substantiated by considerable followup work. It enables couples to discover the nature and source of their problems, to communicate effectively about their sexual relationship, and thereby discard dysfunctional prior learning and develop a new, mutually satisfying form of sexual interaction.

Certainly these approaches must be modified according to the resources available to the social worker as well as the particular needs perceived in each case. Dr. Masters himself anticipated this but commented, "Sure, people will bastardize, but even then what they do has an excellent chance of being better than what's gone before."[13]

Marital sexual problems, which affect and are affected by general marital complementarity, are a legitimate focus of social work intervention and are amenable to change using procedures from social work practice as well as the work of such sexual clinicians as Masters and Johnson. Social work practice that avoids pathologic labeling and focuses on the mutual learning that affects sexual relations can make a marked impact on other aspects of the marital relationship as well as contribute to greater joy in the marriage bed.

NOTES

[1] Margaret Mead, *Male and Female* (New York: William Morrow and Company, 1949), p. 7.

[2] "J," *The Sensuous Woman* (New York: Lyle Stuart, 1969).

[3] William Masters and Virginia Johnson, *Human Sexual Inadequacy* (Boston: Little, Brown and Company, 1970).

[4] *Time,* 25 May 1970, p. 49.

[5] Albert Ellis, "Romantic Love," in *Sex and Human Relationships,* ed. Cecil E. Johnson (Columbus: Charles E. Merrill Books, 1970).

[6] Recently sex books have begun to emerge which do indeed encourage the joy of individual sex styles. A notable example is the significant impact of a very popular book, written by a woman, entitled *The Sensuous Woman.* (See Note 2 above.)

[7] However, it is noteworthy that in many of the "successfully" treated sample (in terms of the sexual problems) other marital problems continued which not infrequently resulted in divorce. This does not negate, however, the improved sexual competence.

[8] J. H. Plumb, "Perspective," *Saturday Review,* 27 July 1968, p. 23.

[9] Harold Lief, "Teaching Doctors about Sex," in R. Brecher and E. Brecher, *An Analysis of Human Sexual Response* (Boston: Little, Brown and Company, 1966), pp. 276–7.

[10] Lee Rainwater, "Attitudes of Patients Affecting Contraceptive Practice," in *Manual of Contraceptive Practice,* ed. M. S. Calderone (Baltimore: The Williams & Wilkins Company, 1964).

[11] J. Wolpe and A. A. Lazarus, *Behavior Therapy Techniques* (London, England: Pergamon Press, 1966), pp. 105–6.

[12] William Masters and Virginia Johnson, *Human Sexual Response* (Boston: Little, Brown and Company, 1966).

[13] Quoted by Will Bradbury from interview reported in *Life,* 1 May 1970, p. 46.

SUGGESTED READINGS

Bach, George R. and Wyden, Peter. *The Intimate Enemy.* New York: William Morrow and Company, 1969.

Belliveau, Fred, and Richter, Lin. *Understanding Human Sexual Inadequacy.* New York: Bantam Books, 1970.

Bird, Joseph, and Bird, Lois. *The Freedom of Sexual Love.* Garden City: Doubleday & Company, 1967.

Cox, R. *Youth into Maturity.* New York: Mental Health Materials Center, 1970.

Eisner, B. *The Unused Potential of Marriage and Sex.* Boston: Little, Brown and Company, 1970.

Folkman, Jerome, and Clatworthy, Nancy. *Marriage Has Many Faces.* Columbus, O.: Charles E. Merrill, 1970.

Greene, Bernard L. *The Psychotherapies of Marital Disharmony.* New York: The Free Press, 1965.

Hollis, Florence. *Women in Marital Conflict: A Casework Study.* New York: Family Service Association of America, 1949.

"J," *The Sensuous Woman.* New York: Lyle Stuart, 1969.

Johnson, Cecil E. *Sex and Human Relationships.* Columbus, O.: Charles E. Merrill, 1970.

Klemer, Richard. *Counseling in Marital and Sexual Problems.* Baltimore: The Williams & Wilkins Company, 1965.

Lederer, William J., and Jackson, Don. *The Mirages of Marriage.* New York: W. W. Norton & Company, 1968.

Masters, William, and Johnson, Virginia. *Human Sexual Inadequacy.* Boston: Little, Brown and Company, 1970.

Satir, Virginia. *Conjoint Family Therapy.* Palo Alto: Science and Behavior Books, 1967.

11

Abortion Counseling

PAMELA LEE LOWRY AND JOAN E. BLANK

Extensive mass media coverage of changing abortion laws has made many women aware that legal abortion services may be available to them, in the event they are faced with an unwanted pregnancy. This awareness has led to greater openness about the problem and has increased their willingness to seek professional help rather than turning immediately to the illegal abortionist.

If a woman has had some contact with a social service or health worker—and if that contact has been one of dignity and warmth—she may turn to this worker for advice on abortion. Health and social welfare personnel throughout the country are finding themselves increasingly involved in such situations. In the past, many agencies were unwilling to acknowledge such problems, and refused to deal with them—but the climate is changing. The question now is not *whether* to handle the problem pregnancy but *how* to handle it.

In trying to answer this question, there are three areas of concern which must be considered. The first is the attitude of the counselor; the second, the attitude of the client; the third, the realities of availability of medical services, costs involved, and the social circumstances of the client.

The Counselor's Attitude

Objectivity is an integral part of social work training, yet it would be foolish to overlook the fact that social workers are human, and they have strong subjective feelings about sexuality and the related issue of abortion. It is very difficult to keep expression of these feelings separate from an interview; this is true whether the social worker is opposed to abortion or in favor of it. A negative view of abortion can show up in the tone of voice or the phraseology used by the worker; too positive a view of abortion may result in the worker's becoming too directive. The primary obligation of the worker is to help the client do what the client feels is best. The worker should explore with the woman all possible alternatives,

138

so that she can make a choice based on fact rather than on superstition and rumor. To withhold assistance to the woman who chooses abortion will not deter her—it will simply increase the risks she faces.

The Client's Attitude

It takes tremendous courage on the part of the client to approach a professional person for help. Society has traditionally been highly judgmental about sexual behavior. The client may fear a disapproving attitude on the part of the worker—indeed she probably expects it. The social worker will therefore want to make every effort to be reassuring and supportive. This may be the first time the client has had an opportunity to discuss her problem openly and to release some of the panic and desperation she may feel.

Confirming the Pregnancy

The social worker may discover that it takes a while for the issue to be raised. The woman may make her approach by a very indirect route, sounding out the counselor's feelings, trying to get some indication of sympathy before she exposes her problem. Sometimes the client will inquire about ways of bringing on a period, about something to "bring her around." She may ask if the social worker knows about "Humphries 11" or other folk remedies, hot baths and castor oil, pounding on the abdomen, hopping up and down stairs. These activities will not cause an abortion; their only therapeutic value is that the woman thinks she is doing something constructive about her unwanted condition.

The worker should spot this immediately and ask: "Do you feel pregnant? Have you had any morning sickness? Have you missed a period?" The worker can then guide the woman to a resource for pregnancy testing. If the woman has missed a period by two weeks or more, she may be referred for a urine test. In most cases a doctor, medical lab, public health clinic, or outpatient gynecology service will do a pregnancy test. If the client is not yet two weeks overdue, she may wish to wait until a urinalysis would be accurate. Alternatively, a doctor might prescribe for her one of the various hormone medications which will bring on a period if she is *not* pregnant. If she is pregnant, there will be no period.

The Interview

The first and most obvious step is to determine how the woman feels about her pregnancy and what she wants to do. The worker will want to explore the pressures which have driven the woman to seek an abortion. By and large, women inquiring about abortion are motivated by strong personal feelings about the pregnancy, and by social pressures. The pregnancy may be out of wedlock, or extramarital; or it may be that she simply has too much to cope with and cannot bear the thought of another addition to the family. The worker should explore alternatives to abortion: financial assistance to help support an additional child, adoption, foster care; but must be careful not to exclude abortion as a solution. Abortion is one alternative; continuing the pregnancy is another. The choice lies with the client not the social worker.

The Referral

If the woman decides on abortion, having considered and rejected the alternatives, the counselor is then faced with helping the client find an appropriate resource. There are several basic facts on which the final choice of a resource depends. The woman's age and marital status may be relevant in that many doctors require consent of parents or husband. Duration of the pregnancy has a direct bearing on what kind of procedure is performed and the cost thereof. If the client isn't sure when she conceived or the date of her last period, she may want to have a physical examination as a guideline to the length of gestation. The social worker should ask if the woman has had any history of medical or psychiatric problems or is taking drugs or other medications. This information will be essential in determining where she might legally qualify for abortion. The last factor is the woman's financial situation. There is little point in referring her to a medical service she cannot afford.

The social worker must now obtain accurate information about laws, policies, requirements, restrictions, and costs of legal abortions both within the immediate vicinity and outside the state. It will be necessary at this point for the worker to make use of a service which deals specifically with this problem.[1]

Legal Guidelines

State abortion laws divide roughly into three categories: (1) abortion permitted to save the life of the mother; (2) abortion permitted to preserve health (mental or physical) and in cases of rape, incest, or probable fetal deformity; (3) abortion available on request with the consent of a physician. If the state where the client resides permits abortion on request, or if she has sufficient funds to travel to such a state, she will have little difficulty obtaining a safe, legal abortion. It is essential, however, to have guidance from a knowledgeable information and referral service such as Planned Parenthood; without it, the client will experience delay and unnecessary expense.

If the client lives in a state where the law requires medical or psychiatric grounds for abortion, she will encounter more difficulty. The social worker will want to encourage her to consult her own physician or a clinic to determine whether her case might be acceptable. If the woman is reluctant to use her own doctor, the worker can suggest another physician for her. Since most abortions in such states are performed on psychiatric grounds, the woman's doctor or clinic may recommend that she see a psychiatrist, either privately or through the clinic service. The hospital considering the case will wish to have as much data as possible, and with the client's permission, it could be very helpful for the social worker to write a letter (or appear with the client) to explain the extent of emotional strain which the pregnancy has caused. The social worker will also want to help arrange appointments, especially when the client is using hospital clinics, because waiting lists are long and delay can be dangerous. The social worker may be able to have the client seen as an emergency case, rather than having her wait four or five weeks for a consultation at the local outpatient clinic. The social worker can also be helpful by handling details of application for payment by the client's insurance company or welfare office. Obtaining an abortion on medical or psychiatric grounds can be a tedious and frustrating experience. The social worker will want to provide every possible support during this process.

In a state where abortions are performed only to save the life of the mother, the probability is that the client will be unable to obtain a legal abortion. If she has the financial resources to explore other states, the social worker can put her in touch with appropriate referral agencies. The worker should be cognizant, however, of the likelihood that the client may instead seek an illegal abortion. This places the worker in a difficult position. No agency wants to make itself party to an illegal procedure. There are ways, however, in which the social worker can, with propriety, provide the woman with information which will protect her in the event that she does seek an illegal abortion.

Illegal Abortion

The term "illegal abortion" has earned its ugly connotation. It has become a lucrative racket for unsavory and incompetent persons eager to make money from people who are desperate. At the same time, it is important to realize that many "illegal" abortionists are competent practitioners with medical training—people who are in business for reasons of personal commitment as well as for the monetary rewards. It is vital, therefore, that the client be given some idea how to distinguish between the good and the bad.

Any abortion performed without legal and immediate access to emergency hospital facilities carries a higher risk than a legally sanctioned hospital or clinic procedure. However, many illegal abortions are performed under sterile conditions and with remarkable competence. While there may be a few paramedical or nonmedical technicians who have achieved skill in this field, it is almost always preferable to seek the services of a trained physician. Only a physician has the knowledge to cope with all the contingencies that may arise.

The woman who turns to illegal abortion should make every effort to ensure that the person she plans to use is in fact a doctor. Once she has a name, she can go to her local library and look up the doctor in the state medical directory or in whatever medical society directory covers his geographical area. If he is not listed, the probability is that he is not a licensed physician.

Some doctors who are performing extralegal abortions will protect themselves by remaining anonymous and using a middleman to arrange the details of the contact. If this is the case, the client should make absolutely certain that somewhere along the line, one of the "contacts" is real—i.e., has a tangible name and address. If there is some way to get back to the doctor or one of his associates, this is a form of insurance that the operation will be competent. If there is no way to reach him or his contact, he has little to lose if things go badly for the client. If he is vulnerable somewhere along the line, he will have far more motivation to be careful in his work.

The client should be advised against trusting anyone further than she has to. She should hold on to her money until the last possible moment. There are many people willing to "arrange" an abortion who manage to disappear the minute the client hands over money to them. She should keep her eyes open at every stage. If she sees or senses something she does not like, she should ask for an explanation. If she is not satisfied with the answer, she should reconsider.

Methods of Abortion

Abortion methods fall into one of two groups: (1) the direct removal of the contents of the uterus (usually by a D&C—scraping the lining of the uterus with a curette; or by the suction method, using a vacuum aspiratory; (2) the causing of a miscarriage (usually 12–36 hours later) through introduction into the uterus of a foreign body or liquid. The former methods, in skilled hands, are far preferable, but the majority of illegal abortionists work with the latter methods. These call for less skill, and they relieve the abortionist of the responsibility of disposing of the products of conception, thereby lessening his vulnerability.

Certain safeguards are essential regardless of the method used. The covering for the operating table should be clean. The instruments used should be sterile. If the doctor does not wash his hands or carefully clean the vaginal area, the client should leave right then and there.

There are certain risks inherent in the methods used to cause a miscarriage. The mechanism of action with the introduction of a foreign object is usually the resultant irritation and infection. A sharp object may damage or perforate the uterine wall, causing excessive bleeding and possible permanent harm. If infection results from the foreign object, and is not checked by antibiotics, this may cause serious threat to the client's future fertility. Severe infection in the uterus is difficult to treat; it can cause sterility if it reaches the ovaries or damages the fallopian tubes, and may even necessitate a hysterectomy. The worker should ensure that the woman knows where to go for emergency medical treatment. If she hemorrhages, runs a high temperature, or encounters any other medical complications, she should seek help immediately. Even if all goes well and she miscarries with minimal bleeding and no fever, she should arrange to see a doctor as soon as possible after the miscarriage.

The introduction of toxic liquids can be highly dangerous. The social worker should make every effort to steer the client clear of such a procedure. The liquids usually have an acid or alkaline base; bleach, lye, and detergents may successfully terminate the pregnancy, but they will also take with them most of whatever tissue they come in contact with. This fact cannot be stressed too much. This type of method is often resorted to by women who plan to perform the abortion themselves or with the aid of a neighbor. If the woman is desperate enough to disregard the workers' warnings about this, it is vital that she immediately be taken to an emergency service to prevent potentially fatal complications.

Other Considerations

Whether she proceeds legally or illegally, the woman who has an abortion needs support before, during and after the procedure. The social worker should ensure that the client has access at all times to accurate medical information and assistance. But it is equally important that the client have someone with whom she can share her experience. The worker can assume certain aspects of this role, but it may be wise to encourage involvement of whatever friends or family the client is willing to trust. Be it boy friend, parents, or others, the woman should have someone as a companion wherever possible—someone to travel with her if she is going out of state; someone waiting to take her home from the hospital; or (where circumstances allow) someone to accompany her to the site of an illegal procedure, stay with her if possible, and take her home afterward.

In the event of complications, she should have someone she can rely on to get her to a hospital or a doctor. Ideally, this person (or persons) should know as much about the procedures and possible complications as possible, and should be reliable enough to act calmly and responsibly if problems arise.

Many women who undergo extralegal abortions are reluctant to seek medical help for postoperative complications because they fear legal consequences. The client should be aware that she has a constitutionally guaranteed right of silence. It may be vital for the physician to know what was done, but he need not know who did it.

Postoperative Guidance

There are several reasons for encouraging continued contact with the client following her abortion. The worker will want to be sure that the woman has arranged for a postoperative examination and will want to guide her to a source of birth control information and help. Some women find it embarrassing to ask for contraceptive help; the social worker might wish to initiate discussion of the subject if the client seems shy, and will want to offer every assistance in finding an appropriate birth control resource.

If there are limited services for this, the client should be advised of nonprescription methods such as contraceptive foams or condoms.

The social worker will also want to be available to discuss any aspect of the abortion or related issues. Often the crisis of an unwanted pregnancy highlights problems in the client's relationship with parents, husband, or boy friend. The reality of pregnancy forces the client to focus on her situation, often for the first time. This can be a jarring experience, and the social worker's support will be essential in helping the woman evaluate the direction she sees her life taking from this point on.

Some women do not appear to encounter such difficulties, or, if they do, they do not wish to discuss them. A sympathetic approach on the part of the worker can usually elicit a response from those who do want to talk and will not be considered offensive to those who consider the issue settled.

NOTE

[1] One of the most accurate sources of information is Planned Parenthood. If there is no local Planned Parenthood office, a call to Planned Parenthood's national

office (810 Seventh Avenue, New York, New York 10019; telephone: 212—541–7800) will elicit information on the most appropriate source of help.

SUGGESTED READINGS

Lee, N. *The Search for an Abortionist.* Chicago: University of Chicago Press, 1969.

Phelon, L., and Maginnis, P. *The Abortion Handbook.* Los Angeles: Contact Press, 1969.

The Social Worker and Family Planning. Proceedings of the 1969 Annual Institute for Public Health Social Workers, University of California, Berkeley, Calif., 1970, pp. 70–76.

12

Early Treatment of Infidelity in the Neurotic Man

Miriam I. Weisberg

Three closely occurring situations in which a neurotic man contemplated divorce to marry the woman he loved aroused my interest in determining an effective early approach to this specific problem.[1] Infidelity, used here to describe an intense extramarital involvement of a neurotic man who has reached the point of wanting a divorce and marriage to the other woman, has multiple determinants that fall into three identifiable, intertwined categories: individual, interactional, and situational.

As a family agency in a society that regards the family as "fundamental to human life and the very cradle of human nature,"[2] we try to preserve a marriage unless it is found to be detrimental to members of the family. Determining the appropriateness of attempts to preserve the marriage and to preserve it without the support of an extramarital affair and motivating the man to a sincere effort to decide for himself if the marriage is workable are interrelated. These efforts constitute a complicated process that not only involves a careful diagnostic assessment of the individual partners, the marriage, and the family relationships, but also requires an understanding of the relationship of both husband and wife to the other woman. In order to invest his energy in such an evaluation, the man will have to give up his active association with the other woman and separate himself from her emotionally.

The three cases that aroused my interest in this subject involved couples at different stages of their marriages. The J's were in their early twenties and had three children under four years of age. The B's had been married for twenty-five years and separated for nine months. They had a married daughter and a son in high school. The R's were in their late thirties, had been married for eighteen years, and had three children from five to eleven years old.

The J Case

The J case particularly illustrates the multiple determinants of infidelity. Mr. J's immaturity, confusions, fears, and anxieties about sex and aggression, and his conflicts about identity and identification were intensified by his wife's problems, by their serious interactional difficulties, by the very existence of their children, and by the children's behavior. Mr. J's girl friend's personality glaringly revealed his pathology.

In individual interviews, we reviewed the J's courtship and their brief marriage. Mrs. J's reaching out to him affectionately and sexually when they were in college had been ego-building. He loved her, felt sympathy for her, and wanted to protect her from continuing conflict with her parents that made her look "sad, like a cocker spaniel." He blamed her for the premarital pregnancy that hastened the marriage, but he recalled a sense of exhilaration in telling his father about the pregnancy and his plans to marry. He still felt the humiliation and pain of an incident in late adolescence when his father had led him like a young child to return a class ring to a girl friend.

Dynamics of Infidelity

The next two pregnancies in quick succession aroused great frustration, anger, and anxiety in both Mr. and Mrs. J. He reproached her for refusing to take birth control pills for religious reasons and he began to avoid being at home by claiming he had business appointments. Regarding her as a "belly" or a "mother" caused him much conflict. The mild depression she brought into the marriage increased, strengthening his identification of her with his depressed mother and arousing anxiety and anger. Tension mounted as his attitude and behavior made her feel deprived and that he disapproved of her. Impulsively, scaring herself, she encouraged him to leave, made suicidal gestures, and even threatened to kill the children—a thought that horrified her. Her anxiety about possible loss made her sexually demanding although at times she was aware of his discomfort and fear. He reacted with panic to her sexual demands. His potency difficulties increased, increasing his doubts about his masculinity.

In contrast to Mrs. J's current demanding attitude, she had refused sex relations during her third pregnancy because of the "evil" it had brought them. Her withdrawal and his consequent masturbation reactivated his guilt feelings about his childhood masturbation in periods of sadness and loneliness when his mother had withdrawn to her room in depression. Mr. J consulted his priest, who advised him to pray and try to be strong to conquer his masturbation, but Mr. J was not always successful. He

decided to sleep with another woman. A dream with some pregenital implications seemed to be a factor in his choice of a partner. Furthermore, an
incident of daytime wetting by his oldest child (that Mr. J attributed to
unhappiness over the marital tension) brought back vividly a beating by
his own father in which he had lost bladder control. (This episode with
his child may have reactivated latent homosexual excitement from his own
father–son relationship, which frightened him and contributed to his occasional absence from the home and to his thinking about breaking up the
marriage.)

Repeating the Past

Although so many determinants were strikingly involved in the J
family's situation, it was the identification of a repetition compulsion in
his behavior that was crucial to the dramatic progress Mr. J made: after
four interviews he decided to discontinue the year-old extramarital affair.
He was horrified at his urge to repeat his father's self-sacrificing life. His
mother's prolonged periods of depression had at times endangered his
father's life and had led to deprivation and virtual desertion of the children—which Mr. J. was now doing to some extent with his children. In
the past, Mr. J had often vowed that he would never sacrifice his life "like
a nut, because of a nut." However, Mr. J had been spending hours with
his girl friend to alleviate her depressions. In recent years, he had been
similarly supporting his mother when his father called on him in times
of crisis. I underscored the urge to repeat the "protection" and "shaping
up" of unhappy women, which initially was a source of gratification but
gradually became a burden and increased his restlessness. He recognized
that his wife's depressions were not so deep as those of his mother or his
girl friend and were precipitated by more serious happenings.

Terminating the Affair

Mr. J's positive fantasy of his future life with his girl friend gradually
crumbled. We discussed how they met, her unhappy background, her continued intense struggle with her mother, the short-lived marriage in which
he had seen her as an innocent victim; the loneliness, confusion, and search
for affection which led her to affairs with many men; and the danger to
her mental health unless she obtained professional help. Mr. J began to
evaluate more realistically his relationship with his girl friend as well as
his relationship with his wife and children. He felt he had to make the
break, even if only for the children. It was for him "a decision in the making of a man and the destroying of the boy." I emphasized that the decision
had to be based on what was best for *him*. However, I supported the idea

of separation from his girl friend because it would lead toward greater maturity and contribute to his goal of understanding himself and his existing marriage, which would be necessary to assure greater success in either this or in another marriage.

A review of past attempts that he and his girl friend had made to end their relationship pointed to the precariousness of her mental state and the intensity of his struggle over separation from her. He was desperate at the thought of the sadness and loneliness he would feel if he gave her up and then the marriage did not work out. He feared that he might not be able to be a good husband and a good father and that he might again become involved with another woman. He tried to brace himself by building up anger at his girl friend, but he soon was able to recognize the strength of his attachment to her and the intensity of his struggle. When he did break off a week earlier than I had anticipated, he handled the situation matter-of-factly to control his feelings. He attributed his timing to the fact that he had learned that his job was in jeopardy because his boss, like his father, had no objection to a casual relationship but disapproved of "a love affair" for a married man. It would seem that he had to repeat the incident of his adolescence and feel that his breaking off was in part imposed on him by a father figure.

After separating from his girl friend, Mr. J felt exhausted and defeated. He could not be alone with his thoughts and therefore welcomed the opportunity to talk about his longing, his sadness, his fantasies, and feelings about his girl friend's life after separation. He resisted her efforts to reinvolve him. He was pleased that Mrs. J welcomed him. Her continued progress in controlling her impulsiveness and her willingness to use birth control pills and to make herself available but not demanding gratified him. He realized that her excessive demands for sex were expressions of her anxiety about losing him and of her insecurity about his love for her, rather than of a strong need for sex per se or a wish to put him in a passive role. However, her improvement and her expectations of radical changes in his functioning as a father and as a husband heightened his awareness of his problems and frightened him. To reduce the pressure and to have a chance to resume some of the normal social activity they had missed in the marriage, he moved out for a month but maintained a close relationship with his wife and children. Then he purchased a set of rings and moved back into the home, symbolically marrying his wife for the first time on his own considered decision.

The B Case

In the second case, the middle-aged B's, the man was not so emotionally involved with the young divorcée "he loved." He talked of planning

to marry her but continued to postpone the step for such reasons as his
birthday, his daughter's wedding, and his son's graduation. He had made
several attempts to reunite with Mrs. B, but these reunions lasted only
a day or two because they immediately revived their long-standing communication problems, their sexual difficulties, and their disagreements over
their eighteen-year-old son. His daughter's marriage and her move out of
town deprived him of some emotional satisfaction because his relationship
with her was better than that of Mrs. B. His impotence problem had been
intensified by his wife's "discovery" of sex in middle age and, as he became
involved in his affair, by the exaggerated fantasies his wife had of the
pleasure she thought he experienced with his girl friend, to whom they
both playfully referred as "it." Actually, in his involvement with the other
woman, sexuality seemed secondary to the opportunity to be a good father
to her two children, seven and nine years old, who had an alcoholic father.
He had been the child of a depriving, alcoholic father himself and he now
had a chance to give to himself symbolically while giving to them. Also
he was given a second chance to be a good father, a role from which he
had been excluded by his wife since his son was seven years old because
he had committed an act of insensitivity that Mrs. B thought was deliberately cruel. It seemed too that by deserting his son he was repeating his
own desertion by both his parents: his father who when drunk would disappear for several weeks and his mother who would spend her time searching for him in bars. The association with the young woman, who was part
of a sophisticated, better-educated group, offered excitement, although he
felt like an outsider. It also offered a chance to undo the adolescent hurt
caused when a girl friend, under pressure from her parents, had broken
off the relationship with him because he was not interested in college.
Moreover the present affair was an expression of anxiety about aging,
which the B's handled in an insensitive fashion with each other.

Mrs. B's Involvement

Mrs. B's own needs contributed to her husband's involvement with the
other woman. The affair was a source of excitement for her as well as
for him. Furthermore she was thrilled by the mildly seductive attention
of her male coworkers (she had started to work when the B's separated).
In addition, her loneliness had caused her to establish a seductive relationship with her son. Mrs. B was not responsive to attempts to develop insight
but she was responsive to an educational, corrective approach.

Although exploration clarified for Mr. B the inadvisability of marriage
to his young girl friend, he decided on a period of "fun." This was understandable in view of his difficulty in gaining even minimal immediate grati-

fication from reunion with his wife and his son. When he returned to treatment nearly three months later, it became clear that he had contrived to be discarded by the young woman (as he had been by a girl friend in his adolescence), who became involved with a man much younger than herself. Recognition of how he had contributed to her rejection of him by continually postponing marriage, which had frustrated her to the point of threats of suicide, and recognition of his need to repeat his earlier rejection as a way of mastering the hurt from the past, served to build up his ego. Although tempted, he made no overtures to her when he later learned that her affair was short-lived. His self-esteem rose because he had never really been comfortable about being involved in an extramarital affair.

Terminating the Affair

Even after the B's had both decided they wanted to make their marriage work, I suggested a two-month exclusive dating period during which they might take initial steps in improving their communication, in increasing mutual understanding and sensitivity, and in reducing their impulsive withdrawals from each other. I also helped each of them assume more appropriate roles with their son, which he welcomed. In general, the emphasis in treatment was on mutual helpfulness.

The R Case

Mr. R's emotional separation from his girl friend, a childless divorcée, was more difficult for him than for Mr. J and Mr. B. A sensitive, inhibited, passive man of thirty-eight who had been married for eighteen years to an equally sensitive, inhibited, depressed woman, Mr. R felt guilty about the extramarital association and about the pain he was causing his wife. Although emotionally unwavering in his desire to marry the other woman, he had agreed more than once to his wife's request that he break off the association, only to resume it on the basis of doubt regarding the permanence of any improvement in the marriage. A number of elements seemed to account for his behavior: his frequent contact with the other woman because they were in the same profession; pressure exerted by the aggressive, skillfully manipulative girl friend who once responded to his attempt to break off with a suicidal gesture; the intensity of his accumulated suppressed anger at his wife, who he felt had been robbing him of his manhood; and Mrs. R's rigid personality.

Mr. R repressed his past, making it necessary for me to depend on his wife's recollections and observations. I had two individual interviews with Mrs. R before I saw Mr. R and three with him before I saw them jointly. Frank discussion of their behavior and attitudes in sex relations presented an opportunity to ease Mrs. R's discomfort over pleasure in activities "bordering on the perverted," which they had given up early in the marriage because of her guilt. In panic over losing him, she was eager to modify her behavior, if not her attitude, but was frustrated by his passivity and ineptness as a lover. Although Mr. R seemed well defended, his reaching out to another woman was to some extent an expression of anxiety and an attempt to protect himself from facing their mutual sex problems.

Dealing with Anger

In the R situation, draining of the anger was crucial. Mr. R actually pounded on the wall and wept hysterically as he related, in a joint interview, the desperate sexual frustration he experienced while waiting for her to take the initiative, which he left to her out of anger and anxiety lest the sexual act become an act of rape. He told of his deep guilt and self-hatred and of his intense anger at his wife for "causing" him to resort to masturbation like "a child sneaking behind the barn." It was a welcome revelation to him that in the best of marriages people occasionally resort to masturbation. The draining of his anger at his wife helped reduce his emotional tie to his girl friend because it reduced his desire for revenge. This increased his desire to give the marriage another chance and impelled him to become appropriately assertive rather than passively resistant. Discussion of the past—his wife's more than his own—was a significant aid in reducing his anger. He was particularly glad to learn that his wife had not been deliberately cruel in her sexual behavior with him.

Casework Techniques

Intensive study of the three situations revealed the specific determinants of infidelity in each case and some of the general techniques for helping the man decide to give up his extramarital relationship and to evaluate the existing marriage. These techniques include encouraging ventilation of anger about the marital relationship, understanding some of the determinants of the extramarital association, understanding the particular choice of the other woman, and evaluating the relationship with the other woman and the expectations in a marriage to her as compared to marriage with his wife and as related to his realistic life goals. They also involve helping him gain hope for future self-fulfillment, whether in the present marriage or another. He needs help with feelings about breaking off the extramarital association. First steps have to be taken in trying to improve the marriage and sometimes in dealing with the personality difficulties of both partners. Both individual and joint interviews should be included, with the nature of the specific situation serving as the guide in determining the timing of and balance between the two methods.

WORK WITH THE HUSBAND: In my initial approach, I convey to the husband a sincere acceptance of his desire for self-fulfillment and an appreciation of how difficult it is to attempt self-examination when one is in love. This attitude reduces his defensiveness. In the R case it was a contrast to his doctor's reference to his involvement as "an infatuation." A sympathetic attitude to the man's girl friend comes as an even greater surprise and is disarming. However, I think it is important to introduce early the idea that any real attempt to improve the marriage necessitates discontinuing the affair; little, if anything, can be accomplished while the excitement and turmoil of the affair continue to absorb the man's energies and keep his wife in a panic. Although in some situations the worker might set a time limit, skillful handling of the exploratory process should enable the man to decide the direction he would like to take. If he chooses to improve his marriage, discontinuing the other relationship would be his own decision. Continuing the affair for a while, however, may be necessary to promote and sustain self-examination and examination of the marriage. Flexibility is needed in the way discontinuation is presented.

WORK WITH THE WIFE: In approaching the wife I try to convey an appreciation of the great crisis she is experiencing and of the strength of her desire to prevent permanent separation. The wife may or may not show her depression but does act upon it constructively or destructively. She needs the chance to express her feelings, to have her destructive behavior weighed against her goals, and her constructive behavior supported. She needs the chance to release her fury at being rejected for another woman and to see how unwittingly she may have contributed to her husband's acting out. Her distrust of her husband may need to be understood in the light of her past, with emphasis on a better relationship as the most effective means to regain trust.

WORK WITH PARTNERS TOGETHER: The marital partners need to be engaged in describing the circumstances of and the reasons for the husband's infidelity. Encouraging each partner to express reactions to the reasons given by the other is a useful technique in both joint and individual interviews. Discussion of the past problems in the various areas of functioning under consideration is invaluable in determining some of the forces that may have instigated the affair. It is important that exploration of the determinants of the infidelity—particularly of both partners' repetition compulsions—be complete enough to insure the stability of the man's decision to end the affair and to secure help in determining whether continuing the existing marriage is best for all members of the family. The unconscious attempts to recreate some frustrating or anxiety-arousing un-resolved conflict situation from the past, with the hope of achieving mastery or gratification in the present, seem to be striking elements in the infidelity. The opportunity for such an attempt, which the other woman's personality and availability seem to offer the man, is a significant factor. Even an in-tellectual awareness of this element in the behavior of both marital partners helps reduce the impact of the present crisis on them. In general, the careful investigative process permits a good deal of ventilation and some mutual and self-understanding. It reduces hurt and anger through depersonalization of the negative behavior. The process also leads both partners gradually to "deromanticize" the extramarital association, permitting the more accurate assessment of realities that is essential for a workable marriage.

The Significance of the Sexual Adjustment

The man often mentions sexual maladjustment in the marriage as the major cause of infidelity. The woman often conceives of the relationship between her husband and the other woman as a continuous sexual orgy. The contrast between the wife's conception of what goes on and the reality of it is revealing not only to her but also to the man, who already may have become aware of some sexual difficulty in the new relationship. Both may see that their fantasies about sexual relationship are not realistic and that they can hope for an improved sexual relationship with each other. It seems helpful to speak of sexual adjustment as having many dimensions and to refer to the unique opportunity marital partners have to help each other with mutual understanding and cooperation. Speaking in this way can reduce anxiety in the man who, burdened by his and society's concept of masculinity, may be defending himself against recognition of his part in the difficulty. It can also reduce anxiety in the woman, who, when threatened with the loss of her husband, sometimes takes to much responsibility and overprotects him, and sometimes takes too little responsibility and attacks him. A direct approach to this subject of sexual adjustment in the early part of the contact when emotions run high and defenses are low can be diagnostically enlightening and therapeutically helpful. One must determine if there are any parts of the subject the persons do not feel free to discuss in joint interviews.

Significant Factors in the Discovery of the Affair

How the wife learned about the extramarital association and the subse-quent reactions of both husband and wife are significant. It took months for one woman to summon the courage to ask. Another was "suddenly" confronted with the man's wish for a divorce and his desire to marry another woman. Once the affair is joint knowledge, both the husband and wife may desire either to share or to avoid the details. It is important to get to the meaning of this behavior, or at least to call their attention to it and question its usefulness. Often the wife is curious about how another woman manages to please her husband when she cannot. Often too, the wife is excited about the husband's affair. Both her curiosity and her fantasies can be used constructively. Oedipal and especially latent homosexual curiosity presents more of a problem.

Some men will be reticent with the caseworker; some, seductively secretive; and others, seductively detailed. Observation of this behavior can offer clues to understanding the man. However, exploration of his affair has to be focused on its meaning to him and how realistic it is in relation to his desire for self-fulfillment.

Identification and Management of Anger and Depression

Reduction of anger stemming from various sources of tension, especially in the man, through ventilation and through depersonalization of each partner's negative behavior to the other is crucial. Reduction of anger reduces the frigidity and impotence problems frequent in these situations as well as improves communication.

Reduction of anger is also important because of the degree of depression that exists in both partners during such a marital crisis. The woman is confronted with the threat of losing her husband to another woman. Her self-esteem is lessened further by the realization that he has two women vying for him while she is feeling lonely and deserted. The man is confronted with pressure from his wife, from his girl friend, and from his conscience. The thought of giving the marriage another chance and in the process losing the other woman may depress him greatly.

Depression must be dealt with directly. It is very important to encourage the man to fully express his fear and anxiety about the future. To reduce this anxiety, the worker must help him with anticipatory and actual mourning for the loss of his girl friend. Gaining some hope for the future of the marriage is another aid in reducing anxiety about ending the affair and in reducing the emotional tie. Perhaps what is most important in reducing depression is helping the man gain a feeling of hope for greater self-fulfillment, particularly hope for a better marriage in the future even if he finds the present marriage unworkable and his girl friend unavailable to him.

From my own limited experience and the experience of coworkers, I have the impression that thoughts of and attempts at suicide are not infrequent in these situations, particularly by the other woman. Questions about past attempts to break off and by whom, each person's reactions to these attempts, and, if necessary, direct questions about suicidal threats need to be raised. This approach will help the man obtain a different perspective of his girl friend, reduce *his* rationalizations and *his* contributions to her suicidal thoughts or drives, and reduce his feeling of responsibility for another adult. If the husband or his wife responds to loss or frustration with suicidal gestures, one can begin preventive counseling.

Fantasies of Marriage to the Other Woman

Dwelling on fantasies of future life in marriage to the other woman is fruitful. Indirectly, it is effective premarital counseling. The man will attain some self-understanding, examine the gratifications and limitations of the courtship period, and contemplate the pros and cons of marriage to the other woman in considering her background, her personality, her current situation, and the problems that would confront them if they had children. These considerations gradually weaken the man's rationalization and strengthen his perceptive powers and his judgment. This change may lead to thoughtful and realistic evaluation of both the extramarital association and the marriage. It may bring to the surface anxieties about marriage to the other woman that have been obscured by the romantic quality of the association. It may clarify and modify the man's conception of his role as a husband and as a father and instill greater awareness of his wife's strength, as was apparent in the J case. In unusual instances, the man's consideration of divorce and marriage to the other woman may be a sign of growth. He may, however, need and want to examine the marriage to determine if, with professional help, sufficient gratification may be possible for him without changing partners.

Discussion

MURRAY A. GOLDSTONE IS CONSULTANT PSYCHIATRIST,
FAMILY SERVICE ASSOCIATION,
CLEVELAND, OHIO.

I have the same problem after reading this article that I have after reading case summaries from Miss Weisberg, that is, "What am I going to add?" Her general study of infidelity—its dynamics and its sociology for men and women, neurotic or character-disordered—surpasses the expectations of the title. The techniques she writes about are adaptable to either sex and perhaps to almost any kind of personality structure. I will comment on those points that seem deserving of special emphasis.

First, I wonder about the phenomenon of being "in love"—whether it differentiates something that might be called "neurotic" from something that would be called "characterologic." I have come to the conclusion that in treating men who are in love as distinct from the acting-out characteriologic sort of infidelity which often is repeated again and again, one is dealing with a more fully developed personality structure and with an individual who is having a new confrontation with his own oedipal situation. The phenomenon of being in love, then, represents an attempt on the part of these persons to effect with a new person a new or similar solution to their own oedipal conflicts. Often this solution appears to the individual to be better than the previous one. Sometimes it becomes evident to the caseworker that it is merely a repetition of the old solution. At other times it becomes evident that no solution is going to be right because the initial oedipal problem is incapable of being resolved. It seems to me that it is worthwhile to identify this phenomenon in the man who is in love, if for no other reason than to demonstrate the intense emotional nature of his problem. The man who is in love in this manner will experience far greater pain in giving up his love than the man involved only in a series of sexual escapades.

Miss Weisberg emphasizes the enormous effect that the correct spontaneous interpretation of the repetition compulsion can have and the great help it can be in freeing the client and enabling him to make a more reasonable decision about his situation. It seems to me that we have a series of potential repetition compulsions in a case of infidelity, both for the wife and the husband. A starting point is the original marriage—that is, each person has sought out a partner who in some ways is satisfying or frustrating certain early needs. Second, the very action of being unfaithful can often be a repetition, both for the husband and the wife—that is, this kind of disenchantment and leaving the spouse for some other person can in itself be a repetition of either an oedipal or preoedipal situation. And then, of course, the choice of the particular new "beloved" offers a third area of repetition which may be operating in exactly the same way as the original marriage, or in some of opposite but equally ineffective way. Curiously, this third repetition—that is, what is involved in the choice of the specific personality for the "beloved"—may actually have significance for the spouse as well. There may be a repetition of certain factors or events in her own past. The caseworker may also ascertain how a repetition compulsion is motivating the other woman. He usually will not see her but can speculate on her needs as he listens to the details. Thus, one can try to gain a framework for understanding infidelity in relation to what is being repeated, by whom, and how it is being done.

The identification of repetition has some additional usefulness, as Miss

Weisberg has shown. It serves as a means to convince the client that there are feelings of which he or she is not aware, unconscious drives that are propelling the person toward an affair or toward a divorce. This revelation can have a very strong effect in diluting the emotions involved. The caseworker, in trying to stimulate a new curiosity as to just what is happening emotionally in the client, can often succeed in making an ally of the client who previously may not have been much of an ally in the casework process. The caseworker is seen as an ally when the client consciously tries to find out "what in the world is going on with me?" From the worker's point of view, it seems to me that this approach is equally helpful in providing time to think and to achieve a better perspective.

There are two other factors discussed in the article that I think are very important to keep in mind and that can apply equally well to almost any characterologic problem in infidelity. These are the matters of anger and depression. I can only emphasize what Miss Weisberg has noted—it is most important to be able to elicit the anger that each person feels. The elicitation of these feelings of anger on the part of both the husband and the wife over what has occurred is of enormous benefit in letting them achieve some distance from their emotional entanglements. It must be recognized also that along with the anger there is always depression.

It is curious that in the situations Miss Weisberg describes, the depressions are often reciprocal. Most of the time, depression for the man will come if and when he decides to end the affair and begin a new attempt at making a go of his marriage. The depression of the wife occurs when she first finds out about the affair. Frequently it does not recur until later, after the man has recovered from the throes of ending his relationship with the other woman, at which time the wife suddenly becomes depressed and angry. This problem of the delayed anger-rejection reaction of the wife is quite understandable. She does not allow herself to feel angry until she is reassured that there will be some reestablishment of the marriage. Then, when the couple are beginning to sit back, sigh with relief and say, "Well, that one's over," the wife's barrage of anger and depression begins. The husband is likely to retort, "You see, here we go again."

In dealing with this reaction, Miss Weisberg introduced a technique I have never tried but am interested in trying: dating. In one of the cases it was an actual suggestion, and in another case it appears to have occurred spontaneously. There was a separation that took place after the reestablishment of the marriage, or at least after the husband's ending the affair. During this period, something happened that allowed these people to return to their marital relationship in a different way. I find this an intriguing idea. It seems to me that it is one way of helping the wife deal with some of her anger, internally or while meeting with the worker, and doing it without giving a day-by-day recitation to her husband. It can also, it seems to me, have a strong symbolic significance for both the man and the woman. If these persons have become strongly aware of the repetitious nature of their behavior, they will be afraid that returning to the marriage will mean a repetition of old patterns. In a resumed dating arrangement, however, a different kind of relationship could symbolically be set up, representing for the couple something different from just going back into the same old relationship.

One final comment: I am impressed with the warmth Miss Weisberg shows for the problems of both the husband and the wife, and her comprehensive understanding of the dynamics involved in infidelity.

NOTES

[1] In analyzing my early thinking, I have had the invaluable help of one of the psychiatric consultants and a group of my colleagues at the Family Service Association of Cleveland, Ohio: Dr. James A. Doull, Jr., Cornelius Utz, Werner Gottlieb, Frances Meshman, Elizabeth Stevenson, and Angela Trannett; plus record material of other staff members.

[2] Anne C. Schwartz, "Reflections on Divorce and Remarriage," *Social Casework* 49 (April 1968): 213.

SUGGESTED READINGS

Constantine, L. and J. *Multilateral Marriage.* Acton, Mass.: Multilateral Relations Study Project, 1970.

English, O. "Values in Psychotherapy: The Affair." *Voices* 3 (1967): 9–14.

Hunt, M. *The Affair.* N.Y.: World, 1969.

Johnson, R. "Some Correlates of Extra-marital Coitus." *Journal of Marriage and the Family* 32 (1970): 449–56.

Neubeck, G., ed. *Extra-marital Relations.* Englewood Cliffs, N.J.: Prentice-Hall, 1969.

13

Silent Sexual Problems

HARVEY L. GOCHROS AND LEROY G. SCHULTZ

Human sexuality encompasses a broad range of attitudes and behavior. In the expression of their sexual needs, populations of people behave in diverse ways toward various sexual objects.

The kinds of sexual behavior tolerated for people in different situations vary from generation to generation and place to place, as attested by the recent emergence of venereal disease as a generally discussable matter, the growing liberality and openness regarding sexual behavior in the Scandinavian countries, and the "live and let live" philosophy of San Francisco. This increased tolerance leaves some groups relatively free to express themselves sexually, such as monogamous married heterosexual young adults, while others—often through no fault of their own—find themselves restrained from sexual fulfillment or placed in a position where they must subject themselves to dangers, social contempt, or major compromises to achieve their sexual goals.

> Man's sexual conduct is surrounded with more taboos, rules and constraints than perhaps any other aspect of his social life. Sexual behavior is rigidly prescribed: The range of persons who are appropriate sex partners is usually narrowly defined, the entry age for sexual activity is restricted, and the context in which it can take place is often specified. While the marriage bed hardly has a monopoly as a place for fun and games, members of the community tend more or less to accept most of the rules on sex behavior that have to do with the characteristics of the partner and exactly what is done. They hold that some sexual encounters are normal or natural, while others are abhorrent and unnatural. The hard impact of these rules is quite evident on our psychological well-being and social adjustment; the sex life of many community members is a compromise between the pressures for expenditure of sexual energies and the constraints of the community.[1]

Some of the sexual problems resulting from these compromises gain prominence and the attention and sometimes even the concern of the general population as well as social workers. Some problems, however, are overlooked, ignored, or given scant attention. These are the silent sexual problems.

This chapter deals with aspects of a few of these problems that social workers may encounter in various settings. They call for such professional roles as counselor, broker, advocate, and social planner, but most of all they call for attention, because they all too often remain unobserved behind a multitude of other more acceptable, resolvable, or perhaps pressing problems. The problems selected are not meant to provide a comprehensive view of the silent sexual problems but, rather, to highlight areas from which generalizations may be drawn.

Early Daters

The years between 13 and 16 are probably the most inherently painful that most human beings endure. While going through awkward physical development, young adolescents are also developing a personal identity and discovering their emerging social and physical sexuality. The trauma of many adolescents in revealing their bodies in gymnasium dressing rooms is a common experience that gives evidence to their painful concern over the adequacy of their own developing sexuality.

Despite the slow liberalization of social attitudes regarding masturbation, the adolescent is still often embarrassed and guilt-ridden about this behavior and possibly even more so over his masturbation fantasies. These anxieties are not appreciably diminished by the usual "It's all right but . . ." philosophy about maturbation that is typically presented in contemporary adolescents sex guides. The not uncommon early homosexual activities create further anxiety and make even more difficult the development of a firm foothold on appropriate sexual identity.

The emerging awareness and concerns of sexuality in adolescents and their perception of the sexual attitudes of parents, teachers, and others in their environment is exemplified in the following excerpt from a preadolescent girl's report on her own developing sexuality:

> In most schools throughout the country, children think sex is something to be laughed and ridiculed at. Sex is a dirty thing, not to be talked about, discussed, or even mentioned to them. It certainly is not the typical thing to talk about in a conversation. For anyone to say anything about sex is usually considered disgraceful, wicked, naughty, shameful and a dirty child. If a teacher hears about a boy or girl saying 'dirty' words or even telling other children how babies are born, etc., the chances are most likely the child will be punished. What's so dirty about sex?

Children will probably never admit how thrilled they are about having their body changing right before their eyes. But I'm sure they are, or at least I am. It's very embarrassing discussing it with the rest of the family. Buying a bra is a very exciting event for most girls, although they will never admit it. If their mother suggests that they buy one, the girl will blush and say, I don't need one of those although they hope they can have one. When they get one, they realize bras are very uncomfortable, but they wear them proudly on their chest.

If a boy asks a girl how she was born or if she menstrates [sic] she would probably blush and be very embarrassed or she might even slap his face and walk away, never to speak to him again. Children shouldn't be blamed for their acts. Society tells them to act this way, Is it time to change society? I believe love is a part of sex or sex is a part of love. I'm not sure which but anyway, love has something to do with it, so I will now talk about love with young children. Love, like sex, is ridiculed, laughed at and teased . . .[2]

The sexual world of a child is even more confusing than that of the contemporary adult. Sex surrounds them in everything from the local newspapers and television to the ads in children's magazines that place a high premium on sexual attractiveness. They become quite aware, early, that sex is a very important matter.

Probably the greatest developmental task for the adolescent is the establishment of heterosexual skills and the acquisition of confirmation of heterosexual competence. The adolescent seeks proof of his adequacy through acceptance and respect from those of his own sex and interest from those of the opposite sex. Early dating experiences are the first major sexual testing ground that the adolescent encounters. The boy wonders how a girl he approaches for a date will respond, while the girl worries if she ever will be approached. Each sees these first formal heterosexual contacts as a test of their ultimate sexual competence: are they truly lovable?

Once a date is contracted, the problems begin. How should they act? What sexual behaviors are expected of them and when? How should they evaluate these advances and how should they respond? "What will he (she) think of me if I do, and what will he (she) think of me if I don't?" When the date is finally, mercifully over, the doubts, fears, and self-recriminations appear and the resolutions for the next foray begin.

Early dating is an experience equally fraught with conflict for many parents, who feel tested by their children's dating experiences or lack of them. They may have the added conflict of not really being quite sure they want their children to date. On one hand they are as eager as their children to gain confirmation of their children's marketability as sexual objects (after all, this is seen as perhaps the greatest test of their own parental performance), yet there is a sadness and a feeling of impending loss accompanying seeing one's children mature to dating age. This problem is further compounded by the parents' anxieties about the dangers of venereal disease, pregnancy, and loss of status resulting from their children's possible sexual behavior on a date.

The perception of their parents' anxieties and ambivalence about their dating only adds to the approach–avoidance conflict of their children in reaction to a social and sexual rite of passage. These problems could provide the core of a relevant sex education program for adolescents. Concerns of what is a man and what is a woman and mutual understanding of the adolescents' and parents' sexual concerns could provide a basis for how to go about making sexual decisions. Many parents are perplexed as to how best to prepare their children for making these decisions in a rapidly changing sexual world. While it has been truly said that the best sex education for a child is seeing his father caress his mother and observe that she obviously enjoys it, a relevant sex education program provided by social workers could help young daters and their parents through a difficult period. Such discussions would make more sense than the typical presentation of the anatomy and physiology of human reproduction and the hazards of premarital sex that all too often is the major product of our hard-fought battles for sex education in the schools.

Adopted Children and Their Parents

Adoption has its psychic risks, not the least of which are related to the sexual aura of adoption. As a result of their own infertility, adoptive parents must resort to adoption as a second-best avenue to parenthood. The infertility, often the result of unknown physiological factors in one or both parents, can create or exaggerate feelings of sexual inadequacy. This problem is compounded when the couple adopts a child who is a product of the union of two unmarried partners. The potential competitiveness of the adoptive parents toward the natural parents is thus reinforced by the fantasy of licentiousness between the natural parents and the threat that their children will prefer and love the fantasy of their natural parents more than the adoptive parents despite their adoptive parents' virtue and the natural parents' fantasied sinfulness. Further, the concept of the "bad seed" is often present in adoption. Sometimes even the adopted child (as well as the adoptive parents) wonders if the "immoral," "sick," "pathological," and "promiscuous" behavior of the mother might be inherited by her children. This is particularly true of an adopted girl as she reaches adolescence. Indeed, adoptive parents often attempt to use a convenient "out" for any feelings of inadequacy as parents by anticipating and then blaming any disturbed behavior of their children on the child's heredity.

The fact that the vast majority of adoptive parents still feel discomfort in dealing with their child's adoption in such areas as answering questions of the child regarding his background, and telling the child about his adoption even after the completion of a year of post-placement visits by a social worker[3] would seem to indicate that social workers have not made so much of an impact on helping adoptive parents resolve basic questions regarding adoption as we would hope. The adoption worker has a responsibility to anticipate and work with potential problems related to sexuality that may be experienced by both the adoptive children and the adoptive parents. Indeed, a sizable number of the parents interviewed in the study reported above indicated an interest in some form of group discussions that focus on sexual matters for themselves as well as their children when their children reach adolescence.

The Aged

A young public welfare worker returned to her agency with a shocked expression after visiting one of her old-age recipients at a home for the aged. "You won't believe it," she said to her coworkers, "but some of the old men at that home actually tried to make a pass at me! And they were in their 70s!" There was a mixture of shock, disgust, and not a little good-natured joking by her coworkers in response to her report. It is difficult—even for those in the helping professions—to perceive the elderly as sexually active. But as people live longer and maintain better health in their advancing years, it becomes increasingly evident that sexual interest and capacity can often be sustained well into the seventh decade and beyond.

A recent study conducted at Duke University Medical Center which investigated the effects of age, sex, and marital status on the sexual behavior of men and women between 60 and 90 years of age revealed that age and sexual activity were not strictly correlated, and while such variables as age-related infirmities and physical illnesses often affected sexual behavior, the incidence of sexual activity was still maintained at 50 percent during the early 60s and from 10 to 20 percent at age 80.[4] Marital status had little effect on the activity or interest of the aging man. It would seem then that sexual activity can be a rewarding experience and a need for men as well as women in their later years, if circumstances permit.

Circumstances, however, do not always permit. Many older people are widowed and isolated. Some have untreated physical conditions which make sexual satisfaction difficult. Some use advancing age as an excuse to terminate a sexual relation they have never really enjoyed. Some perceive an occasional sexual failure as a signal for the termination of sexual relations and avoid subsequent attempts for fear of additional embarrassment. But even when there is interest and opportunity, cultural taboos often prevent sexual experience. Society does not take well to its grandparents' cavorting in bed. Indeed, even the common expression "dirty old man" connotes disgust and disapproval of those interested in sex much beyond 40. Our prevailing cultural attitude is that sex is for the young.

Physiological changes compound social taboos and lack of opportunities for the aged to have a satisfying sex life. As a woman grows older, her vaginal walls become more tender and subject to irritation, while at the same time a man takes longer to achieve an erection which is not so firm as when he was younger. Ejaculation may not be so easy to achieve as formerly. Yet these mutually aggravating physiological problems, sometimes complicated by infirmities, such as heart trouble, need not prevent a continuation of some form of sexual activity. Often medical consultation and treatment will be useful. But there are ways in which social workers can also be helpful. There are some homes for the aged, for instance, which encourage romance and even remarriage, late in life. Social workers can assist elderly, isolated people to develop contact through social clubs and organizations. Sex education may be as useful for the aged as for youth. "Every study of older people has shown that large numbers of them engage in masturbation as an alternative method of gaining release from sexual tension, though some of them feel disturbed because they feel there is something wrong for persons of their age to engage in this practice."[5]

While talking about sex may be alien to many aging clients, the social worker can make attempts, when appropriate, to explore this area of functioning, and help the aged meet their sexual needs whether it is through the reestablishment of interpersonal sexual activity or through permission for masturbatory activity.

The Confirmed Homosexual

Americans have long been committed to pronounced sexual dimorphism: an exaggeration of the differences in the social roles of men and women. We revere the west, "where men are men and women are women." Matt Dillon, with his super masculinity, has been the male ego ideal for the mass of Americans longer than any other television character. From early childhood boys are taught to be "all boy" and girls are rewarded for their femininity. The unisex concept supported by a minority, with its downplay of basic behavioral differences between the sexes, is the subject of ridicule or scorn by most Americans. Long hair on youth is often considered threatening, primarily for its sexual ambiguity and the im-

plicit challenge to the supremacy of the supermale. The Women's Liberation Movement is tolerated, as long as it does not change the basic roles
of men and women in our society.

In view of this preoccupation with assertions of masculinity and
femininity, there is little wonder at the discomfort of many social workers
in working with clients experiencing homosexual wishes or behavior. This
is particularly a problem for many male practitioners whose sexual identity
is already threatened by being in a profession that is still perceived as primarily feminine in orientation. The nervous laughter that often accompanies a discussion of homosexuality is an index of this discomfort. Fortunately for these social workers, the problem does not arise very often,
because confirmed homosexuals are rarely served by social work agencies
and do not perceive social workers as a source for help with the many
problems they experience. Yet the estimated ten million people with a
primarily homosexual orientation represent a sizable oppressed minority
for whom social workers could provide much-needed services.

Even if the worker overcomes his feeling of revulsion and fear of "guilt
by association" with the homosexual and chooses to try to be helpful, he
often tends to approach their situations (regardless of the nature of the
presenting problem) with a therapeutic goal of a "conversion"—that is,
changing their libidinal orientation to heterosexual objects. Putting aside
the issue of whether such a change is therapeutically probable,[6] the fact
remains that many, if not most, homosexually oriented adults do not
choose to change. In fact, to most of them, a change to heterosexuality
is as unthinkable and undesirable as for a heterosexual to change his sexual orientation. Many resent the tendency of those in the helping professions to perceive their goals as changing the homosexual's sexual orientation, regardless of the nature of the problem that they bring to a helping
person.

They also resent the generally held perception of homosexuality as an
"illness." One might question the imputation that a deviation from norms
of sexual orientation implies a pathology of the "total personality." Indeed,
a great many men and women with homosexual orientations lead basically
rewarding, constructive and pleasurable lives (despite the "Boys in the
Band" image), disrupted only by the problems society creates for them
because of their choice of sexual object. As one successful scientist, who
happened to have a homosexual orientation, stated in a paper presented
at a recent meeting of sex educators,[7] "Why does society have to make
such a major issue over what people do with their genital organs? After
all, that only occupies a relatively very small part of life. Yet people seem
more preoccupied with what we do for a couple hours a week in bed than
what we do in the greatest portion of our lives!"

Part of the problem of homosexuals comes from the necessarily secret world they live in. This secrecy, necessitated by the almost universal scorn, intimidations, retributions, and other dangers they realistically fear if discovered, leads to many dysfunctional aspects of their lives: lack of opportunities to meet a wide range of potential partners, difficulty in establishing and maintaining long-lasting relationships, fear of arrest, loss of jobs and social acceptance, and not the least, fear of blackmail.

The relative invisibility of the majority of the homosexually oriented leads to the development of stereotyping. Generally, this image of the homosexual is the very visible deviate from sex role norms: the thin, limp-wristed, high-voiced feminine, sexually preoccupied, bizarre-appearing "queer" man, who hates his sexual identity and is dangerous to children, or the powerful, aggressive, masculine, brutish "butch" woman bent on taking over the world. These attributes are encountered in only a minority of the homosexually oriented. There is no more a "typical" homosexual personality, appearance, or life style than there is a "typical" heterosexual personality, appearance, or life style. Also, Kinsey and others have identified a continuum of choice for sexual objects ranging from exclusively those of the same sex to those of the opposite sex.

The homosexually oriented of either sex can be either gentle or rough, law-abiding or criminal, generally happy or despondent, masculine or feminine in appearance, interested or disinterested in youthful sex partners, hard-working or shiftless, capable or incapable of heterosexual intercourse, married or unmarried, wanting to change their orientation or satisfied with it. They are people who, for a multitude of reasons, to a greater or lesser extent prefer to have sexual relations with people of their own sex, and who suffer from society's sanctions against such an orientation.

As such, many of their problems are similar to those who bear any other social stigma. It is important to bear in mind that this is a stigma not of their own choosing. No one chooses his sexual orientation, any more than one chooses the color of his eyes or which diseases to develop. But they suffer the consequences of these stigmas which can (but do not necessarily) include self-hatred, seeking out others with similar stigmas, familial rejection, striking out against an unjust world, alienation, and relative social isolation.

It is with the consequences of these stigma and the problems of living a satisfying, productive life that the social worker can be of the most help.

The nature of the social work services to the homosexually oriented can be as diverse as the individuals who are so oriented, the unique characteristics of each situation, and the attitudes toward and resources for homosexually oriented in the particular community in which they live. San Francisco, for instance, provides many more social, vocational, and sexual opportunities for the homosexually oriented and less persecution than, say, most small midwestern towns.[8]

The social worker may indeed be quite helpful by assisting his client in deciding whether to remain in his present community or move to a community with more opportunities and safety for those with their sexual interest.

There are other useful roles the social worker can perform. He might be called upon to engage in a form of marital counseling for a crisis in a long-lasting and perhaps basically sound homosexual relationship; or to help a young engaged man with a bisexual history to evaluate the probabilities of marital success and whether, and how, to tell his intended wife about his conflict; or to help a middle-aged professional woman work through her guilt about her homosexual relationships; or to develop some more desirable setting for a community of homosexuals to meet each other than the traditional "gay" bars, steam baths, and public toilets.[9]

Whatever the role, the worker must be willing to accept the sexual orientation of the confirmed homosexual as a given (in adult cases) and work with him on the consequences of that orientation.

With adolescents the situation may be different and more complex. While some may argue that sexual orientation is already fixed by adolescence, the evidence is far from conclusive. Especially if the adolescent wishes to change to a "normal" sexual orientation, the worker should himself, or through referral, help to develop the adolescent's heterosexual orientation. This can perhaps be achieved by approaching the adolescent's fear of heterosexual contacts. Current dysfunctional parental influences should be explored and altered when necessary. The worker can program a series of increasing approximations of intimate heterosexual activities with a high probability of successful culmination. Such an approach is especially useful in those cases, often seen by social workers, in which a young unmarried adult appears in a state of panic, fearing he is homosexual as a result of heterosexual anxieties or failures. Often he interprets his discomfort as evidence of homosexuality even if there has been no specific sexual interest in people of his own sex. The need here is, again, to help the client work through his fears and avoidance of people of the opposite sex.

In cases of seemingly fixed homosexual orientations in adolescents, the social worker, as difficult as it may be for his own personal values, must accept the right of each individual to make his own sexual choices. We also must recognize the potential for social ostracism, loneliness, as well as the physiological limitations of homosexual relationships. We would, therefore, clearly opt for heterosexual orientation for clients where there is both a possibility and a wish for this. The field of behavior modification is developing promising approaches for the conversion of those homo-sexuals who are motivated.[10]

For those who have chosen or who are inevitably fixed in their homo-sexual orientation and wish to maintain that orientation the social worker has a responsibility for helping them achieve as much life satisfaction as possible, working with the problems—vocational, social, and interper-sonal—resulting from their orientation. Further, the social worker should do whatever is possible to alter societal attitudes and sanctions and the behavior of the people in the environment of the homosexually oriented so that their rights as human beings are preserved.

The Hospitalized Mentally Ill

Many years ago visitors to institutions for the mentally ill noted that the chronically psychotic seemed to masturbate openly and regularly. As a result of these observations the logical fallacy developed that if those who are mentally ill masturbate, then masturbation leads to mental illness.

Because of the nature of the behavior exhibited by some hospitalized people with emotional difficulties, another myth developed that those who are adjudicated mentally ill are sexually dangerous as well as incapable of developing and maintaining sexual or interpersonal relationships. This has been compounded by the fear that sexual activity among the mentally ill will produce mentally ill children who will, in turn, become tax burdens.

Certainly our treatment of the mentally ill contributes to both the reality and the myth of these assumptions. Many back-ward state hospital patients have minimal privacy and little to do that is satisfying other than masturbate. And if they are deprived of heterosexual opportunities, they do become preoccupied with sexual thoughts and tend to choose aggressive or deviant sexual activities. Sexual rights are one of the first civil rights that the mentally ill lose.[11] Our fear of behavior labeled as mental illness, as well as our sexual inhibitions lead us to treat the mentally ill in a sexually repressive manner. A humane treatment for the diagnosed mentally ill in hospitals would lead to as many attempts as possible to normalize their heterosexual opportunities, including efforts to maintain normal sexual as well as emotional ties with their spouses and other op-portunities for informal contact between the sexes.

The sexual problems of the hospitalized mentally ill are not dissimilar from many of those experienced by the imprisoned which are discussed next in this chapter. These problems add to the already existing questions about the real therapeutic value for most diagnosed "mentally ill" being confined in institutions.

The Imprisoned

While sexual expression has always been of prime concern to the confined prisoner, it has remained hidden from the public view, and professional prison officials, whether of the custodial or treatment orientation, attempt to avoid its visibility. This is due to America's sexual value system in general, the basically repressive nature of correctional institutions, society's sanctioning of punishment, and the efforts of politically influenced prison administrators to avoid any new programs or policies that may cost the taxpayer more money.

Policies and programs viewing the sexual need satisfaction of prisoners as a "good" have never been acceptable in this country and no American correctional institution, with one exception, appears concerned with meeting the heterosexual needs of prisoners. This exception is the Mississippi State Penitentiary, which since 1918 has had a policy covering "conjugal visiting" and holiday furloughs outside the institution.[12] The conjugal visit allows a "wife" to visit her "husband" in his cell or in an apartment provided by the prison for purposes of sexual intercourse or related sexual behavior. The furlough permits the prisoner to leave the institution to find sexual satisfaction, among other things, in society at large. No American prison permits, as Mexico does, the wife and children of the prisoner to live with the husband in the prison at state expense. No female institution permits conjugal visiting, yet women in confinement are not usually asexual.[13]

The rationale for encouraging conjugal visiting and/or the furlough for sexual purposes is: a) it helps to keep marriages together, creates marital harmony, cuts divorce rates; b) it reduces the likelihood of homosexual behavior, by consent or by force, and, therefore, prison management problems; c) it reduces sexual tension and makes prisoners more manageable; d) it is simply humane; and e) it supports appropriate sexual identity.

Those against conjugal visiting cite the following reasoning:[14] a) it emphasizes only the physical aspects of sexuality; b) it might create security problems; c) it violates society's urge to punish; d) there is no money for staff for such a program and taxpayers would object to public monies being spent to support such "prostitution"; e) it might result in pregnancies and children which the imprisoned father could not support adequately; f) it might create conditions for graft and corruption among prison personnel; g) it would benefit only the married prisoner, not the single person or the homosexual; h) it violates the values of prison managers.

These objections are peculiarly American, since Canada, Mexico, and many European and Scandinavian countries permit conjugal visiting and/or the sexual furlough. Conceivably, if prison officials and correctional professionals would support such programs, along with the American Correctional Association and the National Council on Crime and Delinquency, they would have more of a chance of acceptance by the public. Also, while many of the above objections apply to conjugal visiting, they do not apply to the sexual furlough.

The individual problems posed by the lack of heterosexual release opportunities, and the subsequent forced nature of homosexual rape and sodomy[15] present severe problems for the correctional social worker, even though he remains silent about them.[16] Helping prisoners adjust to this type of deviance is a strain on both treatment methodologies and social work values. To the extent that all helping professions working in correctional institutions contribute to the deprivation of heterosexual relationships, they contribute, indirectly, to a figurative castration through forced celibacy.

Conclusion

This chapter has surveyed problems encountered by some of our society's sexually underprivileged. These groups are among those most handicapped by contemporary society's sexual confusions, stereotypes, and anxieties. Social workers are of this society but have the responsibility to try to heal the wounds it creates. This is no less true for the sexual deprivations experienced by those whose legitimate needs are too often ignored. Some suggestions for social work intervention in these problems have been offered.

The decline of silence regarding these sexual problems can be expected to accelerate as our sex–value confusions gain greater attention, as we become more tortured by uncertainty, as moralistic consensus breaks up, as puritanical constrictions give way to humanistic values based on social science explanations of the real consequences of freer sexual expression, and as all values are opened to critical examination. The healthful assimilation of sexual changes as they evolve, within ourselves and social institutions,[17] may be one of the most substantial challenges to social work in the future.

NOTES

[1] Howard E. Freeman and Norman R. Kurtz, *America's Troubles* (Englewood Cliffs, N.J.: Prentice-Hall, 1969), p. 244.

[2] Susan L. Gochros, *What Eleven Year Olds Think about Sex and Love.* Unpublished manuscript, 1970.

[3] Harvey L. Gochros, "A Study of the Caseworker-Adoptive Parent Relationship in Post-Placement Services," *Child Welfare*, June, 1967, pp. 317–326.

[4] A. Verwoerdt, E. Pfeiffer, and H. S. Wang, "Sexual Behavior in Senescence: Patterns of Sexual Activity and Interest," *Geriatrics* 24, no. 2 (1969), pp. 137–54.

[5] Isadore Rubin, "Sex after Forty—and after Seventy," in *Analysis of Human Sexual Response*, ed. Ruth and Edward Brecher (Boston: Little, Brown and Company, 1966), p. 266.

[6] See: Lawrence J. Hatterer, *Changing Homosexuality in the Male* (New York: McGraw-Hill, 1970).

[7] Franklin Kameny, President of Maryland Mattachine Society, "Conversations with Two Homosexuals," American Association of Sex Educators and Counselors annual meeting, Washington, D.C., April 12, 1970.

[8] Howard S. Becker and Irving Horowitz, "The Culture of Civility," *Trans-Action* 7, no. 6, (April 1970).

[9] Laud Humphreys, *Tearoom Trade: Impersonal Sex in Public Places* (Chicago: Aldine Publishing Company, 1970).

[10] See Chapter 17, "Behavior Modification and Sexual Problems."

[11] Leon H. Ginsberg, "Civil Rights of the Mentally Disabled in Oklahoma," *Oklahoma Law Review* 20, no. 2 (May 1967), pp. 120–21.

[12] C. B. Hopper, *Sex in Prison*, (Baton Rouge: Louisiana State University Press, 1969), pp. 49–63.

[13] D. A. Ward, G. G. Kassebaum, "Homosexuality: A Mode of Adaption in a Prison for Women," *Social Problems*, Fall, 1964, pp. 159–77.

[14] Hopper, *op. cit.*, pp. 1–16.

[15] A. J. Davis, "Sexual Assault in the Philadelphia Prisons and Sheriff's Vans," *Trans-Action*, Dec., 1968, pp. 8–17.

[16] J. E. Herrick, *The Social Worker at the Adult Correctional Institution*, (Northbrook, Ill.: Whitehall, 1969. (Most social work literature avoids the topic of sex).

[17] Carl Rogers, "Interpersonal Relationships: U.S.A. 2000," *Journal of Applied Behavioral Science* 4 (1968): pp. 265–280.

SUGGESTED READINGS

Youth

Ehrmann, W. *Premarital Dating Behavior*. N.Y.: Holt, 1959.

Gagnon, J. "Sexuality and Sexual Learning in the Child." *Psychiatry* 28 (1965): 212–28.

Josselyn, I. "Sexual Education—Is It Wise?" *The Reiss-Davis Clinic Bulletin*, Spring 1970.

Kirkendall, L. "Characteristics of Sexual Decision-making." *Journal of Sex Research* 3 (1967): 201–11.

Packard, V. *The Sexual Wilderness*. N.Y.: Pocket Books, 1970.

Schur, E., ed. *The Family and the Sexual Revolution*. Bloomington: Indiana University Press, 1964.

Toffler, A. *Future Shock*. N.Y.: Random House, pp. 211–86.

Homosexuality

Ellis, A. *Homosexuality: Its Causes and Cure.* N.Y.: Lyle Stuart, 1965.

Cagnon, S., and Simon, W. *Sexual Deviance.* N.Y.: Harper & Row, 1967.

Hatterer, L. *Changing Homosexuality in the Male.* New York: McGraw-Hill 1970.

Hoffman, M. *The Gay World.* New York: Basic Books, 1968.

Rechy, J. *City of Night.* New York: Grove, 1964.

Schur, E. *Crimes Without Victims.* Englewood Cliffs, N.J.: Prentice-Hall, 1965.

Simon, W., and Gagnon, S. H. "Homosexuality: The Formulation of a Sociological Perspective." *Journal of Health and Social Behavior* 8, no. 3, (September 1967), pp. 177–85.

The Aged

Alpert, H. "Love in the Darker Years." *Harvest Years,* June 1970.

Cuber, J., and Harroff, P. *Sex and the Significant Americans.* New York: Appleton-Century.

Cornelia, U. "Sexual Behavior in a Group of Older Women." *Journal of Gerontology* 20 (1965): 351–56.

Rubin, I. *Sex Life After Sixty,* New York: Basic Books, 1965.

S.I.E.C.U.S. *Sexual Life in the Later Years,* New York: Sex Information and Education Council of the U.S., 1970.

Wikler, R., and Grey, P. *Sex and the Senior Citizen.* New York: Fell, 1968.

The Imprisoned

Comfort, A. "Institutions Without Sex." *Social Work* 12, (1967): pp. 107–8.

Hopper, C. B. *Sex in Prison.* Baton Rouge: Louisiana State University Press, 1969.

Sykes, G. M. *The Society of Captives.* New York: Atheneum, 1965.

Vedder, C. B., King, P. G. *Problems of Homosexuality in Corrections.* Springfield, Ill.: Thomas, 1967.

Ward, D. A., and Kassebaum, G. G. *Women's Prison: Sex and Social Structure.* Chicago: Aldine, 1965.

14

The Social Worker and the Treatment
of the Sex Victim

LeRoy G. Schultz

The need for treatment or social service for the victims of sexual offenses is not reported or documented in professional literature[1] and most of the standard professional textbooks dealing with children's services do not cover the topic.[2] Apparently the social work practitioner does not receive such case referrals from the law enforcement agencies, courts, hospitals, or victims' families; or the profession has assumed that such problems are the concern of the medical profession only, specifically the psychiatrist; or the victim cases that occur in social work caseloads have not been researched and published. Possible too is that sex offenders' victims do not want or need treatment or service, or that they and their families are too embarrassed to approach treatment agencies.

The incidence of sexual victimization is very difficult to measure accurately. There is no national statistical system recording the incidence. Estimates run from 4,000 cases of child-sex victimization per year in large cities,[3] a national average of over 5,000 cases of incest per year,[4] and between 200,000[5] and 500,000[6] cases per year of sexual assaults on female children (ages 4–13). Estimates of sexual assaults on male children are even more nonexistent.

Male sexual attacks on female adults have been increasingly reported to law enforcement agencies in the past years, with three rapes reported every hour,[7] or expressed another way, the likelihood of a woman being raped by a male is 1 in 550 per year. Lesbian assaults are almost unheard of but perhaps do occur in female institutions.[8] Male rape is very common in male correctional institutions[9] and may be as statistically prevalent as female rape at large. Possibly 50 percent of all crime is not reported to police by the victim,[10] suggesting that the incidence of sex offenses is much higher than official statistics indicate. The victim may be seen by a family physician or in the emergency room of the local hospital, and therefore no public record is available.

Victim—Topology

Sexual victims may be placed upon a continuum extending from totally accidental victimization at one end to seductive partner at the other. Many victims consent to the offense or offer no resistance, and both victim and offender are symbiotic, or form a cooperative dyad. This relationship shapes the victim's attitude toward the sexual offense and the offender, as well as her willingness to testify against him with subsequent guilt feelings. What type of treatment a victim may request or need appears related to where he is situated along the victimization continuum, with the important factors centered around degree of force employed by the offender and the intensity of the victim–offender relationship prior to the offense.

In past sexual research, female victims were described as having a "collaborative" role in the offense in 7.8 percent of 330 offenses,[11] as "non-objecting" in 40 percent of 1994 offenses,[12] as "encouraging" to the offender in from 66 percent to 95 percent of all sex offenses,[13] as fully "participating" in 60 percent of 73 offenses,[14] and as "seducers" in 21 percent of 185 offenses.[15] While victim precipitation, cooperation, invitation, or seduction may present a problem for the courts in assessing degree of guilt and punishment for the offender, usually relieving him of responsibility, the social service agencies must deal with this type of child as a sex-delinquent. In general, physical force on child victims plays a small role in the offenses (4 percent of 333 offenses[16]), and this may be related to the fact that most offenses against children are by persons they have some relationship with, such as a family member, a family friend, a neighbor, or a teacher,[17] so that physical force is unnecessary to the success of the offense. The lesser incidence of physical force is also related to the fact that the specific type of sex offense does not require physical violence to complete. In the Gagnon study, 1.9 percent of the victims sustained a forced act of penetration and 2.7 percent a general forceful attack on the whole body.[18] By far, the major sexual activity between victim and offender was characterized by exhibition of sexual organs, genital and non-genital petting or fondling, mouth-genital contacts, and attempted penetrattion without force.

In the case of the adult sex-offense victim the factor of physical force is much greater, and the likelihood of the offense being committed by a stranger is much higher. If no force is employed and the act takes place with an acquaintance it probably will not be reported to the police. Important too is that, despite the use of violence, some victims may not report the offense out of shame, embarrassment, mistrust of police, fear of exposure to the community and to relatives and friends. Amir's research indicated that of 646 females raped, only 19 percent were victim-precipitated,

89 percent were committed by nonacquaintances, 31 percent of the cases sustained a brutal beating, and 26 percent were group-raped.[19]

Effects of Victimization

The general direct effects of victimization upon children have been exaggerated in the earlier literature. Generally, sexual assaults on children do not have an excessively unsettling effect on the child's personality development,[20] or a serious effect on his adult adjustment.[21] Of the 5 percent of offenses against children involving physical force and penetration, physical damage may involve sex-organ damage or rupture; general body damages such as bruises, bites, or scratches; venereal disease, vulvitis, or pregnancy. Problems of this type should be treated in the hospital, clinic, or family physician's office, and in general this does not require much time.

Psychosocial effects are not so readily assessed as the physical. The psychosocial negative effects are related to the amount of violence employed by the offender, the depth of the child's relationship to the victim, and the family's and society's reaction to the offense. Immediate reaction to the offense may range from one of simple fright (much like when the child encounters something new but unpleasant) to vomiting and hysteria. Some react without fear or guilt, and some report being sexually aroused. In the Gibbons–Prince Study, 43 percent of 82 cases showed no overt disturbance after the sex act, in 16 percent the child appeared unsettled with behavior problems, 14 percent needed professional treatment, and 6 percent needed correctional institutionalization.[22] In general, the best recovery is made by the child who was sexually assaulted without violence by a stranger. The child's relationship to his offender is very important in understanding the offense dynamics and aftereffects. Most victim children allow or seek out affectionate behavior from their offenders, many feel kindly and lovingly towards them and have established meaningful relationships with their offenders, usually over a period of years with frequent sexual behavior. This situation is particularly true in family incest, where a daughter will not place criminal charges against the father for fear of being responsible for parental separation, divorce, the loss of father, or seeing him sentenced to a correctional institution; or out of oedipal guilt. Female victims are sometimes blamed by their mothers for breaking up the family. The same holds true for the female adolescent victim who manifests strong resistance to bringing charges against her "steady" boy friend. Sometimes victims engaged in behavior that was seductive, out of affectionate feelings, but were naive about its potential as a sexual stimulus, and once the offense was committed, they felt betrayed, shocked, and generally, experienced a negative reaction. The child victim may also feel guilt if she reports some gratification in being the object of love and attention by an older person, whom her family and society all of a sudden condemn.

In the adult victim, having "invited" the offense may take two directions: partial involvement in victimogenesis may actually minimize the traumatic aftereffects; or symptoms may be accentuated as a result of guilt feelings. If the victim feels she was involved in the offense to some degree or stimulated the event, she may feel guilty that society has chosen to prosecute only one-half of the relationship. She may wonder about her reputation or marriageability. If the rape was violent, she may display hysteria, shock, and overwhelming feelings of hostility toward the assailant. Her selfconfidence may disappear as she questions what she did wrong, what precautions she did not take. She may question her possible victimization again by the same man or another one, if she will ever like men again or show a normal interest in sexual relations. Sutherland,[23] a social worker in a mental health agency, reports rape victims' reactions as occurring in the following three phases: phase one—acute reaction characterized by disbelief, dismay, incoherency, agitated and sometimes mute, followed by anxiety; phase two—pseudoadjustment in work, school, and family, through rationalization and denial; and phase three—depression and a need for verbal ventilation.

In general, severe trauma is rare. Hayman reports 12 cases out of 322 rapes suffered trauma, 5 cases of pregnancy, 7 cases requiring surgery, and 26 cases of venereal disease.[24]

By far the greatest potential damage to the child's personality is caused by society and the victims' parents, as a result of (1) the need to use the victim to prosecute the offender, and (2) the need of parents to prove to themselves, family, neighborhood, and society that the victim was free of any participation and that they were not failures as parents.

Society, through its system of administering justice, requires that a person charged with an offense has a right to trial and to confront and cross-examine those who have brought charges against him. What does harm to the victim is society's need to have her repeat the details of the offense several times, to police, prosecutors, and to the jury, sometimes with the assaulter present. This makes what is perhaps in the child's mind a short-lived traumatic event with no permanent consequences become out of proportion to its importance to him, and forces the child to reorient his ideas toward an adult interpretation of the offense, its new importance, and his role in punishing the offender. Most police and prosecutors have no training in nondamaging methods of interviewing children and tend to use adversary approaches appropriate for adults. The offender's lawyer has the duty of defending his client with every tool at his command, and may contribute or induce emotional damage to the victim by attempting to show that the victim is incompetent, seductive, malicious, a "Lolita," or that she brought false charges.[25] The dilemma here is the need to protect the child from the potential trauma of legal proceedings but at the same time to convict and rehabilitate the offender. This dilemma can be somewhat reduced by using special interrogation, as will be discussed later. Even so, many parents might refuse to bring in the legal authorities for fear of reputational damage to the child and family. If courts cannot eliminate the trauma of testifying, then nonreporting may be the best choice.

It is clear from studies of child sexual victims that it is not the sexual assault that usually creates trauma, but the child's parents' behavior upon its discovery and their effect on the child.[26] Parents overreact, develop hysteria, attack the assailant, attack the child victim, berate and punish the victim, demand that the child victim testify that the attack was unprovoked, or threaten court personnel unless they sentence the offender instantly. The Gibbons study indicated that 26 percent of the parents engaged in behavior that aggravated the sex-offense situation or exploited the child's situation for social benefit.[27] As soon as possible after the offense, parents will need help to accept the offense in such a way that horror, panic, and fright are not communicated to the child and a trauma is not created where none existed before. Most single instances of sexual trauma, unless reinforced by court testifying or parental overreaction, produce few permanent consequences.

Social Work Treatment

THE CHILD VICTIM: Once the sexual victim has received medical attention, if needed, and referred to the social agency, the social worker is faced with helping the family decide on the desirability or nondesirability of reporting the offense to the police. A refusal to report the incident is based upon a reluctance to repeat the details of the offense to others; a desire to avoid publicity, social stigma, or revenge from others; or a belief by the victim or parents that the incident created so much emotional disturbance that accurate recounting of the offense is unlikely. The pro and con of these various issues will need to be assessed, and discussed with victim and family in an effort to help them make a decision. The decision involves considering what the effects upon the victim will be if he files charges and is a witness, as against the safety of the community of potential victims if the offender is not prosecuted. If the family and victim decide to bring charges against the alleged offender, they should be instructed in how to do this, and perhaps the social worker should accompany them to the police department and warrant office. The family and victim should be instructed to report the incident as soon as possible. Some introductory effort should be made to make sure the "offense" is not a product of the child's imagination or being reported out of spite or retaliation. Instruction should be given to preserve any physical evidence such as blood- or semen-stained clothing or sheets.

Regrettably, in some jurisdictions the child may be required to testify against the offender without the consent of the child or family, and may be placed in detention until the trial. This situation prevails where the prosecutor feels the alleged offender poses a dangerous threat to the community. In some instances, the child must be placed in detention or in a foster home because the parent is the offender or a neglect charge is filed against the parents.

If the jurisdiction requires the child's testimony, or the family or victim decides to prosecute, the social worker should prepare them for the court experience, easing the anxieties in all legal proceedings. This can be done through traditional role-playing, behavior rehearsal techniques, and mock trials. Efforts should be made to speed the legal proceedings, prevent delays, and insure privacy in court proceedings. The social worker should accompany the child and family at every court appearance.

Casework services for victim *and parents,* if needed, would be of the supportive type. The parents will need supportive but firm assistance in taking a constructive and nondamaging attitude toward the offense, its social repercussions, the possible effects upon the victim, and the role they can play in the reduction of trauma. They may need instruction and direction on "playing-down" the significance of the offense. Many child victims are seeking affection not given by the family or are seeking substitute attachments to compensate for insecurity in the family. Mothers of such victims may need advice and direction on overcoming maternal affection insufficiency. Parents will need an opportunity to ventilate feelings, particularly if there is guilt about parental contribution.

Child victims may need casework assistance in achieving precise understanding of what happened in simple anatomical sexual terms; they may also benefit from ventilation of feelings of anger, guilt, and helplessness with a sympathetic and supportive worker.

Many child victims come from homes and families that are disorganized and lack adequate supervision. Some will have been socialized within homes and neighborhoods with sex codes different from what is reflected in law; others will indicate poor impulse control related to deprivation, rejection, and maternal inconsistency. Later these victims may be the main problem for social work focus and the whole range of traditional protective services of correction and prevention. Incest cases pose a special problem for the family, in that the victim may have developed a strong affection for her father over a long period of time.[28] Courts and social agencies are quick to separate the family members with little preparation for the child's loss of the source of her affection.

Marked efforts at preventing a second victimization or another family member's being victimized should be made through educational measures that are realistically geared to a child's needs and intellectual level, avoiding creation of added fears and anxiety. Particular avoidance should be made of lengthy descriptions of sexual pathology or "dirty old men" generalizations that compound the problem further. The relative harmlessness of certain types of sexual behavior for the victim (exhibitionism, for example) should be reinforced, and a feeling that the child can share his sexual ideas and experience with open-minded parents may prevent concealment of damaging experiences.

THE ADULT VICTIM: As previously indicated, a great deal of brutality and violence characterize the adult female rape. The victim should be taken to a hospital or clinic for proper medical treatment of wounds and injuries and the prevention of venereal disease and pregnancy.

Many of these victims are young and their psychosexual attitudes are quite plastic and in development. Amir reported 51 percent of rape victims under age 19.[29] The offense may shatter the young woman's image of the male as a protective lover and substitute one of sexual man as violent and exploitive. This affects heterosexual trust patterns in the future. Her self-image as a woman may also be changed. She feels used, damaged, and shamed. The police, courts, or family may suggest that she precipitated the event. She will need reassurance that she did not invite the offense, if this is true. She may need help to reaffirm that she is still attractive and feminine. The married victim may need professional help in overcoming feelings of frigidity or that sexuality is distasteful, and the husband will need to develop patience.

The social worker may be faced with the problem of relieving strong, perhaps debilitating, guilt attitudes in the victim, particularly if she felt excited or stimulated by the event or a part of it. Many of these guilt feelings can be handled by reassurance of her value and likelihood of a return to normal. Irrational feelings of guilt can be reduced by discussion and ventilation of the event and its consequences with an accepting sympathetic professional. The adult victim may question reporting the rape to husband or family and may need help in sorting out and weighing the pro and con. The worker will be required to gain and encourage a supportive reaction from important people close to the victim. As a final stage of treatment the victim must integrate a new view of herself based on a realistic appraisal of the rape incident and her role in it.[30]

Reducing the Trauma of Testifying

Most children probably have the strength, stability, and home support to enable them to endure the temporary stress of repetition of the details of the offense before a police officer, prosecutor, or jury, if accompanied by a social worker or other professional; but for a select few, the court proceedings are themselves the chief traumatic event. There appears no effective way of determining which children can sustain the court process and its possible long-range effects. Fortunately, the cases in which repetitious testimony is required are few. Approximately 80 percent to 90 percent of all criminal defendants plead guilty without a trial,[31] so that the child's testimony or appearance is not required. In this majority of cases the child will be spared all but the police, warrant office, and grand jury experience. It remains the court experience with its adversary nature that poses the greatest potential trauma genesis. If violence was employed by the offender, he may not want to risk a jury trial, particularly in states where the jury determines guilt and sets the sentence, and he has an advantage in bargaining for a lighter sentence by pleading guilty. It is when the issue of victim participation or seduction arises that defendants may demand a trial in order to impress the jury with victimogenetic factors in those cases of victims over age 14.

The fact that 75 percent of sex victims or their parents do not report the offense to legal authorities may be the result of the child's contributory behavior or of parents' feeling that the police and court experience will be damaging. The result is that many sex offenders who are perhaps dangerous are not apprehended. If the latter situation prevails, there is a need for reform in the methods of child interrogation following the offense. The mental health of the victim should not be in the hands of untrained police officers, sheriffs, or court personnel.

Since most counties in the United States have at least one trained professional—the child welfare worker attached to the county or regional welfare office—he may be the most practical resource for the professional task of interviewing the child victim. It would appear more practical to teach the social worker a legal perspective than to teach police and prosecutor a mental health orientation.[32]

One country, Israel, has a policy by which a professional person interviews the child victim under age 14 and decides if the child's mental health will be affected by reporting the details of the offense.[33] If he decides that the court experience would be harmful to the child, the social worker may be cross-examined in court instead of the child. The defendant cannot be convicted on the evidence of the probation officer unless supported by other evidence. Naturally, this procedure breaks the fundamental rule of the inadmissibility of hearsay evidence and deprives the accused of the right to cross-examine the accuser. The problem centers around a balance between justice to the child and to the offender. In divorce proceedings, the social consequences to the dependent children involved are taken into consideration and perhaps this concept can be extended to sex offenses against children, although the analogy is far from exact for obvious reasons. Although the welfare and interests of the child–victim and offender seem to clash head–on, neither's legal rights can be abridged. The Israeli law, however, cannot be transplanted here because it would violate basic rights of the accused to face his accuser, the right to cross-examine, the right to exclude hearsay, and the right to equal protection of the law. In addition, Israel has a rigid sex code and a negative attitude towards sexuality, stemming from her religious heritage, which itself may instigate the trauma.

Much of what follows is based on the author's experience in interviewing sex crime victims and is not suggested as rigid format. Modifications in content and style are determined by the situation, the child's personality, and the interviewer's skills. Constant effort must be made, to the extent humanly possible, to prevent overidentifying with the assaulted child.

An appointment should be prearranged with the victim and parents in their home at a nonschool hour. Having the interview in the victim's home has the advantage of providing a familiar relaxed atmosphere, and it places no burden of travel to a strange, perhaps frightening, office or building. The purpose of the interview should be stressed in language compatible to the victim and his parents. My own experience has been that if the child has been informed by his parents that he has nothing to fear (i.e., they endorse the interview) and that he should cooperate with the social worker, then much has already been accomplished. The victim and parents should always be interviewed separately, safely out of hearing and viewing distance of each other. The presence of another person may induce bias, distortions, or omissions in their version of the offense and its consequence. One's manner and choice of language should be natural and appropriate to the child's age, intelligence, and social class. For example, slang or childish terms, if understood, may be appropriate. Reasonable neutrality is basic and the interviewer should avoid prematurely taking sides with or against the child, the child's parents, or the defendant. Some sex victims feel outraged, demoralized, defensive, or outcast. Mutual trust and confidence may be established by sympathetic questions, encouragement, and assurance, aimed at creating a feeling in the victim that you are interested in his current predicament and welfare. Ample recognition and sympathetic acceptance of the victim's opposition to the interview should be made by the interviewer. Some victims will welcome an opportunity to express their views freely, once the purpose of the interview is felt, without the atmosphere, fright, or limitations of the police station or court.

The interview should begin with the consideration of the more objective, tangible, and physical elements of the offense, and after establishing a desirable degree of rapport, the social worker can proceed to emotional considerations of the offense, within the limits of the victim's capacity to tolerate the discussion. The interviewer must be alert to the possibility of disturbing the interviewing relationship by questions that are too abrupt, rapid, or demanding. Conflicts, gaps, or mistruths should be clarified in a moderate, helpful nonemotional manner.

If the case is processed through the courts, the social worker should see as his function the preparation of the victim and his family for the court experience. He may seek to have the case moved up on the docket for early handling, may oppose unreasonable delays or adjournments, may request the case to be heard in chambers or to have the public excluded from the courtroom. He may discuss with the prosecution the advantages in bargaining for sentence or accepting a guilty plea. After the case is disposed of, the social worker's task remains to minimize rehabilitatively the damaging offense and court effects, or if severe trauma results, to refer the family to a psychiatric clinic or family physician.

Conclusion

1. Probably less than 5 percent of all child sex victims are assaulted by violence or penetration.
2. Most of the child sex victims who would be damaged by the court experience indicated personality disturbances before the offense.
3. Most of the sexually assaulted children, in cases where no violence was employed, were engaging in affection–seeking behavior, and do not perceive the event as traumatic.
4. Guilt in sexual victims is fairly absent, but may be engendered by parents, courts, or community *after the fact.*
5. Most sexual assaults do not affect the child's personality development, particularly where neither violence nor court appearance occurred.
6. Where a court appearance is necessary to convict an offender who is dangerous to the community, and such court appearance results in mental or social damage, the child should receive victim compensation from the state or court.
7. With the increase in sex education in elementary schools, victimization may decrease.

8. With rapid value change regarding sexuality, what actually constitutes a sexual offense may change.

9. Communities need sociomedical services for the victims of sexual offenses, and specially trained social workers to handle the child victim's court appearance to prevent or control trauma.

NOTES

[1] *Among the few social work references are:*
Children's Division, American Humane Association, *Sexual Abuse of Children: Implications for Casework* (Denver, Colo., 1967), *Protecting the Child Victim of Sex Crimes* (1966), *Child Victims of Incest* (1968). S. Sutherland and D. Scherl, "Patterns of Response Among Rape Victims," *American Journal of Orthopsychiatry* 40, 1970: 503–11. L. Burton, *Vulnerable Children* (New York: Schocken, 1968), pp. 87–161.

[2] A. Kadushin, *Child Welfare Services* (New York: Macmillan, 1970). H. Gordon, *Casework Services for Children* (Boston: Houghton Mifflin, 1956).

[3] Children's Division, American Humane Association, *Protecting the Child Victim of Sex Crimes* (Denver, Colo., 1966), p. 2.

[4] Children's Division, American Humane Association, *Child Victims of Incest* (Denver, Colo., 1968), p. 5.

[5] Children's Division, American Humane Association, *Sexual Abuse of Children: Implications for Casework* (Denver, Colo., 1967), p. 10.

[6] J. Gagnon, "Female Child Victims of Sex Offenses," *Social Problems* 13 (1965): 191.

[7] Sutherland and Scherl *op. cit.,* p. 503.

[8] D. Jonjack and W. Braden, "A Woman's Story of Jail," in H. Freeman, N. Kurtz, *America's Troubles* (Englewood Cliffs, N.J.: Prentice-Hall, 1969), pp. 436–9.

[9] A. Davis, "Sexual Assaults in the Philadelphia Prison System and Sheriff's Vans," *Trans-Action* 6, no. 2 (1968), 8–18.

[10] A. Biderman, "Surveys of Population Samples of Estimating Crime Incidence," *Annals* 374 (1967): 16–33.

[11] Gagnon, *op. cit.,* p. 176.

[12] L. Radzinowicz, *Sexual Offenses* (New York: Macmillan, 1957), p. 83.

[13] Gebhard, *Sex Offenders: An Analysis of Types,* New York: Bantam Books, p. 747.

[14] J. Weiss *et al.,* "A Study of Girl Sex Victims," *Psychiatric Quarterly* 29 (1955): 1.

[15] B. Glueck, *Research Project for the Study and Treatment of Persons Convicted of Crimes Involving Sexual Aberrations, Final Report,* Albany, N.Y.: Department of Mental Hygiene (1956), p. 296.

[16] Gagnon, *op. cit.,* p. 184.

[17] T. Gibbons and J. Prince, *Child Victims of Sex Offenses* (London, England: Institute for the Study and Treatment of Delinquency, Nell, 1963), p. 11.

[18] Gagnon, *op. cit.,* p. 183. American Humane Association, *Sexual Abuse of Children,* 1967, p. 18.

[19] M. Amir, "Victim Precipitated Forcible Rape," *Journal of Criminal Law, Criminology and Police Science* 58 (1967): 493–502.

[20] Burton, *op. cit.,* p. 155.

[21] Gagnon, *op. cit.,* p. 188.

[22] Gibbons and Prince, *op. cit.,* p. 13.

[23] Sutherland and Scherl, *op. cit.,* p. 509.

[24] C. Hayman *et al.,* "A Public Health Program for Sexually Assaulted Females," *Public Health Reports,* 82 (1967): 499–500. (Included in this volume.)

[25] L. Myers, "Reasonable Mistake of Age: A Needed Defense to Statutory Rape," *Michigan Law Review,* 64 (1966): 105–136. L. Schultz, "The Pre-Sentence Investigation and Victimology," *U.M.K.C. Law Review* 35 (1967): 247–60. J. Rheingold, *The Fear of Being a Woman* (New York: Grune & Stratton, 1964), pp. 100–103.

[26] Gibbons and Prince, *op. cit.,* p. 6.

[27] Gibbons and Prince, *op. cit.,* pp. 14–15.

[28] I. Weiner, "On Incest: A Survey," *Excerpta Criminologica* 4 (1966): 137–55. This article summarizes 74 studies of incest.

[29] Amir, *op. cit.,* p. 498.

[30] Sutherland and Scherl, *op. cit.,* p. 508.

[31] C. Newman, "Pleading Guilty for Consideration: A Study in Bargain Justice," *Journal of Criminal Law, Criminology and Police Science* 46 (1956): 780.

[32] Health, Education and Welfare Conference Proceedings, *The Extension of Legal Services to the Poor* (Washington, D.C.: U.S. Printing Office, 1965), pp. 133–60.

[33] D. Reifen, "The Sex Offender and His Victim," *International Child Welfare Review,* 12 (1958): 109.

SUGGESTED READINGS

Burton, L. *Vulnerable Children.* N.Y.: Schocken, 1968, pp. 87–172.

Gagnon, J. "Female Child Victims of Sex Offenses." *Social Problems* 13 (1965): 176–192.

Gibbons, T. and Prince, J. *Child Victims of Sex Offenses.* London: Nell, 1963.

Halleck, S. "Emotional Effects of Victimization." In Slovenko, R. *Sexual Behavior and the Law.* Springfield, Ill.: Thomas, 1965, pp. 673–686.

McCaghy, C. "Child Molesters: A Study of Their Careers as Deviants." In Clinard, M., Quinney, R. *Criminal Behavior Systems.* Holt, Rinehart and Winston, New York: 1967, pp. 75–88.

Sutherland, S., and Scherl, D. "Patterns of Response Among Rape Victims." *American Journal of Orthopsychiatry* 40 (1970): 503–12.

15

Group Therapy of Incarcerated Sexual Deviants

Irvin D. Yalom, M.D.*

The treatment and rehabilitation of the incarcerated sexual offender is a responsibility presently assigned to psychiatry by the law courts with increasing frequency. A double challenge is presented: the overwhelmingly large number of patients and the recalcitrance of the individual patient. The number of patients requiring treatment calls for more basic research in psychiatric economy; that is, psychiatrists must continue to develop techniques of treatment which provide lasting results in large numbers of patients with the greatest possible conservation of professional manpower. In addition, more accurate methods are needed to predict which patients will respond to a treatment, which, when once undertaken, is lengthy and costly. Dynamic group psychotherapy presents a realistic approach to this problem, for it is a medium that treats large numbers of patients and yet has the potential to effect lasting attitudinal changes.

The committed sexual offender is a notoriously poor candidate for therapy.[1,2] Although periodically appearing articles[3-9] report successful treatment of sexual deviants, these reports by and large deal with voluntary outpatients and leave untouched the far more crucial problem of the incarcerated sexual offender and those specialized techniques germane to his therapy.

The present article stems from a year's work of dynamic group psychotherapy with a group of seriously ill sexual offenders at the Patuxent Institution in Jessup, Maryland. This institution is neither a hospital nor a prison but attempts to combine the best features of each. It has been in operation since 1955 and was provided for in the defective delinquent law passed by the State of Maryland in 1951.[10] In Maryland adult males who show ". . . persistent, aggravated, antisocial or criminal behavior . . . and who are found to have either intellectual deficiency or emotional un-

* The author wishes to express his appreciation to Dr. John C. Whitehorn and Dr. Jerome Frank for their helpful criticisms and suggestions.

balance or both, may, after recommendation by the professional psychiatric staff, be committed to the Patuxent Institution," just as psychotics are committed to a psychiatric hospital. These offenders are given an indeterminate sentence and remain at Patuxent until the psychiatric staff considers them to have undergone sufficient personality change to make a repetition of their criminal activities highly unlikely, at which time they are paroled and meet weekly in group sessions with one of the professional staff. The staff, headed by Doctor Harold M. Boslow, consists of other psychiatrists, psychologists, social workers, and the custodial force.

As a member of the psychiatric staff, the writer formed a group of eight inmates with the only criterion for selection being the existence of a sexual offense. No other criterion was used, and the first eight inmates interviewed were accepted for the group. It is, incidentally, of interest to note that another group of deviants not discussed in this article was formed, using the additional criterion of the existence of neurotic anxiety. To form this second group at least 50 percent of the deviants interviewed were rejected.

The age range of group members was from 21–40. The I.Q. range was 82–135. There were seven white members and one Negro. Only one had been in treatment previously (S. H.). Six of the eight had been in prison previously and the other two had received dishonorable discharges from the military service. There was one alcoholic (S. A.). Only one patient (S. H.) had graduated from high school, although several others were pursuing an education in the institution. The patients' sexual education, incidentally, appeared adequate, there being no lacunae in their knowledge or unusual misconceptions about sexual matters, genital anatomy, reproduction, or childbirth. When the offender was committed to Patuxent, the original temporal sentence was suspended and replaced by an indeterminate sentence.

E. D. is a 28-year-old Negro patient whose original sentence was eighteen months for coercing his six-year-old daughter to perform fellatio on him on many occasions. At present, he has been in Patuxent for two years. This was his first criminal offense, although at the time of arrest he was in possession of obscene pictures and had received a Dishonorable Discharge from the service for repeated bouts of venereal disease. Although he is the only member unwilling to reveal the nature of his offense to the group, he has been an active member, exploring the psychopathology in his marriage and in his interpersonal relationships in the institution. I.Q. is 105. His group behavior is alternately deceptive, sincere, obsequious, and enraged.

D. U. is a 26-year-old, white, married patient who was sentenced to eighteen months for molesting an 18-year-old girl. He has been in the institution for three years. Although he has had no previous convictions, the inmate states that on "at least a hundred occasions" he grabbed the breasts of female passers-by on the street and then fled. He gave himself up to the police because he was afraid of his impulse to rape. Another important problem was his impulsiveness and explosive temper resulting in his discharge from many jobs and a Dishonorable Discharge from the service. Despite his I.Q. of 92, he is able to handle abstract concepts adroitly. He is a spontaneous, active member, who added humor to the group, often good-naturedly baiting the therapist.

G. T. is a forty-year-old, single patient and has spent eleven years behind bars on fifteen convictions for the same offense—making obscene remarks or gestures and phone calls or passing to women obscene notes or photographs. His present offense consists of saying, "I would sure like to eat you," to a woman who happened to be a policewoman off duty. He received a one-year sentence for this and has now been in Patuxent for three years. I.Q. is 105. He is an active group member and takes great pride in recounting his sexual conquests. Preoccupied with his domineering mother, he keeps a scrapbook, which he often brings to meetings, or newspaper clippings about this type of mother.

S. L. is a 20-year-old white, single patient who has spent eight years of his life in penal institutions. His offenses have been arson (age 11), assault and sodomy (age 15), larceny (age 16), and his present offense, assault and sodomy (age 17). He has been in Patuxent for four years, originally obtaining an eight-year sentence. He is the least intelligent member of the group (I.Q. 82), is unable to conceptualize, and was a completely silent member until the last few meetings.

R. T. is twenty-three years old, single, and has spent seven and one-half years of his life locked up for sexual offenses. His most recent offense consisted of forcing at knife point young (8–10 years) boys and girls to submit to sodomy or vaginal intercourse. In addition, he has stabbed a girl and, at the age of ten, set a very costly fire. Originally sentenced for six years, he has been in Patuxent for three years. His I.Q. is 89. He is a pleasant, fairly active member but without curiosity, self-concern, remorse, or motivation.

S. H. is a 36-year-old white, single male who was originally sentenced to three years for coaxing young boys into homosexual practices. He has been in Patuxent for four and one-half years and is the only member who has had previous treatment—twenty months of group treatment at Patuxent and nine months of individual therapy before his imprisonment. He has spent a total of six years in prison for the same type of offense and escaped four other convictions through the influence of his prominent family. He is an intelligent (I.Q. 116), articulate, glib, manipulative patient, often monopolizing the meeting with constant repetitions of historical detail and sterile intellectual unravelings of his problem.

L. I. is a 29-year-old white, married patient who was sentenced to three years for sodomy. He has been in the institution for three years.

He has spent twelve years incarcerated in penal institutions for robbery, burglary and prison escapes. His present charge consisted of performing sodomy and fellatio on two young boys, using both bribery and force. This inmate presented the most difficult problem in the group. He is the "classical" Felix Krull[1] psychopath in his suaveness, his intelligence (I.Q. 135), his handsome physical appearance, his articulateness and his talent for convincing others of his sincerity and the injustices heaped upon him. The group holds him in awe, and frequently the therapist felt trapped and insecure in dealing with him. When he realized that the therapist was not succumbing to his charm and intelligence, his frustration rapidly increased as he reached a near-panic state.

S. A. is a 27-year-old, white, single patient who received a fifteen-year sentence for assault with intent to rape and has been in the Patuxent Institution for three years. As a result of thirteen previous charges (including two charges of rape) and eight convictions for burglary and drunkeness, he has spent a total of seven years in penal institutions. Convinced that his troubles stem only from a desire to drink and from his inability to handle alcohol, he is an exceedingly resistant member. He denies all the rape charges, claims that he was drunk, had a black-out spell, and remembers nothing of the night of the offense except that he "did not rape anyone." During the meetings he was at first negativistic, silent, and spent much of the time looking out of the window. It was only after months that he appeared to be listening to the discussion. His I.Q. is 99. He is pathetically inarticulate, and on a couple of occasions, has had violent outbursts of rage in the group.

The group has met once a week for an hour and a half, and at the time of this writing has met forty times. Although attendance is not compulsory, the members are aware that in some manner their only chance for freedom involves group therapy and there have been no absences.

The ground rules set in the first meeting included the usual brief statements about the desirability of honesty in speech, and the advantages of verbalizing strong feelings. Because of the deeply personal material to be discussed and the destructive irresponsibility of some of the other inmates, the matter of absolute confidentiality was stressed, with discharge from the group cited as the penalty for indiscretion. It is of interest to note that at no time was there any evidence of violation of confidence. The patients were also told that among the things they had in common was that to date their lives have been ruined by their inability to control certain urges, especially those of a sexual nature. They were blindly driven to do things that either gave them no pleasure or a pleasure immeasurably small when compared with the grief of having been imprisoned a considerable portion of their lives.

Philosophy of Treatment

The recalcitrance which one encounters when attempting therapy with
such a group as this, generates respect and gratitude for an often unappre-
ciated ally in treatment—the voluntariness of the patient. Voluntariness
stems from an awareness of personal disequilibrium, from a discomfort
arising from within which leads to a willingness to assume responsibility
for attitudinal changes. Needless to say, it is a prerequisite for successful
therapy, and only after voluntariness has been evoked in the patient does
his treatment begin to resemble the course of therapy of the deviants reported upon in the earlier-cited literature. Soon after the group meetings
began, voluntariness became the all important issue. Treatment begins
when the patient sincerely recognizes that in some way he is responsible
for what has happened to him in life. This concept—disarmingly simple
at first glance—contains the key to the instigation of treatment of the involuntary patient. The query, "What part do you play in this?" repeated
literally dozens of times in the therapy meetings became the entire focus
of the first year's work.

The disclaiming of responsibility was mainly accomplished by the
transfer of blame for the plight onto something outside of themselves—i.e.,
other people, the institution, a "bad record," alcohol, bad luck, an unfair
judicial system, bad company, delinquent neighborhood and poverty. The
lack of a sense of personal responsibility revealed itself in the inmates'
upside-down philosophy—their concept of a universe without causality or
justice. Many long and always animated discussions were centered around
accounts of brutal, evil, immature guards who were invariably the ones
promoted. The rare guard who was a "good guy" always got the bad deal.
The inmates who were the sickest and most dangerous were the ones who
made parole. The ones who went along with the institution were considered
"jailwise" and were left to rot in their cells. "Maybe you have to be bad
to get out of here." This attitude colored a large proportion of the subjects
discussed and was difficult to deal with. Direct disagreement or presentation of the therapist's value system was, of course, always met with unproductive hostility. However, dealing with detailed individual material
directed toward the patient's assumption of responsibility was soon found
to be an effective tactic, as is illustrated by the following examples.

D. U., whose offense was grabbing women's breasts, originally blamed
the bulk of his problem on his wife. She was depicted as frigid, immature,
disloyal, and overly critical of her husband. It was this way right from
the beginning of their marriage, he said. He was offered a lucrative job
in another state but she refused to move that far away from her parents.
Every night when he returned from work, his wife took the car to visit

her parents, who lived thirty miles away. When the situation became intolerable, he felt he got back at his wife by grabbing and hurting strange women on the street, and then by calling her attention to the newspaper accounts of these incidents. This story was received unquestioningly and sympathetically by the group. The therapist asked, "What was it that she wasn't getting from her husband that made her run to her father and mother?" This and similar queries had a staggering impact on the patient. It was a point of view he had never once considered, and shortly thereafter a wealth of pertinent material was divulged. He had married his wife "for spite" immediately after being rejected by another girl, his wife's friend. On the morning after their marriage he accidentally called his wife by her friend's name. He cheated on his wife in a glaringly careless manner so that he was soon discovered. His accounts of how he insulted her, beat her, and was unable to support her made his wife's behavior more understandable. Unable to obtain or hold a job, the patient again transferred responsibility to factors outside of his control. He described in detail how, when hired for a job as a machinist, he had reported early for work spic and span in clean overalls with only a small patch on one knee, but was nevertheless fired on the spot. The group raised a couple of questioning eyebrows at this account. The therapist exclaimed, "Bullshit! There is something we're not hearing," thereby initiating a constructive group discussion. To save face, the patient maintained his position in this instance but discussed how he had sabotaged other jobs. A prospective employer who turned him down "for no good reason" did know he had stolen a jeep from a former employer and did ask the patient if he would steal from him, to which the patient replied, "I don't know." Example followed example of how he lost jobs for insubordination, fighting, and other evidences of his quick uncontrollable temper, until members of the group remarked, "If I were your boss, I'd be damned if I'd put up with that," and other sobering statements to this effect. In this manner, beachheads were established which eventually resulted in the patient's willingness to investigate and even modify his more glaringly self-defeating attitudes.

G. T. is an individual who has spent a considerable portion of his life gesturing or speaking obscenely to females or paying the penalty therefrom. He rationalizes his perversion as a method of seducing women and places the blame for the frantic nature of his sexual quest on his mother, who, he said, had smothered him by restricting all sexual expression. He occasionally brought to the group a scrapbook containing letters which had been published in newspaper advice columns involving domineering mothers. His mother, he said, kept him home until he was 28, prevented him from dating, from talking to girls, and even picked out his clothes and his friends. She even stopped him from masturbating by listening for the squeaking of his bedsprings and then running to his room to protest. The gambit of the therapist was to inquire, "Why didn't you oil your bedsprings?" After the round of laughter had ceased, the therapist solemnly repeated the question, and eventually the group sensed the patient's complex role in this relationship. An ensuing discussion caused the patient to admit that on several occasions his mother, contrary to the original presentation, had tried to force him to leave home, even resorting to calling the police.

E. D.'s offense was the unusual one of influencing his six-year-old daughter to perform fellatio on him. Although he was the only member too ashamed to discuss specifically his offense in the group, he profited considerably in therapy by investigating his relationship with his wife. He described, at first, this relationship as a perfect one and expressed bewilderment and rage at his wife's turning him in to the police and suing for divorce. He admitted afterwards that things between them had not been going well recently but blamed his interfering in-laws. This explanation seemed adequate for the patient and the group. Many of the other members mentioned the hatefulness of their in-laws. The therapist, however, persisted in asking what he had done to warrant so much hate from his in-laws and wife. The patient's many denials were met with the therapist saying kindly but firmly, "There are many things about this that we're not hearing," until he mentioned how he had attempted to seduce his wife's sister. The patient so enjoyed boasting about his sexual exploits that he gave detailed accounts of innumerable infidelities and his glee at his craftiness in deceiving his wife. He mentioned his deserting her six months after marriage because she was pregnant and was "slowing him down" and how he intentionally placed lipstick smeared shirts where she would see them. This information was so extensive that the group and the patient eventually saw how narcissistic and utterly unfeeling he had been towards his wife. One session ended with the patient soberly remarking, "I guess I can't blame her for wanting a divorce." Slowly attitudes of remorse and curiosity about himself were initiated, replacing the stagnating attitudes of blind rage and self-pity.

S. A., a rapist, divorced himself from his actions by employing the offender's favorite scapegoat—alcohol. His closed system was, "I never got into trouble except when I was drunk. To stay out of trouble all I have to do is to stop drinking. I never stopped before because I didn't want to. This long sentence has shook me up and I'm going to stop now. I don't need treatment." One of the group members remarked, "When you go into a bar, do you pick out your liquor by the label on it: robbery, rape, murder, etc.?" This devastatingly lucid comment temporarily punctured the liquor rationalization.

The above discussion highlights the curious paradox that dynamic psychotherapy, so grounded in determinism, begins when the patient accepts the responsibility for his actions. Psychotherapy aims at delivering the patient to a point where he realizes he has a choice—a choice between persevering in certain self-destructive maladaptive habits or engaging in more active helm-taking of the remainder of his life. The realization that a choice exists is a particularly important and difficult aspect of treatment in the present situation, for one can hardly conceive of a more choiceless group of individuals. Although they are obviously limited in choice by reason of their incarceration, they are even more limited by internal factors.

Hopefully, through recognition of their drivenness and discovery of some of the responsible unconscious factors, they would in a sense rebel and achieve a greater measure of freedom. With temptation removed it was difficult for the therapist to assess freedom from the perverse sexual drive except obliquely, for example, from reports of changes in the fantasy life. However, it was possible to work with the concept of greater freedom of choice in one's responses to interpersonal situations and to observe improvements in relationships to the custodial officers and fellow inmates. Since almost every member "graduated" to another tier during the course of therapy, there was an especially propitious opportunity to test out new choices of behavior in new social situations.

As therapy progressed, certain important differences became evident between the therapist's role in this setting and his role in the usual outpatient group. He becomes far more important as he is the patient's only (and sometimes their first) close human contact with nondelinquent society. At the same time, however, great patience was required of the therapist to endure the uncertainty of his efforts. The work was slow, difficult, and frustrating. Meetings were often messy and unrewarding. Only rarely did one have the satisfaction of feeling that a therapy session had been skillfully conducted, and not infrequently at the completion of a meeting the therapist felt that he had wasted his time. It is difficult to maintain one's therapeutic vantage point in the face of an onslaught from a group of angry, resentful, uncooperative, manipulating, deceitful, ridiculing, ungrateful, solipsistic individuals. Therapy can occur only when the therapist can empathize sufficiently to appreciate the assumptive world of the patient. This, of course, is a vital step in any successful therapy but perhaps more difficult to accomplish with this type of patient because of the alien and socially unacceptable territories involved.

Their assumptive world is a more understandable one when one recalls that by and large the world has been a brutal and rejecting one for them. For most, their home environment during their formative years was chaotic. Parents were of the lower socioeconomic class, often divorced or separated, usually promiscuous, alcoholic, rejecting, and brutal. All seemed sufficiently disturbed as to be incapable of satisfying their children's need for attention and affection. For most, this period was followed by years in the Training School where they learned the facts of life of the social structure. In the Training School people are divided into two groups. You are either a "dope" or a 'wise guy." The "dopes" (or "chumps") take the blame and punishment for infractions committed by the "wise guys." They are the "girls" in the forced sexual play and the butt of all the humiliating and often physically punishing horseplay in the "cottage." The "wise guys" are the opposite—the bullies, the sodomists—who from time to time must without provocation beat up a "dope" if they wish to maintain their social status. The therapist is tempted to exclaim, and perhaps with some justification, "But what are you and what do you do to make people treat you so badly?" Historically though, their universe *has* been an unfair one and one eventually hears from the patients, "But I was a child then. What could a child have been or done?" They *have* been unlucky. Friends *have* committed the same offenses and walk the streets freely. There *are* unfair and brutal guards. There *are* unjust judges who are notoriously unpredictable in the severity of the sentences administered.

Their present life situation is an agonizingly uncertain one. They must stay in prison until a psychiatrist, whom they neither understand, respect, or trust, says they are well enough to be released. Even their faith in the penal code has been shaken for, as was seen in the clinical material, most have been incarcerated longer than their original sentences called for. Was the institution a hospital or a prison, they asked. Since the institution was only five years old, most felt that they were guinea pigs—the trial group. Newspapers constantly carried accounts of conflicting opinions as to the constitutionality of the indeterminate sentence.

In the midst of this maelstrom of uncertainty they are ordered to submit to therapy. The therapist is frequently the same individual who was responsible for their commitment to the institution and often, the inmates claim, dishonestly, by quoting them out of context, distorting their statements, and overemphasizing minor remarks which they felt were made confidentially to a physician. Even these charges may not be completely unfounded since at times it is difficult to communicate to a lay jury impressions gained from intuitive sources which are products of long years of experience. Sometimes one *does* emphasize minor, but more accessible and spectacular, issues to the lay audience.

With this view of the patients' assumptive world in mind, the therapist can function with greater understanding and sincerity. With little inner discomfort, no concept of therapy, the prospect of life imprisonment facing them unless they successfully negotiate this vague business of psycho-therapy, and the life attitudes described above, how else could one expect these individuals to react, except by attempting (with their learned social tools) to convince the therapist of their releaseability?

What can be done? If an assumptive world which is the residue of one's life experiences is to be altered, we must supply new, corrective life experiences. These may be supplied in part by their transactions with the therapist whose task is to present himself to the patients as an individual with a different value system but with whom they may identify. The therapist must be honest, sincere, consistent, and yet close enough to them so that identification may occur. One cannot tell patients this: one must show them over a long period of time. Desiring especially to avoid being viewed as aloof, the therapist allowed greater intimacy with the patients than he customarily does in therapy. Trying to close the cultural gap, the therapist adopted the language of the patients in the liberal use of profanity and prison idioms.

The therapist was often baited by the group and participated good naturedly in this play. For example, a patient began a meeting with, "If you're a psychiatrist, suppose you tell me why I like the color blue while so-and-so likes red." Rather than to interpret this as the patient's trying to test or embarrass the therapist, or, God forbid, ask for associations to blue, the therapist usually replied, "I'm a psychiatrist, not a God-damned fortune teller" or "What the hell's eating you today?" Handled in this manner, the bantering was short-lived as the therapist continued to pick up every lead available and doggedly pursue the serious business of therapy.

When serious questions were posed—for example, about the connection between sex and arson, or whether dreams meant anything, the therapist always answered immediately, completely, and with meaningful illustrations for the patients. This practice seemed to increase the group's respect for the therapist, improved rapport, and bolstered their ego as the therapist showed respect for their intellectual curiosity.

Another extremely important factor in treatment was the therapist's position in relation to the administration.[12,13] At the first meeting the group was told that the therapist would at no time communicate any information about the group or any member of the group to the parole board, to the board of review responsible for their institutional privileges, or to the court, and that in no way would he be involved administratively in their release or detention. This is a difficult idea to accept and to fulfill for both inmates and therapist, but in my mind it is perhaps an indispensable condition for treatment. If the inmates know that they must convince the therapist that they are well before they are released, they will attempt to do just that. They will conceal their psychopathology, seal over and control their stronger affects, withhold personal data, pay lip service to theorizing, and, in short, intensively involve themselves in antitherapy.

This is an especially difficult position to maintain when the institution is so professionally understaffed that the parole board receives a shallow and incomplete picture of each inmate's problem and potentialities or when the therapist develops strong feelings that a certain inmate is being unjustly or unwisely incarcerated or released.

It is also important to point out that the concept of the therapist's separateness from the administration was an unfamiliar one to the inmates, since all other groups in the institution are conducted by individuals who are at the same time therapists and administrators. The response of the group members to this position varied; the majority approved but doubted my integrity. In the assumptive world they had constructed they had long since grown to distrust and fear authority figures. Even after months of therapy, statements like the following occurred. "Recently I said that as long as there are cameras and nude women I guess I'll be taking pictures of them and I've been worrying about whether this was the wrong thing to say." This reveals a persisting conviction that the therapist, like the parole board, must be manipulated. The one member who objected to the policy (the objections becoming increasingly vehement as time went by) was L. I. He wished to know at first what *would* my report be if I had to make one; then he deplored the fact that the therapist, the one person who really knew him, would not testify in court. Later, he accused the therapist of shirking his duty and finally announced that he planned to subpoena him to court. This patient revealed much of himself in these maneuvers—his difficulty in relating to another except in such a way as to use him, his disregard for the group rules, his inner feelings of omnipotence in that, if he could force the therapist to testify, the latter would surely advocate release, since he was certain that no one could withstand the onslaught of his charm and intelligence. All of these interpretations were made and discussed in the group.

Group Phenomena

Despite their solipsistic world view and unelaborated social machinery, the members gradually developed a sense of groupness. Chauvinistic comments that this was the institution's "best group" were common. Also heard was, "We may not do much therapy, but we do have a good time." The patients had their own coffee meetings for thirty to forty minutes after the therapy sessions. The therapist's apprehension that the group might be labeled and criticized by other inmates as a "sex group" was never realized.

Attempts to discuss and utilize aspects of the patients' group behavior were ineffectual for the first few months of therapy, which may have been due to an effort on the part of the patients not to appear critical of each other in order to impress the therapist with their good behavior and the extent of their inner controls. The therapist attempted to point out the obvious bravado of certain patients while discussing sexual exploits but the group did not follow up on this. One member of the group, S. H., tended to monopolize the meetings with intellectualizations and repetitious obsequious attempts to please the therapist. No direct discussion of this by the group could be elicited, though they showed their annoyance in oblique ways, for example, by disagreeing with the patient regardless of his stand on any issue; and on one occasion, another group member, S. A., exploded and threatened to hit him. When questioned about this, however, S. A. could carry it no further than, "If you don't like a guy you don't like him." After several months, the therapist noticed another member making imaginary marks on the wall while S. H. was talking. When pinned down on these gestures, the patient reluctantly admitted that he was "jotting down all the points" S. H. had scored with the therapist that day, calling him a phony and deploring the fact that he spent so much time "sucking in." The therapist attempted to change this into a constructive discussion of S. H.'s monopolistic tendencies with the simple approach, "Well, let's see how we can help S. H. with this problem." This episode stimulated further candid discussions of group behavior, which, though often stormy, increased the solidarity of the group.

Unlike the former problem, R. T.'s shyness and reticence to talk became a topic of discussion, opening the important area of his lifelong isolation, his lack of friends, and especially his total inability to approach a female, which may have been one of the factors driving him to satisfy himself sexually in illegal ways.

The most difficult problem which was not resolved was the behavior of L. I., who most closely resembles the popular notion of the psychopath. He is so bright and articulate (his institutional job was that of teaching school) that the rest of the group held him in awe. He spent the first few months helpfully suggesting to the group topics for discussion, making useful interpretations, and occasionally reciting his well-rehearsed formulation of his personal psychodynamics. As time went by he realized that the therapist was serious about his stand on nonintervention in parole proceedings, he grew more concerned, became angry, and demanded continuously that the therapist reveal his impression of the inmate. Upon refusal of these requests, he grew panicky, cried and screamed on several occasions, and became insulting and sarcastic to the therapist. On one occasion he said, "When I get out of here, I'm going to meet you on the street, get you against a wall and make you tell me what you think of me." The therapist's attempts to clarify and interpret his behavior—his use of people, his inability to relate except narcissistically, his anger because the therapist had not been seduced by his charms, and his over-dependence on external props for his self-evaluation were initially of little value. Months later, however, he remembered these interpretations almost verbatim and cited them as the most important thing for him in the year's work.

An especially difficult problem to handle was the patients' tendency to spend long periods of time discussing institutional affairs, injustices or gripes. This was particularly marked during meetings which followed board of review sessions in which one or more members were refused parole or a requested privilege. At these times, tedious, disgruntled, unproductive harangues continued for thirty to forty minutes. No successful method of making better use of this time was discovered. When the therapist directly commented on the time being wasted, there always ensued a sullen, unproductive period. Although it was occasionally possible to pick up leads and direct the discussion to more useful channels, it seems as though one generally has to live through these discussions, implying disapproval by nonparticipation, and allow the group to learn that nothing useful comes from them. Eventually, after several months, these discussions became less frequent and were cut off promptly by the group members themselves. One measure of the success of the techniques described above was the complete absence of utterly unrelated material, i.e., baseball, television programs, which so often appears in nonvoluntary therapeutic groups.

Common Psychodynamic Themes

In the beginning the group seemed to be a band of homogeneous individuals, homogeneous in the general nature of their offenses, in their lower socioeconomic class, in the frequency of a broken or chaotic home during their formative years, and in an antisocial sense of values assimilated during their many years in jail. As the work progressed, though, one became impressed with the enormous diversity in the individual dynamics and with the inability of the psychiatric terminology to communicate this diversity.

An obvious theme and one with which the group worked well was that the sexual drive and offense was actually a substitute for other affects. The expression of rage through sex was an important phenomenon and one which was found operating in every group member. The group responded with great interest when the therapist on several occasions phrased his comments in such a way as to suggest that he and the group together were engaged in an investigative pursuit of the relationship between anger and sex. Abundant data were available for this pursuit. A particularly effective verbal example cited was the most common expression of anger in the institution, the words "fuck you," an expression used several times in the group during some explosive temper outbursts. Many inmates alternate sexual offenses and aggressive, destructive crimes or find one replaced by the other.[14] Three of the group members had set extensive fires and two had been vandalists. Most of the group were unaware of the aggressive components of their sexual compulsion and the uncovering of this in the therapy work was a useful revelation.

G. T. (the obscene gesturist and note-passer) had always looked upon his perversion as "a bit of devilment" and his way of seducing girls. "At least it was direct. You told them what you wanted right off and some women appreciate that." This was a face-saving rationalization in two ways. First, it allowed him to preserve his illusion of being the hyperpotent male whose only flaw was having too much of a good thing—"sex juice." Second, this rationalization allowed him to continue his illusion of self-determination, concealing from himself the fact that he, in reality, was being driven by factors outside of his awareness. This illusion was difficult to deal with, for it served the vital function of warding off the unpleasant, even intolerable, effect accompanying the recognition of the aimlessness and uncertainty of his existence. As is often the case in psychiatrically unsophisticated patients, it was with much bravado and extensive detail that he recounted his erotic adventures. It soon became clear that his offenses were in no way preludes to a sexual relationship. His obscene phone calls and many of his notes were anonymous. He usually set up a situation where the female could not possibly respond to his message (i.e., leaving a note on a restaurant table after finishing a meal), and later came the admission by the patient that on the rare occasions when the recipient of his message did respond favorably, he fled the scene. Eventually the entire group understood that the notes and gestures were angry ones thoroughly insulting and contemptuous of women. The patient knew that his actions were inextricably tied up with his mother and that somehow he was "striking out at her." Though the verbalized grievance, as mentioned earlier, centered about his mother's destructive possessiveness, there was also evidence to suggest that he was reacting to mutual incestual feelings and to the warmth and mothering he did not get. However, the patient was not able to deal with this material in the first year of treatment.

D. U. went out to seize women's breasts after arguments with his wife. He was aware that the act provided little sexual satisfaction; no orgasm was involved, only occasionally was the deed accompanied by an erection, and the compulsion was not influenced by prior intercourse or masturbation. Wanting to hurt his victims, he never caressed but grabbed, while studying their faces for pained expressions. Much of this rage was traced back to a severely rejecting mother and a brutally punishing father, from whom he tried unsuccessfully to escape through an unwise marriage.

Despite his initial description of a perfect marriage, E. D.'s relationship to his wife was obviously a sadomasochistic one, each dedicating himself to the destruction of the other. The patient, as mentioned above, was flagrantly unfaithful, taking great pleasure in deceiving his wife. He attempted to seduce her sister and then "desecrated the thing closest to her heart"—their daughter. His wife retaliated by turning him over to the police in an angry moment some weeks after he confessed to her. Though there seemed to be abundant evidence that under his insatiable search for women lay much doubting of his masculine potential, the patient either rejected or paid mere lip service to this interpretation. Curiously enough, all other members denied feelings of masculine inadequacy, while at the same time all openly admitted homosexual interests, which were almost universal in the institution and therefore socially accepted.

The sexual offense committed as an angry response to a rejection was not uncommon. R. T. was told by his mother that his bags would be packed and outside the front door if he came home without a job. Instead of job-hunting he attemped to rape an eight-year-old girl. S. H. was informed by his "steady" of several years that she was engaged to another and he responded by going out for the first time to cruise for young boys. L. I. discovered what he thought was his wife's unfaithfulness and that evening forced a young boy to submit to a sodomy.

Results

Accurate assessment of any form of psychotherapy is notoriously unreliable and at present is a major and active area of research. Assessing the results of therapy with the group of patients discussed in this article is manyfold more hazardous. These patients are physically separated from the objects of their sexual compulsions and because of their fear of prolonged incarceration are unable to reveal honestly their present mental state. These deficits deprive us of even the usual points of departure for our educated guesses. Though many have been proposed, there are no psychological tests which allow us to predict accurately the offender's behavior when he is again "on the streets." However, there is much to be learned by noting clinical changes occurring in these patients during the course of a year's therapy.

The vignettes at the beginning of this article are printed in the order of the individual patient's response to treatment. The first two patients, E. D. (who had coerced his daughter to perform fellatio upon him) and D. U. (who impulsively grabbed strange women's breasts) were the ones who profited most from treatment. Both had gained considerable insight into the factors responsible for the perverse impulse, had taken steps to remedy these factors (for example, reconciliation and open discussion with their wives) and had worked with understanding on other self-defeating attitudes. In my opinion, both had improved to the point where they were good parole risks provided they continued treatment on an out-patient basis.

G. T. (the obscene gesturist and note passer) was the oldest and, it was thought initially, the patient whose psychopathology was most firmly fixed. During the course of therapy there were many evidences of changing attitudes. After months of bedrock resistance he arrived at the genuine realization that his gestures and notes were not sexual foreplay, as it were, but blind expressions of anger towards women. Hopefully, the driving forces behind his chief symptom have been sufficiently undermined to allow him to stay out of prison. Deeper changes in his way of life were not effected and he will continue to be a lonely, sexually preoccupied transient.

Because of his low intelligence and his reluctance to articulate, S. L. seemed a doubtful candidate for therapy.[15,16] During an individual interview at the end of the year he gave evidence, however, that he had, despite his silence, been an attentive and interested member. This corroborates the experience of others that a silent group member may still benefit from treatment.[17] He remarked then that he had been reluctant to speak because of his shame for his offense (forced sodomy with young boys) and because of shame for his ignorance (during the meetings he frequently heard words he did not know and concepts he could not grasp). Unrealistic but nonetheless encouraging was the extent of his identification with the therapist. He had carefully charted the next fifteen years of his life, planning to become first a hospital orderly, then a practical nurse, a registered nurse, a college graduate, and finally, when enough funds had been saved, a medical student and eventually a physician.

R. T. was little influenced by the year's work except that a sense of curiosity and self-concern were generated, thus motivating him for future treatment. He rarely discussed his offense (forcibly sodomizing children) but was able to discuss the important areas of his aloneness, his shyness, his need for external props to maintain his self esteem, and his inability sexually to approach females who are his contemporaries.

S. H. (also a pedophile) was at times a monopolizer, verbalizing copious but unproductive accounts of his childhood, his Oedipus conflicts, his sense of rejection. His unctuous behavior generated much hostility against himself both in and out of the group. His defenses receded and more honest introspection occurred after these aspects of his interpersonal behavior were discussed. Perhaps through this route he may, in the future, establish a close enough relationship with a therapist to function as an outpatient. Previous outpatient psychotherapy had failed primarily because of his inability to trust and confide in his therapist.

L. I. (who had sexually assaulted two children) is so adroitly manipulative that he is extremely difficult to evaluate. Interpretations of his behavior during the meetings were important to him and if pursued over a long course of therapy might be efficacious in modifying some of his most flagrantly antisocial attitudes. Undoubtedly, though, he will be successful in obtaining his release long before he is ready.

S. A., a rapist and, incidentally, the only severe alcoholic in the group, was a complete therapeutic failure. Unlike the other group members, he maintains that he is innocent of the charge against him and persistently looked upon the group proceedings as nonsense. He was so inarticulate (stammering and possessing an infantile vocabulary) that his silence and resistance may have been a face-saving device. Occasional encouraging signs, such as attentive listening or the sudden recall that his first criminal offense (vandalism and burglary) occurred immediately after discovering his mother in bed with a neighbor, were all short-lived.

It is significant, though of course not statistically so, that in a four-month period immediately preceding treatment the group members received a total of five disciplinary tickets, whereas during the same four-month period following eight months' treatment there was only one infraction, and that a minor one (possession of a photograph of a nude woman). Six of the eight members received a tier promotion during the year. (There are four tier levels at the institution.) This represents a greater number than one would ordinarily expect without treatment. The two members not promoted were S. A. (at the bottom of the list) and S. L., whose silence and degree of withdrawal (as pointed out above) erroneously cause him to appear recalcitrant. Of the two patients at the top of the list, one, D. S., is now being considered for parole, and the other, E. D., has been given the privilege of an outside job. All of these promotions have occurred without the therapist's intervention.

Summary

Experiences with group therapy of incarcerated sexual offenders at the Patuxent Institute in Jessup, Maryland have been presented. The patients, whose offenses included rape, sexual assault of minors, obscene note-passing and incest, were all chronically ill—manifesting their symptomatology for years and usually having served previous prison sentences for the same type of offense.

The results of therapy with a group of patients so often considered untreatable were encouraging. A philosophy of treatment and therapeutic tactics were described. The initial and most crucial step in therapy was to generate in the patients a sense of voluntariness—a sense that they, rather than a host of extraneous influencing, were in some way personally responsible for the misery they were encountering in their lives.

For the therapist to maintain his professional equilibrium he must empathize with and constantly be cognizant of the assumptive world of his patient—a world constructed in a logical manner from deprived and often brutal life experiences. To alter the assumptive world one must supply corrective life experience with one's own person. A sense of unusual intimacy, down-to-earthness, and mutual respect tend to generate a therapeutic identification and trust.

A detailed investigation and analysis of the specific offense was usually a blind alley in therapy. Progress was made instead through discussion of relevant aspects of their physical and psychological worlds. Emphasis was placed upon their social withdrawal, their inability to approach their peers for normal sexual relationsips, and their relationships to their wives and parents.

It is important for the therapist to be only a therapist and separate himself completely from administrative bodies which have the responsibility for privileges and parole.

Discussion of the group behavior of the individual patients rarely occurred for the first several months. However, when the tension had lowered to the point where this material was utilized it was of great importance in demonstrating to the patients their impact on other people. In this way they grew aware of the role of their behavior in the formation of their life environment, which hitherto had been deemed so malevolently unalterable.

NOTES

[1] W. Bromberg, *Crime and the Mind* (Philadelphia: Lippincott, 1947).

[2] B. Cruvant, M. Meltzen, and F. Tartaglino, "An institutional program for committed sexual deviants," *American Journal of Psychiatry* 107 (1950): 190–4.

[3] J. H. Conn, "Brief psychotherapy of the sex offender," *Journal of Clinical Psychotherapy* 10 (1949): 347–72.

[4] A. Ellis, "A homosexual treated with rational psychotherapy," *Journal of Clinical Psychology* 15 (1959): 338–44.

[5] A. Ellis, "The effectiveness of psychotherapy with individuals who have severe homosexual problems," *Journal of Consulting Psychology* 20 (1956): 191–5.

[6] J. S. Poe, "The successful treatment of a forty year old passive homosexual," *Psychoanalytic Review* 39 (1952): 23–33.

[7] L. H. Rubenstein, "Psychotherapeutic aspects of male homosexuality," *British Journal of Medical Psychology* 31 (1958): 14–18.

⁸ D. Silverman, "The treatment of exhibitionism." *Bulletin of the Menninger Clinic* 5 (1941): 85–93.

⁹ I. Stevenson and J. Wolpe, "Recovery from sexual deviations through overcoming nonsexual neurotic responses," *American Journal of Psychiatry* 116 (1960): 737–42.

¹⁰ Article 31 B, Annotated Code of Maryland.

¹¹ Thomas Mann, *The Confessions of Felix Krull* (New York: Knopf, 1955).

¹² R. Corsini, "Psychodramatic treatment of a pedophile," *Group Psychotherapy* 4 (1951): 166–71.

¹³ M. H. Hollender, "The psychiatrist and the release of patient information," *American Journal of Psychiatry* 116 (1960): 828–33.

¹⁴ I. D. Yalom, "Voyeurism, aggression and forbiddenness," *A.M.A. Archives of General Psychiatry* 3 (1960): 305–19.

¹⁵ R. M. Patterson, "Psychiatric treatment of institutionalized delinquent girls," *Diseases of the Nervous System* 11 (1950), 227–32.

¹⁶ K. Yorge and U. O'Connor, "Measurable effects of group psychotherapy with defective delinquents," *Journal of Mental Science* 100 (1954): 944–52.

¹⁷ J. Frank, personal communication.

SUGGESTED READINGS

Hartman, V. "Notes on Group Psychotherapy with Pedophiles." *Canadian Psychiatric Association Journal* 10 (1965): 283–86.

Kadis, A., and Wenick, C. *Group Psychotherapy Today*. New York: Karger, 1965.

Peters, J., et al. "Group Psychotherapy of the Sex Offender," *Federal Probation* 32 (1968): 41–5.

Resnik, H., and Peters, J. "Out-Patient Group Psychotherapy with Convicted Pedophiles." *International Journal of Group Psychology* 17 (1967): 151–8.

16

A Report on a Nude Marathon: The Effect of Physical Nudity upon the Practice of Interaction in the Marathon Group

Paul Bindrim

Although this paper is factual, being based upon tape recordings of the entire session, it must also be regarded as highly tentative. It concerns only one experience with a nude group which may prove atypical, and has been prepared by an author whose past experience as a therapist does not qualify him as an expert on nudity or sexology and to whom these fields represent a minor area among his wider interests.

It hardly need be said that researching the effect of nudity on psychotherapy is highly controversial and is not suited to all therapists in all communities and in all professional settings, nor to all participants, but should be approached in a cautious and sensitive manner by interested individuals, particularly during this early phase when knowledge is sparse, prejudice is strong, and acceptability highly dependent upon the circumstances and the persons involved.

In the group to be described here, therapeutic interaction occurred with the same frequency as would be expected in a clothed marathon. In this regard, extensive discussion has been omitted in the interest of conveying an overall picture of the new vector of nudity.

Theoretical Constructs Leading to the Experiment

The basic concept of the marathon is a minimum period of twenty-four hours of intimate, intensive, authentic human interaction, uninterrupted by subgrouping, structured activities, and the routines of eating and sleeping.[1,2] It is hoped that this round-the-clock pressure will lead the participants to take off their social masks, stop playing games, and start interacting authentically and transparently. Theoretically, the group moves from mistrust to trust, and from polite acceptance to honest critique, from peeping-Tomism to participation, from dependency on the group leader to autonomy, and from autocracy to democracy. During this trial by intimacy, it is anticipated that layer-by-layer, roles, masks, and pretenses will peel away, leaving a more authentic revelation of oneself and of others. Many innovations have been introduced around this basic format, such as lengthening the period of interaction, allowing periods for sleep, and the use of structured activities such as video playback, movement, and sensory awareness techniques.

Over a period of seven years the author noted that there was a growing tendency to disrobe as emotional intimacy and transparency developed between the group members. On a few occasions, when a pool or hot baths were available, the participants spontaneously engaged in nude swimming after the marathon had ended. These spontaneous excursions into nudity seem to increase interpersonal transparency, remove inhibitions in the area of physical contact, decrease the sense of personal isolation and estrangement, and culminate in a feeling of freedom and belongingness. It seemed quite possible that the inviolable sense of privacy that man maintains by wrapping himself in a tower of clothes or retreating to the castle of his home might not only serve to safeguard his individuality, but also perhaps, in effect, be a self-imposed padded cell through which he can limit his contact when he basically distrusts and fears interaction with other persons. It seemed that disrobing might constitute a symbolic attempt to open this cell of isolated psychological privacy to healthy group interaction and intimacy. If a participant disrobed physically he might, by this gesture, also gain the freedom to disrobe emotionally. If this were true, it might be desirable first to disrobe and then interact, thus shortening the process and intensifying the beneficial results. At this point, the author read Maslow's *Eupsychian Management,* in which he stated: "After all, these training groups are a kind of psychological nudism under careful direction. I wonder, as a matter of fact, what would happen as an experiment, if these T-groups remained exactly as they are but only added a physical nudism. People would go away from there an awful lot freer, a lot more spontaneous, less guarded, less defensive; not only about the shape of their behinds, or whether their bellies are hanging or not, but freer and more innocent about their minds, as well. If I can learn not to be conscious about the fact that my ass is hanging or that my belly sticks out too much, if I can throw off this fear, this defense, maybe this act of freedom will enable me thereby to throw off a lot of other defenses—maybe the defense of looking ignorant, or uncontrolled, or something like that."[3]

While this paper is tentative, and subject to the fallacies of clinical judgment, it reports what to the author's knowledge is the first attempt to explore the value of nudity as a facilitator of human interaction in a therapeutic group. I hope it may serve as a guide to others who are willing to risk the negative social and professional pressures that are inherent in conducting an experiment of this type.

It is a common experience in interacting groups that persons hesitate to touch each other. If full body contact of disrobed individuals were to be encouraged, this might well result in a deeper sense of intimacy. If, at this stage, sexual expression was not permitted, this sensory intimacy of skin contact might then be expected to deepen into more meaningful emotional intimacy. This emotional level of intimacy and transparency might then, in some instances, further develop into a sense of intensified personal identity and core unity with all life, which has been described as peak experience, self-transcendence, or the basic spiritual experience of at-one-ment. In structuring the marathon, it was hoped that each individual could be helped to move a little bit further along this chain of increasing authenticity and interrelatedness.

Composition of the Group, Location, and Living Arrangements

Announcements of the proposed nude marathon were sent to psychologists, marriage counselors, participants in group and individual therapy, and persons who had attended previous marathons. Dr. William E. Hartman,[4] professor of sociology at California State College, acted as cotherapist with the author. Dr. Hartman was assisted by Marilyn Fithian, A.B., a college instructor of folklore and marriage classes. The author was assisted by Sara McClure, B.S., a dance therapist. Twenty participants registered for the marathon and were initially screened by telephone interviews. A small reduction in fee was extended to married and unmarried couples, in an attempt to keep an even balance of sexes. This was felt to be important, since it was anticipated that the initial effect of nudity would be expressed in terms of sexual curiosity, which made it desirable that there be an equal number of men and women in attendance. Since more males than females registered, a few single women were offered reduced rates as an inducement for them to attend the marathon, thus maintaining the balance of the sexes—namely ten males and ten females. Minors were not admitted.

The occupations of the persons attending included three engineers, two schoolteachers, four clinical psychologists, a pharmacist, two magazine editors, two social workers, an artist, and a number of housewives. Two of the participants were referred by clinical psychologists who felt that their problems were of a sexual nature and that their symptoms would be helped by the experience of social nudity. A few of the participants had prior experience with social nudity at nudist camps, but the majority either had had no prior experience, or their previous experiences had been limited to one or two occasions when they experienced nudity with a small group of their own selection. Two of the participants were a married couple; others were married but came without their mates; and the majority were single.

The location was Deer Park Nudist Camp near Escondido, California. Deer Park occupies an entire valley between two mountain ranges, is approximately four hundred acres in size, affords privacy, a beautiful natural setting, with abundant fruit trees and wildlife, and is equipped in a fashion comparable to a high-class resort hotel. It had just closed its operation to the general public so that the marathon group had complete privacy on the grounds. Its facilities included a large swimming pool, surrounded by cabanas, and a Jacuzzi bath, which was kept at a temperature of 102 degrees, and was large enough to accommodate the entire group. The group brought sleeping bags and air mattresses and slept in the open around the pool and in the surrounding cabanas. Meetings were held indoors and outdoors, depending on the weather. Climatic conditions were at times unfavorable, occasionally requiring the wearing of clothing for comfort. Meals were served cafeteria style while the group remained in session.

Ground Rules and Scheduled Activities

The participants agreed to conform to the following ground rules:

1. Remain with the group for the entire session and avoid subgrouping;
2. Participate in all scheduled activities;
3. Remain in the presence of persons who would be nude, and feel free to remove their own clothing or to continue to wear their clothing as they wished;
4. Be known by their first name only, if this was their desire;
5. Refrain from any use of alcoholic beverages and drugs throughout the session;
6. Refrain from photography or overt sexual expression which might prove offensive to other participants in the group. Overt sexual expression was defined as any activity which would be socially inappropriate in a similar group wearing clothing. For example, hugging and kissing would be permissible, but intercourse or the fondling of genitals would not be considered appropriate behavior in a group setting.

The leaders reserved the right to refund tuition to any individual if they felt that the experience would be detrimental to his best interest or to that of the group.

It was suggested that the participants bring with them the things that they enjoyed smelling the most, touching the most, tasting the most, looking at the most, and hearing the most, for use as stimuli in a sensory saturation experience designed to induce a peak state of experiencing, which is perhaps best described as a mild "turn-on."

The group was in continuous session from 9 p.m. Friday evening until 3 p.m. Sunday afternoon, with six hours out on Friday evening and six hours out on Saturday evening for sleeping.

The group met on Friday evening with all members clothed. They were asked to share with the group the anxieties, anticipations, and fantasies that they were experiencing as they contemplated nudity. They were again reassured that they did not have to remove their clothing and that our primary interest was the exploration of their emotional attitudes toward clothing and nudity. The interaction took a little over an hour; the group was then informed that the session would move to the Jacuzzi bath and that they could bathe in the nude or wear bathing suits as they chose. They were also informed that following the session in the Jacuzzi bath, there would be an experience with colored lights in the main meeting-room. This would consist of colored patterns being projected on their bodies from a 35 mm slide projector. Those who wished to participate actively could stand in front of the lights and observe the esthetically beautiful patterns and colors in a full-length mirror, while those who preferred to observe could sit quietly in the darkened room.

Following the Jacuzzi bath and the lights, the group retired for the night and was awakened the following morning with the playing of a Bach Brandenburg Concerto. They then had orange juice and coffee, and took a one-hour walk around the grounds to enjoy the natural setting. Breakfast followed and the session continued out-of-doors. After lunch, another encounter was held in the Jacuzzi bath, which was followed by approximately one hour of movement and sensory awareness work, led by Sara McClure. As the weather was becoming colder, the session moved indoors for the evening. There was another brief period in the Jacuzzi bath prior to retiring.

The Sunday morning session included one hour which was devoted to meditation, facilitated by sensory saturation with peak stimuli. In this procedure, the participants chose partners of the opposite sex by gazing into each other's eyes for a few moments and then selecting the person with whom eye contact was the most comfortable and relaxing. They were then seated close to and facing the person of their choice. They were then asked to close their eyes and to keep them closed until asked to open them, following which, they were given suggestions conducive to relaxation. Each participant was asked simultaneously to taste, touch, and smell the items which he enjoyed the most and had selected for the experiment (Bindrim,

1966). For example, one participant simultaneously touched velvet, ate chocolate, and smelled a rose. These items were, of course, different for each participant. During this period, the Prelude to *Tristan and Isolde,* by Wagner, was played on a record-player. This process of sensory saturation led to a mild drugless "turn-on" or peak state of experiencing. In this state, the participants were asked to re-experience in fantasy whatever event in their lives they considered to be the best moment that they had ever lived; a time when they flowed freely in the joy of living and felt close to the core of their being and at one with life. When they each had completed this fantasy recall of a peak experience and were "turned on" within the limits of their capabilities, they were asked to touch the fingertips of both hands with their partners and to quietly gaze into each other's eyes without movement or distraction, allowing themselves to open to each other and experience a growing sense of intimacy and at-one-ment. During this time, the Love Death from *Tristan and Isolde* was played. After twenty minutes of this eye-centered meditation, they were asked to place their chairs in a circle and share their experiences.

A brief period of evaluation preceded the closing of the marathon at 3 p.m.

The Emerging Dynamics of Adaptation to Nudity as Expressed by the Participants

In less than one hour and a half from the beginning of the marathon on Friday evening all participants were bathing nude in the Jacuzzi pool. Although two participants had been referred to the marathon specifically because of anxieties relating to sexuality and nudity, it may be assumed that most of the participants who were willing to attend the marathon were, by and large, ready for the experience. Permitting individuals to remove their clothing if they wished to, but not requiring them to do so, also eliminated issues that normally would be involved. The setting in which nudity was encouraged was a functional setting in which it was natural to remove one's clothing before bathing.

The preliminary ventilation of anxieties regarding nudity also desensitized areas that might have inhibited individuals, had they not been openly expressed and discussed by the group. The following quotes from the tape recording of the session held prior to removal of clothing are typical in this respect:

> Ken: "This is entirely new to me. I've never had any occasion with a group of people to be nude, and I'm scared to death. I think that Lou said it better than I could say it—that I was not so much inhibited as I'm scared of my reaction to other people, and of course scared to death of having an erection."

Greg: "I've never tried it before, and I'll say that I have some inhibitions about it, mild to moderate."

Lee: "I feel quite sensitive, both from the standpoint of being looked at and more so from the standpoint of looking at other people. I don't know exactly why I should, but that's what I want to find out."

Ted: "As I mentioned to Vicky earlier, I wasn't going to be the first, but I wasn't going to be the last one, either."

Joan: "This is my first experience in anything like this, including therapy, but I feel kind of included in the group; I'm not sure, though, if one weekend is quite enough."

The presence of people in the group who had already experienced social nudism also helped. They could allay some of the fears expressed by others. For example:

Leo: "I had an experience seven months ago, just one experience in group therapy which became a nude session. It was a big hurdle, but once I said, 'Oh, the hell with it,' well, it's all over, and everybody's nude and who cares?"

Kathleen: "I had my first experience with social nudism about three years ago—it gave me a great feeling of exhilaration."

Karl: "I've probably been nude longer than any of you here. I can't ever remember not having wanted to be in the nude, because I can remember when I was a very small boy in Germany, we used to swim nude. I look upon people who choose to dress when they don't have to as the odd ones. If, after I met a person at a nudist camp, you asked me under oath whether they were dressed or undressed, I couldn't tell you; it's because it's the normal thing. Nudity is a normal way of life and not something to be consciously made a goal."

Elizabeth: "We regularly have an open house, and at 9:30 the open house becomes a closed house. Everybody continues the conversation, but they take off their clothes. We've been doing this for a number of months and we find that when they remove their clothes, people seem to remove a layer of hypocrisy. The conversation seems to become more meaningful."

Saturday morning participants were asked to share what they had experienced when going into the Jacuzzi nude and when standing in front of the lights on the previous evening. The reports quoted from the tape recording of the session may be grouped under the following headings:

1. A sense of pleasure derived from the freedom to look at other person's bodies and to be looked at:

Lee: "I enjoyed looking at the lovely female bodies last night."

Jack: "It was like one of my fantasies come into reality—all these girls—especially your body, Anita."

Sunny: "I was kind of hesitant, I didn't want to stand up in front of as many people as were there, I felt that was kind of exhibitionistic, and yet I really wanted to."

Walt: "I did find it very difficult to look at people; in there in the light show of course it was easy. I was sitting there in the dark and nobody was looking at me and I could look at anybody, but it's very difficult to look directly. I thought a lot of the women were very attractive and I wanted to look at them directly but I didn't feel able to."

Murray: "I particularly enjoyed looking at the bodies of the women, at their genitals and their breasts."

Vicky: "The thought crossed my mind last night—what a shame it is that this wonderful structure, this human body, created by Nature, has to be covered up for a whole lifetime."

2. A personal sense of comfort, exhilaration, and freedom:

Virginia: "I felt very much more comfortable in the nude."

Anita: "I felt very much more comfortable being undressed than dressed. When dressed, I feel I have to sit up straight, keep my back up and all that. Undressed, I feel it's all open and so I feel very good, being undressed."

Ted: "I felt very exhilarated, not to the point that I was excited, but I just felt good about the whole thing."

3. The desire to touch and experience skin contact and a sense of being inhibited in this respect:

Lee: "I enjoyed the lovely female bodies last night. Many of your breasts—I wanted to touch them, feel them, put my face against them."

Ted: "I was constantly thinking about just this idea of wanting to touch—why can't I touch?"

4. Pleasure arising from the sense of group closeness and the relaxed expressions on the faces of the other participants:

Evelyn: "I've been attending weekly therapy sessions, and I think it's remarkable how much closer I feel to the people here than I have felt in these other encounter groups which I have attended."

Richard: "The pleasure of seeing people in their first experience in nudity—they don't find it a problem—it was enjoyable."

Kathleen: "There seemed to be such a change in personality as the people got into the water. I think everyone who did get into the pool seemed immediately to relax, and to be comfortable."

Lou: "I'd like to tell Jack what a marvelous look of pleasurable wonderment I saw cross his face when he hit the water in the pool last night. I haven't seen an expression like that except on a child's face when something marvelous happened and everything's all right."

5. A sense of the naturalness of the nude condition, and a feeling of relief at not having reacted inappropriately:

Ken: "Just before going to bed I was walking around nude for a few moments, just to get my own reactions, and there were no reactions—the lack of a reaction was my only reaction."

Lee: "My reaction was, 'What's all the goddam fuss about,' and I was pleased and a little bit surprised at my willingness."

Greg: "It seemed like a very normal situation, particularly in swimming, a very comfortable situation, because it seemed for a purpose."

Jack: "And speaking of erections, I looked at a girl, especially your body, Anita, and I could catch myself concentrating on this and I could feel a tickling in my genitals and I found that if I concentrated, if all my thoughts were on this, then I could have an erection very easily, but if it is diffused, it's just like going about everyday life, and I found it quite pleasurable."

Ted: "I had the feeling, 'Why don't I have an erection, why don't I have this sensual urge that I might get when I see somebody in a bikini?'"

6. The experience of being high or unable to sleep for most of the remainder of the night.

Jerry: "Something very strange happened. After we got in the sleeping bags and I fell asleep, after about five minutes, all of a sudden I woke up, and I had this tremendous erection and I felt as if someone had taken this big heavy blanket off me, just pulled it off, and for the next two or three hours, I don't know what a trip is, I don't know what it is to be high, but what a time, my God!"

Ted: "I laid awake the entire night. The stimuli that had been created by the nudity, I think, allowed a great deal of thought in my mind all night."

7. A sense of concern about one's physical body when comparing it with other members of the group.

Walt: ". . . and the other reaction that I was aware of was feeling that my genitals perhaps weren't as large as the other men's, and this was a matter of some concern, although I didn't think about it much, but as I sit here now I know I was concerned."

Peter: "When you were moving with Sandra, Jack, I felt jealous. I thought, 'I'm not as good-looking as this guy is—look at his body, and I'm getting kind of paunchy and aged.' "

Sunny: "I found myself thinking, 'Do I look as good as her?' comparing, and I didn't particularly like that reaction, and I felt like kicking myself for doing it, but I was doing it, and I thought, 'I'm kind of fat here, and this and that, and do I want it to be out in the open and out in the light and have someone looking at me and thinking the same things about me?'—this kind of bothered me, especially when I was looking at Anita. She has such a beautiful body."

Anita: "The funny thing is that I have the same kind of negative feelings about my body."

At first, the experience of colored light patterns on nude bodies permitted the overt expression of voyeuristic and exhibitionistic tendencies. As the marathon continued, the tendency to look excessively or to experience self-consciousness when being looked at diminished to a point where many of the participants would have probably been unable to report whether others were or were not wearing clothing. Full body contact became more spontaneous and less sexually centered. In these respects, physical contact in the warm water of the pool was largely responsible for overcoming the inhibitions that most participants experienced in terms of skin contact in the initial phases of the marathon. Movement work and dance therapy in couples also furthered the process. Overt sexual expression was undoubtedly inhibited by the presence of the group and the ground rules, to which all participants had agreed. The beneficial effect of emotional openness, on the other hand, continued to enhance the depth of interaction in the marathon.

In the sensory saturation meditation and eye contact period on Sunday morning, emotional openness was even more intimate. Perhaps it is best described as a group peak experience or a sense of spiritual at-one-ment. Most participants felt that this was the most profound experience they had in the marathon:

Murray: "I found it to be a very tranquil experience. I got out somewhere on the stream of the universe."

Kathleen: ". . . then in the eyeballing it was as if I were looking into my own eyes. I felt he was very with me—practically every moment—there were times when we were just grabbing for each other—trembling—and it was very difficult to withdraw."

Virginia: "I think the high point was the experience I had this morning. . . . I felt a terrific warmth and tingling sensation up the spine and sometimes a sexual sensation with it—and as the experience built, I again saw the two experiences that I had in your office: the violet eyes followed by the light."

Greg: "Sometimes I would have a hard time telling whether your face was your face or whether I was there—rather that it was myself, rather than any extension or anything else—just merely the self in the same way as any other part of oneself. In many ways there was kind of a relaxing feeling, almost like being asleep for three years."

Evelyn (after a period of time on the floor, going through labor pains and the movements of giving birth): "I feel as though I'm in labor . . . I feel like I created something—it didn't just happen to me . . . I guess God is always right here—I hadn't really believed it before. I have birth but I feel purged at the same time; it's like they're both the same . . . I'm shook up but boy, do I feel good . . . I feel like laughing and crying and everything all over."

Ted: "I've pulled away all my life from people—pulled away. I pulled away from Lou just now—or I felt I did. I don't know whether it's pulling away or whether it's a sort of feeling that I'm standing on my own two feet. I used to have to hold on to somebody because I couldn't stand up. I came closer to seeing God (shouting and weeping). He must be there—why do I shut Him out? I'm seeing God (sobbing) (long pause) . . . (open eyes) I think I see better without my glasses on now."

Sandra: "I was looking at the sky and I thought—I've never been here before and I haven't seen it, and my heart started pounding. And I looked around and I haven't seen any of you, I haven't seen the floor. And at this point I thought 'I'm really tripping out' and then the beauty of the whole thing came through. I feel like a kid!"

The Apparent Permanent Gains as Expressed by the Participants at a Post Session

Fifteen of the twenty participants attended a post session five weeks following the marathon.

The general consensus of opinion of both professional and lay participants was best expressed by Murray, a clinical psychologist, who stated:

I've been telling people that asked me about what happened that I felt there were some people that were helped a great deal, and I didn't see anybody who was harmed. I think that when in a group of twenty-four people you have twenty or twenty-two who were really benefited, and no one really harmed, you have held an effective marathon.

The following comments made by participants are transcribed from the tape recording of the post session:

Lee: "For a period of several months I've been in a kind of metamorphosis. I guess I can call it for lack of a better word, an emerging. If we can think about my emerging like this (gestures, indicating slow uphill plane), our time together kind of did this (indicates rapid upswing), a kind of zoom. Virginia too has been emerging. For the first time in years we talked to each other about things that are important. We're becoming friends for the first time in many years. Virginia and I are divorcing—not as a result of this marathon—but I think as a result of our re-emerging and finally discovering that we can like each other, we can be friends, very good friends, but we just can't be husband and wife any longer.

"And after the meeting of the Humanistic Psychology Forum the other night, this sour old bastard colleague psychiatrist with whom I had tangled violently every time we got together came over to me with a great big smile on his face, put his arms around me, patted me on the back, and said, 'You narcissistic old son-of-a-bitch, you've always been in love with yourself, and I'm delighted that you recognize it.' And George (a psychologist), who is always kind of standoffish, did almost the same thing. I'm alive again! I don't feel as old as I am by a damn sight, and as a therapist I'm many times more effective.

"I ran a marathon with seven couples out of my practice a weekend or two ago. I was open and free, and what I did came from way down deep inside, not from thinking, as I used to—she's thinking this, he's thinking that, now what would be the best way to get at it. I do think that the nakedness, the feeling, what the hell have I got to hide now, might as well let the rest of it come out, I think that this facilitated a lot of it."

Virginia: "On Tuesday night following the marathon I said to Lee, 'This is ridiculous. You're not happy with me and I'm not happy with you. We're making each other miserable. Let's get this divorce,' and from there on it went ahead, and as he said, we have been friends. As he said, this is probably the most friendly divorce anybody ever saw. We can talk together now. It's as though somebody had to make the decision that set all of us free, including our children. It was the best thing I've ever done in my life."

Leo: "At the marathon one of the guys, I forget just who it was now, told me I had a good-looking body, and this surprised the hell out of me, especially a man telling me that that I've got a good-looking body. I had not thought much of myself before this, in fact, I felt pretty much ashamed of myself. I felt I was worthless and all this sort of thing. But I think that, along with a number of other things, has caused me to experience a much greater acceptance of myself since the marathon. Now I don't care too much if I make a mistake or if I'm wrong, or if somebody thinks I'm wrong. It's just too bad.

"And I think I must have had a sort of dependency kind of thing with any woman that I'd go with. I think I'm losing this dependency thing now. If this woman I'm going with doesn't want to go with me, all right, and I didn't feel that way before.

"I've felt a good deal more courage in facing anything that came along since the marathon, more confidence, and steadiness, rather than being all jumpy. And then as a result of this I moved into areas that I avoided because they were too traumatic. I'm just taking on bigger challenges now."

Jack: "I seem less hostile to women, and more natural around them. I feel more open and less afraid of being attacked by them. I have been to two previous clothed marathons and I do believe nudity played a large part in my reaction."

Anita: "The most wonderful thing that happened to me at the marathon was that everybody thought that I was beautiful, and I had never really accepted this because of my relationship with my husband.

"And the marathon also did something to my relationship with my husband. I saw what was going on between he and I. I've been open to him as far as my feelings are concerned. I always felt I had to kind of play my female role—I don't have to do this anymore. If I say *no* it's *no*. My husband's been very dependent on me. I don't want to be a mommy, I want to be a female. He said, 'I was looking at you as a mommy, and I was finding faults with your body like you were my mother.' He catches himself now when he calls me mommy, and I pinch him, you know, to make him aware of it. I'm sick and tired of playing mommy. It's becoming much better now."

Walt: "Sunday morning showed me that I can't open up and relate. I didn't interpret it that way for about two days. I had a whole case built up that it wasn't my fault. But then I became aware that, what the hell, all this came out of me, so I decided to start working on it. I discovered that what I'd been doing all my life was avoiding relationships. My mother died when I was seven and my father started chasing around with women. I saw all these women as bad. They were sexy as hell and I probably wanted them, but I saw them as bad and my grandmother told me they were bad. I think I fabricated stuff about women ever since in order to avoid getting close to them. I married a woman who didn't want to get close, and we're working that through now, but it's seventeen years later. I used to sleep in my mother's bed when my father was working nights. I think I've been true to my goddam mother all this time, and it's ridiculous, but that's what I've been doing. My father certainly wasn't, so somebody had to be. All the opportunities I've wasted! I've just been in constant turmoil for three weeks. I run to the john and I cry at work and I cry over everybody I can get to listen to me. I can talk to my wife, though, and she understands it completely, and I understand it."

Bob (commenting on the telephone conversation that he had just had with Ted, who was not present): "Ted felt the marathon was beneficial in some ways. He said he's been in therapy for seven or eight years and he's never been able to work through his relationship with his father before, and he thought that was the most significant thing that happened at the marathon. He said people are so painful to him, and it's so hard to come and meet them and say good-by. He felt that if he came here tonight he would be in a sense reliving the painful experience of the marathon, so he decided he would not come. He said the religious experience on the last day was very positive for him. It gave him a great feeling of inner spiritual worth and value, not from the standpoint of formalized religion but in terms of personal strength. He said he'd like to go to another marathon, but people are there, and while he likes this group as well as any group, this group is still people, and people frighten him."

Vicky: "Since the marathon I find myself smiling every once in a while, and I think the reason is the memory I have of how I so easily related to the men, without any fear of being rejected. It's really a big thing for me, even though I feel as though I'm doing it very naturally. For many years I've been very stiff, and I haven't related to men at all. Being in the nude did a great deal for me in this respect. I am still a little anxious when I see people clothed."

Conclusion

Nudity apparently facilitates group interaction in a marathon. Seventeen of the twenty participants felt that the factor of nudity increased their ability to open up to each other emotionally and to achieve a greater degree of authenticity and transparency. The group integrated and seemed to become therapeutically functional more rapidly than clothed marathon groups.

Nudity in a group that encourages skin contact seems to be therapeutic in itself. This is perhaps needed to compensate for the sensory isolation experienced by the individual in his normal clothed state. It may be assumed that the social world outside of the home is frequently experienced as a jungle of polite estrangement where physical and emotional contact is prohibited by walls, locked doors, clothing, status roles, and a variety of other masks. Perhaps this is why individuals frequently lack a developed sense of social responsibility and love for their fellow men and are seldom strongly motivated to give of themselves generously and work for the common good. It may also explain why family life at times disintegrates under the extreme emotional demands made by individuals whose relationships with a depersonalized society leave a famine in their hearts and a hunger that cannot be filled by any one person, not even, at times, by their mates. If this is true, nudity in itself may represent a symbolic and factual lifting of the mask which constitutes an invitation to tribal unity and which is most effective when a reversion to the established pattern of private paired relationships is inhibited by blocking sexual expression and subgrouping.

Nudity is apparently of considerable help in dealing with specific problem areas, which often remain unexplored when participants are clothed.

On leaving, Ted indicated that he was considerably less self-conscious when looking at, or being looked at by, other persons. This symptom was probably intensified by nudity and would have been less apparent in a clothed marathon. In addition, it manifested in a more basic sexual form, simplifying therapeutic intervention, which moved to an exploration of his sense of potency and manliness, and to an apparent resolution of an Oedipal complex which had prevented him from identifying with his father, who objected to his being physically close to his mother. In this respect, it would be interesting to see if voyeurs and exhibitionists and other sexual deviates referred by the courts might benefit by a nude marathon.

Self-acceptance, in many cases, is associated with body image. In this respect, much can be accomplished by the open discussion of what the individual feels are his undesirable physical characteristics. These are frequently distortions in his own thinking which can best be remedied by open exposure to group reaction, thus increasing his ego strength and mobilizing his deeper emotional conflicts.

The inhibition of overt sexual expression during the marathon is probably beneficial to individuals who would employ sexual activity as a defense against emotional closeness. For other sexually inhibited participants, it is perhaps unfortunate that our present social mores prevent a more generous sexual attitude in the therapeutic group.

In our society sensual body contact is generally considered to be an invitation to sexual intimacy. The inhibition of sexual intimacy by our mores thus also inhibits body contact. Since body contact is frequently essential to emotional expression, this taboo of touch blocks a vital avenue of communication. This is most clearly observable in relationships between males who are inhibited in their expression of love, since they may not embrace or experience tender body contact without the implication of homosexuality. The nude marathon seems to eliminate this confusion by encouraging sensuality while inhibiting sexuality, thus increasing the range of permissible emotional expression for both sexes. Most of the participants in the marathon were pleasantly surprised to find that they could enjoy sensual pleasure without sexual involvement. The author also observed that when participants in the nude marathon returned to ongoing clothed therapy groups they were more spontaneous in terms of body movement and physical contact. One somewhat inhibited female participant reported that following the marathon men were asking her for dates for the first time in years. Apparently her increased freedom to express emotionally and sensually made her more attractive to the opposite sex. We may tentatively conclude that nude marathons help to differentiate between sensuality and sexuality, thus increasing emotional expressiveness and furthering communication.

The nude marathon apparently requires two steps:

1. A permissive group setting in which participants express their reactions to intimacy which they inhibit in society and in clothed marathons. For example: voyeuristic and exhibitionistic tendencies, the need to touch and to be touched, and the anxieties relative to body image and sexual potency.
2. Once these factors which limit intimacy and authenticity are openly expressed and mobilized in their most basic forms, they are open to the therapeutic intervention of the therapist and the group. This process proceeds in most respects as it would in a clothed marathon.

It is also apparent that the nudist movement itself could contribute more to society if it permitted physical contact and encouraged the formation of encounter groups which would permit the continuation of what has begun as a symbolic removal of defenses in the form of clothing to proceed to the more significant emotional levels of basic human interaction.

NOTES

[1] George R. Bach, "The Marathon Group: Intensive Practice of Intimate Interaction," *Psychological Reports* 18 (1966): 995–1002.

[2] Elizabeth E. Mintz, "Time-Extended Marathon Groups," *Psychotherapy: Theory, Research, and Practice* 4, no. 2 (May 1967), 65–70.

[3] Abraham Maslow, *Eupsychian Management: A Journal* (Homewood, Ill.: R. D. Irwin, 1965), p. 160.

[4] William E. Hartman and Marilyn Fithian, *Nudism in America: A Social Psychological Study*, 1967.

SUGGESTED READINGS

Bach, G. "The Marathon Group," *Psychological Reports* 18 (1966): 995-1002; 20 (1967): 1147–58; 1163–72.

Bindrim, P., "Cultivating Peak Experience," in Herbert A. Otto and John Mann, eds., *Ways of Growth* (New York: Grossman, 1968).

Bindrim, P., "Peak-Oriented Psychotherapy: An Approach to Self-Actualization through the Cultivation of Peak Experiences," 1966. Mimeographed.

Bindrim, P., "Peak-Oriented Psychotherapy: Case Histories and Taped Transcriptions of Therapy Sessions," 1966. Mimeographed.

Howard, J. *Please Touch*. New York: Basic Books, 1970.

Mann, J. *Encounter*. New York: Grossman, 1970.

Mintz, E. "Time-extended Marathon Groups." *Psychotherapy: Theory, Research, and Practice* 4 (1967): 65–70.

17

Behavior Modification and Sexual Problems

Ernest A. Vargas

Behavior modification therapy is a cluster of techniques with origins in twentieth-century learning theory. What is emphasized in diagnosis and treatment is the overt behavior of the individual, what he does and says. A behavior disorder is not presumed due to some inner disease of which the behavior is a symptom. It is the behavior itself that is causing trouble. What is to be changed in therapy is the relationship between the behavior and the circumstances in which it occurs.

Focusing on behavior leads to stating explicitly what is to be changed. The objectives are spelled out prior to initiating therapy. Clear-cut criteria are stated that help the client as well as the therapist in judging degree of success. Behaviors to be changed or learned may be specified in a performance contract. Disturbing areas in the client's life not specified may be deferred for later attention. Treatment is thus concentrated on behavior found troublesome for personal or social reasons in a given situation.

A behavior disorder is any behavior having aversive properties for the individual or others. There is no *a priori* reason, however, for a need to correct that behavior to accord to some set of social norms. A person's sexual behavior may deviate from some norm; for example, he may be sexually attracted to persons of his own sex. But he may be concerned not with the deviation but with the fact that he is impotent under such circumstances. Correcting the impotence, not the homosexuality, may be what he explicitly contracts for with the therapist.

As a technology, behavior therapy is nonnormative. Like any technology, however, it can be used for a variety of value-laden ends. A person's behavior may be "corrected" not because it is uncomfortable for him but because it is uncomfortable for others. Whether a technology has social utility is a very different question from whether it is effective. Clearly, however, the more powerful a technology the more social concern there should be about its use. What has been learned scientifically is used technically only if it means social profit—to someone.

Because of their experimental origins, the behavioral therapies empha-

size the functional analysis of disorders. Changes in behavior are a function
of changes in the circumstances in which that behavior occurs. New behaviors brought about by deliberately manipulating these circumstances are
called learned. What is known of this process is summarized in the learning
theories that are the basis for the behavioral therapies.

Respondent and Operant Learning

A tone is sounded and food is presented to a hungry dog. This is done
a number of times. After a while the tone is sounded without presenting
the food. The dog now salivates to the tone alone. A juicy lemon is cut
and a slice given to a person who has never tasted a lemon before. He
takes a big bite of the slice. Thereafter whenever he sees the yellow shape
of the lemon, smells its citrus odor, or even thinks about a lemon, he
immediately begins to salivate. A young adolescent is taught to masturbate
by another boy. Soon this boy and others began to excite him sexually.
A formerly neutral stimulus, boys, now elicits sexual behavior.

The above are all examples of Pavlovian or respondent conditioning.
A natural or unconditioned stimulus (the food) elicits a response. A
neutral stimulus that at first produces no response occurs just before the
unconditioned stimulus. Thereafter the neutral stimulus (the tone) becomes a conditioned stimulus also eliciting the response (salivating), even
in the absence of the original unconditioned stimulus. Through this conditioning procedure of substituting one stimulus for another, the range of
new stimuli that control a response is extended. (Skinner, 1953)

Operant conditioning is different. The reinforcer is paired with the
response instead of the stimulus, and occurs as a result of the response.
A dog that has not eaten for some time comes into the kitchen and sees
some meat. He barks. He runs about. He finally sits up and begs. He is
given some meat as a consequence of this behavior. On the next occasion
he is more likely to engage in this action rather than any other. A woman
who likes lemons buys a dozen at a fruit stand. They all turned out to be
rotten. From then on, she avoids that fruit stand. Because of religious
scruples a young man is impotent when attempting sexual intercourse with
women. While in the overseas military he visits brothels where prostitutes
masturbate him. When masturbating himself, he uses this memory because
it was his first experience with a sexual partner. Later in the jungle,
reluctant to approach native women, he induces children to masturbate
him. When released and back home he has young boys masturbate him.
After getting married he has intercourse to fantasies of prostitutes or boys
masturbating him. He comes for therapy when his wife discovers he has
made his four-year-old child masturbate him. (McGuire, *et. al.,* 1965) The

deviant behavior was produced through both operant and respondent conditioning, illustrating how human behavior gets shaped through its consequences.

Most human behavior is operant behavior. Operants are responses that operate on the environment and are defined by their effect. To understand the behavior not only must the response be observed but also its consequences. Responses may differ but if they have the same result, they are the same operant. A child may knock at a door, turn its knob, or call for someone to open it. If all these responses succeed at gaining entry, at least occasionally, then the operant is "opening the door," though the form of the response differs. By beginning with what the person does and what happens after he does it, it is possible to analyze the complexity of what has traditionally been called "voluntary" behavior.

A child spills his milk, interrupts his parents' conversation, makes faces, and drops his fork on the floor. Each of these responses may be said to be from the same operant class, "annoying his parents." Each of these responses is followed by a scolding, which involves his parents' attention. As a consequence, while a particular response may not be repeated, the general class of behavior increases in frequency. Often when contracting for a specific performance, for example, hair grooming, other related behaviors, such as neat dressing, also improve. Through the common operant a response has with others, an individual improved in one behavior will improve in all behavior of like function. The consequences of grooming actions were reinforcing. In the child's case, attention was reinforcing. Any behavior followed by a reinforcer is likely to increase in frequency.

There are two types of reinforcers, positive and negative. An event that increases the frequency of responses when *presented* is positive. An event that increases the frequency of responses when *removed* is a negative reinforcer. If instead of taking away the negative reinforcer, we apply it, then the response frequency will go down. Another way of lowering the response rate is to take away a positive reinforcer. These latter two situations are called punishment. In short, whether a stimulus event is punishing or reinforcing depends on whether it increases or lowers the frequency of a response when presented or taken away.

A young man stands on a street corner. He whistles at a pretty girl going by. She ignores him. So does the next one, and the next two or three. Finally, one of the girls turns and gives him a tentative smile before going on. The smile was, of course, a reinforcer. More important, it was given after a number of other opportunities where there might have been smiles but were not. The result is a tenacious perseverance in the young man's whistling behavior. The example illustrates that the schedule of reinforcement determines the persistence and frequency of most behavior. A high-density reinforcement immediately increases the response rate. If, however, the reinforcing stimulus is no longer presented, the response rate eventually drops off, and soon responses are no longer made. The behavior is extinguished. However, when a number of responses are made before reinforcement occurs, the behavior persists for a long period of time before it ceases. It only slowly extinguishes. This is also true if an interval of time goes by before another reinforcement is given since the last one. Most sexual behavior, including deviant behavior, is sometimes reinforced, sometimes not. Once a pattern is set up, it tends to be persistent. It is maintained by very infrequent reinforcement.

Specific Techniques

Behavioral therapy techniques emphasize either bringing a person's behavior under control of new stimuli through respondent conditioning or constructing new behavior through operant conditioning. In the actual clinical situation, techniques utilizing both approaches are used, depending on circumstances and the stage of treatment. Masters and Johnson, for example, use a subtle blending of both operant and respondent conditioning in their work, without explicitly naming them. The case studies presented in the literature usually describe one or two techniques and interpret events from their perspective. Convenient labels are then attached, underlining the critical events stressed or the method used.

In aversion therapy, noxious stimuli are emphasized. They are applied when the preferred stimulus is presented or the undesired behavior performed. A truck driver who was a weight lifter and physical culturist had dressed in women's clothing, his sister's initially, since early youth. He derived erotic satisfaction from his actions, either directly or through fantasy when masturbating. Pictures were taken when the client was dressing and a tape made by him describing his actions. These were shown and played while nausea and vomiting were induced by a drug. The client stopped dressing as a girl. Six months later the client still was not inclined to cross-dress. (Lavin, et. al., 1961)

Changes in attitude occurring during aversion therapy were researched by Marks and Gelder. Three sorts of attitude changes occurred. Attitudes about the self initially worsened and then improved. Attitudes about the sexual deviancy significantly worsened. And attitudes about neutral concepts—for example, doctor or girl friend—had little change. Changes in attitude preceded physiological changes directly measured by degree of erection in the penis. By using this autonomic measure, Marks and Gelder were able to observe directly how effective they were in changing the client's behavior when having him fantasize his sexual disorder.

Marks and Gelder were concerned with the ethical propriety of using aversive techniques. As they state, "Unpleasant treatments should not be used if they are only elaborate vehicles of suggestion. Aversion is only justified when no other effective treatment is available . . ." (Marks and Gelder, 1967). In operant conditioning, a reinforcing stimulus is applied only after an individual has made a response. Because shock is dependent on the person's signaling his thoughts, his cooperation is needed. If the individual refuses to cooperate or behave appropriately, reconditioning is impossible. This provides an ethical safeguard against unreasonable manipulation as far as Marks and Gelder are concerned.

What is the relationship between using an aversive stimulus, such as electric shock, and masochistic behavior? A client had

> . . . a shoe fetishism for 25 years, associated masochism for 15 years and impotence of 3 months duration . . . Since age 19 he had fantasies of being kicked by men or women wearing rubber boots or high heeled shoes and actually slapped his genitals with boots. He married at 21 and repeatedly urged his wife to kick or stand on him; this she did with great reluctance, though once she broke his coccyx in the process. For six months prior to admission, she had refused to cooperate in this behavior. His masochistic fantasies were associated with sexual excitation, and included visions of being beaten to death. (Marks *et al.,* 1965, p. 253).

Marks, Rachman, and Gelder wondered whether using a painful stimulus, such as shock, would simply contribute to the client's masochistic inclinations. Using a basic operant procedure, they assessed experimentally whether the shock was reinforcing. It was found that the client "was clearly avoiding the shock even in the presence" of sexual objects connected with his masochism. (Marks, Rachman, and Gelder, 1965, p. 254) The client was later found to avoid shock even in a neutral situation. The stimuli used for masochistic purposes were clearly restricted. Being kicked or beaten with boots were the only painful stimuli associated with sexual excitement. (Marks *et. al.,* 1965)

"Noxious" stimuli that might be positively reinforcing are specific in their effect on an individual's behavior, as are all reinforcing stimuli. Not all men find women sexually attractive, and of those who do, not all women are appealing. What is an effective reinforcer is very much an individual affair. For any social group, certain classes of events are seen to be reinforcing, but this may not be true for any individual within that group. An event is presumed reinforcing, but it is not known to be so until its effect is observed. An event or stimulus is reinforcing only if the behavior increases in frequency. Since reinforcement in operant psychology is not dependent on the notion of satisfying some need, it cannot be stated why an event is reinforcing. It can only be observed that it has been reinforcing.

Systematic desensitization is a more complex case of reconditioning. Taken into account is man's extensive use of imagery and the powerful hold it has on him. The patient is taught to engage in deep muscular relaxation. A ranked listing of events that produce anxiety is constructed. The patient is then relaxed and asked to imagine a scene producing the least anxiety on his ranked list. As soon as this can be done without fear, the next event on the list is taken up. The relaxing responses are incompatible with those of anxiety, and the client is conditioned to relax to stimuli previously producing fear. The patient learns that responding to the events portrayed in the hierarchy will not be punished. Positive reinforcers in the situation will then shape the desired behavior. For example:

> A frequent practice was to hide completely nude in a small wooded area in the centre of the town where he then lived, and spring out and expose himself to the first woman who passed. Another was to hide himself in the cloakroom of a girls' school, exposing himself to the first girl to use the lavatory. If the door were latched, he would lie on the floor and thrust his erect penis under the door for the occupant's view. While driving a car, he would entertain exposure fantasies of such intensity that his driving was a public danger. These fantasies led to turning up a side street to get out of the car and expose. Passing an attractive female when driving led to exposure also . . .

> Previous treatment had included individual and group psychotherapy and CO_2 abreaction therapy conducted over an 18-month period at a reformatory clinic. He had received a few weeks of individual psychotherapy and 10 months of group psychotherapy at the Forensic Clinic. During this period he wore a "chastity belt" which he decided to have made by a prosthetics manufacturer to prevent his exhibiting. His wife locked the belt in the morning and unlocked it at night. The treatment was interrupted by a conviction for indecent assault. While wearing the belt, the patient had attempted to grasp the legs and breasts of a young woman he saw in a crowd. (Bond and Hutchison, 1965, p. 247)

Numerous arrests and convictions were also ineffective.

Systematic desensitization was used with a hierarchy of provoking stimuli "of types of female, her physical attributes and place of exposure." The patient was relaxed and the milder stimuli eliciting exposure presented. Following the first session the patient was instructed to practice relaxing at home. As the sessions proceeded, stimuli increasing in intensity were presented.

After a dozen sessions, the patient was sent through a department store where there were many young women of the type to whom he would expose. He simply involuntarily relaxed and when he could not, gave himself the command, relax. During the next week he sought employment. He was unsuccessful and this, in conjunction with his wife's illness, made him despondent. He entered a small park to expose, unbuttoned his trousers, and hid behind a clump of bushes. But when a girl approached, he involuntarily relaxed and lost his erection. "He then adjusted his clothing and continued on his way feeling foolish."[6] (Bond and Hutchison, 1965, p. 248)

After this he improved rapidly. He enjoyed social activities, mixing with women who were provocatively dressed without feeling tense. When treatment ended, he obtained a job and did quite well at it, but was dismissed after ten months due to discovery of his previous exhibitionism. Two hours later, he left the welfare office and

> feeling depressed, he saw a woman in the street and found himself following her. She went into an office building and eventually to a washroom. The patient followed her inside with urges to look under the door and perhaps expose as he had done in the past. The woman had heard him enter and shouted an alarm frightening the patient away. (Bond and Hutchison, 1965, p. 249)

Soon thereafter he began exposing again in women's washrooms.

The therapist had concentrated on desensitizing the patient to the kind of woman who excited him. "This was successful in that provocative females in public places as for example, streets, parks, or department stores ceased to be effective stimuli insofar as initiation of tension was concerned. Situations giving rise to feelings of inadequacies were ignored, and these were allowed to retain strength as had weaker stimuli of washrooms . . ." (Bond and Hutchison, 1965, p. 250) When both the correct situation and a provocative female were present, the patient was likely to expose himself and did. A more elaborate listing of these stimuli was constructed and the patient desensitized to them.

New behavior can be constructed by using positively reinforcing stimuli. A terminal objective is decided upon, and any approximation in this direction reinforced. Sexual stimuli are powerful reinforcers and are used this way. Prime considerations are not having the person try too much at any one time and doing only what he feels strongly impelled to.

> The therapeutic use of sexual responses is illustrated by a case drawn from Wolpe's series. The patient, a forty-year-old, unmarried male, had after many years of normal sexual activity, undergone a progressive decline in his sexual satisfaction. He had, for a period of four years, been complaining of premature ejaculations and failure to obtain an erection in sexual situations . . . He was advised to explain his sexual difficulties to his

current girl friend, and to obtain her cooperation in a gradual, therapeutic programme which was designed to resuscitate his sexual performance. After three failures, in which the patient failed to obtain an erection because he had attempted to go too quickly and had on these occasions experienced anxiety, he was advised to confine himself to preliminary love-play until such time as he felt a strong sexual urge and obtained a full erection. He was told that he was showing too much urgency about having successful intercourse and that he should, instead, concentrate on enjoying the preliminary love-play. The following week, the patient reported that he had twice been with his girl friend in the nude without intercourse being intended, and he had obtained several erections of varying quality. He was then told that if his erection was sufficiently good after manual handling, he could attempt coitus in the presence of a strong desire to do so. He achieved satisfactory sexual intercourse within the next two weeks, and after that continued to improve progressively. He eventually married his girl friend and, at follow-up eight months later, he reported that he was happily married and that their sexual activities were entirely satisfactory. (Eysenck and Rachman, 1965, p. 143)

When new responses are being built through operant conditioning, instruction can promote occasions where positive consequences can occur. Assertive training is a technique quite explicit in this procedure. Initially the client's ineffectual responses are made aversive. Instructions are then given on how to assert one's right without being too aggressively nasty. The therapist may act as a model for the client, portraying how he should act in the social situation giving him difficulties. There may then be behavior rehearsal in which the client practices the actions he later will engage in, meanwhile reinforced by the therapist.

Assertive therapy is only one of a number of techniques in which the client takes an active role in managing his own behavior. A young college man's only sexual behavior was to masturbate to sadistic fantasies involving women. He was instructed to obtain a sexy, nude picture from *Playboy* magazine and masturbate to it. If he began to lose his erection he was to engage in his sadistic fantasy but return to the *Playboy* nude and concentrate on it at orgasm. Pictures of girls in bathing suits or lingerie were then used for masturbating, with the *Playboy* nude as a supportive stimulus much as the sadistic fantasy had been. However, he was reluctant to give up his sadistic fantasy, and an imaginary noxious scene was made a consequence of it. He soon masturbated successfully to the bathing suit pictures and was no longer able to achieve an erection with his former sadistic fantasies. Assuring the client he was not diseased, and advising him how to date accompanied this procedure.

Davison (1968) and Jackson (1969) found that next after peeping, a voyeur was stimulated most by pornographic pictures. The voyeur was instructed to masturbate to pornography next time he wanted to peer through bedroom windows. If he wanted to, he could imagine his voyeuristic activities, but at orgasm he was to look at the pornographic pictures and concentrate on those. Soon thereafter he no longer felt inclined to peep. He next masturbated to the stimulus of a *Playboy* magazine centerfold, using the pornographic picture if necessary to maintain an erection, but concentrating on the *Playboy* nude at orgasm. Eventually he engaged in normal heterosexual behavior (Jackson, 1969). The therapist specified the shaping procedure away from his voyeuristic activities and fantasies, but the client did his own conditioning. Cautela (1967) had his patients imagine aversive consequences whenever they were in situations where nonacceptable sexual stimuli became urging. He also had alcoholics and delinquents do this. Stuart (1970) had a woman attempt to control her eating by imagining her husband in the arms of another woman. In short the client manages the consequences of his own behavior, either covertly or overtly, and thus increases or decreases the probability of its reoccurrence. If one says this is common sense, it is; but it is common sense correctly applied.

Some Sexual Disorders

Behavior modification techniques have been used with fetishism, frigidity, homosexuality, impotence, transvestism, pedophilia, sadistic fantasy, and exhibitionism. The range of techniques and some pertinent issues in their use for any sexual dysfunction will be illustrated with a few commonly reported examples.

FETISHISM: The specific nature of fetishistic behavior facilitates using behavior therapy. The usual treatment is to pair some noxious stimulus with the fetish or fetish behavior. In some cases, classical and operant conditioning methods have been combined with psychotherapy. Psychotherapeutic methods by themselves have not been too successful in treating this type of behavior deviancy. Long-term behavioral changes with conditioning techniques are yet unknown. Short-term success has been good, and long-term studies are in process.

Fetish behavior is often found in conjunction with other sexual disorders. An Englishman's fetish was dressing in women's clothes. After laying a silken garment on the inner side of his thighs, he would straddle a chair and through friction, reach orgasm. The individual was extraordinarily ashamed whenever he did this but found the urge unresistable. He had been fired from his last place of work when discovered engaging in his fetish in the ladies' cloakroom. Prior to behavior therapy he had been treated unsuccessfully for eighteen months with psychotherapy and hormones. (Cooper, 1963)

During his long courtship of his wife, he never attempted intercourse because he felt strongly that this was against his moral code. The honeymoon was a failure. On their first occasion together he felt tired and had a slight headache. But when intercourse was first attempted, he had only a partial erection and in his anxiety, rushed to penetrate her and on initial contact, ejaculated. Further attempts at intercourse were as disappointing as the first. On the last day of the honeymoon, when his wife was out, he dressed in her clothes, had a strong erection with a great deal of pleasure and relief from anxiety, and ejaculated. His sexual relations after the honeymoon were poor and he had premature ejaculation and no (or very poor) erections.

The fetish and the impotence were treated separately. While performing his fetish and shortly before completing it, he was given a drug to cause nausea and vomiting. While ill, moral exhortations were given on how despicable fetish behavior was, and an explicit connection was made between the fetish objects and his illness. He was refused permission to get rid of the fetish clothes. There was a strong aversive reaction to the clothes, and nine months later there was still no desire to engage in his former behavior. The effects of the reconditioning process were specific only to his fetishism. His impotence was treated successfully by using sexual stimuli as reinforcers.

Kushner (1965) also reconditioned an individual for both impotence and fetishism. A 33-year-old male had had a fetish since he was 12. He masturbated while wearing women's panties or, if these were not available, while viewing pictures of women in them. He developed this fetish when, as a boy, he had become sexually excited viewing the panties of little girls as they slid down the slide. At this time he was introduced to masturbation and recognized the same sensations. His fantasies while masturbating focused on what he had observed, and panties soon came to have their special sexual properties.

Some careful distinctions had to be made during relearning. It was made explicit to the individual that masturbation per se was not being attacked, but the type of fantasies engaged in. Further a distinction was made between the wearing of panties for purposes of masturbation and women in panties. Care was taken here, as in all behavior therapeutic situations, to be very specific on the behavior being reconditioned.

Panties, pictures of women in panties, and panties imagined under different sets of circumstances were paired with shock. The shock was applied until the individual could not stand any more, at which point he could end it by saying stop. After forty-one sessions over a period of fourteen weeks, the fetish behavior was no longer present. One month later, there was a spontaneous recovery of this fetish but in mild form. The individual had been prepared for this by the therapist and was not alarmed. Later in a period of stress he was again having fetish thoughts, but he could easily dismiss them from his mind. Another session was held, and eighteen months later the patient was still free from his fetish.

Near the end of his treatment for his fetish, a desensitization procedure for his impotence was initiated. Within a short period of time, he had satisfactory sexual relationships. Kushner remarks on Freud's and Stekel's point that removal of fetishistic objects would result in homosexual behavior or impotence or strong sadistic drives. Nothing like this happened. On the contrary, the client had formerly been very aggressive, acting out constantly, and engaged in proving his masculinity; now he no longer did so. Further, he now had a full and satisfactory heterosexual life.

Behavior therapy works as well with inner behavior as with outer. The only necessity is that the inner fantasy should be explicit enough so that the therapist will know when and how to apply a reinforcing stimulus and what is occurring when it is applied. Not only may the response to be treated be inner, but the stimulus may be applied in a cognitive fashion. All that is necessary is to maintain the basic learning paradigm on which behavior therapy is based—either two stimuli in conjunction with each other or a stimulus contingent upon a response.

Kolvin (1967) illustrates this in eliminating the fetish behavior of a 14-year-old. Instead of a shock or a drug, which have social, personal, or professional drawbacks, a stimulus was used that was personally aversive. A list was made of experiences the boy found unpleasant. The two most unpleasant events on the list were falling in a dream and looking down from a precarious height. The client was relaxed in a darkened room and asked to imagine vividly the fetish event portrayed by the therapist. When the client was suitably excited, the aversive image was described graphically. The aversive effect was usually immediate, as indicated by the client's gestures of discomfort. Seventeen months after the treatment, there had been no reoccurrences of his former behavior, and the boy was doing well.

Correct timing of both stimulus and response is needed to achieve optimal effect, especially when both are most vivid, but this is difficult to obtain. (Kolvin, 1967) However, the method has the great advantage of needing only the patient's repertoire to work with. It is another version of the principle that a response more likely to be made can be used to reinforce a less likely one. In this case, any behavior of greater noxious intensity can be used to suppress that of lower. It is an unstated but commonly used technique in everyday behavioral management. With skill it could be used in those situations where social or professional propriety or lack of technology does not permit using other techniques involving an aversion stimulus.

FRIGIDITY: Sixteen cases of chronic frigidity treated by Lazarus (1963) touch on most of the major points involved in this sexual disorder. All the cases were characterized by a good deal of anxiety and, in some instances, intense hostility, which inhibited pleasurable sexual behavior either of themselves or others. Frigidity was the primary concern. The reasons varied, and there was no common cause. Most women had no idea as to how the problem had developed, though a few had. However, insight had little or nothing to do with whether treatment was successful. The women differed from each other in personality, temperament, background, and life styles.

All had received some form of prior treatment.

> Five had received detailed instruction from their family doctors concerning sex technique. Three were treated by means of hormonal injections and topical ointments. Three of the patients had consulted marriage guidance counselors who had embarked on a course of reassuring discussions with both husband and wife, supplemented by a recommended list of books on sex hygiene. One of the patients had undergone four years of psychoanalysis. Two had visited psychiatrists at weekly intervals for approximately 6 months and the remaining two patients had been treated by clinical psychologists for one year and 5 months respectively. (Lazarus, 1963, p. 274)

All were treated through systematic desensitization. All were taught to relax. Stimulus hierarchies were made up, and items from these lists presented, progressively from the mildest anxiety-provoking stimulus to the strongest. Lazarus gives one of his cases in detail to illustrate the therapeutic procedure, and it is quoted in full here for that purpose.

> Mrs. A, age 24 years, had been married for 2½ years during which time she claimed to have had coitus on less than two dozen occasions. She always experienced violent dyspareunia during intercourse as well as 'disgust and anxiety of the whole messy business.' She could tolerate casual kissing and caressing without anxiety and at times found these experiences 'mildly pleasant.' The background of her problem was clearly one of Puritanical upbringing in which much emphasis was placed on the sinful qualities of carnal desire. Mrs. A's husband had endeavored to solve their difficulties by providing his wife with books on sex techniques and practices. Mrs. A had obligingly read these books but her emotional reactions remained unchanged. She sought treatment of her own accord when she suspected that her husband had developed an extramarital attachment.

After diagnostic interviews and psychometric tests, systematic desensitization was administered according to the following hierarchy:

1. dancing with and embracing husband while both fully clothed.
2. being kissed on the cheeks and forehead.
3. being kissed on the lips.
4. sitting in husband's lap, both fully dressed.
5. husband kisses neck and ears.
6. husband caresses hair and face.
7. shoulders and back being caressed.
8. having buttocks and thighs caressed.
9. contact of tongues while kissing.
10. embracing while semiclothed and being aware of husband's erection and his desire for sex.
11. breasts being caressed while fully clothed.
12. naked breasts being caressed.
13. oral stimulation of the breasts.
14. caressing husband's genitals.
15. husband's fingers being inserted into the vagina during precoital loveplay.
16. manual stimulation of the clitoris.
17. having intercourse in the nude under the bed covers.
18. having intercourse in the nude on top of a bed.
19. having coitus in the nude in the dining room or living room.
20. changing positions during intercourse.
21. having intercourse in the nude while sitting in husband's lap. (Lazarus, 1963, pp. 275–276)

Whether these events took place in the light or dark played an important part in the patient's reactions. For example, the patient was able to visualize being caressed on the buttocks and thighs in the dark, but it took several desensitization sessions before she could accept this behavior in the light. During the desensitization treatments, Mrs. A's husband was requested not to have intercourse with her. This was to avoid resensitizing her to the anxiety in their sexual relationship.

Of the sixteen patients, nine became sexually adjusted. They looked forward to sexual intercourse, almost always had an orgasm, and felt free to initiate sexual activity. Instruction took approximately six months and twenty-nine sessions on the average. As Lazarus puts it, even though the results were anything but spectacular, the degree of success was much better than usually achieved with this disorder.

Extensive changes often take place in other spheres of a patient's life beside the specific sexual disorder being treated. Kraft and Al-Issa (1967) used systematic desensitization with a young woman who had never made a satisfactory sexual adjustment to men. A hierarchy of twenty-six items was made—ranging from talking to a man to sexual intercourse. After the first nine sessions, the woman became more friendly to other people as well as to men. Soon the pervasive anxiety she usually felt had disappeared. By the middle of her training, she was not only beginning to enjoy male company but she was tolerating events of a sexual nature, such as watching kissing scenes in a movie and relating better to her parents. At this time she also acquired a part-time job. Later she took a full-time job and felt sufficiently adjusted to end the treatment. However, she began seeing an ex–boy friend, and there were further sessions on more intense and intimate sexual interactions. By the end of treatment she became engaged and reported no difficulty with sexual intercourse. Soon thereafter she was married. A followup nine months later revealed no problems.

Frigidity may often be imbedded in the complex of other behavioral disorders, which may have to be corrected before moving on to the frigidity. Cooper (1964) gives a case of a young woman treated for bronchial asthma initiated by stress conditions. She had had an attack of asthma during intercourse, and it had been so severe she felt she was going to die. It was not feasible to make up desensitization lists to stressful events because almost any one would set off an attack, and they were extraordinarily prevalent. Therefore, she was desensitized to her emotional states. During the desensitization sessions, verbal suggestions were made by the therapist that she was feeling anxious, but at the first sign of anxiety, the suggestions were stopped. Each session ended with deep relaxation. Increasing emotional states were portrayed until she could tolerate them. When her asthma was corrected, the sexual problem was then taken up.

How fear was conditioned to her sexual responses was explained to her. She was instructed to practice relaxing deeply when in bed with her husband and not to initiate any sexual activity unless she felt calm enough to proceed. As she obtained confidence, she was to proceed only when she felt capable and desired. She was successful the first time she did this. There were no further problems in her sexual relations.

Madsen and Ullmann (1967) recommend that the husband be brought into the desensitization procedure, both in constructing the hierarchy and in presenting items from it. When the husband is a partner in the treatment, he is better able to behave appropriately and to communicate with his wife. He is also less fearful and may understand social problems confounding the sexual relationship. Madsen and Ullmann, unlike other behavior therapists, also suggest that intercourse take place during the desensitization process. They feel this may reinforce any progress the client is making and that it is only common sense in light of the client's desire to perform well. The critical consideration is only that activity be engaged in that the person eagerly wants.

HOMOSEXUALITY: Homosexuality is a form of sexual behavior difficult to change. Presumably it is as hard to change as heterosexual behavior. Individuals vary a good deal in the complexity of the reinforcers governing their homosexual activity. The problem of treatment is confounded further because differing sorts of aversive consequences may be attendant on sexual activity. People may come to treatment because of court order or voluntarily. Freund (1960) states that therapy is most effective with those who come voluntarily and not under court order. Others support this contention. However, to come voluntarily means that homosexual behavior has an aversive consequence, as it has for the individual under court order. The difference might be in degree of pervasiveness of punishment, especially through the "self," but this has not been studied systematically in its relationship to types of therapy.

There are a number of different behavioral techniques used with homosexuality. Most therapists have used some form of aversive conditioning with drugs or shock. Only the simplest classical or operant techniques are used and, though the rate of effectiveness is low, it is perhaps surprising that there is any effect at all, especially as many of the cases presented in the literature turned to behavioral therapy as a last resort. However, MacCulloch and Feldman (1967) obtained a 60 percent improvement well above the 27 percent "achieved by experienced psychotherapists in a comparable series." (MacCulloch and Feldman, 1967, p. 597) They attribute their success to the use of a more sophisticated operant method, the anticipatory avoidance technique. In this method the individual terminates a stimulus which signals that an aversive event will occur. By so doing he prevents the event, and is thus reinforced for avoiding a situation in which something unpleasant may occur. In this case the signal is the sexual aspects of social interaction with the same sex.

Most of the behavioral therapeutic work with homosexuality, as with other sexual problems, has been done in the last decade. It has become increasingly sophisticated. At first, respondent conditioning was used, as noxious stimuli were paired with preferred objects. The technique was unknowingly muddled with operant features. Improvements have led to techniques producing changes more resistant to extinction, techniques in which no aversive stimuli are presented, or in which these stimuli are covert or symbolic.

Thorpe, Schmidt, and Castel (1963) used shock, after attempting to positively condition a homosexual to females. The individual was to masturbate to whatever fantasy he wanted. Shortly before reaching orgasm, a female picture was presented. Despite a number of trials, his imagery remained homosexual. It was then decided to present the female picture randomly throughout his masturbation. However, this also did not alter his use of homosexual fantasy while masturbating. There was then a series of negative conditioning trials in which male pictures were presented and the individual occasionally shocked. Positive conditioning with female pictures was then tried again. This time the individual showed reluctance to use homosexual imagery when masturbating and used heterosexual. After a short relapse and some further positively conditioning trials, he continued to use heterosexual imagery solely. Eight months later he was expressing an interest in finding the right girl to marry.

Thorpe, Schmidt, and Castel's objective was to have the client fantasize females while masturbating. He would have to take further steps with females by himself. They were successful in their limited objective, even though the client engaged in some homosexual activity in a minor way.

The points they make with respect to the objective of behavioral therapy and how it is to be evaluated are pertinent.

> The patient has, however, technically relapsed and will be regarded in this way by many. It is therefore important to examine the meaning of this concept. Its main usage is in the field of medicine when people who seem to be recovering from their disease are overcome by it once more. If we consider our attempt to treat our homosexual as a straightforward exercise in the psychology of learning, then the big problem is one of behavior manipulation and change. Are the changes, which are to be achieved, being maintained or not? The medical concepts of relapse, therefore, are inapplicable within this framework.
>
> In a similar way, if we regard homosexuality as a learned behavior pattern, and not as a disease, then the medical concept of cure is also inapplicable. If anything has been achieved with this patient, it is simply that he has been taught to use females in a way completely new to him and more in line with the requirements of the existing social structures. (Thorpe, *et al.*, 1963, p. 361)

Behavioral modification techniques with homosexuals have not been restricted to aversion conditioning using shock or drugs. Assertive training, systematic desensitization, and the use of aversive images have all been successful. These and other techniques do not require elaborate equipment or hospitalization.

Systematic desensitization was used with a 32-year-old homosexual who had had a number of unpleasant heterosexual experiences. After leaving an orphanage he met his mother, a drunken prostitute, who invited him to have intercourse with her. As a young man he engaged in a number of homosexual activities, many with sadistic overtones. He was married after a courtship of two weeks, and the marriage was a failure. He had premature ejaculations and difficulty in obtaining erections. The marriage lasted only nine months, and he returned to his homosexual activity. (Kraft, 1967)

Kraft felt that if the client was desensitized from anxiety in behaving in a normal heterosexual manner, he would lose his homosexual inclinations without treatment of the homosexuality directly. A hierarchical list of events involving normal heterosexual behavior was drawn up. He was asked to imagine these vividly. Over a period of six sessions they were gone over in detail. At the last session it was realized that the client could not imagine having intercourse unless the therapist was present. The client had formed a very strong attachment to the therapist. Another stimulus list was drawn up involving separation from the therapist. The items were stated in terms of the patient coping on his own—that is, without contact with the therapist. The list went as follows:

1. Coping on his own for 24 hours.
2. Coping on his own for 24 hours and increasing by 1-hour intervals to 36 hours.
3. Coping on his own for 48 hours, 72 hours, 96 hours.
4. Coping on his own for 4 days and then increasing by 1-day intervals to 10 days. (Kraft, 1967, p. 817)

Approximately a year later the patient was continuing to have sexual intercourse with women and had no return of his former homosexual activity.

Gold and Neufeld (1965) combined a number of behavioral techniques in reconditioning a 16-year-old homosexual. The young man's life seemed to be characterized by a good deal of personal inadequacy and fear of failure. He was first desensitized to events in which these feelings occurred. Attention was then directed to his homosexual activity. He was asked to imagine himself in a public toilet with a repugnant old man. It was suggested to the client that under no circumstances would he solicit him. When the client agreed, he was reinforced verbally with words such as, "well done." The image of the old man was changed slowly to that of more attractive males but under prohibitive circumstances such as a nearby policeman. When the image was most attractive, the prohibitions were slowly removed until there was no desire for soliciting, even in the absence of a policeman. He was then given a choice between an attractive young man and an attractive young woman. The circumstances surrounding the young man were full of unpleasant cues, while the young woman always appeared in pleasant circumstances. The patient eventually chose the young woman consistently, even though the prohibitive cues had been removed progressively from the situation with the young man. A year later there was no desire for homosexual contact. The client was succeeding scholastically and socially and was dating a girl.

Cautela (1967) has used covert sensitization successfully with a number of behavioral problems. The client is first relaxed and a listing of desirable events made. His problem is discussed, and he is told that a noxious stimulus will be associated with the actions he finds so pleasurable. He is asked to visualize his homosexual activity and when he sees himself engaged in it, he is to indicate this, usually by raising an index finger. The therapist then portrays some extraordinarily noxious circumstances associated with his actions and the object of his actions. Cautela gives the following as an example of what he says:

> I want you to imagine that you are in a room with X. He is completely naked. As you approach him you notice he has sores and scabs all over his body with some kind of fluid oozing from them. A terrible foul stench comes from his body. The odor is so strong it makes you sick. You can feel food particles coming up your throat. You can't help yourself and you vomit all over the place, all over the floor, on your hands and clothes. And now that even makes you sicker and you vomit again and again all over everything. You turn away and then you start to feel better. You try to get out of the room but the door seems to be locked. The smell is still strong but you try desperately to get out. You kick at the door frantically until it finally opens and you run out into the nice clean air. It smells wonderful. You go home and shower and you feel so clean. (Cautela, 1967, p. 164)

After training in the office he is instructed to go through the procedure at least ten to twenty times twice a day at home.

Again, this is a type of operant conditioning in that aversive consequences follow the patient's responses. It is all done with verbal behavior much as traditional psychotherapy is, but the arrangement is different. Desired objects and actions are given such aversive properties that the individual is reinforced for leaving them, and after sufficient conditioning these properties become occasions for the individual's avoiding them.

Cautela cites a number of benefits derivable from covert sensitization. It can be applied by the individual outside of the therapist's office; hence a greater number of conditioning trials can be made. Since it is under the individual's control, he can initiate it in difficult or tempting situations. It helps relieve the anxiety that is so pervasive in behavioral disorders, and this helps in correcting the disorder and maintaining new behavior.

An experimental test of the effectiveness of covert sensitization was made by Barlow, Leitenberg, and Agras.[24] The subjects were two males who had engaged in pedophilic and homosexual behavior. Measures of their usual level of sexual activity were obtained over five sessions. A ranking list of sexually exciting scenes was made and placed on cards. For the homosexual, some of these scenes involved his current boy friend. Three measures of sexual arousals were taken. First, the clients counted the number of times they were sexually aroused by a young girl or a mature male. Second, they placed their cards in a set of categories valued from 0 to 4, from which an arousal score was calculated. Third, galvanic skin responses to sixty imagined scenes from their list were recorded.

The patients were told that they had developed a bad habit and that techniques would be used which had been successful in similar cases in breaking that habit. However, to ameliorate discouragement during extinction, they were told not to get too upset if there were relapses. In each session, four scenes chosen from their hierarchy were presented. In the first four the patient was described as approaching his sexual object, getting nauseous, and vomiting. The following was used as one of the noxious stimuli with the homosexual subject.

> As you get closer to the door you notice a queer feeling in the pit of the stomach. You open the door and see Bill lying on the bed naked and you can sense that puke is filling up your stomach and forcing its way up to your throat. You walk over to Bill and you can see him clearly, as you reach out for him you can taste the puke, bitter and sticky and acidity on your tongue; you start gagging and retching and chunks of vomit are coming out of your mouth and nose, dropping onto your skin and all over Bill's skin. (Barlow, *et. al.*, p. 598)

A second set of four scenes was then presented in which the individual again gets nauseous, but as he walks away he feels relieved and relaxed.

During extinction, no noxious stimuli were described; the sex scenes were simply presented. The therapist actively kept the subject from imagining aversive consequences. In reacquisition the noxious stimuli were again an aversive consequence of the sexual behavior, and the same procedure was repeated.

The data showed that imagined noxious stimuli were successful in changing sexual behavior. There was a sharp drop in sexual behavior from the baseline rate during acquisition. When aversive consequences were taken away, sexual behavior increased to its former level. The subjects reported being depressed, and the homosexual subject had an affair for the first time since conditioning began. When aversive consequences were again introduced during reacquisition, deviant arousals dropped to zero.

Of course, a positive experimental test is not final proof of the efficacy of a method, but it does help to give confidence that what one is doing is relevant to the changes observed.

Conclusion

The relationship between the individual and the circumstances in which he behaves may be altered by changing the circumstances or some surrogate of them. In an institutional setting we commonly change only the circumstances. We alter the procedures of a welfare office, the action of the government in its income program, and the employment practices of business, confident that people will then live their lives differently. But with the individual in the clinical setting, a different problem appears to present itself. He is apart from the "real-life" circumstances in which he normally behaves, and so we try to alter *him*.

The individual is placed or portrayed in circumstances not really present. In psychotherapy, different forms of his behavior in various situations are described in detail either to point out their consequences or to give the individual insight—i.e., knowledge of how circumstances govern him. The psychoanalyst considers himself to be curing disorders in the mental apparatus presumed to govern the person's behavior. The psychotherapist "changes ego structures," "promotes reality testing," "helps unlock unsolved conflicts," and so on, but it is very hard to specify either the changes in behavior or the measures that bring changes about.

In behavioral therapy, events are portrayed more concretely, and specifically to the behavior observed. It is not necessary to go into history; to explain why the individual behaves as he does is to describe how he presently behaves under certain circumstances. History is useful in obtaining some idea of the reinforcement schedules that have shaped a behavior, but analysis and reeducation proceed in the current situation, within the learning framework of respondent and operant technology.

Whatever the modification technique, the sexual behavior to be changed must be defined in behavioral detail. Sufficient situations must be delineated to relate the behavior to the reinforcement contingencies governing it. The sexual behavior to be changed must be pinpointed to apply aversive consequences to the narrowest possible range of the response repertoire. It hardly needs saying that causing impotence as a result of punishing undesired sexual responses is not a preferred therapeutic outcome. By pinpointing behavior we can apply positive reinforcers more effectively in part because they should be applied immediately.

The range of techniques is growing, and growing more sophisticated, as more transfer is made from the laboratory to the everyday situation.

The detailed procedures of any one of the prevalent techniques should be obtained from the literature. Those techniques, however, in which the client conducts his own therapy are best. The client can make counts of his own behavior outside the therapeutic setting. He can chart these to note progress and follow the influence of the treatment variable. The "therapeutic setting" is now wherever the client happens to be, because he can now apply his own conditioning techniques by arranging positive and negative reinforcers appropriately.

The aim of behavioral therapy is self-control. The correction of a sexual disorder must be a byproduct of this. The justification of a behavior technology is freedom from painful compulsion. Only when the individual is able to manage his own behavior, without destruction to himself or others, has the therapist been successful.

NOTES

Bandura, A. (1961) "Psychotherapy as a Learning Process." *Psychological Bulletin,* Vol. 58, no. 2, pp. 143–59.

Bandura, A. (1969) *Principles of Behavior Modification.* (New York: Holt, Rinehart and Winston, Inc.)

Barlow, D. H., Leitenberg, H., and Agras, W. S. (1968) "Experimental Control of Sexual Deviation through Manipulation of the Noxious Scene in Covert Sensitization," *Journal of Abnormal Psychology,* 74, no. 5, pp. 596–601.

Bond, I. K., and Hutchison, H. C., (1965), "Application of Reciprocal Inhibition Therapy to Exhibitionism," in *Case Studies in Behavior Modification,* ed. L. P. Ullman and L. Krasner. (New York: Holt, Rinehart and Winston, Inc.) pp. 246–50.

Cautela, J. R. (1967) "Covert Sensitization." *Psychological Reports* 20: 164, 459–68.

Cooper, A. J. (1964) "A Case of Bronchial Asthma Treated by Behavior Therapy." *Behavior Research and Therapy,* vol. 1: 351–6.

Cooper, A. J. (1963) "A Case of Fetishism and Impotence Treated by Behavior Therapy." *British Journal of Psychiatry,* 109: 649–52.

Davison, G. C. (1968) "Elimination of a Sadistic Fantasy by a Client-Controlled Counter Conditioning Technique," *Journal of Abnormal Psychology* 73, no. 1, pp. 84–90.

Evans, D. R. (1968) "Masturbatory Fantasy and Sexual Deviation." *Behavior Research and Therapy,* Vol. 6, pp. 17–19.

Eysenck, H. J. and Rachman, S. (1965) *The Causes and Cures of Neuroses* (San Diego, Calif.: Robert R. Knapp, 1965).

Feldman, M. P. and MacCulloch, M. J. (1964) "A Systematic Approach to the Treatment of Homosexuality by Conditioned Aversion: Preliminary Report." *American Journal of Psychiatry,* Vol. 121, pp. 167–72.

Feldman, M. P. and MacCulloch, M. J. (1965) "The Application of Anticipatory Avoidance Learning to the Treatment of Homosexuality—I. Theory, Technique and Preliminary Results." *Behavior Research and Therapy,* Vol. 2, pp. 165–183.

Franks, C. M., ed. (1969) *Behavior Therapy.* (New York: McGraw-Hill Book Company.)

Freund, K. (1960) "Some Problems in the Treatment of Homosexuality," in Eysenck, H. J., *Behavior Therapy and the Neuroses* (Oxford: Pergamon Press, 1960).

Gold, S., and Neufeld, I. L. (1965) "A Learning Approach to the Treatment of Homosexuality." *Behavior Research and Therapy* 2: pp. 201–4.

Grossberg, J. M. (1964) "Behavior Therapy: A Review." *Psychological Bulletin,* 62: no. 2, pp. 73–88.

Jackson, B. T. (1969) "A Case of Voyeurism Treated by Counterconditioning," *Behavior Research and Therapy* 7: 133–4.

Kolvin, I. (1967) "Aversive Imaginary Treatment in Adolescents," *Behavior Research and Therapy* 5: 245–8.

Kraft, T. (1967) "A Case of Homosexuality Treated by Systematic Desensitization," *American Journal of Psychotherapy* 21: 815–22.

Kraft, T. and Al-Issa, I. (1967) "Behavior Therapy and the Treatment of Frigidity," *American Journal of Psychotherapy* 21: 116–20.

Kushner, M. (1965) "The Reduction of a Long-Standing Fetish by Means of Aversive Conditioning," in *Case Studies in Behavior Modification,* ed. L. P. Ullmann and L. Krasner. (New York: Holt, Rinehart and Winston).

Lavin, N. I., Thorpe, J. G., Barker, J. C., Blakemore, C. B., and Conway, C. G. (1961) "Behavior Therapy in a Case of Transvestism," *Journal of Nervous and Mental Diseases,* 133: 346–53.

Lazarus, A. A. (1963) "The Treatment of Chronic Frigidity by Systematic Desensitization," *Journal of Nervous and Mental Diseases* 136: 272–8.

Lazarus, A. A. (1965) "The Treatment of a Sexually Inadequate Man," in *Case Studies in Behavior Modification.* Edited by L. P. Ullman and L. Krasner. (New York: Holt, Rinehart and Winston, Inc.), pp. 243–245.

MacCulloch, M. J. and Feldman, M. P. (1967) "Aversion Therapy in Management of 43 Homosexuals." *British Medical Journal* 2: 594–7.

MacCulloch, M. J., Feldman, M. P., and Pinshoff, J. M. (1965) "The Application of Anticipatory Avoidance Learning to the Treatment of Homosexuality—II. Avoidance Response Latencies and Pulse Rate Changes," *Behavior Research and Therapy,* Vol. 3, pp. 21–43.

Madsen, C. H., and Ullman, L. P. (1967). "Innovations in the Desensitization of Frigidity," *Behavior Research and Therapy,* 5: 67–68.

Marks, I. M. and Gelder, M. G. (1967) "Transvestism and Fetishism: Clinical and Psychological Changes During Faradic Aversion," *British Journal of Psychiatry* 113: 711–29.

Marks, L. M., Rachma, E., and Gelder, M. G. (1965) "Methods for Assessment of Aversion Treatment and Fetishism with Masochism." *Behavior Research and Therapy* 3: 253–8.

McGuire, R. J., Carlisle, J. M., and Young, B. G. (1965) "Sexual Deviations as Conditioned Behavior, a Hypothesis," *Behavior Research and Therapy,* 2: pp. 185–190.

Rachman, S. (1961) "Sexual Disorders and Behavior Therapy." *American Journal of Psychiatry,* Vol. 118, pp. 235–240.

Rachman, S. and Teasdale, J. (1969) *Aversion Therapy and Behavior Disorders.* (Coral Gables, Florida: University of Miami Press.)

Skinner, B. F. (1953) *Science and Human Behavior.* (New York: The Macmillan Company).

Stuart, R. B. (1970) "Behavioral Control of Overeating." In *Control of Human Behavior.* Edited by R. Ulrich, T. Stachnik, and J. Mabry. (Glenview, Illinois: Scott, Foresman and Company.)

J. G. Thorpe, E. Schmidt, and D. Castel, "A Comparison of Positive and Negative (Aversive) Conditioning in the Treatment of Homosexuality." *Behavior Research and Therapy* 1 (1963): 357–62.

J. Wolpe and A. A. Lazarus, *Behavior Therapy Techniques* (New York: Pergamon Press, 1966).

SUGGESTED READINGS

Bandura, A. "Psychotherapy as a Learning Process." *Psychological Bulletin* 58 (1961), no. 2, pp. 143–59.

Bandura, A. *Principles of Behavior Modification.* New York: Holt, Rinehart and Winston, 1969.

Bruck, M. "Behavior Modification Theory and Practice: A Critical Review." *Social Work* 13 (1968): 43–50.

Evans, D. R. "Masturbatory Fantasy and Sexual Deviation." *Behavior Research and Therapy* 6: 17–19.

Feldman, M. P., and MacCulloch, M. J. "A Systematic Approach to the Treatment of Homosexuality by Conditioned Aversion: Preliminary Report." *American Journal of Psychiatry* 121: 167–72.

Feldman, M. P., and MacCulloch, M. J. "The Application of Anticipatory Avoidance Learning to the Treatment of Homosexuality—I. Theory, Technique and Preliminary Results." *Behavior Research and Therapy* 2: 165–83.

Franks, C. M., ed. *Behavior Therapy.* New York: McGraw-Hill, 1969.

Grossberg, J. M. "Behavior Therapy: A Review." *Psychological Bulletin* 62 (1964).

Lazarus, A. A. "The Treatment of a Sexually Inadequate Man," In *Case Studies in Behavior Modification.* Edited by L. P. Ullmann and L. Krasner. New York: Holt, Rinehart and Winston, 1965, pp. 243–5.

MacCulloch, M. J., Feldman, M. P., and Pinshoff, J. M. "The Application of Anticipatory Avoidance Learning to the Treatment of Homosexuality—II. Avoidance Response Latencies and Pulse Rate Changes." *Behavior Research and Therapy* 3 (1965): 21–43.

Morrow, W. and Gochros, H. "Misconceptions Regarding Behavior Modification." *Social Service Review* 44 (1970): 293–307.

Rachman, S. "Sexual Disorders and Behavior Therapy." *American Journal of Psychiatry* 118: 235–40.

Rachman, S., and Teasdale, J. *Aversion Therapy and Behavior Disorders.* Coral Gables, Fla.: University of Miami Press, 1969.

Tharp, K., and Wetzel, K. *Behavior Modification in the Natural Environment.* New York: Academic Press, 1969.

Thomas, E., *The Sociobehavioral Approach and Application to Social Work.* New York: Council on Social Work Education, 1968.

Wolpe, J., and Lazarus, A. A. *Behavior Therapy Techniques.* New York: Pergamon Press, 1966.

18

Educating Graduate Social Work Students to Deal with Sexual Problems

Harvey L. Gochros

There are few areas of human behavior that can create as much pain and anguish for as many people, rich and poor, young and old, black and white, as human sexuality. American society is undergoing a major change in its openness and attitudes regarding sexuality, if not in its actual behavior. Yet sex is still a subject which social workers, with few exceptions, prefer to ignore.

There is little taught in our graduate schools about sexual behavior problems and their treatment. A study of graduate social work students concluded that any knowledge or attitudes regarding sexuality development by the students during their graduate program were "not due to any known factor for which [social work] educators are responsible."[1] There are few vigorous social work programs being offered relating to contemporary sexual problems, and social workers have failed to take an active role in improving societal attitudes and sanctions regarding sexual behavior.[2]

Explicit references to human sexual problems are rare in social work literature. When these references do appear, they are generally presented as one aspect of a client's behavior which is incorporated into an overall psychosocial diagnosis, or they are regarded as "symptoms" of a more general disease process which cannot be treated as a specific entity. Sexual dysfunctioning is rarely portrayed as a discrete entity in itself, amenable to and *requiring* social work intervention. Social workers have made little visible effort to undertake the epidemiological or practice research necessary to understand more effectively the nature of sexual problems and how to deal with them. Such collective avoidance among the profession's educators and leaders supports the individual practitioner's reluctance to engage in this area of practice, deprives him of adequate practice models, and gives him a justification for his own avoidance.

Yet much of social work practice involves people with specifically sexual problems: for example, the husband and wife who can speak with each

244

other about anything but their sexual relationship; the young man with anxieties about masturbation; the adolescent who uses Saran wrap, thinking it will serve as an adequate contraceptive; the young married woman who wants an abortion; the homosexual whose life satisfactions are blocked by social disapproval, job insecurity, and self-hate; the rural mother of multiple unwanted children who feels compelled to have more; the victim of a rape; the aged couple whose sexual adjustment no longer works; the community divided over the introduction of sex education in its schools; and the people of all ages and social groups whose ignorance and biases interfere with their own and others' sexual satisfactions. The list of the social consequences of sexual behavior is a long one which emphasizes the need for social workers to recognize and deal directly with the problems associated with human sexuality rather than to deny the centrality of the sexual component in these problems.

Such a recognition is beginning to appear, as evidenced by these comments from *Child Welfare:*

> While revolts against poverty, racism and other social ills attract much of our time and attention, a deeper, if less spectacular revolt is occurring against the long established standards governing relations between the sexes. . . . Young people are more sexually permissive, they are confused and looking for standards by which to govern their sexual behavior and they need help. . . . What is the responsibility of child welfare agencies in relation to this situation? What are agencies doing to help young people deal with the social pressures toward sexual acting-out that surround them?[3]

Many social workers use a number of rationalizations to cover their basic discomfort and unwillingness to engage in this particular cluster of social problems. "Sex is just a symptom" (the medical concept of sex as just a symptom is being questioned with increasing frequency). "It's not within the area of social work competence" (but it should be—social functioning certainly includes sexual functioning). "Cases like this should be referred to physicians" (is sex only physiological?). "It's basically a religious issue" (only in part—and that is subject to widely varying interpretations). "Clients really don't want to talk about it" (often true if the social worker is uncomfortable about it). "I don't know how to deal with it or talk about it" (then learn!).

These arguments sidestep the major reason for the avoidance of this material, which is that we are influenced by our society's general attitudes about sexuality. Sexual activity unrelated to reproduction is still considered sinful, especially for poor people, a necessary evil to be performed in secrecy, a biological necessity. It is something to be talked about in whispers, snickers, and boasts by men—but women, good women, do not even think

about it (and many social workers are good women). Those who are concerned about sexual problems are branded as sexually obsessed "dirty old
men," or as frustrated, voyeuristic women. It is not surprising, then, that
social workers have avoided the topic of sexuality as have, indeed, most
other helping professions.

Until recently, for example, most physicians were not prepared in their
own education to offer counseling for the sexual problems that were
brought to them by many of their patients. Yet clients have regularly been
referred to physicians by social workers, with the mistaken idea that they
are the best source of counseling in sexual matters. The medical profession
has recognized this gap in their educational program. Within the last few
years, more than half of the 82 medical schools in the United States have
introduced courses on human sexuality, whereas ten years ago, less then
ten of them offered even a single lecture on sexual behavior and problems.
Furthermore, programs are being developed which will prepare medical
educators to present these courses to their students.[4]

If social workers are to accept the responsibility of working adequately
with sexual problems, graduate education must show similar initiative. The
first step could be to offer a specific course on human sexuality in graduate
social work programs.

Why a Separate Course?

If one were to agree that sexual behavior is a component of many of
the problems experienced by social work clients, and that problems in the
sexual area are indeed common, would it be sufficient to encourage the
human behavior and social environment instructors to focus more on the
nature and variation, both normal and dysfunctional, of sexual experience;
the social welfare and policy instructors to address themselves to needed
legal and policy reforms regarding sex; and the practice instructors to include more material on intervention in sex-related problems? Eventually,
such a dissemination of sexual content may be desirable, with sexuality
being treated as just another aspect of social functioning requiring social
work attention. To the extent that sexual material is now discussed in graduate education, this is the manner in which it is presented. At this point
in time, however, sexuality is not "just another" facet of human behavior.
It is a unique one, which often brings out discomfort, confusion, resistances, biases, and ignorance on the part of the students and the faculty
who deal with it. For this reason, it seems more effective to offer a separate
course specifically entitled Human Sexuality, at least as an elective study.
Separate, discrete courses generally serve the function of highlighting
slighted areas of social work interest and provide an opportunity to pin-
point, develop, and then integrate areas which are otherwise ignored, into

the general curriculum. Such a separation also provides students who take the course with an opportunity to develop specialized interest and competence.

The remainder of this paper presents a model for such a course based on electives which were recently introduced in two schools of social work.

Objectives of the Course

The primary objective of a course in human sexuality taught within a graduate school of social work is to familiarize students with the range of expression of human sexuality, how sexual behaviors are learned and developed, the potential resulting individual and social problems, and the practice and social policy interventions which can alleviate individual and collective sexual problems. The course has the more general purpose of helping students to feel comfortable and to accept the appropriateness of their professional involvement in this area, and perhaps also of helping them to accept the challenge of addressing part of their practice to human sexual problems.

Knowledge Objectives

The student is introduced to current ideas of how sexual behavior—functional and dysfunctional—is learned. He is then helped to review how and why society attempts to control sexual behavior. Particular focus is placed on cultural variations and on the range of individual differences in sexual expression (for example, masturbation, extramarital intercourse, sex crimes, abortion, prostitution, homosexuality, and sexual incompetence), and how these problems may be understood by the social worker. The knowledge base of the course is broad. In addition to applying knowledge from other courses and from previous learning, the course attempts to familiarize the student with such diverse areas as developments in contraceptives, Masters and Johnson's research on the physiology and modification of sexual response, and the studies of sexual behavior reported by the University of Indiana's Institute for Sex Research.

Attitudinal Objectives

Such a course as this recognizes that the sexual attitudes of students cover a wide range and are deeply set. It is therefore incumbent upon the instructor to clarify his own attitudes for the class, and allow the students to express theirs fully. Essentially, the interrelated major attitudes to be communicated are:

1. Both acceptable sexual behavior and sexual disturbances are learned, and to a large extent socially and culturally determined. There are

few absolutes as to sexual "normalcy," and one has to be careful to discriminate between individual and collective biases and the actual results of various sexual activities.

2. Adults should have the right to express themselves sexually in private in any manner they choose without legal or social recriminations or labels of "sickness," as long as such self-expression does not interfere with the reasonable rights of others.[5]

3. The social worker has the responsibility to seek ways to support the sexual rights implicit in these statements. He has a further responsibility and competence to provide and aggressively deliver social work services in connection with problems related to human sexuality, and to work toward affecting community knowledge and attitudes in what he and the profession consider appropriate directions.

Skill Objectives

The course attempts to enable students to practice comfortably, effectively, and assertively in areas related to human sexuality. This involves not only developing clinical skills, including the basic skills of communication regarding sexual material, but also macro-intervention procedures such as working with a police department, school board, county AMA, or state legislature, as particular problems dictate.

Content of the Course

By the very nature of the course, content will include material relating to practice, human behavior, and the social environment as well as social welfare policies and services. The following outline summarizes the range of such content.

I. Human Sexual Behavior and Environment Influences
   A. The nature and varieties of sexual expression
   B. The vocabulary of sex
   C. Social, class, and cultural differences in sexual behavior
   D. Sex and age differences in sexual behavior
   E. Sexual expression in marriage
   F. Rural–urban differences in sexual behavior
   G. The nature of "deviance"
   H. Pregnancy out of wedlock
   I. Sex offenders and their victims
   J. Physical aspects of sexuality; the anatomy and physiology of sex
   K. Nature of sex–related diseases and dysfunctioning

II. Social Policy and Sexuality
   A. Sexual rights
   B. The effects of social policy on sexual behavior: the formulation of a national policy
   C. Family planning policy
   D. Abortion policy
   E. Pornography and censorship policy
   F. Laws pertaining to sexuality
III. Social Work Practice Approaches to Sexual Problems
   A. Problems
      1. Unwanted pregnancies
      2. Deviance
      3. Common sexual disorders
      4. Sexual offenders
      5. The sex offenders' victims
      6. Sexual aspects of adoption
   B. Approaches
      1. Prevention: relevant sex education
      2. Individual approaches
      3. Group approaches
      4. Interviewing techniques
      5. Planning and conducting research in human sexual behavior

The above outline is only suggestive of the various topics that could be included in such a course and does not imply a particular sequence. Time limitations and the need to enable students to explore emotionally charged areas adequately require selectivity in content.

Format of Course

In the past experiences of most students (and perhaps faculty), discussions of sex have frequently been conducted in either of two ways:

1. As clandestine sessions in which the Victorian fear of sex as something dirty, evil, mysterious, and perhaps frightening, still hangs in the air, or
2. As formal, dry, antiseptic, medically oriented lectures, exemplified by the vague biologically focused content of high school and college physical education and preparation–for–marriage courses.

The course suggested here must avoid both approaches. It must be communicated to the students and subsequently by them to their respective client groups that sex need be neither dirty nor dull.

The instructor of this course sets its tone. By his directness, comfort, and honesty, he creates the opportunity for the class to involve itself actively in the material. His words and the appropriate use of humor are critical. If the student is to be helped to develop a comfortable approach to exploring and working with sexual problems, he will need a knowledgeable teacher with whose attitudes and manner he can identify and after whom he can model his own professional behaviors.

It would defeat the purposes of the course if it were taught mainly through lectures. Rather, small group seminars would be the ideal format. The class itself must create an atmosphere in which the student can reveal and discuss his uncertainties, anxieties, and disagreements, or his lack of information regarding human sexuality.

Among the most effective teaching procedures are discussions and exercises early in the course geared explicitly to desensitizing the students to speaking about sex[6] (one ingenious group of students developed a sexual crossword puzzle to enhance and desensitize the use of a sexual vocabulary); video tapes; in- and out-of-class research which gives students the opportunity, sanction, and requirement of exploring sexual matters openly and of talking about them candidly and professionally; discussions of cases carried by the students in field placements and in previous work experiences; critiques of current literature, motion pictures, novels, and even advertisements having sexual content; and guest experts such as gynecologists, law professors, and anthropologists, who generally welcome the opportunity to speak freely to a group explicitly interested in the subject of sex.

Conclusion

There are problems associated with introducing a graduate social work course in human sexuality such as the one outlined here: a crowded curriculum, administrative and educational concerns, anxieties, and limitations; inadequate literature; and the difficulty of obtaining instructors who admit an interest in what is often a taboo topic. Both teacher and class become suspect by their involvement in the class. But by its very existence, the course serves the purpose of bringing sex into the open in a graduate program. As Virginia Johnson has noted, "People must learn that they are sexual beings and learn to be comfortable with that fact."[7]

Students who have taken a course such as that outlined here have described it as a worthwhile experience that fills a gap in their formal education and is consistent with their perception of social work practice.

Despite the image of today's graduate student being knowledgeable and objective about sexuality, if not bored by it, some are unsophisticated and more are uncomfortable about it. Many are concerned about this area of their future professional responsibility and have had little or no structured opportunity or sanction to learn conscientiously about, discuss, and understand human sexuality. The problems cited here in introducing this course are minor in contrast to the contributions such a course could make to the students' education, to the possible enhancement of a major area of human functioning, and to the potential diminution of human suffering.

NOTES

[1] Kay Cajacob and Edwin Rill, "A Study of Social Work Students' Attitudes Toward Marital-Sex Problems" (Research Project, unpublished, School of Social Work, University of Missouri, June, 1964), p. 54.

[2] A notable exception to these criticisms is in the area of family planning and birth control, in which social workers have become increasingly involved. See, for instance, the section on Family Planning in *Public Welfare* 27, no. 1 (January 1969).

[3] Editor's page, *Child Welfare* 47, no. 7 (July 1968), p. 380.

[4] Tom Buckley, "All They Talk about Is Sex," *New York Times Magazine,* 20 April 1969, p. 98.

[5] As an illustration of the danger of the "sickness" label, students review the changing knowledge regarding clitoral orgasm (as compared to vaginal). Traditionally, preference for clitoral stimulation was perceived as "neurotic." Social workers engaged in marital counseling often supported this assessment and contributed to the guilt feelings of the client. The recent work of Masters and Johnson, however, suggests that a preference for clitoral stimulation may be physiologically based.

[6] Excellent discussion guides and literature on sexual subjects are obtainable through the Sex Information and Education Council of the United States (SIECUS), 1855 Broadway, New York, New York 10023.

[7] Buckley, *op. cit.,* p. 104.

SUGGESTED READINGS

Haselkorn, F. "Family Planning: Implications for Social Work Education." *Journal of Education for Social Work* 6 (1970), no. 2, pp. 13–20.

Lief, H. "What Medical Schools Teach about Sex." *Bulletin of the Tulane Univ. Medical Faculty,* Vol. 22 (1963), pp. 161–68.

Lief, H. "Teaching Doctors About Sex." In *An Analysis of Human Sexual Response.* Edited by Ruth and Edward Buecher. Boston: Little, Brown and Company, 1966.

Lief, H. "New Developments in the Sex Education of the Physician." *Journal of the American Medical Association,* 15 June 1970.

Rapoport, L. "Education and Training of Social Workers for Roles and Functions in Family Planning." *Journal of Education for Social Work* 6 (1970), no. 2, pp. 27–38.

Social Policy and Sexual Behavior

In this section, concern is with the policy of sexual behavior, which is usually of a proscriptive nature as determined by the legislature or court, and also with policies to control the unintended or undesirable results of sexual intercourse, such as family planning policy and service policy for society's sexual casualties.

In general, sex behavior norms are codified in the law and can be changed by the legislative process by adding new ones and voiding old ones, or by the judicial process through a changing interpretation of individual rights as against those of the state. In addition, public agencies, such as those of the prosecutor or police, effect sexual policy by choosing sex laws they will or can enforce and ignoring others.

Another type of policy is that of the medical, educational, or social agency which provides service to sexual victims or assists in the prevention of victimization.

Because most policy regarding sexual behavior is made by the legislature and the courts, these two sociopolitical institutions will be emphasized here. Policymaking may be defined as the process of setting courses of action intended to implement the values, ordinarily of a large group, on a given issue without compromising other values on other issues. The diversity of interests and values in America precludes any sort of determinate identification of a single "best" or "good" policy. The mission of the public policymaker is to allocate scarce resources and mediate among conflicting sets of interests and values. Goal-oriented action toward policy statements is governed by a shared value orientation and some degree of political consensus. The shared value orientation in this country regarding sex behavior is that law should place restraints upon it through the fear of punishment, that law should define "normal" acts and "normal" sex objects. The majority is generally capable of forcing its sex value system upon the minority through law, with scant attention being paid to other values, such as separation of church and state or the concept that certain illegal sex behavior does not injure the public welfare and that punitive action is therefore an invasion of privacy. Consensus in the past seems to have provided an agreed-upon *minimal* range of sexual policies that change only in incremental steps, most of which appear to be based upon a fear of sexual freedom, its consequences, and public costs. Examples are the "moral policeman" services for unwed mothers in public welfare agencies, harsh restrictions on eligibility for abortion service, and "asexual" sex education in public schools. Most of society's sexual policies reflect a repressive controlling value; and the majoritarian-prone legislator is safe in ignoring minority pleas for change (and such proposals are electorally dangerous). Perhaps it is more expedient to let unpopular sex policies abrogate themselves into nonenforcement.[1]

Nonincremental sexual policy changes through the legislature are not likely because such proposals for change lack sufficient "leverage" to influence proximate policymakers who are the public officials. This means that sexual issues calling for change lack relevance for enough people, or for those with power, to energize them to act collectively for change.

Theoretically, policy formation may be divided into the following stages: identifying the problem requiring a policy solution; data gathering and data analysis; publicity about and communication of the policy issues; building support and gaining institutional sanction; organizing intra-elites; financing; and gaining compliance to the policy. It can quickly be surmised from these lengthy and costly processes that few sexual issues can generate the resources necessary to engineer a policy change. Legislative response to sexual issues that result in changed legal norms tends to occur:

a. when the proposed policy change has a well organized and articulate interest group pushing for change.

b. when considerable harm is occurring as a result of legislative inaction and the proposed policy is a practical solution.

c. when the political consequences that are anticipated by the policy change favor taking action.

d. when such things as personal relationships and "rules of the game" favor taking action.

Again, this set of conditions does not exist for advocates of sexual policy change—witness the efforts of homosexual groups to influence public policy. Even modest changes, such as initiating family planning policy, have had a very difficult and lengthy struggle to gain sanction.

Policy may also be made by changes and alterations through the judicial process and the courts. Law is a social institution for achieving desired ends and its policy pronouncements take the form of decisions recognizing interests, settling disputes, and allocating values. Courts appear attractive to interests favoring change because access is more readily available than to the legislature. Note the recent use of courts to change policy minorities, poverty groups, students, and consumers. Courts must hear the disputes and cannot dodge them as the legislature may through self-interest. Even if the sexual issue or dispute lacks a constituency or interest group, the court must hear the individual case and render a decision on its merits. It is also handicapped in that it must wait for the parties in the case, state and citizen, to define the policy issues to be adjudicated. Each litigant must have the resources to initiate and press his claim, and this may be costly and protracted. Subsequently, interests favoring change may lack the means or inclination to suffer the requisite ordeal. With the exception of the few cases defended by the American Civil Liberties Union and radical legal aid groups, recourse to the courts to change sexual policy by challenging its constitutionality is an illusionary source for change for most citizens.

In summary, we can account for the retardation of sexual policy change in the legislature by its unwillingness to act in new areas and its "wait and see" attitude born of political reservation. The courts, on the other hand, are not really designed to solve sociosexual problems through broad comprehensive policy change.[2]

The conflicting and pluralistic nature of various sexual value orientations and the state's historically repressive role in human sexuality are made abundantly clear in the first selection in this section on social policy. Hugh M. Hefner's article, "The Legal Enforcement of Morality," is a catalogue of the state's efforts over time to repress, control, and overcriminalize its citizens' sexual behavior, its own hypocritical stance, and a supreme reluctance to respond humanely to sexual minorities. He closes with a plea for a sane sexual policy for the state.

Three articles are included on public policy designed to help control fertility. Dr. Vera Shlakman's contribution analyzes a host of problems surrounding effective birth control policy and services, highlighting the differences between family planning and population control. She indicates that any policy proposal may be emasculated by poor funding or by a lack of trained personnel to carry out policy objectives. The second contribution, "Abortion: A Social Policy for Prevention," is a rationale for a policy change protecting women from the effects of sexual intercourse resulting in unwanted pregnancy when the more traditional methods of family planning have failed or when the expected child will be deformed or handicapped. Having abortion laws liberalized will require even more medical services, and existing ones are already in short supply.

The third article on fertility control by Alice Taylor Day, a sociologist at Yale University, suggests the possible failure of citizens' voluntary efforts to control family size and the future need for state control of population to ensure its own survival. She emphasizes that effective policy cannot be made today because we lack sufficient knowledge of the psychosocial factors affecting fertility and choice of family size.

Following these are three articles dealing with service policy in various areas. The first by Dr. Charles R. Hayman et al. deals with a sexual problem for which almost all communities fail to provide help or specific treatment. He describes the need for a special program for sexual victims involving expansion of the concept of public health, and he includes the results of a nine-month pilot program. The second of the three articles on service policy cites the imperative for a social welfare policy to cover an unmet need, and a rationale for a public policy compensating victims of sex crimes. A civilized affluent society can afford psychologically and physically to mend those victimized by sexual violence and in the truest of capitalistic traditions to compensate them for their injuries. The absence of a service policy is due to the lack of issue relevance, a small interest group, and state fiscal conservation. The last selection on service policy deals with sexual education in our schools. It indicates what happens to policy when it is made by a professional elite *without* an effective supporting constituency. When sex education policy moves from a repressive, controlling psychology to one stressing the healthy and liberated nature of sexuality, communities (mostly of adults) rise up in opposition and overreaction. Policy means are difficult to determine because consensus on what sex education goals are has never been reached.

The last contribution to the policy section is "Sex and Social Policy," by a pioneer advocate of sex and family life education. Dr. Lester Kirkendall reports four broad changes in America that will affect future sexual policy. These are: attitudinal changes based on the new sexual abundance; cultural intermingling; changing sex roles; and the distribution of sex research results. He suggests that while a more rational and humane management of our sexuality is possible today, our puritanical value system remains steadfast. A more democratic distribution of sexual opportunity remains for the future.

L. G. S.

NOTES

[1] Arthur E. Bonfield, "The Abrogation of Penal Statutes by Nonenforcement," *Iowa Law Review* 49 (1964): 398–440.

[2] H. Friendly, "The Gap in Law Making—Judges Who Can't and Legislators Who Won't," *Columbia Law Review* 63 (1963): 787–807.

19

The Legal Enforcement of Morality

Hugh M. Hefner

No human act between two people is more intimate, more private, more personal than sex. One would assume that a democratic society that prided itself on freedom of the individual, whose Declaration of Independence proclaimed the right of every citizen to life, liberty, and the pursuit of happiness, and whose Constitution guaranteed the separation of church and state, would be deeply concerned with any attempted infringement of liberty in this most private act.

But how successful have we been in protecting these ideals for ourselves and our fellow citizens? Just how personally free is each one of us in modern America? The dream of individual freedom persists, but are we actually allowed to live our own lives, rejoice in our liberty and pursue our personal concepts of happiness—limited only by the extent that we infringe upon the like rights of others? Even the most cursory examination of our sex laws indicates that, at least in the area of sexual behavior, we have long been denied such freedom.

We will consider, in this article, some of the specific statutes regulating private sexual behavior and the extent to which these laws are at odds with the sex practices of a sizable portion of the population—making us a nation of criminals. Some consideration will be given, too, to the wide disparity in the sex laws of the various states—making it possible, quite literally, for a couple to indulge in intimacies within the privacy of their home that are perfectly legal, while another couple engaging in the same activity in a house a block away (but in the jurisdiction of an adjoining state) is guilty of a crime that carries a ten-year prison sentence. We will also discuss the wholly arbitrary manner in which these various laws are enforced, or not enforced, and the effect such capricious law enforcement has upon the entire fabric of law and order.

In our examination of America's sex laws, it should not be assumed that we necessarily approve of all of the behavior thus brought under legislative control of the state. The point to be made here is not that we find this sex behavior either moral or immoral, but that the moral questions

256

involved—when they relate to private sex between consenting adults—are the business of the individual and his personally chosen religion, and not the business of government.

This view of the matter is shared by a number of our most highly respected religious leaders and by the American Law Institute, which excluded consensual sex relations between adults in private from its draft of a Model Penal Code in the late 1950s (the American Law Institute officially adopted the Code in 1962). The logic underlying the recommended omission of consensual conduct from the criminal law was that "no harm to the secular interests of the community is involved in atypical sex practice in private between consenting adult partners"[1] (and, as we shall see, much of the behavior legislated against is anything but atypical); and, further, that "there is the fundamental question of the protection to which every individual is entitled against state interference in his personal affairs when he is not hurting others."[2]

Although the section of the Model Penal Code governing sexual behavior was drafted a decade and a half ago, no state has yet reshaped its laws wholly along the lines recommended by the Law Institute—despite the fact that one of the primary purposes of this illustrious advisory body in the drafting of such model codes is to "promote the clarification and simplification of the law and its better adaptation to social needs."[3]

1. Proscription of "Natural" Sex Acts

A. FORNICATION: Nonmarital and extramarital sexual intercourse between consenting adults is prohibited under statutes covering fornication, adultery, and lewd cohabitation in forty-eight of the fifty states and the District of Columbia (excluding only Louisiana and Tennessee), as well as under the federal Mann Act[4] where interstate activity is involved. Of these, eighteen states and the District of Columbia have fornication statutes that cover even a single act of intercourse between unmarried adults in private.[5] The penalties range from $10 fine in Rhode Island[6] to $1,000 fine and six months in prison in Georgia.[7]

In addition, four other states prohibit fornication when it is "open and notorious"[8] or "habitual,"[9] and a large number of states have statutes misleadingly labeled "Fornication" or "Adultery," but that actually are concerned with "Lewd Cohabitation"[10] (discussed further on in this article).

Two states lacking fornication statutes compensate for the oversight with extremely novel rape and "enticement" laws: Tennessee deems intercourse with a girl under twenty-one statutory rape[11] (nowhere else in this country is there such a high "age of consent"); and in Kansas, any male who entices a female of any age for the purpose of fornication can be punished with one to five years at hard labor.[12] An intriguing aspect of this law is that the "enticement" need not be successful!

Nonmarital intercourse, publicly condemned throughout most of our society and forbidden by both state and federal law, is privately practiced—not by a select minority—but by a considerable majority of our adult population. Fornication is engaged in by approximately 90 percent of adult males, according to Dr. Alfred C. Kinsey and his research associates at Indiana University, in their monumental study of sex behavior in the United States, published in two volumes, *Sexual Behavior of the Human Male*[13] and *Sexual Behavior in the Human Female*.[14]

Dr. Kinsey and his associates found that sexual activity varies greatly, in both form and incidence, depending upon educational and social background. Among males who go to college, some 67 percent have sexual intercourse prior to marriage; among those who receive some high-school education, but do not go further, approximately 84 percent have premarital intercourse; and among males who do not go beyond a grade-school education, the accumulative incidence figure is 98 percent.[15] Kinsey reports that in some groups among the lower social levels, it is virtually impossible to find a single male who has not had sexual intercourse by the time he reaches his mid-teens.[16] In addition, nearly all men (about 95 percent), who have been initiated into regular coital experience in marriage, continue to engage in sexual intercourse after their marriages have been terminated by the spouse's death, by separation, or by divorce. According to Kinsey, they

> repudiate the doctrine that intercourse should be restricted to marital relations. Nearly all ignore the legal limitation on intercourse outside of marriage. Only age finally reduces the coital activities of those individuals and, thus, demonstrates that biological factors are, in the long run, more effective than man-made regulations in determining the patterns of human behavior.[17]

Although our society places strong taboos on women engaging in sexual intercourse outside of marriage, approximately 50 percent of all females have premarital coitus.[18] Unlike the men, however, the higher educational and social level females tend to have a higher, rather than a lower, percentage with nonmarital sex experiences; among women with a college education, approximately 60 percent have premarital intercourse.[19] Postmarital sex for females who have lost their spouses through death, separation, or divorce, follows the same general pattern as that of males[20]—once a woman has engaged in regular coital experience as a part of marriage, she tends to continue to engage in such experience after the marriage has ended. Significantly, with both men and women, the percentage of total sexual outlet through coitus continues to be approximately the same after the conclusion of a marriage as it was within it.[21]

In contrast to laws in the United States forbidding nonmarital sex, Kinsey comments, in *Sexual Behavior in the Human Male:* "Premarital relations have also been more or less openly accepted in most of the other civilizations of the world, in the Orient, in the Ancient World, and among most European groups apart from the Anglo-American stocks."[22] And in *Sexual Behavior in the Human Female,* Kinsey states:

> There is no aspect of American sex law which surprises visitors from other countries as much as the legal attempt to penalize pre-marital activity to which both of the participating parties have consented and in which no force has been involved. . . . [T]here is practically no other culture, anywhere in the world, in which all non-marital coitus, even between adults, is considered criminal.[23]

B. LEWD COHABITATION: Cohabitation is usually defined as a relationship in which two persons not married to each other live together as man and wife. The requirement that the relationship be "open and notorious" is sometimes added to this definition. Thirty-one states have statutes that specifically prohibit cohabitation.[24] A few of the cohabitation prohibitions are found in "lewdness" or "gross lewdness" statutes[25] and many are mislabeled "adultery" or "fornication," but the text of these statutes makes it clear that the penalty is applicable only to cohabitation and not to an occasional act of nonmarital intercourse.[26]

It would seem logical for society to prefer sexual liaisons of a more permanent nature to the more casual, indiscriminate variety, but logic has very little to do with our sex laws and, in general, the penalties for cohabitation are more severe than for random fornication. Arizona, which has no statute prohibiting fornication, does have one against cohabitation, with a maximum sentence of three years' imprisonment;[27] Massachusetts, with $30 or three months for fornication,[28] raises the sentence to a maximum of $300 or three years for cohabitation;[29] Arkansas, with no statute prohibiting either fornication or adultery, stipulates a penalty of $20 to $100 for cohabitation on the first conviction, a $100 minimum plus an optional one-year maximum for the second conviction, and one to three years' imprisonment for the third.[30]

The Alabama law against cohabitation is written specifically to discourage a continuing relationship between the same two partners. The punishment for such conduct is:

> Not less than one hundred dollars and [the offender] may also be imprisoned in the county jail . . . for not more than six months; on a second

conviction for the offense, with the same person, the offender shall be fined not less than three hundred dollars, and may be imprisoned in county jail, or sentenced to hard labor for the county, for not more than twelve months; and, on third, or any subsequent conviction, with the same person, shall be imprisoned in penitentiary for two years.[31]

C. ADULTERY: In our society, adultery is generally held to be a worse sin than fornication. This is reflected in our state statutes that tend to treat this behavior as a crime warranting more severe punishment.

Adultery is forbidden in the Ten Commandments,[32] which play an important part in both the Christian and Jewish religions. It doesn't matter that the original Judaic injunction against adultery was primarily concerned with property rights (when a wife was considered her husband's possession), nor that the admonition historically applied only to women (it was not thought improper in olden times for married men to have sexual intercourse with other than their wives). The antisexualism of the Middle Ages imbued adultery with its present moral significance and broadened its prohibition to include male and female alike (though even today society is more tolerant of the adulterous husband than wife).

Statutes forbidding fornication and adultery have no historical basis in common law—traditionally this behavior has been dealt with by the ecclesiastical courts—consistent with their origin as violations of property; however, common law has permitted the innocent spouse to claim damages through civil action.[33]

Fornication is easily defined as illicit sexual intercourse between two unmarried individuals, but a legal definition of adultery is not quite so simple. What distinguishes adultery from fornication? Morris Ploscowe, a former judge of the Magistrates' Court of the City of New York and presently Adjunct Professor of Law at New York University, wrote in his book, *Sex and the Law:*

> The Roman law, which influenced much of our thinking on this question, differentiated between the illicit sexual intercourse of a married man and that of a married woman. A married man might have sexual intercourse with a single woman and not be guilty of adultery or any other crime. A married woman was guilty of adultery whenever she had sexual intercourse with a man who was not her husband, whether that man was married to someone else or was single. In such a case, both the married woman and the paramour were guilty of adultery.

> These Roman-law conceptions may be encountered in common-law views on adultery. While adultery, as we have seen, was not generally regarded as a crime at common law, it might still be the subject of a civil suit for damages . . . [I]f an Englishman wanted a divorce by Act of Par-

liament he had to bring an action first for criminal conversation based on the adultery of his wife. Only a husband could bring such an action. A wife could not sue another woman for damages because the latter had made love to her husband. Adultery was therefore defined at common law as at Roman law; the sexual intercourse with another man's wife was adultery.

Many of our modern criminal statutes on adultery are interpreted in the same way, making sexual intercourse by a married man with a single woman fornication or no crime at all [e.g., Connecticut and Indiana]. The justification for this distinction between married men and married women, with respect to extramarital sexual intercourse, has come down to us from medieval times as is reiterated by modern cases. For example, in the case of State v. Armstrong, the court stated: ". . . the gist of the crime, independently of statutory enactments, is the danger of introducing spurious heirs into a family, whereby a man may be charged with the maintenance of children not his own, and the legitimate offspring be robbed of their lawful inheritance. That an offense which may entail such consequences upon society is much more aggravated in its nature than the simple incontinence of a husband, few can doubt . . ."[34]

But Ploscowe notes,

If this rationale were adequate, sexual intercourse with a married woman who was unable to bear children should not be adultery. We have been unable to find any judicial decision which makes such an exception to the adultery statute.

The English ecclesiastical law took an entirely different approach to adultery than the Roman law . . . Adultery was defined by the ecclesiastical [court] as "the inconstancy of married persons, a sin arising out of the marriage relation," which was equally great whether the offender was male or female.[35]

This view of adultery was adopted by the early American courts, For example, in the Massachusetts case of *Commonwealth* v. *Call*,[36] the defendant, a married man, was found guilty of having sexual intercourse with Eliza, a single woman. Call contended that this did not constitute adultery. The Massachusetts Supreme Judicial Court decided, however, that this was adultery, stating in its opinion,

Whatever . . . may have been the original meaning of the term adultery, it is very obvious that we have in this Commonwealth adopted the definition given to it by the ecclesiastical courts . . .We hold the infidelity of the husband as well as that of the wife the highly aggravated offense constituting the crime of adultery.[37]

This religious interpretation of the word has also received express statutory sanction in a number of states; for example, the Delaware statute reads: "Adultery is the sexual intercourse of two persons, either of whom is married to a third person."[38] Under this type of statute, both the man and the woman are guilty of adultery, even if only one of the parties is married.

There are other states, however, that hold husbands and wives to the same standards of sexual fidelity, but make distinctions between the guilt of the single partner in illicit intercourse and the married one. In these states, the single partner may be deemed guilty of fornication while the married one is declared guilty of adultery. Pennsylvania is a prime example.[39]

To further complicate the picture, at least two states (Massachusetts[40] and Oregon[41]) appear to combine the above definition with the Roman law definition of adultery and, thereby, find any party guilty except a single girl.

But whichever definition we apply to the term, the Kinsey studies of our sexual behavior make abundantly clear that all of the combined church and state prohibitions have been notably unsuccessful in suppressing adultery in America. Kinsey's statistics on extramarital coitus of married adults and coital experiences of the partners in these relationships, when the partners are themselves single, appear in the studies as part of the premarital and postmarital calculations, even though this behavior is legally termed adultery by a number of the states. If these additional statistics were added to those that follow, the incidences for adultery would be, of course, much closer to those of other nonmarital intercourse.

Kinsey's research indicates that approximately 50 percent of all married males have intercourse with women other than their wives at some time while they are married.[42] Kinsey and his associates found a higher degree of cover-up and reluctance to supply answers on questions related to extramarital sexual experience than was evidenced in any other part of their studies.[43] The 50 percent figure is therefore considered a minimum one and the real figure is probably somewhat higher. Nearly three-quarters (72 percent) of the married males in a study conducted by Terman in 1938 expressed an interest in extramarital relations and Kinsey's extensive study revealed a "similarly high proportion" who expressed such desires.[44] The gap between the desire for such experience and actual behavior must be viewed as the result of the strong taboos placed upon adultery in our society and on lack of opportunity.

In the study of the American female, 26 percent admitted extramarital intercourse;[45] among women with a college education, the incidence is somewhat higher, amounting to 31 percent.[46] Here again, the cover-up evidenced in this portion of the studies suggests that the true percentages are somewhat higher than those reported.[47]

There are a variety of psychological and emotional, as well as some physical, causes for extramarital intercourse in both sexes. We will not attempt to evaluate the effect that extramarital sex may have upon a marriage relationship, though obviously the effect is far more dependent upon the attitudes of the persons involved than on the sexual activity itself. The only point to be emphasized here is that these problems are personal ones and should remain the private business of the people involved; they are not the proper business of government.

Nevertheless, thirty-one of the fifty states and the District of Columbia have adultery statutes directed against individual private acts of extramarital intercourse.[48] In addition, two states proscribe "open and notorious" adultery[49] and two others prohibit "habitual" adultery.[50] Only eight of these statutes specify that prosecution may be initiated solely on complaint of the injured spouse.[51] The others permit state authorities to interfere with the marital relationship by initiating prosecutions with attendant embarrassing publicity, even though neither party requested it. Indeed, even in the former states, the injured spouse usually cannot halt prosecution once it has begun.[52] The adultery laws are, in general, more severe than those for fornication and range in punishment from a $10 fine in Maryland[53] to a maximum penalty of $1,000 or five years' imprisonment in Maine.[54] Arizona, Idaho, Iowa, Massachusetts, New Hampshire, New Jersey, North Dakota, Utah, and Wisconsin all have statutes with a maximum prison sentence of three years for conviction of adultery;[55] in Michigan it is four years;[56] in Connecticut, Oklahoma, South Dakota, and Vermont, it is five.[57]

Only four states have the same penalty for adultery as they do for fornication.[58] In Wisconsin, fornication may bring $200 and six months,[59] while adultery may be good for $1,000 and three years.[60] Connecticut penalizes fornication with a maximum fine of $100 and six months' imprisonment,[61] but the prison sentence for adultery can be five years.[62] In Rhode Island, the fine for fornication is $10[63]—more like a tax than a penalty—but adultery can cost a year in prison or a $500 fine.[64]

Fourteen states have no law against fornication, but do have statutes prohibiting adultery;[65] only Florida has a law against fornication,[66] but no law for adultery. Several states have laws for neither, but prohibit illegal cohabitation.[67] As we commented earlier, only Louisiana and Tennessee have no statutes prohibiting any of the three. Hawaii is the only state that has different adultery penalties for men and women—$30 to $100 or three to twelve months or both for men; $10 to $30 or two to four months for women.[68] Hawaii is doubly unique in that the greater penalty applies to the male, whereas society is generally more severe with women for such behavior (as exemplified by the two years' imprisonment for women for adultery in Italy, with no comparable penalty for men).[69]

D. Enforcement of "Natural" Sex Laws: A study of the statutes of the various states affords us only a portion of the true picture of things, of course, since many laws exist that are not actively enforced. These sex statutes are, in fact, among the least enforced and least enforceable of any in existence in these United States. For example, during the fiscal year of July 1965 through June 1966 (the last year that New York's old divorce law was in effect), approximately 3,500 divorces were granted in New York City on grounds of adultery, but an analysis of the Annual Report of the Police Department for the same period fails to disclose a single arrest for the crime,[70] which was then punishable in New York with a fine of up to $250 or six months in jail or both.[71] The same evidence of adultery that is legally acceptable for the granting of a divorce is rarely then applied to a criminal prosecution for the activity.

However, some arrests and convictions for fornication and adultery do take place. For the year 1960, for example, the following typical municipal arrests for adultery were reported: Baltimore, two (both dismissed); Dallas, ten; Seattle, thirty-one (adultery and fornication).[72] In 1966, Boston reported that six people were arrested for fornication and seven for adultery.[73] Sheboygan, Wisconsin, may hold a per capita record for arrests in the area of consensual sex behavior: a total of nine prosecutions for fornication, adultery, or cohabitation were reported in this small community (population 45,747) during a one-month period in 1966.[74]

The arbitrary and often capricious manner in which these laws are enforced constitutes a serious problem for the nation. By making the sexual behavior of the majority of adults illegal, these laws breed contempt for all law and the fact of their being so widely unenforced induces disrespect for all law enforcement, in much the same way that Prohibition did in the Twenties. In addition, their existence permits them to be used by the unscrupulous for purposes of intimidation and blackmail.

Dr. Kinsey states in *Sexual Behavior in the Human Female:*

[T]he current sex laws are unenforced and are unenforceable because they are too completely out of accord with the realities of human behavior, and because they attempt too much in the way of social control. Such a high proportion of the females and males in our population is involved in sexual activities which are prohibited by the law of most of the states of the union, that it is inconceivable that the present laws could be administered in any fashion that even remotely approached systematic and complete enforcement . . . The consequently capricious enforcement which these laws now receive offers an opportunity for mal-administration, for police and political graft, and for blackmail which is regularly imposed both by underworld groups and by the police themselves.[75]

II. Crimes Against Nature

It is in our laws against sodomy, or what some state statutes refer to as "the abominable and detestable crime against nature," that our religiously generated aversion to sex proved most pronounced. Sodomy historically and medically refers to anal intercourse, or buggery,[76] but the statutes on sodomy include all manner of sexual activity conceived by someone, somewhere, at one time or another, to be "unnatural"; and this means, of course, in this sexually repressed society, almost every variety of sexual activity other than "natural" coitus. Sodomy laws thus cover, in one state or another, not only buggery, but fellatio (oral–genital contact with the male,[77] cunnilingus (oral-genital contact with the female),[78] homosexual behavior, bestiality (sex contact with animals),[79] necrophilia (sexual contact with the dead),[80] and even mutual masturbation. The very concept of "natural" and "unnatural" sex is, of course, a religious–moral one. Among all these "crimes against nature," only necrophilia is relatively rare and a certain symptom of a serious psychosexual disorder. We will offer no personal moral judgments on the rest of this behavior, but psychiatrists, without making any moral determination on the subject, would consider almost all of this activity normal (and, therefore, "natural"), and Kinsey found a far greater frequency for most of it than was previously assumed.[81]

Nearly all fifty states and the District of Columbia have sodomy statutes and they include some of the most emotion–tinged language to be found anywhere in the law.[82] The phrase "abominable and detestable crime against nature" appears with such regularity in the sodomy statutes that it has the effect of being an alternate title for the offense, and Rhode Island actually lists the crime under that heading.[83] In Arizona, California and Montana, it is also referred to as the "infamous crime against nature."[84]

The "abominable and detestable" phrase also becomes, in some instances, the sole description of the offenses prohibited under the law.[85] Some of the legislators responsible for initiating and passing the statutes were apparently so embarrassed by the whole business that they offered no further clue to the nature of the crime, except to state that it was illegal if perpetrated "with mankind or beast."

Various state courts have displayed a similar distaste in dealing with the subject. Thus, the judge in *State v. Whitemarsh*[86] commented, "We regret that the importance of this question [Whether or not oral-genital contact can be considered a crime against nature] renders it necessary to soil the pages of our reports with a discussion of a subject so loathsome and disgusting as the one confronting us."[87] Morris Ploscowe states in *Sex and the Law:*

> Ever since Lord Coke's time, the attitude of judges has been that sodomy is "a detestable and abominable sin among Christians not to be named." The result of this attitude is a sharp departure from the usual rules of criminal pleading. It is one of the basic canons of criminal procedure that a defendant is entitled to know the particulars of the crime charged against him so that he can adequately prepare his defense. If the indictment is not sufficiently specific, the defendant has a right to demand a bill of particulars. But when a man is charged with sodomy or a crime against nature, an indictment in the language of the statute is enough. It is enough that the indictment alleges that at a particular time and place the defendant committed a "crime against nature" with a specific person. The defendant need not be informed of the particular sexual pervision which is charged against him. As the Court put it in the case of Honselman v. People, [186, Ill. 172, 174 (1897)],
>
> "It was never the practice to describe the particular manner or the details of the commission of the crime, but the offense was treated in the indictment as the abominable crime not fit to be named among Christians. The existence of such an offense is a disgrace to human nature. The legislature has not seen fit to define it further than by the general term, and the records of the courts need not be defiled with the details of different acts which may go to constitute it. A statement of the offense in the language of the statute is all that is required."[88]

A. HETEROSEXUAL SODOMY: Although English common law, from which our own statutes on the subject are derived, defined, and prohibited only buggery with mankind or beast as "the crime against nature," which act carried the death penalty, a majority of the present-day American statutes include both oral and anal intercourse under sodomy.[89]

Moreover, in none of the states with sodomy laws do the statutes make any distinction between heterosexual and homosexual sodomy—both are prohibited; and what is even less clearly recognized is that of all these statutes forbidding sodomy, only New York makes a distinction between the married and the unmarried.[90] Our state governments thus specify, quite literally, where a husband and wife may, and may not, kiss one another and the manner in which the sex act may be initiated and carried out in the marriage bed without becoming illegal.

Modern insights into human behavior have radically changed society's views on the subject of perversion, of course, and what was once considered "unnatural" in sex is now recognized as perfectly normal and, in many instances, desirable. A majority of our contemporary marriage manuals, courses in sex education, and counselors on the problems of sex and family stress a natural freedom in the love play that accompanies marital coitus; both husband and wife are informed that the intimate preliminaries of sex can be important in achieving the full satisfaction of both partners; every part of the loved one should be dear and free from shame, and the sexual foreplay may quite properly include kisses and caresses wherever desired; no act of intimacy that brings pleasure to both members of the mating should be considered improper or taboo.

In offering such psychologically sound advice, the marriage manuals, educators, and counselors of America are actually inviting husbands and wives to commit criminal acts in their bedrooms—acts that are prohibited by law almost everywhere in the United States, with lengthy prison sentences prescribed for offenders.

Since the relations between a man and his wife are most often kept private, relatively few instances of such behavior come to public attention. Kinsey reports in *Sexual Behavior in the Human Male,* however, that:

> While the laws are more commonly enforced in regard to such relations outside of marriage, there are instances of spouses whose oral activities became known to their children and through them to the neighborhood, and ultimately led to prosecution and penal sentences for both husband and wife.[91]

More often this behavior comes to light as the result of a divorce action, although Ploscowe comments that it has been customary for the courts to view such charges with skepticism when they are a part of a suit for divorce, since they are inherently unprovable and rest solely upon the assertion of the party seeking to end the marriage.[92] Sometimes the behavior comes to light through charges lodged by an unwilling partner in oral or anal sex, because the act was allegedly performed under duress.

Kinsey states in his second volume, *Sexual Behavior in the Human Female,* that "We have cases of persons who were convicted because one of the spouses objected, or because some other person became aware that oral or anal play had been included in the marital activities.[93] He goes on to observe that there have been relatively few actual convictions of husbands or wives under the sodomy laws, but adds,

> [A]s long as they remain on the books, they are subject to capricious enforcement and become tools for blackmailers. In those states where the definition of cruelty as one of the grounds for divorce includes "personal indignities" or "mental cruelty," divorce cases involving either the husband's or the wife's desires or demands for the use of oral techniques are not infrequent.[94]

For the unmarried, the chances of discovery and possible prosecution are obviously greater. Completion of the act to orgasm with either the male or female is not required for a person to be guilty of the offense—the act itself is sufficient. In some states, a conviction may be based upon circumstantial evidence or simply an *attempt* to commit the act. An Alabama opinion interpreting the state's statute on the "Crime Against Nature" held that the essential element of the offense may be proven by circumstantial evidence when positive proof is wanting, and that a conviction may be had for an attempt to commit an act denounced by the statute.[95] In some states the mere suggestion or solicitation to engage in such behavior is a crime. Kinsey reports, "[O]ne case even goes so far as to uphold the conviction of a man for soliciting his wife to commit sodomy.[96]

Considering the obvious abhorrence with which both the legislative and the judicial branches of our government have dealt with the subject, and the prohibitive penalties prescribed for the assorted nonprocreative acts collected together under the "Crime Against Nature" statutes (the most severe of any of our laws dealing with sexual activity between consenting adults), it is especially interesting—and significant—to consider how prevalent at least some of this behavior is in our society.

Kinsey reports, "Mouth–genital contacts of some sort, with the subject as either the active or the passive member in the relationship, occur at some time in the histories of nearly 60 percent of all males."[97] in an Accumulative Incidence Table for Oral Contacts[98] in *Sexual Behavior in the Human Male,* Kinsey found that 18.4 percent of the males had premarital heterosexual oral-genital relations of an "active" nature (cunnilingus performed by the male on the female) and 38.6 percent had "passive" mouth-genital relations prior to marriage (fellatio, performed on the male by a female); in marital relations approximately 45.3 percent of the males engage in cunnilingus with their wives and 42.7 percent experience fellatio.[99]

On this Kinsey comments,

Often the female makes such contacts only because she is urged to do so by the male, but there are a few females who initiate such activity and some who may be much aroused by it. A few may even reach orgasm as they manipulate the male genitalia orally. This greater inclination of the human male toward oral activity is duplicated among other species of mammals. Contrary to our earlier thinking . . . we now understand that there are basic psychologic differences between the sexes; and although cultural traditions may also be involved, the differences in oral behavior may depend primarily on the greater capacity of the male to be stimulated psychologically. . . .[100]

One of Kinsey's most interesting findings related to oral eroticism has to do with the decade in which his subjects were born—a comparison of the incidence of this activity among both the males and females of the present and previous generations. Quite clearly the *public* attitude toward such behavior has changed radically during the past fifty years and what was once considered "perversion" is now recognized and accepted throughout much of our society as both natural and good; such a lessening of the taboos connected with this sexual activity might be expected to produce a noticeable increase in the activity itself.

In addition, the antisexual might argue that the prevalence of such "sophisticated" nonreproductive variations on the sexual theme offers evidence of a sexually jaded society that requires such "abnormal" psychosexual stimulation, because the unnatural contemporary obsession with the subject has dulled our capacity to appreciate sex and be aroused by it in its simpler forms.

It is significant to note, therefore, that in the accumulative–incidence tables in both the *Male*[101] and the *Female*[102] studies, the oral-genital activity is relatively the same for past and present generations. Society's publicly proclaimed attitude on the subject has undergone a dramatic change, but the actual private behavior of the individual has remained almost constant. There were significant variations based upon educational background, but for both males and females of similar education in this and the previous generations, born in each decade back to 1900, Kinsey comments, "There were surprisingly few differences . . . ."[103]

The fact is important, we feel, both in establishing the essential naturalness of the behavior itself and in pointing out how relatively ineffective social and legal taboos are in suppressing natural sexuality.

B. HOMOSEXUAL SODOMY: The same oral and anal techniques that may be used to introduce variety and additional pleasure into a heterosexual relationship are the primary means of sexual gratification in homosexual associations.

As we have already stated, none of the state statutes dealing with sodomy and/or "the abominable and detestable crime against nature" make any distinction between the heterosexual or homosexual practice of such activities. In the enforcement of the laws, however, a disproportionately high percentage of sodomy arrests and convictions involve homosexual contacts—presumably because a heterosexual cop and a heterosexual judge find a homosexual crime against nature a good deal more "abominable and detestable" than a heterosexual one.

We confess to a strong personal prejudice in favor of the boy–girl variety of sex, but our belief in a free, rational, and human society demands a tolerance of those whose sexual inclinations are different from our own—so long as their activity is limited to consenting adults in private and does not involve either minors or the use of any kind of coercion. Lenny Bruce expressed our viewpoint with typical satiric bite and insight when he said: "I'm not prejudiced against homosexuals, but I wouldn't want my brother to marry one."

Actually, we Americans are—as a nation—more intolerant of homosexuality than almost any other country in the world. Dr. Kinsey states in *Sexual Behavior in the Human Female:* "There appears to be no other major culture in the world in which public opinion and the statute law so severely penalize homosexual relationships as they do in the United States today."[104] You can call an American male a scoundrel and a thief with less chance of eliciting an emotional response than if you simply question his manhood.

Quite obviously, however, any attempts society may make to legislate homosexuality out of existence are doomed to certain failure and may actually perpetuate and encourage sexual deviation rather than diminish it.

To whatever extent homosexuality—an erotic attraction to members of the same rather than the opposite sex—represents an emotional disorder, it must be dealt with psychiatrically; you do not successfully treat a neurosis by passing a law against its manifestations. In addition, homosexual behavior is not necessarily symptomatic of any emotional aberration; far too great a percentage of our adult population have engaged in some form of homosexual activity at some time in their lives to permit it to be scientifically defined as abnormal.

Kinsey points out that homosexual contacts occur frequently in all other species of animal life, and that were it not for the strong cultural taboos affixed to such behavior, the incidence would presumably be equally high among human beings. Kinsey states that a perfectly normal man or woman may be erotically attracted to, or aroused by, a member of the same sex and that prolonged separation from the opposite sex (as in prison or some assignments in the armed services) may significantly increase these homosexual responses.[105]

The individual whose homosexual activity becomes known is apt to find himself an outcast in much of our heterosexual society and forced into a nether world inhabited almost exclusively by homosexuals; it thus becomes increasingly unlikely that he will ever find his way back to a predominantly heterosexual life. In this way, we unwittingly support a system calculated to maximize the spread of homosexuality rather than reduce its incidence, at the same time linking the behavior with feelings of guilt and shame conducive to emotional conflict, anxiety, and perhaps serious psychological disorientation.

Kinsey makes this further appeal to reason regarding our attitude on the subject:

> Condemnations of homosexual as well as some other types of sexual activity are based on the argument that they do not serve the prime function of sex, which is interpreted to be procreation, and in that sense represent a perversion of what is taken to be "normal" sexual behavior. It is contended that the general spread of homosexuality would threaten the existence of the human species, and that the integrity of the home and of the social organization could not be maintained if homosexual activity were not condemned by moral codes and public opinion and made punishable under the statute law. The argument ignores the fact that the existent mammalian species have managed to survive in spite of their widespread homosexual activity, and that sexual relations between males seem to be widespread in certain cultures (for instance, Moslem and Buddhist cultures) which are more seriously concerned with problems of overpopulation than they are with any threat of underpopulation. Interestingly enough, these are also cultures in which the institution of the family is very strong.[106]

The general condemnation of homosexual relationships originated in Jewish history in about the Seventh Century B.C., as a part of the extensive antisexualism that permeated Judaism after the Babylonian exile. Kinsey comments,

> Both mouth–genital contacts and homosexual activities had previously been associated with the Jewish religious service, as they had been with the religious service of most of the other peoples of that part of Asia, and just as they have been in many other cultures elsewhere in the world. In the wave of nationalism which was then developing among the Jewish people, there was an attempt to dis-identify themselves with their neighbors by breaking with many of the customs which they had previously shared with them. Many of the Talmudic condemnations were based on the fact that such activities represented the way of the Canaanite, the way of the Chaldean, the way of the pagan, and they were originally condemned as a form of idolatry rather than a sexual crime. Throughout the Middle Ages homosexuality was associated with heresy. The reform in the custom (the mores) soon, however, became a matter of morals, and finally a question for action under criminal law.
>
> Jewish sex codes were brought over into Christian codes by the early adherents of the Church, including St. Paul, who had been raised in the Jewish tradition on matters of sex. The Catholic sex code is an almost precise continuation of the more ancient Jewish code. For centuries in medieval Europe, the ecclesiastic law dominated on all questions of morals and subsequently became the basis for the English common law, the statute laws of England, and the laws of the various states of the United States.

This accounts for the considerable conformity between the Talmudic and Catholic codes and the present-day statute law on sex, including the laws on homosexual activity.[107]

We share a common Judaeo-Christian heritage with Europe, but American Puritanism has carried this country well beyond the antisexualism still to be found in the Old World. In much of the United States, the legal penalties for sodomy are surpassed only by those for kidnapping, murder, and rape.

And yet, despite the severest sort of social and statutory prohibitions, Dr. Kinsey and his research associates of Indiana University found a remarkably high percentage of both American men and women who admitted to having had some homosexual contacts. On the opening page of the chapter entitled "Homosexual Outlet," in *Sexual Behavior in the Human Male,* Kinsey states:

> [A] considerable portion of the population, perhaps the major portion of the male population, has at least some homosexual experience between adolescence and old age. In addition, about 60 percent of the pre-adolescent boys engage in homosexual activities . . . and there is an additional group of adult males who avoid overt contacts but who are quite aware of their potentialities for reacting to other males.[108]

The data in this study indicate that a maximum of 37 percent of the total male population have had overt homosexual experience to the point of orgasm after puberty and prior to the age of forty-five.[109] Among all males approximately 30 percent have been brought to climax at least once through mouth–genital contact with other males and 14 percent have brought other males to climax in the same manner.[110]

When the sampling is limited to those men who remain single until the age of thirty-five, half (50 percent) have had overt homosexual contact resulting in orgasm since puberty; when educational level is taken into consideration for this same group of single males, 58 percent of those who went to high school, but not beyond, 50 percent of the grade school level, and 47 percent of the college level have had homosexual experience to the point of orgasm after the onset of adolescence.[111]

Among females, 20 percent of the total population have had some overt homosexual experience prior to the age of forty-five.[112] and 13 percent have had homosexual experience resulting in orgasm.[113] When the sampling is limited to those females who are still unmarried at the age of forty-five, the incidence of overt homosexual experience rises to 26 percent.[114]

For any oldsters who may find these statistics shocking evidence of the immorality of the modern generation, it must be reported that—as with the data on similar heterosexual nonreproductive techniques—males and females born prior to 1900 (and in each decade since) evidence almost identical percentages for homosexual activity.[115] Grandma and grandpa would have been shocked beyond words by any open discussion of the subject, but their actual sexual behavior was little different from our own today.

Quite obviously, Kinsey's statistics do not represent the number of "homosexuals" in society, as we usually understand and use the term, but the amount of "homosexual experience." The great majority of the men and women who have had such experiences are primarily heterosexual in their behavior, and the most significant point to be understood from this data is that almost all of us have, within ourselves, the capacity to respond to both heterosexual and homosexual stimuli.

On this point, Kinsey states,

> It would encourage clearer thinking on these matters if persons were not characterized as heterosexual or homosexual but as individuals who have had certain amounts of heterosexual experience and certain amounts of homosexual experience. Instead of using these terms as substantives which stand for persons, or even as adjectives to describe persons, they may better be used to describe the nature of the overt sexual relations, or of the stimuli to which an individual erotically responds.[116]

This point is best illustrated by the following facts: While 37 percent of the total white male population—or nearly two males out of every five—have at least some overt homosexual experience to the point of orgasm between adolescence and old age, only 25 percent of this male population have more than incidental homosexual experience or reactions over at least a three-year period between the ages of sixteen and fifty-five; only 18 percent have at least as much homosexual as heterosexual experience in their histories for at least a three-year period between the same ages; 10 percent are more or less exclusively homosexual for at least a three-year period; 8 percent are exclusively homosexual for at least three years; and only 4 percent are *exclusively homosexual throughout their lives.*[117]

But related to the subject presently under discussion, we must remember that it is not *being* "homosexual" that is illegal in almost all of the fifty states, it is the single "homosexual experience"—of the sort engaged in, at one time or another, by nearly two out of every five adult males in society—that is a crime.[118] In most states, it is a crime punishable by a lengthy prison sentence.

C. PENALTIES FOR "CRIMES AGAINST NATURE": The irrational nature of American sodomy statutes emphasizes the lack of logic that pervades almost all of our sex laws; the severity of the penalties for what our law-makers have deemed to be "crimes against nature" emphasizes the ex-treme, religiously inspired superstition and emotionalism that still persist in our attitudes toward sex in this supposedly modern, rational, scientifically enlightened, just, humane, and free society.

Most of our fifty states have sodomy statutes.[119] Almost all of them make illegal the variety of noncoital sex activity discussed in this article—at least some of which is engaged in, at one time or another, by a majority of our adult population. Almost none of these statutes make any distinction between a prohibited act when it is performed by members of the same or opposite sex (the single possible exception may permit certain activity between two females that is prohibited between a female and a male).[120] Of these statutes only New York's exempts the prohibited act when it is performed within marriage.[121] The penalties for behavior covered under sodomy are among the most severe of any in the law.

Several states and the District of Columbia specify that imprisonment for "crimes against nature" be spent at hard labor.[122] The maximum sen-tence in the following states is fourteen or fifteen years: California (oral copulation only, with no maximum for other forms of sodomy), Colorado, Indiana, Oregon, and Tennessee.[123] Ten states specify twenty years (Ari-zona, Florida, Hawaii, Massachusetts, Minnesota, Nebraska, New Jersey, Ohio, Rhode Island, and Utah).[124] In Idaho and Montana the *minimum* penalty for sodomy is five years, the maximum life;[125] in Pennsylvania the maximum ten years may be spent "[in] solitary confinement at labor."[126] In Nevada the possible maximum penalty is imprisonment for life.[127]

III. Conclusion

Incredible as it should seem, and despite all constitutional guarantees to the contrary, we do not enjoy a true separation of church and state in the United States today. Each citizen in our democracy has a right to expect that the laws of his government have been established and will be enforced in a rational manner consistent with the aims and protections of the Constitution. But many of our laws are not based on any such premise.

Currently, in the United States, we have statutes regulating personal sex behavior, marriage, divorce, birth control, abortion, and prostitution that are based not upon a concern for the health, happiness, and welfare of the individual, but upon various concepts of religious morality. Thus sin and crime become intermixed and confused—and the religious views of a portion of society are forced upon the rest of it—through government coercion—whether they are consistent with the personal conviction or practice of the individual or not.

Concern over our irrational sex laws was reflected in the drafting of the Model Penal Code by the American Law Institute. The pertinent sections of this code were apparently predicated on the premise that in a free society all sex relations entered into freely by adults in private should be excluded from our criminal law. In the fifteen years since this code was drafted, the legislatures of only two states—Illinois and Connecticut—have made any serious attempt to correct their statutes on consensual sex behavior. In 1961, Illinois legislators replaced their sodomy statute with a new law patterned after the one suggested by the Institute;[128] and in 1969, Connecticut adopted a new penal code, which excludes virtually all private acts between consenting adults.[129] Illinois and Connecticut are, therefore, the only states in the Union that have repealed their statutes for the "abominable and detestable crimes against nature." (Recently, a U.S. District Court in Texas declared the state's sodomy law void for overstepping the Constitution by interfering with the private consensual acts of married couples; hence the law remains on the books, but is unenforceable.)[130]

These examples of modern legislative acumen are not without irony, however. The Illinois lawmakers did remove the state's sodomy statute, but they left standing the statutes against fornication and adultery.[131] Illinois is thus in the unusual position of permitting all so-called "perversion," both heterosexual and homosexual, while prohibiting normal sexual intercourse.

It is obvious that we are still a very long way from establishing sane sex law *anywhere* in the United States.

NOTES

[1] Model Penal Code 207.5, Comment at 277 (Tent. Draft No. 4, 1955).

[2] *Id.* at 278.

[3] ALI By-laws 2 (1923). See, however, text accompanying notes 128 and 131, *infra*, for a discussion of the partial revision recently enacted by the State of Illinois.

[4] White Slavery Act, 18, U.S.C. 2421 (1964).

[5] Conn. Gen. Stat. Rev. 53-219 (1958); D.C. Code Ann. 22-1002 (1961); Fla. Stat. 798.03 (1965); Ga. Code Ann. 26-5801 (1953); Hawaii Rev. Laws 309-10, 309-12 (1955); Idaho Code Ann. 18-6603 (1947); Ky. Gen. Laws ch. 272, 18 (1932); N.H. Rev. Stat. Ann. 579:4 (1955); N.J. Rev. Stat. 2A:110-1 (1937); N.D. Cent. Code 12-22-08 (1959); Pa. Stat. tit. 18, 4506 (1963); R.I. Gen. Laws Ann. 11-6-3 (1956); Utah Code Ann. 76-53-5 (1953); Va. Code Ann. 18.1-188 (1950); W.Va. Code Ann 61-8-3 (1961); Wis. Stat. 944.15 (1961). See Model Penal Code 207.1, Comment at 204 (Tent. Draft No. 4, 1955).

[6] R.I. Gen. Laws Ann. 11-6-3 (1956).

⁷ Ga. Code Ann. 26-5801 (1953).

⁸ Ill. Rev. Stat. Ch. 38, 11-8 (1963); Mo- Rev. Stat. 563.150 (1959).

⁹ S.C. Code Ann. 16-408 (1962); Tex. Pen. Code art. 508 (1948).

¹⁰ E.g., Colo. Rev. Stat. Ann. 40-0-3 (1963); Ind. Stat. Ann. 10-4207 (1956); Mont. Rev. Codes Ann. 94-4107 (1947).

¹¹ Tenn. Code Ann. 39-3706 (1955).

¹² Kan. Gen. Stat. Ann. 21-937 (1963).

¹³ A. Kinsey, W. Pomeroy, and C. Martin, *Sexual Behavior in the Human Male* (Philadelphia: W. B. Saunders Company, 1948), pp. 550–51 [hereinafter cited as "Kinsey, *Male*"].

¹⁴ A. Kinsey, W. Pomeroy, C. Martin, and P. Gebhard, *Sexual Behavior in the Human Female* (Philadelphia: W. B. Saunders Company, 1953) [hereinafter cited as "Kinsey, *Female*"].

¹⁵ Kinsey, *Male*, 549–52.

¹⁶ *Id.*, 552.

¹⁷ Id. 295.

¹⁸ Kinsey, *Female*, 286.

¹⁹ *Id.*, 293.

²⁰ *Id.*, 536.

²¹ *Id.*, 562.

²² Kinsey, *Male*, 547.

²³ Kinsey, *Female*, 326.

²⁴ Ala. Code tit. 14, 16 (1958); Alaska Stat. 11.40.040 (Suppl 1962): Ariz. Rev. Stat. Ann. 13-222 (1956); Ark. Stat. Ann. 41-805 (1947); Cal. Pen. Code 269a (West 1956); Colo. Rev. Stat. Ann. 40-9-3 (1963); Fla. Stat. Ann. 798.02 (1965); Ga. Code Ann. 26-5801 (1953); Idaho Code Ann. 18-6604 (1947); Ill. Rev. Stat. Ch. 38, 11-7 (1963); Ind. Ann. Stat. 10-4207 (1956); Kan. Gen. Stat. Ann. 21-908 (1963); Me. Rev. Stat. Ann. tit. 17, 2151 (1964); Mass. Gen. Laws Ch. 272, 16 (1932); Mich. Comp. Laws 750.335 (1958); Miss. Code Ann. 1998 (1956); Mo. Rev. Stat. 563.150 (1959); Mont. Rev. Codes Ann. 94-4107 (1947); Neb. Rev. Stat. 28-928 (1964): Nev. Rev. Stat. 201.200 (Supp. 1965); N.M. Stat. Ann. 40A-10-2 (1953); N.C. Gen. Stat. 14-184 (1953); N.D. Cent. Code 12-22-12 (1959); Ohio Rev. Code Ann. 2905.08 (Page 1953); Ore. Rev. Stat. 167.015 (Supp. 1965); S.C. Code Ann. 16-408 (1962); Tex. Pen. Code art. 499 (1948); Va. Code Ann. 18.1-193 (1950); W.Va. Code Ann. 61-8-4 (1961); Wis. Stat. 944.15 (1961).

²⁵ E.g., Fla. Stat. 798.02 (1965 Me. Rev. Stat. Ann. tit. 17, 2151 (1964); and Mo. Rev. Stat. 563.150 (1959).

²⁶ E.g., Colo. Rev. Stat. Ann. 40-0-3 (1963); Ind. Ann. Stat. 10-4207 (1956).

²⁷ Ariz. Rev. Stat. Ann. 13-222 (1956).

²⁸ Mass. Gen. Laws ch. 272, 18 (1932).

²⁹ Mass. Gen. Laws ch. 272, 16 (1932).

³⁰ Ark. Stat. Ann. 41-805 (1947).

³¹ Ala. Code tit. 14 16 (1958).

³² Exod. 20:14.

[33] M. Ploscowe, *Sex and the Law,* rev. ed. (1962), 140 [hereinafter cited as "Ploscowe"].

[34] *Id.,* 139–40.

[35] *Id.,* 140.

[36] 38 Mass. (21 Pick.) 509 (1839).

[37] *Id.* See Ploscowe, 140.

[38] Del. Code Ann. tit. 311 (1953).

[39] Pa. Stat. tit. 18, 4505-06 (1936).

[40] Mass. Gen. Laws ch. 272, 14 (1932).

[41] Ore. Rev. Stat. 167.005, 167.010 (Supp. 1965).

[42] Kinsey, *Male,* 585.

[43] *Id.*

[44] *Id.,* 584.

[45] Kinsey, *Female,* 416.

[46] *Id.,* 421.

[47] *Id.,* 416.

[48] Alaska Stat. 11.40040 (Supp. 1962); Ariz. Rev. Stat. Ann. 13-222 (1956); Conn. Gen. Stat. Rev. 53–218 (1958); Del. Code Ann. tit. 11, 311 (1953): D.C. Code Ann. 22-301 (1961); Ga. Code Ann. 26-5801 (1953); Hawaii Rev. Laws 309-8, 309-9 (1955); Idaho Code Ann. 18-6601 (1947); Iowa Code 702.1 (1962); Kan. Gen. Stat. Ann. 21-908 (1963); Ky. Rev. Stat. 436.070 (1963); Me. Rev. Stat. Ann. tit. 17, 101 (1964); Md. Ann. Code art. 27, 4 (1957); Mass. Gen. Laws ch. 272, 14 (1932); Mich. Comp. Laws 750.29 (1948); Minn. Stat. 609.36 (1961): Neb. Rev. Stat. 28-902 (1964); N.H. Rev. Stat. Ann. 579:1 (1955); N.J. Rev. Stat. 2A:88-1 (1937); N.Y. Pen. Act 255.17 (McKinney 1944); N.D. Cent. Code 12-22-09 (1959); Okla. Stat. Tit. 21, 871 (1961); Ore. Rev. Stat. 167.005 (Supp. 1965); Pa. Stat. tit. 18, 4505 (1936); R.I. Gen. Laws Ann. 11-6-2 (1956); S.D. Code 13.3002 (1939); Utah Code Ann. 76-53-3 (1953); Vt. Stat. Ann. tit. 13, 201 (1959); Va. Code Ann. 18.1-187 (1950); Wash. Rev. Code 944.16 (1961).

[49] Ill. Rev. Stat. ch. 38, 11-7 (1963); Mo. Rev. Stat. 563.150 (1959).

[50] S.C. Code Ann. 16-407 (1962); Tex. Pen. Code art. 499 (1948).

[51] Ariz. Rev. Stat. Ann. 13-221 (1956); Iowa Code 702.1 (1962); Mich. Comp. Laws 750.31 (1948); Minn. Stat. 609.36 (1961); N.D. Cent. Code 12-22-10 (1959); Okla. Stat. tit. 21, 871 (1961); Ore. Rev. Stat. 167.010 (Supp. 1965); Wash. Rev. Code 9.79.110 (1950).

[52] See, e.g., State v. Allison, 175 Minn. 218, 220 N.W. 563 (1928); State v. Beck, 52 N.D. 391, 202 N.W. 857 (1925); State v. Austin, 106 Wash. 336, 180, p. 394 (1919).

[53] Md. Ann. Code art. 27, 4 (1957).

[54] Me. Rev. Stat. Ann. tit. 17, 101 (1965).

[55] Ariz. Rev. Stat. Ann. 13-221 (1956); Idaho Code Ann. 18-6601 (1947); Iowa Code 702.1 (1962); Mass. Gen. Laws ch. 272, 14 (1932); N.H. Rev. Stat. Ann. 579:1 (1955); N.J. Rev. Stat. 2A:88-1 (1937); N.D. Cent. Code 12-22-11 (1959); Utah Code Ann. 76-53-3 (1953); Wis. Stat. 944.16 (1961).

[56] Mich. Comp. Laws 750.29 (1948).

[57] Conn. Gen. Stat. Rev. 53-218 (1958); Okla. Stat. tit. 21, 872 (1961); S.D. Code 13.3002 (1939); Vt. Stat. Ann. tit. 13, 201 (1959).

[58] Ga. Code Ann. 26-5801 (1953); Ky. Rev. Stat. 436.070 (1963); S.C. Code Ann. 16-407, 16-408 (1962); Va. Code Ann. 18.1-180 (1950).

[59] Wis. Stat. 944.15 (1961).

[60] Wis. Stat. 944.16 (1961).

[61] Conn. Gen. Stat. Rev. 53-219 (1958).

[62] Conn. Gen. Stat. Rev. 53-218 (1958).

[63] R.I. Gen. Laws Ann. 11-6-3 (1956).

[64] R.I. Gen. Laws Ann. 11-6-2 (1956).

[65] Alaska, Arizona, Delaware, Iowa, Kansas, Maryland, Michigan, Nebraska, New York, Oregon, Oklahoma, South Dakota, Vermont, and Washington. For these states' adultery statutes see note 48 *supra*.

[66] Fla. Stat. 798.03 (1965).

[67] E.g., Alabama, Arkansas, Colorado, Montana, and New Mexico. For statute citations see note 24 *supra*.

[68] Hawaii Rev. Laws 309-9 (1955).

[69] Ploscowe, 141. See text at note 42 *supra*.

[70] 1967 Annual Report of the Judicial Conference of the State of New York 413.

[71] Ch. 583, 1, 1907 N.Y. Laws 1330.

[72] Ploscowe, 148.

[73] Letter from Police Commissioner Edmund L. McNamara to Hugh Hefner, October 5, 1967.

[74] *Sheboygan Press*, July 1966.

[75] Kinsey, *Female*, 20.

[76] *Black's Law Dictionary*, 4th ed. (1951), 243.

[77] *Id.*, 743.

[78] *Id.*, 456.

[79] *Id.*, 203.

[80] *Id.*, 934.

[81] Kinsey, *Male*, 574.

[82] See notes accompanying text, *infra*. See generally N. St. John-Stevas, *Life, Death and the Law*, 310-324 (1961); Bensing, *Comparative Study* of American Sex Statutes, 42 J. of Crim. Law 57 (1951).

[83] R.I. Gen. Laws Ann. 11-10-01 (1956).

[84] Ariz. Rev. Stat. Ann. 13-651 (1956); Cal. Pen. Code 286 (West 1956); Mont. Rev. Codes Ann. 94-4118 (1947).

[85] E.g., Fla. Stat. 800.01 (1965); Ind. Ann. Stat. 10-4221 (1956); Kan. Gen. Stat. Ann. 21-907 (1963); Mass. Gen. Laws ch. 272, 34 (1932).

[86] 26 S.D. 426, 128 N.W. 580 (1910).

[87] *Id.*, 429, 128 N.W. at 581.

[88] Ploscowe, 184.

[89] E.g., Colo. Rev. Stat. Ann. 40-2-31 (1963); Iowa Code 705.1 (1962); Minn. Stat. 617.14 (1961).

[90] N.Y. Pen. Act. 130.00 (McKinney 1944).

[91] Kinsey, *Male,* 577.

[92] Ploscowe, 189.

[93] Kinsey, *Female,* 370.

[94] *Id.*

[95] Tarrant v. State, 12 Ala. App. 172, 67 So. 626 (1915).

[96] Kinsey, *Female,* 370.

[97] Kinsey, *Male,* 371.

[98] By which is meant the sexual experience of the subject up to the time of the interview.

[99] Kinsey, *Male,* 368.

[100] Kinsey, *Female,* 257-58.

[101] Kinsey, *Male,* 368.

[102] Kinsey, *Female,* 281.

[103] *Id.,* 257.

[104] Kinsey, *Female,* 483.

[105] Kinsey, *Male,* 612-22.

[106] Kinsey, *Female,* 483.

[107] *Id.,* 482-83.

[108] Kinsey, *Male,* 610.

[109] *Id.,* 650.

[110] *Id.,* 373.

[111] *Id.,* 650.

[112] Kinsey, *Female,* 490.

[113] *Id.,* 454.

[114] *Id.,* 490.

[115] Kinsey, *Male,* 402; Kinsey, *Female,* 495.

[116] Kinsey, *Male,* 617.

[117] *Id.,* 650-51.

[118] *Id.*

[119] See note 83 *supra.*

[120] E.g., Ga. Code Ann. 26-5901 (1953).

[121] N.Y. Pen. Act 130.00 (McKinney 1944).

[122] Hawaii Rev. Laws 309-34 (1955); Kan. Gen. Stat. Ann. 21-907 (1963); La. Rev. Stat. 14:89 (1950).

[123] Cal. Pen. Code 288a, 286 (1956); Colo. Rev. Stat. Ann. 40-2-31 (1963); Ind. Ann. Stat. 10-4221 (1956); Ore. Rev. Stat. 167.040 (Supp. 1965); Tenn. Code Ann. 39-707 (1955).

[124] Ariz. Rev. Stat. Ann. 13-651 (1956); Fla. Stat. 800.01 (1965); Hawaii Rev. Laws 309-34 (1955); Mass. Gen. Laws ch. 272, 34 (1932); Minn. Stat. 617.14 (1961); Neb. Rev. Stat. 28-919 (1964); N.J. Rev. Stat. 2A:143-1 (1937); Ohio Rev. Code Ann. 2905.44 (Page 1953); R.I. Gen. Laws Ann. 11-10-1 (1956); Utah Code Ann. 76-53-22 (1953).

[125] Idaho Code Ann. 18-6605 (1947); Mont. Rev. Codes Ann. 94-4118 (1947).

[126] Pa. Stat. tit. 18, 4501 (1936).

[127] Nev. Rev. Stat. 201.190 (Supp. 1965).

[128] Ill. Rev. Stat. ch. 38, 11-2,3 (1963).

[129] Conn. Modified House Bill 7182 Public Act No. 828; (effective Oct. 1, 1971).

[130] Buchanan v. Batchelor; U.S.D.C. N. Texas; (4/30/70).

[131] Ill. Rev. Stat. ch. 38, 11-7-8 (1963).

SUGGESTED READINGS

American Law Institute. *Model Penal Code.* Philadelphia, Pa.: American Law Institute, 1962.

Cantor, D. J. "Deviation and the Criminal Law." *Journal of Criminal Law, Criminology and Police Science* 55 (1964): 441–54.

H.M.S.O. Report of the Departmental Committee on Homosexual Offenses and Prostitution (The Wolfenden Report). London 1957.

S. H. Kadish. "The Crisis of Overcriminalization." *Annals of the American Academy of Political and Social Science* 374, (1967): 157–70.

Packer, H. L. *The Limits of Criminal Sanction.* Stanford, Calif.: Stanford University Press, 1968.

Wheeler, S. "Sex Offenses: A Sociological Critique." *Law and Contemporary Problems* 25 (1960), no. 2.

20

Family Planning and Social Policy

Vera Shlakman

The auspices, the announced themes, and the composition of this conference proclaim that social work does, indeed, have a role to play in family planning, its contribution is not in question. Approval of a national family planning policy and of active social work participation in its implementation was expressed in a policy statement adopted by the National Association of Social Workers in 1967. Similar declarations have been made by the American Public Welfare Association, the American Public Health Association, the American Nurses Association, the Family Services Association, and other professional groups. Thus there is widespread agreement that as a matter of public policy, family planning services should be brought within the reach of all who want them. While we are no longer required to debate yea or nay in the same terms as in the past, we nonetheless face some problems that are the social policy analyst's responsibility to identify.

Some of these problems are the heritage of past policies; some can be attributed to the structure of social and medical service delivery systems; some to the narrow mandate given to the public health mission thereby reinforcing its separation from curative medicine. Some of the problems stem from past failure to provide family planning services, with consequent shortages of skilled professional cadres around whom services could now be expanded. And there are problems that derive from the traditional second-class status assigned to medical programs for the indigent. From one point of view, the problems are simply one phase of the difficulties that attend the progressive expansion of social welfare and health services under the characteristic conditions imposed by dominant American values. We need only forget about family planning for a moment and observe what problems we encounter in trying to remove the economic barriers to any health service—for example, in building Medicare and Medicaid programs—to realize that we are dealing with a general problem. As a matter of fact, if some of these broader issues were settled, one could probably deal rather easily and effectively with the institution and expansion of family planning services. In this sense, there is nothing peculiar about removing the economic barriers to the use of family planning services. This is not to underestimate the sensitivity of an area marked by the interplay of values based on attitudes toward sexual morality, religious belief and practice, economic dependency, and racism.

Broadly speaking, the issues that concern us present themselves at two levels. At one level are the questions that cluster around social purpose. How clearly does policy formulate the ends toward which provision is to be directed? Is the consensus to encourage the control of fertility through wider use of contraceptives matched by agreement on the primary reasons for the policy, and if there is divergence, does it matter?

Another range of questions is encountered at a second level. What prevents attainment of the stated or desired objectives and how can obstacles to their achievement be removed or circumvented? What service structure will most efficiently facilitate delivery of services? How and where should funds be sought for the implementation of policy? What factors should govern the selection of priorities with respect to the population to be offered services? What delivery systems should carry the major burden of policy? What alternatives are available?

In the course of its history, the family planning movement was motivated by several strains of opinion. Some family planners saw it as the means of establishing the economic, legal, political, and social rights of women. But there were also the neo–Malthusian advocates of population control, and those who favored eugenic selection. The sheltering umbrella of planned parenthood (or family planning) in concept, if not organizationally, has covered different viewpoints and motives. The means of achievement, however, were the same, for control of fertility can serve diverse ends. Moreover, for a great part of its history, and this is a point of no small importance—although conditions were not everywhere the same—the birth control movement had to work in a climate of partial or total illegality, and against the sanctions of respectability and religion. The name by which the movement was known at different times reflected the need to divest its advocates of the cloak of non-respectability.[1] Such changes also reflected the desire, or the need, to modify emphasis, or to differentiate one type of program from that of fellow travelers who cherished somewhat different objectives. In addition, the climate of illegality or social condemnation encouraged the formulation of alternative argumentation that could be used to legitimate purposes which it might have been difficult to achieve by reference to openly stated objectives. In Victorian England, and in the United States when Social Darwinism represented the conventional wisdom, it was permissible to say things about the poor that a later era came to regard as outrageous. The democratic temper required new vocabularies even if underlying content changed somewhat less than its architects realized. But changing vocabularies sometimes mask undercurrents of opinion that still owe something to their ancestry. To plan a family and to exercise responsible parenthood have more appeal than to control births.

The attainment of official sanction for fertility control has probably been facilitated by an unofficial or tacit coalition of diverse interests, and the arguments marshaled in support of different approaches persuaded different publics. As a tactical maneuver (or as a calculated adaptation to political realities), this was understandable. But, the process has left us with a residue of confusion that could hamper effective policy development. Hence the circumstances in which we now come to project policy with official sanction and in a climate of social approval, demand clarification of purpose, partly because of past and present political requirements, and partly because we are dealing with the same means for the attainment of possibly different ends.

One does not have to examine many policy declarations or read very deeply into family planning literature of the past few years to discover that policy is being advocated for overlapping and sometimes apparently contradictory purposes. Briefly, the following themes can be identified: Family planning policy is being urged (1) to assure that every child is "wanted"; (2) to free women from the drudgery of chronic pregnancy and the requirement of bearing children against their will; (3) to reduce child dependency, that is, to cut public welfare costs; (4) to reduce the social costs of child rearing; (5) to reduce poverty; (6) to prevent illegitimacy; (7) to foster the health and happiness of families by spacing pregnancies; (8) to encourage families not to have more children than they can afford; (9) to enhance family well–being by reducing the size of families; (10) to protect maternal health; (11) to prevent defect through reduction of births to very young or older mothers, and to others who are at risk, and through genetic counseling; (12) to offer to every couple the opportunity to realize the size of family to which it aspires; and (13) to control total population.

The use of efficient contraceptive methods is probably relevant to the attainment of each of these objectives, but hardly sufficient in some cases and not necessarily primary in others. Control of fertility is not exactly a broad–spectrum remedy to which the different social problems and private troubles that are implied in my enumeration will easily yield. The counsel of wisdom would seem to advise against arousing public expectations of a simple remedy for complex problems. More important, in the immediate context, is the fact that the public has been given two well–defined and incompatible messages.

Control of population, for example, is not a necessary consequence of child spacing; every child may be wanted and planned for, but to an extent that results in rapid population growth. Now, population control, whether aggregative or selective, about which there has been great expression of interest, is not on the agenda of this conference. This was a sound decision, but it has not, in practice, been excluded from conceptualization of the problem, nor from the rationale for action. President Johnson has made frequent references to population problems in developing countries and has raised the issue, by association at least, for the United States. Former Secretary John Gardner announced HEW policy in this area by reference to "population dynamics, fertility, sterility and family planning," an interesting sequence, and he created the post of Deputy Assistant Secretary for Science and Population.[2] The National Association of Social Workers policy statement of April 1967 emphasizes freedom of choice, but also invokes "the unprecedented rate of population growth, especially in the crowded urban centers." The American Nurses Association points to "public concern over implications of the expanding world population and the human and natural resources available to maintain this population."[3] The American Public Health Association stresses family planning as a public health service, but also refers to population problems.[4] A declaration of policy of the Minneapolis Board of Public Welfare in 1965 stated: "Unprecedented population growth is a matter of increasing concern to public and private agencies on the international, national and local levels. The problems of imbalanced population increase has been amply demonstrated as existing in Minneapolis, as well as in Latin America, India and Appalachia." By way of contrast, it is interesting to compare the statement of philosophy of the Maryland Department of Health: "The purpose of the Family Planning Service is to promote and safeguard family health, happiness and security through the application of scientific knowledge about conception in order to enable parents to have children and to space the birth of children. . . . Family planning service is a component part of public health service and of maternal care . . ."[5]

A population policy has many components, but, historically, it has not been neutral as to numbers; it has been either pro-natalist or anti-natalist. The currently fashionable rhetoric of the "population explosion" is being invoked to encourage birth control for a range of stated purposes, but not in direct, candid support of a defined anti-natalist population policy. The adoption of such a policy may be desirable, but there are dangers involved in approaching it surreptitiously, either because of carelessness of formulation or in the belief, right or wrong, that it would conflict with other social purposes, or because it would create political embarrassments. The difficulty arises most sharply at the point of intersection between population control and family self-determination.

The main theme that marks current development of family planning policy at operational levels bases itself on the principle that all families, by free choice, should have the opportunity to space pregnancies and limit family size. Such self-determination has not been enjoyed by low-income families, just as they have not enjoyed equal access to other health services that are available to families of higher income levels. This is a reasonable, viable public health position. But the rate of population growth is influenced, of course, by private decisions through which family-size aspirations are realized. If our objective is to check population, then we have to be prepared to be concerned about the social and demographic consequences of such private decisions. It would follow that the thrust of policy then ought to be directed toward *all* classes by seeking to modify the ideal of what the "right-size" family should be,[6] an attitude that is shaped by many social and economic factors.

If self-determination is the goal, then it would seem wise to refrain from talking about the population explosion. Because, if we link the need to control total population to the goal of giving poor people the opportunity to eliminate excess fertility (that is, to choose how many children they will have), we open the door to dubious policies. Then we give entry to the proposition that, after all, couples should not have more children than they can afford, and larger families are seen to be the privilege of the well-to-do, because they can afford them. It follows, then, that policy should direct services toward the poor, or toward the residents of the inner city—for which read minority groups—to have fewer children. It is one thing to do this in the interest of enabling a deprived population to realize its family-size aspirations by helping it to have access to a basic health service which it wants, which it has difficulty in getting, and which has been enjoyed for years past by better-off families. It is another thing to use this approach as a carrier of, or as a blind for, a concealed, selective anti-natalist policy. Clarity of purpose is therefore important to assure that we do not signal population policy, selective or general, if that is not our intention. There is some evidence that the receipt of such signals could deter some women of the black ghetto, for example, from using family planning services.[7] We should not permit our discomfort at the extravagance of the language with which some Black Nationalists have charged genocidal intentions against family planning policy to lead us to underestimate the realities of the situation.

It would therefore seem wise for professionals to refrain from discussing family planning policy by reference to population issues, unless and until they propose to advocate pursuit of population policy openly, and on its own merits. On the other hand, if we are prepared to place population policy on the agenda, that is quite another matter, but it would open for consideration the full range of social and economic policies that impinge on family formation, family-building, and family well-being. Family planning is only one component of population policy, which, as social policy for families, is very much a central social work concern.[8]

This has been a lengthy *caveat* on the need for more precise definition of the goals of a family planning program and for greater honesty in its articulation. The wisest and the most widely accepted frame of reference from which it is possible to proceed seems to be that of self-determination. The family-size aspirations of low-income couples are not significantly different from those of the middle class, but low-income couples have been less successful in avoiding excess fertility because they have not had access to efficient contraceptives. They have not had access to them because of lack of money or information, or because of lack of health services. And low-income couples will use effective family planning services if they are provided in an acceptable way, that is, with dignity and respect. Finally, family planning is a basic health service that should be available through subsidized public provision like other health services.

Numerous studies have established the facts regarding the family-size aspirations of low-income couples.[9] Information derived from attitude and opinion surveys is supported by historical evidence. The impressive reductions of fertility in working-class populations in industrial countries could hardly have been achieved without planned limitation.[10] The reduction in average size of family in England, for example, was described by Titmuss as "representing nothing less than a revolutionary enlargement of freedom for women brought about by the power to control their own fertility. This private power, what Bernard Shaw once described as the ultimate freedom, can hardly have been exercised without the consent—if not the approval—of the husband."[11] Further evidence in support of the desire to control family size is suggested by the prevalence of illegal abortions, as well as by the response to the provision of contraceptive services in various low-income localities as it becomes available.[12]

Thus the goal is to equalize opportunity by making subsidized family planning services available to those who have difficulty in gaining access to them. The population to be served consists of those medically indigent women of child-bearing years who are defined by Social Security Administration standards as poor and near-poor, and who are not infertile, pregnant, or seeking to be pregnant. We are indebted to Planned Parenthood/World Population for a useful analysis of the composition and distribution of this group, estimated to number 5.3 million medically indigent women. Of these, only 700,000 receive subsidized help in family planning, with Planned Parenthood clinics serving about 250,000. About 37.5 percent live on farms or in rural areas; 50.4 percent live in large metropolitan areas, and twelve percent in cities of less than 250,000 population. Seventy percent are white, and public welfare assistance is the major support of only about fourteen percent of the total. Almost twenty percent work full time. Thirty-one percent are under 25, and about half are under 30. And 60 percent are married and living with their husbands.[13]

These 5,000,000 women in low-income families have been unable to buy medical care in the market economy, the only sure source of supply. And in any case, until quite recently, even assuming no legal or political obstacles, family planning has not been regarded as a basic health service to be provided free or at nominal cost. Family planning has long been identified as a medical service, but an attitude that impeded the development of public financial support for it, even in England, with a history of national health insurance, is suggested by the "idea that as self-control ought to be possible, a birth control service is a form of self-indulgence which ought to be paid for by the individual as are other luxury goods."[14] In the United States, fewer than 30 percent of local health departments provide any kind of family planning service, and only twenty percent of hospitals with large maternity services.[15] Thus, low-income families who have had to rely on public provision have been cut off from family planning information, advice, and service. The fact that they have not been provided with *any* medical services of reasonable quality and acceptably delivered, deserves emphasis. Medical care for the poor has been fragmented and emergency-oriented.[16] How, then, in the new climate, should family planning be financed, and where located, and how related to general family medical care?

It is useful to ask, first, where, if we had free option, it would be desirable to place responsibility for the provision of family planning services. If we had a rationally organized health care structure, family-oriented and coordinated by a family doctor, and backed up by specialists, hospitals, and clinics, delivering preventive and curative health services to everyone, then we could assume the automatic inclusion of family planning, and this is where we would want to lodge the service. But such a system does not yet exist, and certainly not for low-income families, who, in some areas, have no access to public medical facilities of *any* kind, good or bad.

When our new family planning policy was announced by former Secretary Gardner in January 1966, he declared that the Department of Health, Education and Welfare aimed "to improve the health of the people, to strengthen the integrity of the family and to provide families the freedom of choice to determine the spacing of their children and the size of their families."[17] Other official statements of a similar nature have been made. But while policy has been loudly proclaimed, it has not yet been implemented by appropriations on any significant scale, and such funds as are available have to be filtered through the existing fragmented medical care structure.

Some $3,000,000 of the sums provided under formula grants for maternal and child health were used for family planning services in fiscal 1966. Most of the 51 Maternity and Infant Care projects under the 1963 "Retardation Amendments" provide some family planning services as part of comprehensive maternity care. State and local welfare agencies are starting to facilitate services by referral and authorization of payment to health agencies and physicians. Some funds have also become available through the Public Health Service general health grants to the states. And the Office of Economic Opportunity, by last summer, had funded 121 family planning programs.[18] Thus, funds are being channeled to special projects with family planning components, or to specialized clinics. The largest potential source of support may be through Title 19 of the Social Security Act.

Title 19 has, of course, a very considerable potential for meeting health needs of the medically indigent through purchase of services. But whether it will effectively bring family planning to low-income families will depend on state definitions of medical indigence. Liberal interpretations have been countered by Congressional cutbacks. Not all the states can be expected to go beyond the limits of Federal reimbursement, and the requirement that groups be categorically related would seem effectively to exclude married low-income women. Title 19 does not itself create health facilities, but pays for their use; nor does it guarantee access to private physicians.

Thus, even with such financial help as is forthcoming under Title 19, the starting point for a drive to make family planning accessible to the medically indigent is a hodge-podge of good to bad facilities—hospital clinics, maternal and infant care programs, maternal and child health facilities, voluntary Planned Parenthood clinics—these could be enlarged and improved and made more functional or imitated as their characteristics warrant. However, to the extent that this results in the separation of family planning from the full range of other health services, it could lead to some long-run, undesirable consequences that merit attention.

First is the danger of institutionalizing family planning services outside the mainstream of medical care provision. Patterns develop that are hard to reverse. The fact is that Great Britain, with a universal National Health Service in operation since 1948, and before that with considerable experience with health insurance, has only this past year taken the steps necessary to incorporate family planning advice and prescription into the family doctor's practice. The failure early to lodge the service where it belonged helped to institutionalize the exclusion. For many years drugs and advice could be paid for under the National Health Service if avoidance of pregnancy was medically indicated, but not otherwise.[19] In the present stage of development of our health services it would be desirable, wherever possible, to take steps that might prevent bad practice from acquiring a vested interest. While we may have no choice but to proceed with specialized and separate family planning provision, we should be aware of its implications for the continuing fragmentation of medical care.

Another reason for concern at the separation of family planning from family health supervision lies in the popularity of the pill. Whatever reservations there may be in some medical circles regarding the safety of the pill, there is complete agreement on the need for medical supervision while the patient is taking the drug.[20] The middle-class woman who habitually uses preventive health service has regular access to a family physician or to a gynecologist. But the patient of the subsidized family planning clinic may be out of touch with medical advice except on return visits for a new supply of pills. This, to be sure, provides a measure of health supervision. But the fact should not be burked that the contraceptive which has been gaining the widest acceptance requires more medical supervision than have some so-called traditional methods. Therefore, the separation of family planning from other medical practice could raise issues that deserve attention.

Title 19, which may play an important role in some areas in bringing family planning services to medically indigent women, did not create, nor will it heal, the fragmentation of our health services. It is a reflection of our traditional approach in coping with health and, indeed, other social problems. We are committed to disturbing the traditional arrangements as little as possible, at the same time as we are ready to innovate creatively on a small scale, through demonstrations, and to place quite undeserved confidence in the powers of coordination. The great defect of Title 19, however, lies in its confusion of health services with the welfare structure. At the national level, administrative responsibility was given to the Welfare Administration, and in most states it has likewise gone to welfare departments instead of making medical care the direct responsibility of health authorities.[21] The structure of service therefore remains in the tradition of medical provision for the indigent.

Health care facilities, like other institutions that have been designed and operated for the poor, have always reflected upper-class views of the nature of poverty, and upper-class perceptions of how use is made of them, and, of course, upper-class opinion of what is good, or good enough, for the poor. We are now more sophisticated in our knowledge of how class-conditioned bias can distort delivery of health services, but we could afford to be more precise in defining the assumptions about poverty on which intervention strategies and priorities are based. One of the first questions to be addressed, and perhaps one that some professionals may have prejudged or answered too quickly, is whether a major obstacle to use of services inheres in those for whom the services are designed, or in some other factor like the structure of delivery systems. Consideration should be given to whether policy development has been unduly influenced by untested hypotheses about "the poor," poorly defined. "Poor" should not be substituted, like an interchangeable part, for welfare clients, or problem families. And the literature is negligent in specifying how, without reference to income levels, but with implied differentiation as to personal traits, the "very poor" or the "lower-lower class" differ from just the "poor."

Poor people are likely to be undereducated, that is, unlettered as well as inexperienced and unsophisticated in the use of social and health services; when in a client position, they are likely also to be intimidated by officialdom, including teachers, school principals, policemen, social workers, and so on; for the client, unlike the customer, is not always right. But poor or deprived (and client or not) does not necessarily mean disorganized, apathetic, unmotivated, given to magical thinking, and unable to reason. Poor people are not necessarily chronically dependent, or irresponsible, or fatalistic. Poor people are estimated to number over 30,000,000, so obviously they are more numerous than those in the thin stratum of the demoralized "hard-to-reach." These exist, of course, and they stand greatly in need of family planning services, as they are in need of other social and health services. One is entitled to question the editorial judgment of a recent government publication that reviewed behavioral research relevant to family planning. The title is "Poverty and Family Planning,"[22] but it quickly slips into repeated and almost exclusive references to the "very poor," whoever they may be. And one may also question how practically useful for family planning policy is the suggested guideline, based on these behavioral findings, that "programs that focus only on women would seem likely to add to the family problems of all people, especially those of the very poor."[23]

Effective implementation of family planning policy may depend on the extent to which professionals are able to disengage from this tendency to attribute to the poor as a whole some of the traits of the disorganized, problem-ridden sector, a consequence of faulty conceptualization of the problem of poverty, and of careless usage of the category. Until such time as services are available, until they are offered in a respectful manner in a helpful way, at times that are convenient and in places that are acceptable, it would seem to be wise, certainly in planning over-all strategy, to suspend sweeping judgments about poor people's alleged lack of motivation, and to concentrate on provision of service. Thus an issue that merits discussion may be how to strengthen the conviction of the serving professionals that their primary task is to enable people to use a service that they want, and to provide it in the most usable form. In this connection it is interesting to compare Kenneth Clark's conclusion regarding teachers who lack conviction in the ability of their pupils to learn, and hence fail to teach.[24]

The difficulties that low-income families have experienced in trying to use public health facilities, and their discouragement, have been well documented, and criticisms of dysfunctional clinics have not been without effect. In Children's Bureau demonstration programs and in the Office of Economic Opportunity community action programs, admirable progress has been made in developing better and more acceptable systems, designed specifically for the poor, with convenient locations, evening clinic hours, and with an attempt to maintain continuity of health care. However, it is not always clear if such modifications of practice which are designed to make health service delivery more functional for the poor represent a transitional stage on the road to better integrated health services for everyone, or whether they are intended only as improved, second-track systems for the poor, declared to be better for them than the mainstream system. This case was recently put by Lisbeth Bamberger, an official of OEO, who argued that "the neighborhood health center seems to be providing a workable means of dealing with the issue of so-called 'mainstream' medical care versus a separate system for the poor." Referring to the patient's need for respect, and granting that for the poor patient "respect is considerably harder to come by" than for the nonpoor, Miss Bamberger concluded that "the neighborhood health center can be structured in ways that communicate respect to the persons using the center."[25] Possibly this is so, but respect is hard to sustain when the rest of life is an insult.

These various attempts to make delivery systems more functional for the poor are obviously well-intentioned, desirable, and often creative; they are improvements over past practice. One can only applaud some of the OEO-financed attempts to structure special health facilities so as to make them more effective and comfortable for the poor to use. But it is not out of order to suggest that there may be a tendency here to romanticize them, together with the poor, and to suggest caution about rationalizing practice by reference to another set of untested hypotheses about the characteristics of the poor and their need for separate, second-track systems. And one can also raise questions about basing such facilities for poor people on the assumption that they are so different from the nonpoor as to require separate public facilities which our experience tells us will remain second-track and inferior. Long ago, social workers were criticized by some for allegedly helping clients to adjust to their condition instead of helping them to change it. Are we today, in fact, devising service systems adjusted to the poor, or to our perceptions of them, instead of putting pressures on the philosophies, as well as the operations, of mainstream systems?

These cross-currents of poverty theory affect practice and the structure of service, and their relevance and validity merit careful professional assessment. In addition, decisions will have to be made at state and community levels about the structure of the delivery systems that will be used for family planning, how they can be made to relate to each other, how responsibilities will be shared between agencies, how social work skills and knowledge and expertise will be used in planning and in working with other professionals and with non-professionals. Such skills will have to be deployed in very different kinds of situations and agencies, in traditional Planned Parenthood clinics, maternity wards of hospitals, ante-natal and post-partum clinics, comprehensive maternal and infant care projects, neighborhood poverty program centers, in mobile health units in rural areas, and perhaps also in work with private medical practitioners to whom patients are referred. The common thread, apart from the objective, is that all these systems are designed for that sector of the population called poor, traditionally served by public health agencies to which reference has been made, and by public welfare departments to which I now turn.

When I was invited to participate in this Institute, my first thought was, "Is this conference necessary?" I have to confess that the question still nags at me. Why should there be any special question about the social work role in connection with the organization and delivery of a basic socio-medical service like family planning? Does it mean that social work has not done what it should have been doing? Does it mean that social work does not know how to do it? Does it mean that social work does not know what it should be doing? I find it difficult to believe that these questions should be answered in the affirmative. And so I am led to wonder if we have a hidden agenda. Is the real question, not what shall be the role of the social worker, but what shall be the role of the department of welfare? How shall we get it tooled up for family planning action?

There are two policy issues that ought to be resolved in defining public welfare's role in family planning programming. The one that has received major attention has been the question of *if, when,* and *how* caseworkers should take the initiative in discussing family planning with their clients. Congress seems to be on its way to settling the *if* and *when* by mandate. The other policy issue has to do with what we want the over-all role of public welfare to be, not only in relation to family planning, but in the larger sense of public welfare's mission.

While women on the welfare rolls are entitled to more help in controlling fertility than they have so far received from public welfare departments, it does not follow that public welfare should be the fulcrum on which family planning policy turns. As we have seen, only a small segment of the medically indigent women of child-bearing age receive financial support from departments of welfare. Hence, provision should not be structured as though most of the women who are in need of service can be reached through public welfare channels; this approach would only miss the larger target. Moreover, we must decide whether we want to convey the impression that family planning is primarily a public welfare responsibility or a matter of special interest to the welfare authorities. There are very good reasons for avoiding this, unless we have reason to suggest openly what is already implicit in much discussion of family planning policy; namely, that for many of its advocates, the primary purpose is the pursuit of an anti-natalist policy in the interest of cutting welfare costs.

To raise questions about the welfare department thrust in family planning strategy is not to dismiss its responsibility for service to its clients. Good policy requires that information and referral be available, and that they be provided in the same way as for any other medical, educational, or social service. This includes taking the initiative in discussion with the client and being supportive when necessary, again, as in good practice in other situations. But in considering how to facilitate use of service, the client's perception of the agency cannot be overlooked. In this respect, departments of welfare may be at a disadvantage. Throughout its history, public welfare has been deterrent in philosophy and practice; it has been so by definition and mandate. Stigma attaches to the receipt of its services, and this is inevitable so long as the applicant is required to declare, document, and certify his poverty. The attachment of social services to the process does not necessarily open the client's eyes to the benevolence of the agency. How has the client been educated to perceive a social service? What notions about social services are conveyed by the process of eligibility determination? Do we reach out to the client, eager to be helpful and enabling as regards only the one particular service that we now want him to use? Does equal zeal attend the offer of all services?

In view of the historic deterrent philosophy and sometimes punitive practice of welfare departments, and in deference to the attitudes and feelings of some clients, consideration might be given to methods of by-passing the department, or of reinforcing its informational services so as to make it possible for the client to connect with family planning services without the direct intervention of the department.

While some critics have pressed departments of welfare to act more effectively to enable their clients to have access to family planning, on the other hand, fears have been voiced that some departments might press clients against their will to accept family planning services under penalty of loss of financial support, or in the belief that a child might be removed from the home. The possibility cannot be lightly dismissed that coercive referrals might be used, not to impose an unwanted service, but as a lever to separate clients from the rolls, or to prevent them from applying in the first place. There is precedent in the way that "suitable home" and "man in the house" regulations have been used.[26] Taking into consideration the context of some of its punitive recommendations, the Report of the House Ways and Means Committee on HR 12080 revealed a temper that could be potentially congenial to advocacy of coercive referral for contraceptive counseling.[27] This is the subject of an appeal currently being taken from a judgment of a circuit judge in Maryland. When mothers charged with child neglect by reason of having given birth to more than one illegitimate child were brought before his court, he was reported to have required them "to study and understand the methods of birth control and to practice them at the risk of losing their (other) children."[28] While this case did not apparently originate in the local department of welfare, it points up situations in which departments may be placed under pressure which, it is to be hoped, they will be able to resist.

The initiation of new family planning policies raises priority questions. We do not yet have the appropriations, the trained physicians, or the supporting professional staffs for implementation. Nor do we have them, incidentally, for other medical and social services, and family planners are understandably concerned about the possible neglect of family planning if it is absorbed into general maternal and child health operations and has to compete for limited funds.

With regard to the logistics of bringing family planning services to medically indigent women, a schedule of priorities has been elaborated by Planned Parenthood.[29] It is recommended, on the basis of clinic experience, that a strategy should be designed to meet, first, the needs of those who can be reached with minimal effort. The largest concentration of women are to be found in and near the poverty neighborhoods of metropolitan areas. Here experience suggests that the opening of central hospital clinics, with minimal informational supports, is sufficient to reach 15 to 25 percent of the population. When a wanted service is made available, the multiplier effect of word-of-mouth advertising by satisfied patients enables programs to reach optimal operational efficiency with relatively little additional effort. Similar consideratons apply to a second group, 35 to 50 percent of the target, which can be reached by neighborhood clinics backed up by intensive educational and referral programs. A third group yielding another 20 to 30 percent is seen to require still more attention, including home visits and help in attending clinics through provision of transportation and babysitting services. This would leave a residual group of families who carry more than their share of problems and pathology. To reach them will require disproportionate effort, including counseling and various supportive measures well beyond the requirements of the first three groups.

The strategy suggested makes sense, in light of what is known about the heritage of inadequate or shoddy medical services for the poor, including, especially, family planning services. The first requirement is that the services become available. In urging this approach, Frederick Jaffe, a persuasive and knowledgeable spokesman for Planned Parenthood—World Population, has charged that an obstacle to moving in this direction lies in a consistent failure of professionals to focus on delivery systems because of their preoccupation with the apparently intractable problems of the hardest to reach. (A British social worker is triumphantly reported to stop in to see a client every day on her way to work to remind her to take her pill. Whether this would be regarded as good practice, I do not know.) Jaffe argues that most communities are not ready to work at the level of the hardest-to-reach because they have not yet instituted services for the easiest-to-reach, with whom successful efforts would help to create a climate of acceptance among the others. "In New York City, Washington and perhaps several other U.S. cities," he says, "it has become feasible to begin working creatively and systematically on outreach programs to serve the so-called 'hard to reach.' In almost every other community, to place any substantial emphasis on this aspect of the problem is a diversion of attention and scarce resources from the most productive lines of program development."[30] Whether this is a position that social workers can readily endorse, or whether it presents value issues that require resolution, may merit discussion.

It remains to suggest some issues of another order that will require consideration and decision. At the moment, Planned Parenthood affiliates are a repository of experience in the organization of clinics and in training of personnel which they are ready to place at the service of public agencies. Their expertise is needed for program development in many communities. Some mutual accommodation between Planned Parenthood groups and the social work profession may be necessary. For a variety of reasons, Planned Parenthood groups have not always been seen as entirely respectable agencies; for example, their facilities have not commonly been used for field work placements. But in many communities they may now assume a leadership role. Social workers may have to be prepared to look at them differently and establish new relationships. And by the same token, it may be that Planned Parenthood will have to modify some of its perceptions about social work.

It has been said that not only have some social workers been reluctant, or resistant, to initiate discussion of family planning with their clients, but by exaggerating the complexities of family planning counseling, they may contribute to distortion of program development.[31] The issue arises often enough to make discussion necessary in professional circles. But a point of equal, or greater, importance may be not so much the question of the social worker's role in the technical sense, as how to develop a greater concern in the profession with matters of policy and provision, including assessment of their strategy and relevance: these need social work judgment. Is a differential service required for different age groups? What kind of information services should be planned for teen-agers? What are the relative claims on scarce professional resources of the older women as against the needs of the younger ones? Are different strategies necessary to meet the needs of different stages of family building? How much emphasis should be placed on child spacing as appropriate for younger couples, as against family limitation, which may be the concern of the older age group? Is this a matter of educational effort or of differential service structures and locations? Where and how, in the interest of the family economy, should couples first be reached? Is reinforcement of clinical educational methods by means of school programs and the popular media indicated for those couples who might postpone birth of the first child while family resources are being conserved through savings and earnings of the wife?

If professional social workers have been failing to serve clients who need help in availing themselves of service, how, and in what particulars? Is it only in the public welfare setting that services are needed? Are there other settings in which it has not been customary practice to raise the issues? Whose responsibility, for example, is it to give family planning advice or to make a referral of clients in psychiatric settings, either at point of discharge from hospital, or in after-care or community facilities?[32] What responsibility falls to social workers in settlement houses or in schools? And, to suggest the opposite tack, is it always necessary to require social work mediation, and, when not, what alternatives may there be for providing adequate information?

These seem to be appropriate questions for social workers to address, and it is important that they should find the means for making their professional judgment count.

I have left until now consideration of the role of family planning in relationship to the classic concern of social policy, namely, the relief and prevention of poverty. While few family planning authorities pretend to offer it as an anti-poverty policy, except as prescription for individual families, there is a pervasive tendency to suggest its usefulness as a preventive in the basic sense. We can grant that control of fertility is a strategic component in family welfare and family economy, without endowing it with superordinate powers. It can contribute to maintaining a better balance between family income and family responsibilities; it can prevent an income squeeze from jeopardizing family cohesion in individual cases; it can permit more low-income mothers to choose, if they wish, to ease problems of family economy by taking jobs; it may enable some low-income families to escape some of the most oppressive features of poverty. But it will not cure poverty nor prevent it so long as poverty-generating factors still operate in the social-industrial structure.

Family planning makes it possible for low-income families to attain higher per capita income within the family than could be sustained if fertility were not controlled. But it is possible to make the income meet the needs of the family, no less than to tailor family size to fit the income. Large families are in poverty, not just because they are large, but because their incomes are insufficient. If, as a matter of policy, we want to persuade potential users of service that family health and welfare will be enhanced by child spacing, or by limitation of family size, we will have to concern ourselves also with other social measures that are relevant to the objective, if only to prevent inaction from giving the lie to our slogans. If we really want to continue to use that sentimental and possibly ambiguous slogan, "every child a wanted child," we have many policy issues to work out and much work to do. If wages are inadequate, and medical care lacking, and housing dilapidated, then our concern about family health may be less than convincing. Family planning should therefore be located in a range of services that are supportive of healthy family life. Family planning is no substitute for children's allowances, for adequate housing, for preventive medical and dental care, for day care for working mothers, and perhaps for shopping mothers, too; for schools that teach, for social support in the event of incapacity or absence of a breadwinner, and for adequate family income, whether earned or socially provided. These are objectives that cannot be attained without some reduction of the gross inequities of affluent society.

Without these social supports, family planning provision will be more difficult to use by those who need and want it, or who would use it if given a fair chance. That chance could be frustrated if low-income communities are made to feel that we are not so much interested in child spacing as in population control, particularly of those who are poor and black, and the frequently cited unwanted child, so called because unplanned by his parents, emerges, in truth, as the child unwanted and rejected by society.

Thus we are on the threshold of a new policy development for family planning. We have not made the necessary financial provision for developing it as a health service, and the Congress is in process of looking at it as a welfare program. The executive branch and the welfare bureaucracy talk very grandly of self-determination and equalization of opportunity and show signs of having been unduly influenced by some "culture of poverty" approaches. Presumably we will have to wait to hear from the provinces to see what directions are taken.

In keeping with the history of the family planning movement, its ideological auspices are still mixed. There are those who advise that the fact that it started as social reform in the interest of women ought to be forgotten, now that it has ended up as a medical service. Others might counsel that we would do better not to forget the continuing relevance of the social reform past for the social and economic problems of low-income women. These problems are at least as real as the alleged ego and virility problems of low-income men.

We are in a complex situation, presenting opportunities as well as dangers. The latter should not be exaggerated, but neither should they be underestimated, particularly because we are not building policy during a positive, social-reforming climate congenial to the best in the family planning tradition, but in a restrictive, budget-trimming climate dictated by the prior needs of an indecent war. In threading its way through ideological crosscurrents, service complexities, and contradictions of policy, it is possible that one of the most important contributions that social work could make would be in the exercise of its professional social guardianship function.

NOTES

[1] Elizabeth Draper, *Birth Control in the Modern World* (Harmondsworth, England, 1965), p. 13.

[2] Wilbur J. Cohen, "Family Planning: One Aspect of Freedom to Choose," *HEW Indicators*, June 1966.

[3] Board of Directors, American Nurses Association, September 1966.

[4] American Public Health Association, *Policy Statement on Population*, October 4, 1964.

[5] Maryland, Department of Health, *Memorandum from the Commissioner to Local Health Officers*, May 12, 1966.

[6] Report on Family Planning Conference, *Children*, July-August 1966, p. 161.

[7] See remarks of Miss Wilma Johnson, R.N., in *Public Family Planning Clinics, Report of Second Conference*, San Francisco, September 19-20, 1966 (New York, 1967), p. 13; also, remarks of Rep. Eugene Gelfand of Pennsylvania in U.S. Department of Health, Education and Welfare, Region II, *Proceedings of Regional Conference on Family Planning*, December 14-15, 1966, p. 108.

[8] Alva Myrdal, *Nation and Family* (New York, 1941), *passim*.

[9] Frederick S. Jaffe, "Programming for Community Needs," in *Proceedings of Regional Conference on Family Planning*, pp. 27–38.

[10] Norman B. Ryder, "The Character of Modern Fertility," in *World Population,* ed. John D. Durand, *Annals of the American Academy of Political and Social Science* 369 (January 1967), pp. 26–36.

[11] Richard M. Titmuss, *Essays on "The Welfare State,"* 2nd ed. (London, 1963), p. 91.

[12] Joseph D. Beasley et al., "Attitudes and Knowledge Relevant to Family Planning Among New Orleans Negro Women," *American Journal of Public Health,* November 1966, pp. 1947–57; Richard Frank and Christopher Tietze, "Acceptance of an Oral Contraceptive Program in a Large Metropolitan Area," *American Journal of Obstetrics and Gynecology,* September 1, 1965, pp. 122–127; Robert H. Browning and L. L. Parks, "Childbearing Aspirations of Public Health Maternity Patients," *American Journal of Public Health,* November 1964, pp. 1831–33; Jaffe, *op. cit.*

[13] Planned Parenthood-World Population, *Five Million Women* (New York, 1967).

[14] Draper, *op. cit.,* p. 201.

[15] Planned Parenthood-World Population, *op. cit.*

[16] Alonzo S. Yerby, *The Disadvantaged and Health Care,* paper presented at White House Conference on Health, November 3-4, 1965.

[17] U.S. Department of Health, Education and Welfare, *Indicators,* June 1966. Reprint.

[18] U.S. Department of Health, Education and Welfare, *Report on Family Planning,* Activities of the U.S. Department of Health, Education and Welfare in Family Planning, Fertility, Sterility and Population Dynamics (Washington, D.C.: Government Printing Office, September 1966); information received from Office of Economic Opportunity, letter, August 7, 1967.

[19] Robert E. Dowse and John Peel, "The Politics of Birth Control." *Political Studies,* 1965, pp. 179–197; Draper, *op. cit.,* pp. 254ff; *Family Planning Miscellany,* No. 1 and 2 (London, England: Family Planning Association, January and July, 1967).

[20] Draper, *op. cit.,* pp. 58ff.

[21] Eveline M. Burns, "Some Major Policy Decisions Facing the United States in the Financing and Organization of Health Care," *New Directions in Public Policy for Health Care,* reprinted from *Bulletin of the New York Academy of Medicine,* Second Series (December 1966), pp. 1067–1242.

[22] Catherine S. Chilman, "Poverty and Family Planning in the United States: Some Social and Psychological Aspects and Implications for Programs and Policy," *Welfare in Review,* April 1967, pp. 3–15.

[23] *Ibid.*

[24] Kenneth B. Clark, *Dark Ghetto: Dilemmas of Social Power* (New York, 1965).

[25] Lisbeth Bamberger, "Health Care and Poverty," in *New Directions in Public Policy for Health Care.*

[26] Winifred Bell, *Aid to Dependent Children* (New York, 1965), *passim.*

[27] U.S. 90th Congress, 1st Session. House Report No. 544. Report of the Committee on Ways and Means on H.R. 12080. Social Security Amendments of 1967 (Washington, D.C.: Government Printing Office, 1967).

[28] *New York Times,* 22 September 1967; and *Welfare Law Bulletin,* No. 10 (October 1967), p. 10.

[29] Jaffe, *op. cit.*

[30] *Ibid;* see also, Jaffe, *Family Planning and Rural Poverty: An Approach to Programming of Services* (paper prepared for the National Advisory Commission on Rural Poverty, June 1967).

[31] Gitta Meier, "Research and Action Program in Human Fertility Control: A Review of the Literature," *Social Work,* July 1966, pp. 40–45.

[32] *Family Planning and Mental Health.* Summary of discussions held at National Institutes of Health, January 13, 1966. See, particularly, comments by Mrs. Gitta Meier.

SUGGESTED READINGS

Haselkorn, F., ed., *Family Planning: The Role of Social Work,* Garden City, New York: School of Social Work Publications, Adelphi University, 1968.

Jaffe, F., "Family Planning, Public Policy and Intervention Strategy," *Journal of Social Issues* 23 (1967): 145–62.

Journal of Marriage and the Family, "Family Planning and Fertility Control," 30, no. 2 (1968) (entire issue).

Manisoff, M. T., *Family Planning Training for Social Service.* New York: Planned Parenthood—World Population, 1970.

Public Family Planning Clinics: How to Organize/How to Operate, New York: Searle Co., 1966.

Sheppard, H. L., *Effects of Family Planning on Poverty in the U.S.* Kalamazoo, Mich.: Upjohn Institute, 1967.

21

Abortion: A Social Policy for Prevention

LeRoy G. Schultz

The preventive function of social work, while the most sought-after goal of all the helping professions, has received relatively scant attention despite its basic imperative nature to any successful social work in the long view.[1] The semi-professions dealing with social and personal problems have not developed a mature knowledge base to accommodate prevention as a concept, and as a practice tool. The value of prevention has characterized the profession from its historical beginning. More recently and specifically one of social work's functions is "the elimination of conditions which potentially could hamper social functioning."[2] Rapoport has clearly and appropriately warned the profession to "guard against legal structure and administrative usage which, in actuality if not by intent, undermine and impair the independent striving of individuals . . ."[3] And more directly, "The mission of family planning impinges directly on the mission of preventive social work: to bypass a measure of personal and community ills by eradicating some of the root causes of social pathology."[4] It is the thesis of this paper that the current abortion laws of most states rule out to any effective degree meaningful prevention within the current social work definition, that current abortion law is a socially dysfunctional policy, and that social work has neglected to help formulate abortion policy as a proper preventive.

American social work literature contains almost no mention of abortion as a problem, a policy, or as a preventative instrument, even though social workers presumably have been picking up its casualties. Abortion is not solely the problem of any one profession, or of all the helping professions, but of all citizens, as it involves public morality, and theology, as well as social work, law, and medicine. No profession should or can have a monopoly over what goes into the formation of policy,[5] but social work has made little effort to mobilize the capacity of affected groups to have their own impact on their own destiny. Even so, the problem of abortion has as much relevance for social work as any other profession, if not more.

Abortion is medically defined as the expulsion of a nonviable fetus, i.e., one not sufficiently developed to live outside the uterus. Concern here is for criminal and therapeutic abortions, not those of a spontaneous origin. Therapeutic abortion refers to a simple surgical procedure (first trimester) performed by physicians or paramedical personnel, usually after consultation and hospital approval, which is protected by law. All other abortions are criminal. Although criminal abortion has become a major cause of maternal death in the United States and a liberal abortion policy would prevent considerable social, psychological, and physical pathology,[6] it has only been in the past several years that social work has paid any effective attention to abortion.[7] This, on the surface, appears a paradox in a profession whose early history can literally be told in terms of its impact on provisions, programs, and policies protecting the welfare of mothers, families, children, and the emancipation of women. Our functional blindness in neglecting this problem is related to both the profession's enforced predisposition to treating problems after they are created and the reluctance of a budding profession looking for social acceptance and sanction to become involved in controversial and taboo areas, where goals are chosen only after near total consensus.

The Population at Risk

Although there are some 10,000 to 18,000 legal and therapeutic abortions per year in the United States, there is one "criminal" abortion every minute, and criminal abortion constitutes one of the most lucrative criminal enterprises in this country.[8] The majority of abortions, both legal and criminal, are performed upon legally married women who have conceived by their husbands, and who have two or more children. Approximately 80 percent of all abortions, legal and illegal, are performed by competent licensed physicians in what amounts to the "medical underground"[9] in those states without reformed abortion laws. In a large sample of married women researched, some 22 percent admitted to at least one abortion by the time they reached age 45 years.[10] The unwed mother, because she is the most discriminated against as to the legal abortion services,[11] must in 88 to 95 percent of the cases seek out a criminal abortion to terminate her pregnancy.[12] Some 8 to 10 percent of pregnant women become so emotionally upset that they attempt to self-abort with crude instruments or chemicals, in the absence of an adequate abortion service, with lethal results to from 5,000 to 10,000 women each year.[13]

No state allows a pregnant woman the complete choice to have an abortion, even when it is medically safe, although half of all the states are surveying the problem with a view to possible changing policy.[14] Obviously, millions of pregnant women are rejecting involuntary motherhood each year by either requesting a physician to break the law, seeking out a criminal abortionist, aborting oneself, or (if affluent) flying to Europe, Japan, or Scandinavia for medical service. The difference between having an abortion or a child is contingent upon having the fees, or not, and knowing or not knowing the right person for referral. The result is a direct ratio between income and abortion, with the poor being the most excluded from the service availability.[15] This inequality in medical services forces the lower-class patient to resort more to the untrained criminal abortionist or self-abortion, with a subsequently higher mortality.[16] Some private hospital patients are aborted twenty times—more frequently than "charity" patients.[17] Private hospitals perform one abortion for every 35 deliveries, while public hospitals nearby perform one abortion for every 2,864 deliveries.[18]

It appears improbable that medical opinion and diagnosis could vary so widely between indigent and affluent patients. There is an obvious class discrimination in the availability of the medical service of abortion that is difficult to reconcile with our belief in the right to the highest attainable health standard for each, despite his economic condition.

What the above grim statistics do not reveal is the degree and extent of human misery for the pregnant female who is being coerced by the physiological processes of her body into having a child against her wishes and perhaps her rights, and not in the best interests of social welfare. In summary, we have a law which is felt to be antiquated and unjust to the degree that millions of women and many physicians choose to violate it, a law which indirectly results in forcing pregnant women to seek out the criminal abortionist, or attempt self-abortion, with lethal results for 5,000 to 10,000 per year, a law so differentially defined so as to result in an unfair distribution of a needed form of surgery, and a law which unintentionally legislates against prevention.

Medical-Psychiatric Indications

No one can agree on what time in the pregnancy process a life begins.[19] Many people think life refers to the physical, never the mental or social. Present abortion law commands the physician to consider the patient's health up to the time when she will normally deliver, but absurdly rules that her health afterwards is of little significance; yet life depends on health. The result of current interpretation of abortion law is the forcing of physicians to determine if a physical illness coupled with pregnancy will kill the patient, or determine whether carrying the pregnancy to term will result in suicide. Most states will not permit abortion for fetal indications, even where it is well established that the infant will be born deformed and handicapped, either mentally or physically, or both, due to the pregnant woman's use of drugs, the presence of rubella (German measles), radiation, or genetic factors.

In the past thirty years, nearly all hospital surveys have reported a sharp decrease in therapeutic abortion for somatic indications, due to advancing medical technology.[20] However, there has been, during the same time period, a steady increase in abortion on psychiatric grounds—i.e., threats of suicide.[21] Yet research has demonstrated that the suicide rate among pregnant women is considerably lower than that of the general population of nonpregnant women.[22] It appears that suicidal threats, real or imagined, are being used by both patient and physician as a method of circumventing what is to them an unrealistic law.[23] No physician should be required to break a law in order to render good medical practice.

Socioeconomic Indications

The primary and most viable reason the majority of American women ask for and receive abortions, both here and abroad, is the socioeconomic one.[24] It is in this area that social work has a sizable body of knowledge and practice and much to contribute, yet no social workers are called upon to sit on hospital abortion committees or to act as consultants to physicians on the abortion question, nor have we asserted the initiative. The result is that the physician must alone make a decision to abort in most cases for reasons he neither has the time nor the understanding to determine properly. The fact remains that the physician has felt so concerned about the abortion problem and so outraged by a harsh antiquated law that he has taken upon himself the unpopular task of doing something about it, occasionally at great personal cost.[25]

For social work to continue to remain silent and inactive on this problem indirectly condones it through communication by default. We seem to have left the problem to the medical profession, as if we have nothing to say or do, yet we stand to profit just as greatly from its solution.

Although physicians may not be the best judges of socioeconomic factors, they know that these factors are important to health. Both social work and medicine have learned that we cannot merely respond to ills, because the absence of disease does not consitute health. Most current abortion law prohibits this kind of practical thinking.

Naturally, medical, psychiatric, and fetal factors can be stated in terms of their social interest and they tend to overlap. Most socioeconomic indications for abortion are for the following reasons:

1. Cases where the expected child has a reasonable chance of being born deformed, mentally defective, or incapable of living a normal

life, or if the child will be born into a highly detrimental environment that cannot be reasonably compensated for.
2. Cases of extreme poverty, particularly where organic and mental illness decrease the mother's ability to care for a larger family.
3. Cases where the economic well-being of the whole family would be adversely affected if the same resources must be stretched to care for another member.
4. Cases where females are impregnated through forcible or statutory rape or incest.
5. Cases where it appears probable that the pregnant female may be under such emotional stress as to appear likely to resort to a criminal abortionist or risk self-induced abortion.

We can force women to give birth to children, but a quarter century of social work research has demonstrated that mothers cannot be forced to love unwanted children. It is not desirable even if it were possible. The consequences of an abortion are usually limited in time,[26] the consequences of ill-advised parenthood are paid for by society for generations.[27] Scandinavian studies comparing the welfare of children of mothers refused abortion with those who made no such request, reveal that the destiny and interests of children are best met through a liberal abortion law.[28] Socioeconomic indications for absorption should be made legal for those who want them, and where it is safe (first trimester), and a reformed abortion law should become part of the general social welfare legislation for the support of mothers and families.

Policy Alternatives

A complex pluralistic society is continuously faced with the problem of making differing systems of values compatible. One social institution that molds group and individual values is the church, and it has finally come to realize that it cannot force its moral ideals upon other citizens through secular criminal law, and that morality is poorly reinforced by fear of punishment.[29] What the citizen views as a possible solution to the abortion problem, in the absence of religious values, depends on one's general attitude towards abortion, the right to family planning, the population explosion, costs of unwanted children on the tax system, and concepts of women's rights. The policy considerations stressed reflect individual tastes, inconsistencies, and how well the problems are publicized. Legislators shape their policy inputs in terms of their guesses as to constituency choice and pressure and reelection anxiety. No fact or argument based upon the current law's social evils or its mental of phycial casualties will make the

slightest impact upon the moral absolutist who asserts that abortion is murder.[30] However, for many in social work and other helping professions as
well as among the citizenry there are those who subscribe to a differing
morality. To them our present abortion laws are unnecessarily harsh, restrictive, violative of true dignity, and unsupported by social work logic.

Two styles of policy are currently being attempted in approximately
half of the states[31] by citizen–professional social action groups. The first
approach consists of retaining the restraining spirit of the present law, but
adding amendments to include more grounds for abortion. The basic and
somewhat conservative policy model used in this approach is that of the
American Law Institute Penal Code, according to which abortion would
be made legal if there was a substantial risk that the expected child would
be born with grave physical and mental defect, or if pregnancy resulted
from rape, incest, or illicit intercourse with a female under age sixteen.[32]
No further justifications were included in the Code for fear that additional
amendments would not be acceptable to Catholics.[33] The Code further requires two physicians to certify in writing to the hospital that in their judgment the abortion is needed and legal.

The second policy approach consists of removing all abortion law restriction, leaving the decision to abort to the pregnant female and her
husband, if married, or to her parents if she is under age, and a physician.
The reformed law in New York, passed on April 10, 1970, is the best
example of this approach, providing that within the first twenty-four weeks
of pregnancy, the decision to abort is between the female and her physician, and after the twenty-four weeks an abortion can be done only to
save her life. Most reform bill proposals in the various states reflect the
Code provisions and are incremental. Each social action group working
for reform has to bargain politically for what amendments are likely to
pass in a given state. Likely issues in the future that may determine the
national abortion policy will probably center on the right of self-determination for the women or couple, or whether the public has a right to interfere
with abortion as a family planning method, or whether the state is invading
the privacy of its citizens through current law.

The Role of the Social Worker

Whatever policy alternative is chosen will require, for legislative passage, professional commitment and sociopolitical action for reform. Man
is a cultural animal, his society is not solely determined biologically, and
he is constantly discarding, editing, changing, and creating new methods
in accord with new experiences and changing environments. Social action
is the link between individual man and this cultural flux. An abortion takes

little time, is comparatively economical, is more safe than normal delivery, and has few serious side-effects.[34] As a preventive procedure and service, it holds great value for every setting of social work practice. Although we admit these ideas as facts in private, and although we are more exposed to antiquated abortion policy casualties, we have not shared either the facts or our values with the public. Nor have we engaged (with slight exception) in the legal and political combat necessary for change. Our preventive goal should be directed toward modification of environmental factors, including the values of various groups influencing policy formation. We should not be forced to ask a client or physician to break the law in order to practice preventive social work. However, reform, repeal, and revision of current abortion law, despite its being flouted by millions, is not a popular cause and is electorally dangerous to legislators. The present law rules out a potent tool of prevention, a possibility of choice and partial control over our destiny heretofore unthought of. Some of us will view the freedom of choice as a burden and resent the freedom that makes us responsible for our own fate. Others will see it for the preventive opportunity it offers for the public welfare, as the aim of mankind must be to act as agent for its own improvement.

There is no question of imposing conformity to community consensus on a few women and their families, but rather of continuing to employ the machinery of the state to force a major group to conform to the ideals of others, and to cease restriction upon the self-determination of millions of citizens having differing but equally respectable sensibilities. Democracy remains the sum total of social and political structures, the sum total of the practices of creating, distributing, and balancing *all* socially significant values through which true human dignity and individuality may be realized. It is the greatest possible working harmony with the greatest possible diversity.

The really seminal minds of early social work professionals combined passion about social problems in their time with rigor in matters of social action, holding no illusions about the possibility or even the desirability of neutrality in laying down the superstructure of welfare liberalism through law reform. All law is a tool, a mere instrumentality, never the driving force of society. It must remain an intelligent servant, never becoming absolute master of the people.

There appears little precedent in past social work history to assist us with solutions to the abortion problem. Perhaps it was not so severe a problem in the past, and no doubt our forefathers would view abortion law repeal as revolutionary. Important to recall is that all social institutions like social work, unless constantly revised and revitalized, are prone to grow hard, inelastic, and unrealistic. They crystallize upon their own historical premises, gradually developing a tendency to become patterned on their own past rather than adjusting themselves to existing conditions of real life. We cannot remain staring fixedly into rear-view mirrors that block the view ahead. The emancipation of the present generation of social workers from an immature dependence on the past is forcing us into the perhaps uncomfortable position of having to think and decide for ourselves on many issues unknown to earlier professionals.

The professional and civic obligation to social reform is preliminary to any significant social work, just as was for our forefathers. There are many ways and levels of participating in real social reform of our devitalizing abortion law that suit the diverse personalities involved, but all require extroverted action with other citizens in all their chaotic individualism and irrationalism. Militant social action is a time-honored method of dealing with entrenched evils that defy orderly change.

No matter what role we choose to play in abortion policy formation, we should continue to strengthen our professional efforts in sex education, birth control, and genetic counseling, which lessen the need for abortion. Marked professional effort should be made to correct the historical and self-serving mistake of separating abortion from family planning and family planning from population control.[35]

Even after passage of a prevention-oriented abortion law, our professional contribution will be required. Hospital and clinic policy will have to be altered to accommodate the new medical service; medical and paramedical staff, client groups, and hospital administration attitudes will have to be altered and information distribution methods developed. A new abortion law have little effect upon America's rural areas where there are few physicians and hospitals. Compounding this difficulty is the reluctance of the medical profession to deliver abortion services in clinics rather than hospitals, or to support the training and certification of paramedical personnel as abortionists despite the simplicity of this "surgical" procedure. Already New York physicians are expected to discourage abortion because of limited resources and overcrowded facilities. Who should receive an abortion in preference to someone else is a *social,* political, and medical question.

If the new abortion laws require the patient to submit the eligibility question to a hospital board, certainly social worker representation on such a board is necessary in view of the already mentioned socioeconomic motivation for abortion. One would hope that social work's contribution would consist of trying to avoid the hospital committee approach completely, since the profession has witnessed with chronic horror the "needs test" and "residence requirements" in public welfare programs. Like a welfare recipient, a woman applicant for abortion is forced to show her weaknesses and her inability to cope with stress in requesting service from the hospital committe and may need social work representation in making her claims to service. Already some qualified abortion applicants are being denied medical service in California and Colorado.[36] This increases anxiety, incites some to seek out criminal abortionists, or results in the loss of precious time. Hospital bureaucracy is just as bad as bureaucracy in general. Our help is needed to determine indigency and fees, to clear medicare and private insurance issues, and work closely with referral services in Europe for those from "no-abortion" states.

Conclusion

"Admonishing physicians for permitting social and economic factors to influence their decisions [to abort] indicates a blindness toward the modern concept of social medicine which embraces all aspects of sickness and health."[37] Although social workers do not suffer this kind of blindness in conceptual theory, we do lack this vision in practice. If abortions are to be made on socioeconomic indications, certainly our contribution and responsibility are ncessary, and we as well as the medical profession stand to profit by a law revision. From a social work standpoint, moralizing about abortion is not profitable. Constructively, our task is to try to understand abortion in relation to human needs, values, and institutions and to assist actively the decision-makers in determining the best policy in terms of our values and knowledge. Each social worker has the responsibility as citizen and professional not only to support, with others, general public welfare, but to seize the initiative in seeking the elimination of specific ills, in our role as molders and partners in social realtities. The least we should expect is to recognize the values for family life that other countries and their social workers have found in abortion law reform, and to speak out for the value that a similar system might have in this country.

"Perhaps the most important influence on the future of social work will be the seriousness of its concern with prevention . . ."[38] Working to ward amending or repealing our abortion law could well start the profession toward making one type of prevention a reality. The reproductive renaissance may yet make this the century of the wanted child.

NOTES

[1] F. Haselkorn, "An Ounce of Prevention," *Journal of Social Work Education* 3 (1967), 61–71. This article is an excellent summation of the status of "prevention" in the social work profession.

[2] W. Boehm, "The Nature of Social Work," *Social Work* 3 (1958), 16–17. NASW, *Goals of Public Social Policy,* New York: NASW, 1959, p. 5, 12, 13, 19.

[3] L. Rapoport, "The Concept of Prevention in Social Work," *Social Work* 6 (1961), 12.

[4] K. Oettinger, *The School of Social Work's Responsibilities in Family Planning Education* (Washington, D.C.: HEW, 1968), p. 3.

[5] C. Levy, "The Social Worker as Agent of Policy Change," *Social Casework* 51 (1970), 102–108.

[6] K. Niswander, "Medical Abortion Practices in the U.S.," *Western Reserve Law Review* 17 (1965), 403. L. Lader, *Abortion* (Boston: Beacon Press, 1967), pp. 1–42.

[7] M. Zeppetello, *et al.* "The Social Problem of Abortion in the U.S.: Its Significance for the Social Work Profession," (MSW Thesis, School of Social Work, Syracuse University, 1967), pp. 45–55.

[8] H. Rosen, "Psychiatric Implications of Abortion: A Case Study in Social Hypocrisy," *Western Reserve Law Review* 17 (1965), 436.

[9] *Ibid.,* 436–437.

[10] P. Gebhard *et al., Pregnancy, Birth, and Abortion,* (New York: Hoeber, 1958), Chapter 4.

[11] E. Schur, *Crimes Without Victims* (Englewood Cliffs, N.J.: Prentice-Hall, 1965), pp. 21–22.

[12] Gebhard, *op. cit.,* Chapter 4.

[13] M. Trout, "Therapeutic Abortion Laws Need Therapy," *Temple Law Quarterly* 37 (1964), 178.

[14] J. Voyles, "Changing Abortion Laws in the U.S.," *Journal of Family Law,* 7 (1967), 496–511.

[15] Niswander, *op. cit.,* pp. 417–18.

[16] E. Gold, *et al.,* "Therapeutic Abortions in New York City: A 20-Year Review," *American Journal of Public Health,* 55 (1965), 964–72.

[17] Niswander, *op. cit.,* 417–418.

[18] *Ibid.*

[19] A. Knutson, "The Definition and Value of a New Human Life," *Social Science and Medicine,* 1 (1967), 7–29. D. Giannella, "The Difficult Quest for a Truly Humane Abortion Law," *Villanova Law Review,* 13 (1968), 257–302.

[20] Niswander, *op. cit.,* 415–417.

[21] Niswander, *op. cit.,* pp. 413–418. Rosen, *op. cit.,* 444–449.

[22] Niswander, *op. cit.,* p. 417. E. W. Anderson, "Psychiatric Aspects of Abortion," *Proceedings, Third World Congress of Psychiatry,* 1963, p. 1172.

[23] Rosen, *op. cit.,* p. 448. S. Bolter, "The Psychiatrist's Role in Therapeutic Abortion: Unwitting Accomplice," *American Journal of Psychiatry* 119 (1962), 312–16.

[24] Niswander, *op. cit.,* p. 414, Rosen, *op. cit.,* p. 438, 449, 450, 451. T. S. Szasz. "Bootlegging Humanistic Values Through Psychiatry," *Antioch Review,* 1962, pp. 341–449; J. L. Rapoport, "American Abortion Applicants in Sweden," *Archives of General Psychiatry* 13 (1965), 24–33; E. W. Anderson, "Psychiatric Indications for the Termination of Pregnancy," *Postgraduate Medical Journal* 34 (1958), 70.

[25] L. Freeman, *The Abortionist* (New York: Grove Press, 1963), Chapter 6.

[26] J. M. Kummer, "Post-Abortion Psychiatric Illness—A Myth," *American Journal of Psychiatry* 119, no. 10 (1963), pp. 980–983. G. Hardin, *Abortion and Human Dignity,* Lecture, University of California, Berkeley, April 29, 1964.

[27] R. Jenkins, "The Significance of Maternal Rejection of Pregnancy for the Future Development of the Child," in H. Rosen, ed., *Therapeutic Abortion* (New York: Julian, 1954), p. 269. H. D. Bryant, *et al.* "Physical Abuse of Children—An Agency Study," *Child Welfare,* March 1963, pp. 125–130. L. Adelson, "Homicide by Starvation," *Journal American Medical Association* 186 (1963), pp. 458–460.

[28] H. Hoffmeyer, "Medical Aspects of the Danish Legislation on Abortion," *Western Reserve Law Review* 17, no. 2 (1965), pp. 548–50.

[29] "Abortion Law," *Commonweal* 83 (1966) 685. W. Hooft, "Pluralism, Temptation, or Opportunity," *Ecumenical Review* 18 (1966), 129–49.

[30] N. Stevas, *The Right to Life,* (New York: Holt-Rinehart and Winston, 1964), Chapter 5.

[31] National Association for the Repeal of Abortion Laws, New York, *News,* Summer 1969, pp. 3–5.

[32] American Law Institute, Model Penal Code, Section 230.3, 1962.

[33] L. Schwartz, "Moral Offenses and the Model Penal Code," *Columbia Law Review* 63 (1963), 686.

[34] Niswander, *op. cit.,* 420–422; C. Tietze, "Abortion as a Cause of Death," *American Journal of Public Health* 38 (1948), 1434.

[35] A. Rossi, "Abortion and Social Change," *Dissent,* August 1969, pp. 338–346.

[36] *Ibid.,* p. 343.

[37] H. Rosen, *Therapeutic Abortion* (New York: Julian, 1954), p. 295.

[38] N. Cohen, *Social Work in the American Tradition,* (New York: Holt, Rinehart and Winston, 1958), p. 352.

SUGGESTED READINGS

Callahan, D. *Abortion: Law, Choice and Morality,* New York: Macmillan, 1970.

Cooke, R., et al. *The Terrible Choice.* New York: Bantam, 1968.

How to Set Up a Legalized Abortion Committee. Legalize Abortion, Post Office Box 24163, Los Angeles, Calif., (n.d.)

Lader, L. *Abortion.* Boston: Beacon, 1967.

Lee, N. *The Search for an Abortionist.* Chicago: University of Chicago Press, 1969.

McCaghy, C. et al. *In Their Own Behalf: Voices from the Margin.* New York: Appleton-Century-Crofts, 1968, pp. 10–21.

Phelon, L. and Maginnis, P. *The Abortion Handbook.* Los Angeles, Contact, 1969.

Simms, M. *Abortion, the Campaign, the Bill, the Aftermath.* London: Owen, 1967.

Western Reserve Law Review 17 (1965) no. 2 (entire issue).

22

Population Control and Personal Freedom: Are They Compatible?

ALICE TAYLOR DAY

The twentieth century may well be remembered as the last period in which man could reproduce without regard for the social consequences of his behavior. Few developments in history have so challenged the ability of man to live harmoniously within his social and physical environments as has the unprecedented increase of his own species. Recognition of the penalties of unlimited reproduction is leading increasingly to the demand that action be taken to alter the ruinous course of present demographic trends. The rising pressure for action is reflected in the expansion of programs to influence reproductive behavior, and in the growing discussion of broad questions about population policy itself. The important question is now no longer whether man should curtail his excess reproduction, but how best to induce him to do so. The urgency of the problem is even more pronounced in view of Pope Paul's Encyclical, "On Human Life."

Replacement or Expansion?

Two leading American demographers have recently offered different views about the means necessary to end the current population expansion. Differences in their outlooks can be traced to their differing judgments about the adequacy of current family-planning programs to effect a genuine long-term decline in population growth. Asserting that action programs now under way are successfully bringing birth rates under control, Donald Bogue claims that within the brief span of five years a change amounting to "a social revolution" has taken place both in the acceptance of the need for birth control and in the growth of knowledge and research activities concerning the techniques of effective family planning. Crediting organized family-planning programs with most of the declines in the birth rate in Korea, Pakistan, Taiwan, and Colombia, he goes on to say that, considering the rapid pace of "fertility control" over the past few years, ". . . it is quite reasonable to assume that the world population crisis is a phenomenon of the twentieth century, and will be largely if not entirely a matter of history when humanity moves into the twenty-first century."

Kingsley Davis is much less sanguine. Even if we accept the judgment that the next few decades will witness the rapid adoption of contraception all over the world, there are firm grounds, he believes, for skepticism about whether the widespread use of family planning will signal an end to the population explosion. He notes first that despite the enthusiasm about the spread of family planning, birth rates in many underdeveloped countries are rising, not falling. Moreover, he continues, the responsibility of family-planning campaigns for falling birth rates in particular areas may well have been exaggerated, for in many such instances birth rates were beginning to decline well before family-planning campaigns were under way. Declining fertility could be attributed, therefore, at least as much to the influence of social change and modernization as to the introduction of birth control.

In fact, claims Davis, talk about "population control" or "fertility control" in connection with family-planning programs is misleading. Such programs make no attempt to influence the factors actually determining levels of reproduction. Their aim is, instead, to enable individual couples to bear the number of children they want when they want them. Any program designed to enable parents to have no more than the number of children they want can reduce a population's growth rate only if couples have been having more children than they want to have. Though such conditions of excess childbearing seem to exist in many (if not all) underdeveloped countries, the numbers of children desired are well above those needed for replacement only. In the developed countries, moreover, recent studies of reproductive motivation show that the numbers of children couples say they want are frequently *above* those they actually have. So far as is known, there is no population—whether in an underdeveloped or a developed country—whose childbearing aspirations are currently low enough to halt population increase. The prevention of unwanted births (the actual result of a successful family-planning program) could still leave a rapid rate of population growth.

Needed: A Change in Attitude

Extension of control over childbearing to individuals is obviously an important preliminary to population control, but it is only a preliminary. To effect a substantial decline in growth rates there must also be a fundamental change in the size of the families couples want. Present action programs avoid persuading couples to reduce their desire for children. Family planning is urged as a means to improve personal family interests: the health of the mother and the quality of the children born. The demographic results of such programs are at the best ambiguous. Appeals to control reproduction couched in terms of personal interests may reduce high-order births in the short run, but the long-run consequences may be to encourage couples to bear more children as their economic and social fortunes improve. Once couples possess the means to plan their families, a crucial question still remains: What, in fact, influences a couple's decision to have a given number of children; and where population limitation is clearly indicated, what are the attributes of that social setting that will prompt couples to have no more than the number needed to replace themselves?

By failing to come to terms with this question, warns Davis, we are evading the real issue of population policy, "which is how to give societies the number of children they need." Demographic history has demonstrated repeatedly that the family-building habits of couples are almost totally uninfluenced by demographic considerations. In European countries the biggest advances in the spread of family limitation came in the 20s and 30s against a background of official alarm about the possibility of underpopulation. During the 1960s, in many of these same countries, the three-or-four-child family has been gaining in popularity, particularly among certain higher socioeconomic groups, and this at a time of increasing public concern with the threat of overpopulation. Projection of the average family size of 2.6 recently given as "ideal" by a sample of newly married British couples would lead in two centuries to a United Kingdom population of 400 million, a number ten times the 40 million proposed at the 1966 Conference of the British Association for the Advancement of Science as the maximum those densely settled islands could sustain at reasonably comfortable levels of living. The gap between private behavior and public needs becomes even more obvious when we realize that to achieve that figure of 40 million the British population would have to experience an actual decline over the next two centuries to three-fourths of its present size.

Clearly, individual assessments of the number of children conducive to family welfare do not necessarily add up to a population size conducive to collective welfare. Demographic man, making isolated personal choices about his family size, is ill-suited to create demographic conditions beneficial to himself and his progeny. Ultimately, genuine control over population would require a judicious arrangement of the sociocultural context in which family formation takes place along lines that would promote the family whose size is most congruent with social needs.

Before specific measures to meet this challenge can be intelligently considered, we must have clearly in mind what it is we hope to achieve by a cessation of population increase. We must remember that population control is itself only a means to broader human goals. The ultimate goal of population control is survival of the human species. Any rate of population increase would eventually exhaust the earth as a human habitat. But suppose for a moment that (though they have not yet done so) developments in the provision of food, clothing, and shelter did manage to keep abreast of today's population increases. Would a world of, say, 20 to 30 billion be fit for human life? Under conditions of such high density, human behavior of all kinds would have to be rigidly controlled. Spontaneity could not be permitted; individual variation would have to be virtually nil. What is at stake here is no less than the survival of human society as we know it.

Fortunately, such an extreme is quite improbable demographically. Before an age of encapsulated man could become reality, the pressure of human numbers would so depress levels of living that mortality would rise to preindustrial heights. Population would cease to grow because mankind would no longer exercise control over death.

Much more pertinent to our present concern is the immediate threat of population growth to conditions of life that are essential to the fulfillment of goals sought by the 3.5 billion people who already inhabit the earth. Such goals as health, longevity, material well-being, the rule of law, and the orderly settlement of conflicts are generally preferred to their opposites by men everywhere, regardless of the particular social setting in which they live. The attainment of these goals is, in fact, coming to be recognized as requisite to the pursuit of most other individual interests—intellectual, spiritual, and esthetic. Underlying the agitation for population control is the growing conviction that, above all else, the continued addition of human numbers diminishes the capacity of society to provide those conditions that serve individual interests and offer the greatest possibilities for the full development of human faculties.

At the most general level the means chosen to control human reproduction must be consistent with the goal of promoting the kinds of social conditions that are hospitable to human development and the satisfaction of individual interests. So far, instructing parents about how to plan the number of their children to coincide with their personal family interests has been relied upon as the only policy consistent with this goal. But, as we have suggested, the family-planning approach to population policy, while it advances individual interests in the short run, will be self-defeating in the long run (and not so very long at that) if it fails to accomplish that reduction in population growth that is essential to the improvement of conditions of life throughout the world. To what avail is nurturing the family if the individual members of the family are unable to satisfy their needs for good health, education, employment, and recreation? In short, it may be necessary to alter the traditional emphasis on the family in order to safeguard the individual from deterioration of the social conditions through which most of his goals as both a human and a social being must be met.

Possible Solutions

A value choice of this sort seems to underlie Davis' admonition that what is required to halt population growth is not family planning as such, but rather, "selective restructuring of the family in relation to the rest of society." To this end Davis proposes two broad changes in present family systems: 1) raising the age at marriage, and 2) encouraging further limitation of births within marriage. Although some of the measures he proposes to spur change in these directions are in the nature of inducements to refrain from childbearing, the general tenor of his proposals is decidedly negative. The majority of them involve the imposition of some kind of restraint and hardship not only on family life but on all individuals in the society. Davis himself acknowledges this in noting:

> A realistic proposal for a government policy of lowering the birth rate reads like a catalogue of horrors: squeeze consumers through taxation and inflation; make housing very scarce by limiting construction; force wives and mothers to work outside the home to offset the inadequacy of male wages, yet provide few child-care facilities; encourage migration to the city by paying low wages in the country and providing few rural jobs; increase congestion in cities by starving the transit system; increase personal insecurity by encouraging conditions that produce unemployment and haphazard political arrests.

But as a long-term policy of population control, would these measures be any more effective than the extension of current family-planning programs? The adequacy of such measures, imposed by themselves, seems, in fact, to be open to question on two counts: 1) Many of these measures are patently inconsistent with the basic aim of improving conditions of life, and 2) In the absence of pertinent research, their consequences for population growth are by no means clear. Such measures, for example, as "increasing congestion in cities" or "increasing personal insecurity by encouraging conditions that produce unemployment and haphazard political arrests" (while undoubtedly included by Davis to highlight the barrenness of current ideas about how to encourage a limitation of childbearing) would obviously in the long run promote certain of the very conditions that population control is designed to alleviate. Moreover, a policy of indirect repression (i.e., limiting the supply of housing and squeezing consumers) might have quite different consequences for the birth rates of successive age groups. Major fluctuations in family size very likely occur more as a response to changes in social conditions than as a response to any particular elements in the social situation. What one age group experiences as a change may be taken for granted as facts of life by those who follow. Given the breathing space afforded by the lower reproductivity of their parents, succeeding age groups might be encouraged—unless different and even more stringent measures were applied—to have larger families than did their ancestors.

Actually, even the short-run consequences of all such specific measures is uncertain. One of the difficulties in devising a national policy for lowering the birth rate is that specific measures may have quite different consequences for the childbearing of different groups. The effectiveness of specific measures for lowering family size would vary with the social setting in which they were applied and the needs met by childbearing for couples in different socioeconomic categories. Depending on the social context, for example, increasing child-care facilities to encourage women to take jobs after bearing one or two children might be a more effective (as well as a less repressive) policy than denying women access to the possibilities of leaving their children in competent hands (which could discourage them from pursuing interests outside the family). For a great many women in the United States, facilities for the care of preschool children are now so rudimentary that this indirect method of influencing family size may be considered to be already in effect.

In fact, the conditions Davis enumerates already exist for a large minority of the American population. The Negro migrants to American metropolitan centers (and to a lesser extent the urban poor of all description) are daily subjected to such "horrors"; and, indeed, the birth rate of urban Negroes is substantially lower than that of their rural counterparts. Though the burden of blighted living conditions falls heaviest on the Negro and the poor, Americans from all social strata are increasingly experiencing the weight of certain of Davis' measures: the congestion of cities, higher taxes and inflation, and increased personal insecurity. It is hard to avoid the conclusion that this spreading of hardship may have some bearing on the fact that American fertility rates have been steadily declining since 1957. It is such evidence as this—piecemeal observation of the economic and social conditions that have in the past accompanied intervals of low birth rates—that, in the absence of systematic sociological and demographic research on the matter, demographers have been obligated to use in support of their contention that only a repressive population policy will be effective. Certainly, in historical perspective, the lowest birth rates appear to have been associated with periods of rapid changes and conditions that contribute to general insecurity, such as economic depres-

sion, housing shortages, migration to cities, and economic and political in-
stability of the sort found today in certain Eastern European countries—
predominantly Catholic countries, by the way—which have the lowest birth
rates in the world.

But does this necessarily mean that to be effective a program of population control must be coercive, or, as a minimum, draw its provisions
extensively from Davis' "catalogue of horrors"? Or is it possible that potential parents might choose to have small families as a response, instead,
to a healthy adjustment to their surroundings, and confidence that their
lives can be rewarding without resorting to childbearing in excess of the
number necessary for replacement? Whether limitation of childbearing to
the necessary degree could indeed come about as such a positive response,
and what the conditions are that would bring it about and maintain it,
should become the target of intensive research, supported generously as
contributing information about population policy of the most practical
kind.

Substitutes for Childbearing

If population policy is to emphasize inducements for limiting reproduction rather than sanctions against parenthood, it is necessary, first, to have
a clear understanding of the rewards now presumed to be secured through
childbearing. Given the apparent preference for more than two children
among populations in which birth control is widely practiced, the question
we must ask is why the desire for families of moderate size remains so
durable? As a start, we suggest that children be viewed as a source of
satisfaction of personal interests, rather than regarded chiefly in terms of
the costs they represent to their parents. What, then, are the interests
served by childbearing among the different groups in the population, and
can alternatives be provided that would reduce dependence on children
as a means of satisfying these interests? Specific inducements to limit childbearing may have to be geared to the needs of couples in particular social
environments; but any policy designed to have more than a random, short-
term influence on demographic behavior would have to consider as well
the effect on family building of more general sociocultural conditions. To
suggest that the meaning of childbearing for the Negro urban mother on
welfare might be somewhat different from that for the white wife of a business executive living in suburbia is not to diminish the importance to family
size of influences these two may have in common. Both, by reason of their
residence in the same country, are exposed to certain of the same general
cultural themes and social arrangements. Both, by reason of their common
humanity, presumably seek to satisfy through childbearing certain of the

same general interests: support (psychological if not financial) in periods of crisis and old age, interest and variety, meaningful activities to fill in time, self-esteem and a sense of unique contribution, a shield against loneliness.

In line with the purpose of seeking positive measures to curtail reproduction we suggest that one way to reduce incentives to childbearing might be to increase the opportunities for finding these rewards in situations outside the family. This is not a new idea. The provision of financial security in old age and expanding educational and occupational opportunities for women have already been proposed as measures to lower fertility. But there are many other measures that might at once increase the individual's scope for satisfying his interests and at the same time lower fertility by reducing his dependence on marriage and childbearing. Such changes as improving public transportation to community facilities, increasing the access of urban populations to outdoor recreation, providing more opportunities for people of all ages to engage in socially useful activities, and increasing opportunities for adults to have meaningful relationships with children other than their own could all conceivably have this effect—in addition, of course, to enlarging access to a variety of birth-control techniques. Some have proposed the establishment of a permanent national service corps, the ostensible purpose of which would be to alleviate pressing domestic needs—from the tutoring of educationally disadvantaged children to the beautification of public places, and even the maintenance of clean public toilets. If such a program could offer genuinely attractive provisions for such interests as a satisfying social life for single individuals, a respite from routine work, accessible employment for married women, productive activities for the elderly, a chance for urbanites to spend time in the country, it could have important indirect consequences for repressing fertility. Among other things, it could provide an alternative to early marriage, and also reduce the temptation to resort to childbearing for want of other meaningful options.

In the long run, assuming that the demographic and social conditions found today in industrialized countries (i.e., low death rates, early and near-universal marriage, and high material levels of living) eventually spread throughout the world, stability in population size could be maintained, short of coercion, only in a social climate in which the family of three children was considered large. I suggest that, as a minimum, there are two conditions necessary to achieve this favorable predisposition to the replacement-sized family: 1) much greater accessibility to effective means of limiting births and 2) much greater concern for the well-being of each individual at all stages of life. The relation of the first to a reduction in births is clear; the second is as yet only a hunch. If adults are to be content with a long life relieved by the diversion of but few of their own children, they must have confidence in their own and their children's chances to fulfill themselves in whatever terms the society defines as worthwhile. I suggest that a more solid foundation for the small-family system is a population policy designed to foster attractive alternatives to marriage and childbearing rather than a policy aimed at increasing the already substantial burdens of everyday living. Such a policy would also be more consistent with human needs and human goals. Surely, there may be limits to the effectiveness of indirect repression in reducing childbearing. Though low fertility has in the past been associated with insecurity and hardship, excess childbearing seems actually to thrive most in a context of indifference to human potential. The population policy that stifles human interests may well boomerang by enhancing the role of the family as a source of security and personal intimacy. To avoid this impasse, much research is needed to determine both the needs that are presumed to be met by childbearing and the measures that would provide real substitutes for childbearing in meeting these needs. At this transitional stage in our attitudes toward population control, what is needed is a bold sense of the future, in terms of both the sort of demographic and social conditions we can expect and the part man should play in shaping demographic behavior to realize more nearly his individual and collective goals.

SUGGESTED READINGS

Barnett, L. D. "Population Policy: Payments for Fertility Limitation in the U.S." *Social Biology* 16 (1969): 239–48.

Blake, J. "Population Policy for Americans: Is the Government Being Misled?" *Science* 164 (1969): 522–29.

Davis, K. "Population Policy: Will Current Programs Succeed?" *Science* 158 (1967): 730–39.

Ehrlich, P. R. and Ehrlich, A. H. *Population, Resources, Environment.* San Francisco: Freeman, 1970.

Heer, D. M. *Readings on Population.* Englewood Cliffs, N.J.: Prentice-Hall, 1968.

23

A Public Health Program for Sexually Assaulted Females

CHARLES R. HAYMAN, M.D., M.P.H.
FRANCES R. LEWIS, B.S.
WILLIAM F. STEWART, M.S., AND
MURRAY GRANT, M.D., D.P.H.

The following abstract from the clinical records of the District of Columbia Department of Public Health points up a situation which is occurring with increasing frequency throughout the United States.

> A 2½-year-old girl was taken to a local hospital after she was attacked in her home by an unknown man. She suffered deep vaginal tears. She was given a sedative and transferred to the municipal general hospital where she was examined, treated, and discharged. Her parents were instructed to give her sitz baths and to apply a vaginal cream. Four months after the incident, the child had recovered physically.

The Situation in D.C.

In September 1965 a woman who had been raped was questioned by members of the Metropolitan Police Department's sex squad and taken to the District of Columbia General Hospital for examination and treatment. In subsequent statements to the newspapers, she complained strongly about the emergency police and medical procedures.

The patient stated that the initial questioning by the police was too lengthy and detailed, and it delayed her transportation for medical examination. It took three hours from the time of her arrival at the police station for questioning, return by police car to the scene of the crime, and then to the hospital. She felt that the police treated her more like a "cold statistic than a human being."

At the hospital emergency room the patient had to wait one hour and forty minutes for examination, which was accomplished in ten minutes. The examining physician did not offer a douche or other cleansing mate-

. His services were confined to the medicolegal examination. The patient stated that "the medical search for evidence coldly ignores the patient," and that the entire medical procedure was inhumane.

The police then asked the patient to return to headquarters for questioning, but she refused and insisted on going to her private physician. Finally, seven hours after the assault, the patient received treatment.

An investigation was immediately made of the current practices, and certain procedures were changed. The most important change was that of reducing preliminary questioning by the police to the essential minimum and taking the victim to a hospital as soon as possible thereafter. Medical procedures for initial examination and treatment were revised by the health department and distributed to its staff at the District of Columbia General Hospital and to all other hospitals in the District. All were asked to provide the emergency service. For various reasons, however, particularly staff physicians' fear of having to testify in court, among the voluntary hospitals only the Children's Hospital responded.

According to the police department, 90 cases of rape or attempted rape were reported to the FBI in 1964. However, about 150 sexual incidents had been thoroughly investigated by the sex squad and dropped for lack of enough evidence to warrant prosecution. About 200 investigations were terminated immediately after initial questioning and medical examination because they did not merit further police consideration, and in about an additional 160 cases, the police questioned the complainants but did not consider them in need of medical examination. Except for victims who required emergency treatment, the police requested the examination only to determine sexual penetration for proof of rape—if the penis touches within the labia minora, against the extreme will of a female of a certain age[1]. In the District of Columbia, a girl under 16 years of age cannot legally consent to sexual intercourse (statutory rape).

The 90 cases reported to the FBI consisted of rape and attempted rape, but the additional 500 or so complaints to the sex squad included for adult victims forced genital contacts other than intercourse, voluntary intercourse (rather than assault), and imaginary assault. For adolescents and young children, the complaints also included statutory rape, incest, concubinage, seduction, and molestation. We considered all of these cases to be of possible medical and public health significance.

To determine whether assault victims needed further assistance after the emergency period, the department of health initiated a followup program on September 15, 1965. We intended to test the hypothesis that patients need emotional support and that they would welcome guidance from nurses and referral for psychiatric and medical assistance. We anticipated that these measures would be needed particularly for the prevention and treatment of emotional trauma and also for detection and treatment of pregnancy, venereal disease, and injury after the original assault.

Procedures

When a complaint is received, the patient (or parent) is questioned by a member of the sex squad to establish the type of incident, a description of the assailant, and other pertinent information. If the police decide that the complainant needs a medical examination to determine sexual penetration or emergency treatment, they take her to District of Columbia General Hospital, or, if she wishes, to another local hospital, or to a private physician. A policewoman escorts the patient.

The liaison public health nurse receives the report of the medical examination from the sex squad on the following day. Within a few days, the nurse contacts the patient by telephone, visit, or both, and if necessary, by a followup letter. The patient is then referred to the senior public health nurse in her district. (A senior public health nurse was selected for each of the nine nursing districts to maintain contact with patients.)

Each patient is seen or telephoned as often as indicated, in the nurse's judgment. Many patients also telephone or visit the nurse. Medical and psychiatric consultation is available to the nurse to help her serve the patient. The nurse refers patients to public and private physicians or health facilities, and she checks to find out if the patient has kept her appointment and what kind of treatment has been prescribed.

After ninety days from the first contact, the nurse continues to make periodic telephone calls or visits to patients who need further counseling or referral or whose cases are being processed further by the police, because these patients are considered to be under great emotional strain.

Findings

During the nine-month period, September 15, 1965 through June 15, 1966, the sex squad received 668 complaints. Of the complainants, 335 had a preliminary questioning, an initial medical examination, and were referred to the bureau of nursing. Thirteen of these complainants were boys and 322 were women and girls.

After reviewing the police, medical, and nursing records, we classified the 322 female patients as probably victims of the following types of assault: forcible rape, 232; statutory rape, 26; seduction (under 13 years of age), 20; forced genital contact, 12; attempted rape, 7; incest, 2; molestation, 2; seduction of adult, 1; voluntary intercourse (age 18), 1; and other, 1. In 7 instances the incident was imagined, and in at least 11 the incident was fabricated.

Our classification follows the descriptions given by Oliven[1]. We could not use the police classification because two-thirds of the 668 complaints were not classified according to legal categories. They were considered miscellaneous complaints, primarily because there was not enough evidence to warrant further investigation toward prosecution; for example, a woman obviously raped might be entirely unable to identify her assailant.

Number and rate of sexually assaulted women and children, by age and color, Washington, D.C., September 15, 1965 to June 15, 1966

Age group of victim (years)	Number of persons			Case rate		
	Total	White	Nonwhite	Total	White	Nonwhite
0–4.............	11	1	10	25.6	10.0	30.3
5–9.............	36	4	32	101.0	56.8	111.9
10–14..........	81	1	80	294.1	17.7	365.6
15–19..........	75	9	66	247.0	99.4	309.9
20–24..........	43	13	30	129.2	94.5	153.6
25–29..........	12	2	10	42.5	19.1	56.2
30–34..........	20	1	19	69.7	10.5	99.0
35–44..........	21	3	18	34.7	14.0	45.9
45–54..........	11	4	7	20.5	15.5	25.1
55–64..........	6	1	5	13.7	3.7	29.3
65 and over......	6	3	3	13.5	9.8	21.9
All ages.......	322	42	280	75.0	24.7	108.0

Note: Rates (per 100,000 females in specified groups) are for a nine-month period, which excludes the summer months of peak incidence.

Of the 322 females referred for nursing service, however, 145 were classified as having cases warranting prosecution or already adjudicated.

The nurse attempted to find each victim within 72 hours after she received the report from the police department; 97 were contacted within 24 hours and 216 within 48 hours. A number were interviewed in the office of the sex squad. In some instances the patient or family was greatly upset and had gone to visit relatives or had moved out of town for a few days to a week. On the other hand, others had returned to work and thus initial contact was delayed.

Thirteen adults could not be located because they had moved or had given a fictitious address. Six patients refused assistance at initial contact: three said they had not been assaulted, two mothers refused nursing assistance for their daughters, and another mother stated that her daughter was too disturbed to talk to anyone. On second contact, the last mother said that she would take her daughter to a private physician. None of these victims or mothers were overtly hostile to the nurse. Fourteen other victims or mothers did not want nursing assistance, but accepted referral to a physician or clinic. Thirteen children had been taken to welfare facilities by the police, and followup information was obtained from the nurses at these facilities.

Of the 322 females referred to the nursing bureau, 23 were children 2 through 6 years old, 53 were 7 through 12 years old, 113 were teenagers under 18, and 133 were adults—the oldest was 88. Only 13 percent were white (see table). Initial examinations were performed on 308 patients at the District of Columbia General Hospital, on 12 at other local hospitals, and on 2 at physicians' offices.

During assault, 12 patients suffered severe trauma. Two patients with severe vaginal tears required hospitalization, one for repair of a digital nerve and the other for a fractured nose and scalp laceration. Surgery was performed on two patients in the emergency room: one had a severe vaginal tear and bleeding and the other had severe laceration of the buttocks. Six other patients were treated for less severe lacerations and bruises.

The following conditions were found at initial examination: 5 patients were pregnant, 15 had positive serologic tests for syphilis, and 11 others has positive smear tests for gonorrhea (9 had a vaginal discharge). All of these patients were referred for evaluation and treatment. Most of their conditions were pre-existing: for example, one 13-year-old had been impregnated three months before by her adult boyfriend, who was later charged with statutory rape.

One 15-year-old became pregnant as a result of the sexual assault, and she and her mother became severely disturbed. The girl was placed under the supervision of a private physician, and, with the health department's assistance, arrangements were made for a therapeutic abortion. She was followed up by the school nurse, who reported that the girl was doing well at the end of the school term.

A 4-year-old girl who had a positive smear test for gonorrhea at initial examination became infected with primary syphilis after the assault. She was treated successfully. Gonorrhea developed in 13 other patients, and they were treated. (Prophylactic penicillin was not given routinely at the time of emergency treatment.)

Thirteen patients who became significantly disturbed were referred to private psychiatrists and public clinics. One was a 15-year-old who had been raped by a boy she knew and his brother. Three days after the assault she attempted suicide by ingesting seven aspirin tablets and preparing to drink a glass of ammonia. All of these patients are still under psychiatric supervision, except for a 9-year-old who was recently discharged when her mother refused to assist with the treatment procedures.

A total of 290 patients accepted the public health nurse followup service, and they were referred to various facilities for evaluation and treatment. A number of patients were referred to more than one place. Thus, as shown below, 336 appointments were made through August 15, 1966, and 245 or 73 percent were kept.

Place of referral	Number of referrals	Number of appointments kept
District of Columbia Department of Public Health clinics	231	155
Venereal disease	116	87
Maternity	83	46
Pediatric	24	15
Mental health	7	6
Dental	1	1
Private physicians	59	46
Children's Hospital	32	30
Other hospitals	8	8
Other facilities	6	6
Total	336	245

The nurses discontinued followup for 165 patients because there was no evident need for medical or police followup, the patients were under the care of private physicians, the patients did not wish further services, or the patients had moved. Some of the cases were reopened when the patients called for assistance. Still being followed are 157 patients who need medical or psychiatric followup or who are being processed by the police or both. (Patients, especially children, being prepared for or undergoing court appearances are considered to be under significant emotional strain.)

The nurses have observed that the patients and their families are most receptive to the initial contact when it is made within two or three days after the alleged assault. There appears to be a definite need for emotional support at that time. The major concern of the patient and her family during the first month is the possibility of pregnancy and, secondarily, of syphilis. Also, the sexual incident itself or the fact that it is reported to the police seems to cause much stress for the family and frequently evokes submerged emotional difficulties. Some patients show emotional signs and symptoms, and some mothers express concern that their parental supervision has been inadequate.

Many patients telephone or visit the nurses to request information or help with other problems such as housing, finances, and health supervision for other members of the family. Many have had no previous contact with the health department, particularly those who have moved to the District of Columbia within the year. Visits by the nurses uncover health and social problems often unrelated to the sexual incident.

The telephone calls decrease when the family begins to relax, which is usually soon after the patient menstruates and a negative serologic test for syphilis is reported. After ninety days, responsiveness to nursing followup usually decreases, unless an emotional problem has occurred or a court appearance is expected, and most patients and families express a desire to forget that the incident occurred.

During the nine-month period, the program required the entire time of one senior public health nurse and half of the time of one consultant nurse. The nine selected public health nurses spent about 5 percent of their time for followup. The members of the sex squad, particularly the two policewomen, devoted up to 5 percent of their time for discussions with the liaison nurse about individual patients.

Members of the clinic and administrative staffs at the District of Columbia General Hospital devoted about 500 hours to examination and treatment of victims, and the associate director for preventive services and the deputy director of the department of public health devoted about 250 hours for administrative direction and medical consultation.

In a letter to the health department, Chief John B. Layton of the Metropolitan Police Department stated:

> Since September 1965, when the present public health department program was inaugurated to provide followup medical and psychiatric care for victims of sexual assault, the value of this type of assistance has been evident in several ways. The program, as presently administered, demonstrates a human interest in the welfare of the victims, but more specifically, members of the sex squad have observed tangible benefits accruing from the services thus far provided. For example, sexual assault victims appear more composed and better prepared for the ordeal of a public trial. Victims are not as fearful and apprehensive regarding the possibility of pregnancy or disease after counseling by a health department representative . . . Interviews and visits by the nurses have uncovered and tend to alleviate social and family problems of victims which, if allowed to develop and continue, could result in future police action.

> As a result of the quality and scope of the services provided by the health department for victims of sexual assault, better public relations between members of the community and the police have developed as a side effect. Victims and their families originally are in contact with the police and,

when they subsequently receive assistance and guidance, the premise is established that the police have participated in the solution of their problems and are interested in the welfare of the citizens.

The National Picture

According to a report by the Federal Bureau of Investigation, 22,470 females in the United States, or 11.6 per 100,000 population, were forcibly raped or assaulted in 1965.[2a] The number of forcible rapes increased by 36 percent from 1960 to 1965. Of the seven offenses listed in the FBI's "Index of Crime," in 1965 the highest percentage of increase was shown for forcible rape; about two-thirds of the cases reported were actual rape and the others were attempted rape. The report states: "Many offenses of this type are not reported to a law enforcement agency primarily due to fear and/or embarrassment on the part of the victim." Although most reports of such offenses come from large cities, the suburban rates are increasing rapidly.[2a]

The following standard metropolitan statistical areas showed the highest rates per 100,000 inhabitants in 1965 for forcible rape and assault.[2b]

Los Angeles-Long Beach, Calif.	32.9
Oxnard-Ventura, Calif.	30.3
Galveston-Texas City, Tex.	26.9
Detroit, Michigan	26.8
Lansing, Michigan	26.8
Bakersfield, Calif.	25.7
Sacramento, Calif.	24.9
Kansas City, Mo.-Kans.	24.8
Flint, Michigan	22.8
Chicago, Illinois	21.6

The Washington, D.C., Metropolitan area reported 339 offenses, a rate of 14.2 per 100,000 population in 1965[2b], and the District of Columbia 140 offenses, a rate of 17.3[2c].

To learn whether other communities provided any services for victims of sexual assault, we sent inquiries to seventeen city and county health departments, including those which serve the areas listed by the FBI as having the highest rates for 1964. Fourteen departments responded (Board of Health, Chicago; Allegheny County Board of Health, Pittsburgh; City and County Health Department, San Francisco; Maricopa County Health Department, Phoenix; Atlantic County Health Department, Atlantic City; Health Department, Detroit; County Health Department, Los Angeles; Chatham County Health Department, Savannah; Health Department,

Kansas City, Missouri; Health Department, Houston; City Health Department, Baltimore; Kansas City-Wyandotte County Health Department, Kansas City, Kansas; City and County Health and Hospital Department, Denver; San Joaquin Local Health District, Stockton).

Only four of the departments reported an organized effort by the police department to take the victim to a hospital or physician for examination and emergency treatment. None of the respondents reported having a formal program for nursing followup, and they also indicated that no specific community efforts were being made to provide medical and psychiatric assistance beyond the emergency service for women and girls.

Discussion

Our experience documents the fact that sexual assault is a significant medical and public health problem. During nine months, 335 victims in the District of Columbia received emergency examination or treatment or both (as of September 15, 1966, this figure rose to 473). The public health nurses provided emotional support to many of these patients and insured that all patients who wanted or needed medical and psychiatric assistance received it. From the psychiatric viewpoint, even when sexual assault is imagined the complainant may need help.

The District of Columbia General Hospital is providing almost all of the emergency examination and treatment. However, voluntary hospitals have an obligation (which only the Children's Hospital is accepting) to provide this service, and private physicians who have cared for these patients previously have a similar obligation. Fear of having to testify in court seems to be the main deterrent for private physicians, but many patients went to them for followup and treatment.

Only the health department is in a position to provide public health nursing followup to see that medical and psychiatric assistance is obtained. The department does not need to provide the assistance, but may refer to and call on private physicians and voluntary hospitals.

A detailed epidemiologic analysis will be presented in another report. However, preliminary analysis indicates that the common picture of sexual assault, that of an adult woman raped by a strange adult, is far from being complete. About one-fourth of the victims were children 2 through 12 years old, and about one-half were under 17. Many of the children were assaulted by close relatives or other persons they knew—these are the victims who suffer the greatest emotional trauma. Most of the reported victims were nonwhite and medically indigent. Nevertheless, the societal disease of sexual assault may strike anyone.

We believe that only the health department is able to study the entire problem and see that a comprehensive program is carried out. In most communities the health department does not operate general hospitals, but it can obtain reports of initial examinations from them and from private physicians. The police department can do the same, but it cannot analyze the reports medically and epidemiologically. The health department is best equipped to analyze epidemiologically the sexual–assault incidents and the characteristics of the aggressors and victims, a procedure which is essential to determine preventive measures. The health department can also provide leadership to work with the police, education departments, and other agencies to institute preventive measures throughout a community.

The pilot program reported here was undertaken as a basis for a more comprehensive program for which Federal and voluntary funds are being sought. In the larger program, in addition to providing the services described, we hope to also carry out the following procedures.

1. Test methods of establishing the medical diagnosis of the incident, apart from the police classification, by determination of the diagnosis at the time of emergency service, or during subsequent visits of the nurses, or by psychiatric interviews, or by a combination of these.
2. Determine the epidemiology of sexual assault by such indices as rates of occurrence, by socioeconomic levels of victims, and by characteristics of known aggressors and of the victims.
3. Determine the procedures necessary for complete medical, psychiatric, and nursing followup, and the cost of carrying out such a program.
4. Measure not only the immediate but the transitory and permanent physical and, particularly, emotional effects on health.
5. Determine from the study findings practicable preventive measures and institute these measures throughout the community to lessen the incidence of sexual assault.

Review of the Literature

A search by the National Library of Medicine of 381,000 citations in the international literature disclosed only 33 periodical titles under RAPE for the period March 1962 through January 1966. Most of these articles were either clinical or dealt with medicolegal aspects.

A review of *Index Medicus* from January 1957 through April 1966 showed that during that period none of the public health journals contained articles on rape. Also, none of the medical literature described epidemiologic aspects on any demographic basis, or community health and medical services for immediate care, or followup of victims for continued care. Literature on the prevention of sexual assault is sparse.

The best overview is given by Oliven,[1] who describes the medical types of assault encountered, methods for immediate diagnosis and treatment, measures for medical followup, and possible outcomes. He states that death has followed assault, particularly among young children, and that permanent emotional damage may occur, especially among victims who have been provocative and among children who have been repeatedly seduced. Oliven describes precautionary rules for children and preventive measures which may be applied by various segments of the community.

In another comprehensive article written for family physicians, the psychiatrist Halleck stresses the important role they can play in giving immediate assistance and in referring victims for early psychiatric consultation and treatment.[3] He indicates, however, that most victims, especially children, come from the lower socioeconomic levels which have no family physician. (In the District of Columbia, the department of public health acts in this capacity.) Halleck feels that psychological equilibrium is always disrupted and that serious damage occurs frequently, particularly when personality disturbance or family disruption has existed previously, when assault has been invited, or when incest has occurred.

One of the few retrospective studies to assess outcomes was undertaken by Brunold.[4] He calls the study a "simple" one, from which significant conclusions cannot be drawn. However, he concluded that 6 of 62 children suffered permanent emotional damage fifteen or more years after the incident. Brunold believes that it is difficult to reduce the number of potential assaulters and that children may be protected by sex education and warnings by parents, schools, and family physicians. If parents are unable or unwilling to provide them, supervision and education must be provided by other sources.

Wells reviews her 27 years of experience as a police surgeon and classifies about 2,000 cases of sexual offenses.[5] She feels that further emotional trauma can be prevented if the initial examination is made by a female physician assisted by a policewoman, and if court practices are improved, such as hearing cases in chambers or in closed courtrooms.

De Francis makes a strong plea for social work protective services for "child victims of sexual offenses [who] are exposed to serious emotional damage, not only from the crime but from police questioning and court appearances." He states that only five or six Societies for the Prevention of Cruelty to Children in the United States have accepted such responsibility.[6] He is conducting a research project to investigate the differences in consequences between a community with a well–developed service for child victims of crime and a comparable community lacking such protective services.

Summary

Women and girls are being sexually assaulted in large numbers and with increasing frequency, especially in large cities. Comprehensive health services for these often tragically neglected victims are needed in every community. Many health departments serving areas which had the highest rates for sexual assault in 1964 have indicated that they have no program to provide the needed emergency care and followup assistance.

In September 1965 the District of Columbia Department of Public Health, which provided almost all emergency treatment for victims, initiated followup by public health nurses to determine if sexually assaulted females need psychiatric or further medical assistance.

During the first nine months of the program, 322 women and girls were seen and questioned by the police department, given an initial medical examination, and referred to the nursing bureau. Their ages ranged from 2 to 88 years; 24 percent were under 13 and 53 percent were under 17. Only 13 percent were white. The sexual incidents varied from forcible "gang" rape by strangers to incest with the father and imagined assault.

Fourteen patients suffered severe trauma requiring emergency treatment, and four of these also required hospitalization. As a result of the assault, one 15-year-old became pregnant, one 4-year-old became infected with syphilis, and 13 other patients contracted gonorrhea. Thirteen patients became emotionally disturbed, and one of these attempted suicide.

A total of 290 patients accepted the public health nurse followup service, and they were referred to various facilities and private physicians for psychiatric and medical evaluation and treatment. As of August 15, 1966, 73 percent of the appointments were kept.

The nurses observed that emotional support during the first three months after the incident was particularly needed and appreciated by the patients.

Still being followed by the nurses are 157 patients who need medical or psychiatric followup or who are being processed by the police or both.

Epidemiologic analysis of the incidents, the aggressors, and the victims is necessary to develop community measures to prevent sexual assault.

NOTES

[1] J. Oliven, 2nd ed. *Sexual hygiene and pathology* (Philadelphia: J. B. Lippincott Company, 1965), pp. 55–71, 272–276.

[2] Federal Bureau of Investigation "Uniform crime reports for the United States" (Washington, D.C.: 1965) (a) p. 9, (b) table 4, (c) table 51.

[3] S. L. Halleck, "The physician's role in management of victims of sex offenders," Journal of the American Medical Association 180 (April 28, 1962): 273–8.

[4] H. Brunold, "Beiobachtungen und Katamnestische Festellungen nach im Kindesalter erlittenen Sexualtraumen," *Praxis* 51 (Sept. 27, 1962): 965–71.

[5] N. H. Wells, "Sexual offenses as seen by a woman police surgeon." British Medical Journal no. 5109 (Dec. 6, 1958): 1404–1408.

[6] V. De Francis, "Protecting the child victim of sex crimes." Publication No. 28, Children's Division, American Humane Association, Denver, Colorado, 1965.

SUGGESTED READINGS

Amir, M. "Victim Precipitated Forcible Rape." *Journal of Criminal Law, Criminology and Police Science* 58 (1967): 493–502.

Brunold, X., "Observations after Sexual Traumata Suffered During Childhood." *Excerpta Criminologica* 4 (1964): 5–10.

Defrancis, V. *Protecting the Child Victim of Sex Crimes Committed by Adults.* Denver, Colo.: American Humane Association, 1969.

Ploscowe, M. "Rape." In Sagarin, E., and MacNamara, D. *Problems of Sexual Behavior.* New York: Crowell, 1969, pp. 203–40.

Sutherland, S. "Patterns of Response Among Rape Victims." *American Journal of Orthopsychiatry* 40 (1970): 503–11.

24

A Compensation Policy for Sex Victims

LeRoy G. Schultz

The history of criminal law, corrections, and criminology in the United States is characterized by a lack of effective concern for the victim of the offense. What little interest has been indicated regarding the victim in criminal law centers on "consent," "culpability," and "provocation"[1] as factors in the defense of the offender and, in criminology, on the psychosocial factors in the etiology of the offense.[2] One loks in vain for any concern by the criminal law for the specific welfare of the victim. The law of torts is essentially concerned with compensation between individuals where the primary issue is the propriety of granting damages to a specific plaintiff and against a particular defendant. As will be demonstrated later, this is an illusory source of redress for victims of sex crime. In criminal law the wrong done to the victim is absorbed in the wrong done the whole of society. The state monopolizes punishment and, by its criminal court processes, all but eliminates any possibility of victim restitution by the offender.

Admittedly, court processes are not necessarily appropriate for the solution of all social problems. The ability to admit this limitation need not offend the integrity of the law. Since neither the institutions of law nor social welfare have indicated any real concern for the general problem of victim welfare, now may be the appropriate time for these two institutions and their professions to bring their talents to bear jointly on this neglected and unresolved problem, particularly after the relevant experiments in England, New Zealand, California, and New York. This chapter will attempt to explain the current phenomenon of the lack of effective means for victim compensation and offer a rationale for change and remedy. Compensation as used here is limited to crimes of physical sexual violence against the person.

A Brief History of Compensation

Financial penalties, confiscation of the offender's property, and compensation or restitution of the victims of crime have existed from the beginning of most literate societies. One such early compensation plan was provided in the Code of Hammurabi, enacted about 2250 B.C.[3]

The concept of victim compensation in Western civilization may be thought of as developing in three broad phases.[4] First phase: The injured individual claimed damages directly from the offender, the amount depending on the extent of injury and social status of the injured party. Second phase: The state or king claimed from the offender the costs of prosecution and/or the costs of injury done to the state. Third phase: Payments to the state by the offender became an important source of revenue, so that by the year 1200, the victim's share from the offender had decreased and the exactions of the state had increased until the state took all. In short, the victim of crime came more and more to be viewed as the state, not as an individual. The state's right to punish was substituted for the injured individual's right to recover damages.[5] Early societies were primarily concerned with the individual loss caused by the criminal act, but as civilization progressed the consequences of the criminal act became divided from the intent of the actor. Criminal law, as it developed, concerned itself primarily with the guilt and the offender's responsibility toward the more abstract concept of society; the individual victim was forced into a lesser and lesser role in criminal justice, until finally he was forced to seek remedies through civil law. Compensation for injury and punishment for crime were indistinguishable until the division of wrongs into tort and crime developed. When the distinction appeared, indemnity slowly disappeared.[6]

Both the Classical and the Positivist Schools of Criminology endorsed victim compensation by the nineteenth century as a welfare goal independent of punishment. The English classicalist Jeremy Bentham felt that when society failed in protecting citizens from criminals, it owed them an indemnity.[7] He based compensation upon the failure of police protection, a view which was later echoed by Sir Samuel Romilly.

The Italian positivists, Garofalo and Ferri, made abundantly clear that any criminal law system concerned with full justice must acknowledge the state's responsibility for victim compensation. If the state could not collect the victim's compensation from the offender, the state should still be responsible.[8] Garofalo's plan would have the victim and state compensated by the offender. The victim was to be awarded compensation for "material damages and mental suffering."[9] The state was to be compensated because it suffered morally from the fact of the crime and materially from the cost of prosecution. Garofalo and Ferri were the foremost agitants for victim compensation in the nineteenth century.

Ferri based his compensation plan on the Code of the Grand Duke Leopold of Tuscany (1786). He proposed that compensation funds be administered by social welfare agencies called "Councils of Patronage," possibly suggesting a dole or relief aspect. Ferri put great emphasis on the offender's duty to compensate his victim through prison labor. Each prisoner was to be paid wages equal to those paid in free society for similar work. The prisoner's wages were to be divided, with one-third going to the state, one-third to the victim, and one-third to the offender's dependents. No nation adopted the Ferri plan completely, although some Latin American countries adopted certain parts.[10] Perhaps, as Childers suggests, it took the industrial revolution to develop sufficient national wealth before government could realistically support a compensation plan.[11]

The English put two laws into effect, one in 1826 and another in 1870, which provided compensation to certain victims for certain crimes.[12] By the Criminal Act of 1826 compensation was to be awarded to persons, whether injured or not, who were active in apprehending offenders; and by the Forfeiture Act of 1870 the courts were empowered to compensate for personal injury.

The concept of victim compensation has lain dormant for the past half century in common law countries. In 1954 new life was pumped into it by the English social reformer, Margery Fry, when she recommended serious consideration of a compensation plan for her country.[13] Following her proposal a White Paper was published in 1959, stating:

> [Our penal Law] . . . must consider the fundamental concepts underlying our treatment of offenders, and examine not only the obligations of society and the offender to one another, but also the obligation of both to the victim, a concept of which modern criminal law has almost completely lost sight . . . indeed, in the public mind the interest of the offender may not infrequently seem to be placed before those of the victim.[14]

In 1959 a Working Party was appointed to study the problem of victim compensation in England, and in 1961 a commission policy statement was offered which was very skeptical of a compensation program and only very weakly endorsed it.[15] Despite this, England instituted a compensation program in 1965, and New Zealand a year earlier.[16] In New Zealand a "Crime Compensation Tribunal" can award financial compensation in lump sum or installments for attempted or completed rape, sexual intercourse, or sexual indecency with a female under age 12, infecting with a disease, and sexual assault of male or female.[17] The English plan calls for a Compensation Board to award compensation for any sexual offenses (unless committed by a family member) and the pain, suffering, and shock resulting. The state will not pay for the maintenance of a child born as a result of a sexual offense.

The first American attempt at victim compensation occurred in California in 1965.[18] Like so many other American welfare policies, it seems to have been drawn up on the almost paranoid assumption that it will attract fraudulent applicants. Financial compensation was to be paid to victims of crimes of violence *provided they needed it*. "Need" was to be determined by the public welfare agency under AFDC qualifications. In view of the low AFDC payment scale that has characterized public welfare since its inception, the California program can be expected to neglect most victims.

The New York program went into effect in 1966 and echoed the California concept of economy. Both of these American examples made compensation a "matter of charity" rather than an assumption by the state of responsibility for the loss suffered by the victim.

The Rationale of Compensation

The early rationale and motives for victim compensation during Garofalo's and Bentham's time were based on society's failure to protect its citizens from crime. This rationale took on added significance when the state prohibited its citizens from going about armed for self-defense. The state now exhorts citizens to protect property against theft, but generally discourages self-protection of the person by prohibiting the carrying of weapons. The reason for state intervention in this area stems from the basic contract between citizen and government, a contract that implies the right to be reasonably secure in one's person and not to be unjustly deprived of life, liberty, or property.

Because society is presently not sufficiently advanced to know what causes crimes of violence or how to prevent them, prematurely to saddle society with control and prevention is fruitless and unfair.[19] It is doubtful if even a totalitarian state with all the electronic devices of "Big Brother" could ever prevent the majority of violent crimes. It is possible that a police state may give rise to an even greater incidence of such crime. Any compensation scheme will have to be based on reasons other than society's duty to prevent crime.

This is not to infer that society is not to some degree responsible for violent crime, particularly when it tolerates well-established and well-known crime ghettos, narcotics–centered slums, and syndicated crime. Society is made up of many citizens who will not take a normal citizen's role in crime prevention.[20] In some areas citizens feel they must break the law in an effort to protect themselves from violence.[21] Certainly when a crime is committed by a man who has been excluded from civilization, as is true of some crimes in our slums, that civilization is an accomplice to the offense.

It will be indicated later that all civil and criminal court measures and provisions fail to compensate adequately the majority of victims of criminal violence. These measures overconcentrate on the "individual responsibility" approach, and therefore cannot account for those violent crimes in which the offender is not apprehended or for those in which the offender is acquitted for various reasons.

The real and vital rationale for victim compensation rests on a moral, realistic concern for the welfare of the injured citizen. Society has clearly admitted a collective responsibility for the costs of sickness, industrial injury, and old age; and it has in these instances developed the machinery of compensation. Our society compensates veterans injured outside our borders but not citizens victimized at home. Though the veterans may have been injured in defense of the society, the sick, the industrially injured, and the old were not incapacitated in defense of the society. All of us have an equal chance to fall in the victim roulette.[22] Social isolation is difficult in a mobile society. Should not compensation costs for crime victims be likewise spread out among all potential victims? The state has a definite interest in protecting and maintaining certain standards of well-being for all its citizens. Social legislation, such as veterans' compensation, workmen's compensation, and the whole range of public welfare programs, is the culmination of a democracy's conviction regarding responsibility for human welfare. Certainly common sense calls for grouping together for mutual protection through a system of shared risk in the area of victims of criminal violence. This is one problem in social relationships which seemingly, in the light of man's ingenuity, should not have defeated him. This is one welfare gap that should be bridged. We cannot, in our abundance, do as our predecessors did and plead poverty. Nor is there a need to support the claim for compensation by a flight into the constitution.[23] In short, the present lack of any effective provisions for compensation unintentionally results in punishing the victim of crime, often more effectively than the criminal.

Present Provisions

Very few states provide a social welfare program to cover victims of sex crimes. Victims are forced to seek compensation through tort actions, which usually prove meaningless, because most sex offenders are insolvent or indigent. If the sex offender does have money or property it is quickly exhausted on bail and/or legal defense expenses. Crimes of sexual violence are not ordinarily committed by the rich as they have funds to purchase various types of sexual services. Yet compensation should not depend on the wealth of the aggressor. Because the wages of most offenders, should they be employed, hardly pay their normal living expenses and those of their dependents, garnishment of wages is not a practical remedy. Once a sex offender is sentenced to a correctional institution he is considered "civilly dead"[24]—that is, almost impossible to sue. If the victim should try to sue the state, city, or county for damages—either because the government failed to protect the victim from a crime, or removed the offender from society so that he is no longer financially responsible—she finds that the government is sovereign and cannot be sued without its consent.

The only other alternative to the damage suit in most states lies in the possibility of restitution by the offender to the victim as a legal condition of probation or parole. Most criminal courts and parole boards may impose the condition of restitution of a specific amount to be paid to the victim as a condition of release of the offender.

This provision is likewise ineffectual in meeting the compensation needs of the great majority of victims because probationers and parolees are either insolvent or, if employed, do not earn enough to exceed basic needs. In addition, not all offenders are apprehended; many may be juveniles; some will be incapable of responsibility due to mental illness; others may be acquitted due to technical or legal reasons; many will not be granted probation or parole; and some are unemployable.

Professional probation and parole officers are reluctant to recommend an order for restitution to the court unless they are reasonably sure it can be collected. Although restitution need not always be financial, other types raise many more problems.[25] If restitution is ordered but not paid, many probation officers are reluctant to recommend probation revocation to the court, because this type of revocation is analogous to being sentenced to debtor's prison. Restitution poses many problems for defendants convicted of violent crimes, because the stigma of this type of conviction makes employment very difficult.[26]

Parolees who have served a part of their sentence in confinement are very resistant to paying restitution; they make the same mistake as the rest of society does by inferring that the offense was against the collective whole and not against the individual victim. Convicts often speak of paying "their debt to society."

Day parole, known more generally as the Huber Law, by which the offender works at large during the day and returns to prison at night has as its prime concern the support of the offender's dependents and minimizing the negative effects of imprisonment.[27]

In summary, all of the presently available legal provisions for victim compensation in most states are illusory and fall considerably short of adequately meeting the compensation needs of the great majority of victims. Either society compensates victims or they suffer the consequences alone.

Prison Wages as Compensation

Another method sometimes suggested for compensating victims of criminal sexual violence is the use of prison wages for the victim. Wages for prison labor commenced in this country in Massachusetts during the early eighteenth century, but from its inception the wage plan has had the sole aim of paying the maintenance costs of the prisoner or the support costs of his dependents.

The earliest form of prison labor in this country was the contract system, whereby prisoners were hired out to private contractors who furnished materials and machines. Shortly after this system began, organized labor and its potential lobbyists raised objections.[28] Ex-prisoners revealed the system as a corrupt, merciless means for profit at the expense of helpless prisoners, and the plan was discontinued.[29]

In the mid-1830s the leasing system began, whereby the prisoner was turned over to a lessor who controlled employment and discipline outside the prison. This system gave rise to the infamous "chain-gang." Many legislatures objected to prisoners working outside prison walls and the leasing system was described as dangerous. By 1936 all states had abolished the leasing system.

The last and present system of prison labor is the "state-use plan," whereby the state controls the employment of its own prisoners inside the prison. Despite opposition from business and labor, this system functioned well financially until the end of the 1920s. The passage of the Hawes-Cooper Act of 1929, the Ashurst-Summers Act of 1935, and the Act of October 14, 1940 all but buried prison industries as a profit-making enterprise. These three laws restricted the sale of prison-made goods to state institutions only.

All prison industry has failed as a profit-making wage plan for prisoners, due to competition and resistance by organized labor and business, plus inadequate equipment and capital. Indeed, no country has been able to resolve the question of prison wages satisfactorily.[30] Before prison wages can be considered as a practical source for victim restitution, there must be a vast improvement and updating of prison industries with "equal pay for equal work." Even so, no prison in the United States has been able to employ more than half its population, and the time will probably never come in this country when a prisoner will be able to earn a wage comparable to that of free labor.[31] Perhaps the results of cybernation will ultimately render all prison labor too expensive for the state to maintain.[32] At any rate, the average amount paid to the majority of employed prisoners rules out restitution of any adequate size.

Some Policy Problems

The literature on victim compensation indicates that the opposition to it centers around its cost and unintended side effects rather than the state's moral duty to provide it.[33] These side effects consist of the possible negative effect on the victim's interest in assisting the state in prosecution, the danger of fraudulent claims, the high cost of such a program, and the fear that such a program is another step toward the welfare state through "creeping socialism."

While victims of crimes against property might not be motivated to assist in prosecution if compensated, victims who sustained physical or mental damage or pain, disablement, or hospitalization would probably assist in such prosecution. Actually the prosecution of crime and victim compensation are distinctly different and unrelated governmental services to its citizens. Such an argument against compensation is similar to the old argument of many years ago which erroneously inferred that if courts grant probation, police will see no value in making arrests. In all likelihood the criminal charges against a defendant would be disposed of before compensation could or would be awarded.

The fear of fraudulent claims may be assuaged by effective criteria to determine "victims" and by careful investigation of all claims. Some deterrents to fraudulent claims would consist of penalties such as those already provided under workmen's compensation, unemployment compensation, or the crimal code in every state.

The real problem is how to determine who is a victim and to what degree he should be compensated. The contrast of Cain against Abel is an oversimplification which the law has long recognized. Any compensation plan will have to deny claimants who willfully engage in violent activity designed to injure themselves. Though defendants' lawyers would probably argue the point, few people would voluntarily wound themselves for a modest compensation.

The criminal law has long recognized the culpable victim, the consenting victim, and the victim injured through his own provocation. Although research in American criminology has largely ignored the victim, the conclusion reached from such sparse research as has considered him has been that responsibility for a given act of violence is one of degree involving both offender and victim, referred to as the "penal couple." Of all types of crime, the one requiring the closest investigation of the offender–victim relationship is the sex offense.[34] Research has demonstrated that many so-called "victims" are, in fact, seducers or aggressors. Damage, either physical or mental, is usually rare.[35] In many instances the psychological damage following a sex offense is unrelated to the event itself but conditioned by what follows the crime.[36]

To think of the victim and offender as opposites in a victim–precipitated offense is pointless. It appears necessary when dealing with a compensation plan to discard or drastically redefine the traditional concept of blameworthiness. It is significant to remember that an injury resulting from violent crime is no less an injury because the offense was victim-precipitated. Although precipitation may change the legal aspects, the factual situation remains unaltered. Many of us seem born victims, or society has made us such. If 25 percent of all violent crime is victim–precipitated,[37] it certainly is socially more meaningful to compensate this 25 percent in order to do full justice to the remaining 75 percent who are blameless than not to compensate at all. Emphasis should be on the injury and not solely on how it occurred. In view of the diverse range of victim–precipitation possible within any penal couple's relationship, the compensation commission should be allowed discretion in adjusting compensation size in accordance with their appraisal of the relationship. In New Zealand the compensation commission uses the presentencing investigation of the probation and parole officer as a guide in determining factors of victimology.[38]

Although a compensation plan may be justified in not covering all sex offenses, it should include forcible rape; it should also cover to some degree pain and suffering and all expenses of any pregnancy, including birth and child support, especially because most states prohibit abortion.

What would a compensation plan cost? The answer lies in the eligibility criteria, the number of claims, the size of the claims, and the costs of administration. Costs can be controlled by setting limits on each of these areas. It is surprising that during the first year of operation of the New Zealand compensation plan, only seven claims were made, and all seven were granted.[39] Although New Zealand and Missouri have relatively equal populations, the crime rate in Missouri is higher. In England a survey of 3,700 crimes of violence in 1950, 1957, and 1960, of which 90 percent were at the felony level, revealed that only 3 percent could be considered serious.[40] Here, as with the New Zealand data, comparison is hazardous and there appears to be no substitute for a statewide appraisal of victimology in all its aspects before budgeting for a compensation plan.[41]

The amount of compensation awarded to each claimant is probably the most sensitive area of any compensation plan. There is ample reason for avoiding any comparison to United States welfare grants, which have as their prime motive the forcing of recipients back to work through payments so small as to hardly maintain life. Compensation is unrelated to poverty or indigency, and compensation claimants should not be forced to exhaust their money or property resources before becoming eligible, as is the case in state public welfare. Although current welfare grants are too low, common law damages are too high and involve factors unrelated to compensation as discussed here. Compensation should be restricted to the victim's loss of income and the value of services lost as a result of criminal violence. As a ceiling, the average family income of the United States for the last year could be used; or, if this is objectionable, a flat rate or maximum sum could be provided for all victims regardless of income. With the experience the states have had with workmen's and unemployment compensation scales and with public welfare programs, there should be little difficulty in deciding on grant size; or perhaps the commission should be allowed discretion in deciding the size of the grant between a maximum and minimum, with the element of victim precipitation taken into account.

Added to the direct cost are the expenses of administration. Good, effective administration costs money as any other good service will, and any administrative staff should be paid the prevailing rate for work of this complexity and skill. A staff of from three to five members made up of lawyers, one of whom has had compensation experience, social workers experienced in income maintenance aspects, and members of the courts would probably be sufficient, depending on the extent of victimology found prevalent by a survey of the state.

"Creeping socialism" is a phrase that has been applied to every effort of government to exercise its duty of citizen welfare in past decades, and all such efforts are viewed by those fearing "creeping socialism" as a treasonable weakening of the American way of life. Our twentieth century has witnessed many departures from traditional attitudes and an increasing acceptance of the view that it is the responsibility of the state to concern itself with the welfare of the individual. The state need no longer rely on the great welfare mistake, the Elizabethan Poor Law, to prevent complete destitution. Finally government has begun to cease its passive role and to undertake its affirmative obligations, and has moved from mediator and regulator to a dispenser of services. All social acts have social costs. We often pay dearly for what seemed like a good policy at the time. We gladly accept governmental responsibility in a host of significant welfare areas already mentioned. No great revolution is required to accept the simple principle of victim compensation from the state. Nor can such a program be viewed as a threat to the free enterprise system or a total abandonment of all concern for individual responsibility. The "Affluent Society" need no longer proffer the thin tokens of minimal concern in this area as in the past. The dilemma is one of ideology and values, not technology and money. The greatest task of the next one hundred years will be to humanize government in its goal, directing it from self-centered to socialized ends. The fate of victim welfare ought not to depend on irrelevant arguments or unreasoned suspicions.

Conclusion

The increase in violent crime is forcing society to evaluate more realistically the plight of the victim. The offender is an illusive source for compensating victims. Usually he is insolvent or not apprehended, or in sentencing him the state all but prohibits effective restitution. The victim, in effect, is a victim of society as well as his individual aggressor ". . . and society should assume some responsibility for making him whole."[42] To be paid for one's injury is not alien to the capitalist system and the duty of the government to do so is but the proper extension of the welfare system. The time has come to recognize effectively the justice of the claims of citizens wronged by criminal violence.

NOTES

[1] G. Hughes, "Consent in Sexual Offenses," *Modern Law Review,* 25 (1962): 672–686.

G. Hughes, "Two Views of Consent in Criminal Law," *Modern Law Review* 26 (1963): 233–248.

B. Hogan, "Victims as Parties to Crime," *Criminal Law Review,* October 1962, pp. 683–95.

[2] B. Mendesohn, "The Origin of the Doctrine of Victimology," *Excerpta Criminologica,* 3 (1963): 239–42.

H. Ellenberger, "Psychological Relationships Between Criminals and Victims," *Archives of Criminal Psychodynamics* 2 (1955): 103–110.

[3] *Code of Hammurabi,* Section 22-24, allowed compensation to victims of robbery, provided the robber was not arrested.

[4] L. Hobhouse, et al., *The Material Culture and Social Institutions of the Simpler People* (London: Routledge and Kegan Paul, 1915), pp. 86–119.

[5] H. Silving, "Compensation for Victims of Criminal Violence," *Journal of Public Law* 8 (1959): 191–250.

[6] *Ibid.,* p. 240.

[7] *The Works of Jeremy Bentham,* Vol. 1 (London: Routledge and Kegan Paul, 1962), p. 589.

[8] R. Garofalo, *Criminology* (New York: William Sloane Associates, 1914 ed.), p. 413.

[9] *Ibid.,* p. 227.

[10] R. Childres, "Compensation for Criminally Inflicted Personal Injury," *New York University Law Review,* 39 (1964); 444–472.

[11] *Ibid.,* p. 451.

[12] Command Paper 1406, *Compensation for Victims of Crimes of Violence* (London: HMSO, 1961), Sections 2, 3.

[13] The "Fry Scheme" is reprinted in Silving, *op. cit.,* p. 194.

[14] Command Paper 645, *Penal Practice in a Changing Society* (London: HMSO, 1959), p. 7.

[15] *Supra,* Note 12.

[16] New Zealand Act 134, 1963.

[17] S. Schaefer, *The Victim and His Criminal* (New York: Random House, 1968), pp. 118–119.

[18] *Ibid.,* p. 131.

[19] S. Ferracuti, M. Wolfgang, "The Prediction of Violent Behavior," *Correctional Psychiatry* 10 (1964): 56–62.

D. Pittman, "Patterns in Criminal Aggravated Assault," *Journal of Criminal Law, Criminology, and Police Science,* 55 (1964), 462–470.

[20] E. Bruen, "Controlling Violence versus Compensating Victims," *American Bar Association Journal* 50 (1964): 855–856.

[21] L. Schultz, "Why the Negro Carries Weapons," *Journal of Criminal Law, Criminology, and Police Science* 53 (1962): 476–483.

[22] K. Schuesslar, "Variation in City Crime Rates," *Social Problems,* 9 (1962): 314–320.

[23] Justice Felix Frankfurther once remarked, "The ultimate reliance for the deepest needs of civilization must be found outside of their vindication in courts of law. . . ." Dennis *v.* United States, 341 US 494, 556 (1951).

[24] S. Rubin, *Law of Criminal Correction* (St. Paul, Minnesota: West, 1963), p. 618.

[25] A. Eglash, "Creative Restitution," *Journal of Criminal Law, Criminology, and Police Science,* 48 (1958): 619–622.

[26] R. Schwartz and R. Skolnick, "Two Studies in Legal Stigma," *Social Problems,* 10 (1962): 134–140.

[27] S. Grupp, "Work Release," *Prison Journal,* 44 (1964): 4–26.

[28] H. Barnes and N. Teeters, *New Horizons in Criminology,* (Philadelphia: Lippincott, 1959), p. 592.

[29] M. O'Hare, *In Prison* (Chicago: Sadler, 1923), p. 100.

[30] M. Lopez-Rey, "Some Considerations on the Character and Organization of Prison Labor," *Journal of Criminal Law, Criminology and Police Science,* 49 (1958), 10–21. R. Evans, "The Self-Determinant Sentence," *Magistrate* 20 (1964): 142–151.

[31] Barnes and Teeters, *op. cit.,* p. 541.

[32] B. Seligman, *Most Notorious Victory* (New York: Free Press, 1966).

[33] S. Schafer, *Restitution to Victims of Crime* (Chicago: Quadrangle, 1960).

G. Geis and R. Weiner, "Compensation for Victims of Violent Crime," National Commission on Causes and Prevention of Crime, December 1968.

[34] L. Radzinowicz, *Sexual Offenses* (New York: Macmillan, 1957), pp. 83–109.

[35] X. Brunold, "Observation after Sexual Traumata Suffered During Childhood," *Excerpta Criminological* 4 (1964): 5–10.

[36] D. Reifen, "Protection of Children Involved in Sexual Offenses," *Journal of Criminal Law, Criminology and Police Science,* 49 (1959): 222–230. D. Libai, "The Protection of the Child Victim of Sexual Offense in the Criminal Justice System," *Wayne Law Review,* 1969, pp. 977–1059.

[37] H. Weihofen, "Compensation for Victims of Criminal Violence," *Journal of Public Law,* 8 (1959), 209–229.

[38] New Zealand Criminal Injuries Compensation Act of 1963, Section 10 (2).

[39] Correspondence from A. J. Dronke, Secretary, Office of Crimes Compensation Tribunal, New Zealand, Department of Justice.

[40] J. McClintock, *Crimes of Violence* (New York: Macmillan, 1963), pp. 103–176.

[41] A. Biderman, "Surveys of Population Samples for Estimating Crime Incidence," *Annals* 374 (1967): 16–33.

[42] Justice Goldberg, "Equality and Governmental Action," James Madison Lecture, New York University Law School, New York, February 1964.

SUGGESTED READINGS

Harvard Journal of Legislation 4 (1966): 127–47. "A state statute to provide compensation for innocent victims of violent crime."

Minnesota Law Review 50 (1965), no. 2. Six articles on victim compensation.

Schafer, Stephen. *The Victim and His Criminal.* New York: Random House, 1968.

Schultz, Gladys. *How Many More Victims?* New York: Ballantine, 1965.

Smith, Kathleen. *A Cure for Crime.* London: Duckworth, 1965.

25

Sex Education Policy in Schools

LeRoy G. Schultz

While formal education has not been classified as a form of social service or social welfare in this country, at least since 1900, social work contributions to education have been substantial in the form of school social services. These have included the function of visiting teacher, truant or attendance officer, counselor and therapist, community organizer, and policy formulator along with others. The social worker may work professionally with students as individuals or as groups on issues of classroom misbehavior, or help students organize to change an undesirable school policy regarding dress or hair; or he may work with a parent who is contributing to a student's inability to take advantage of his learning environment, or with a school administrator experiencing communication problems with staff and PTA.

More recently school social workers have begun establishing policy and services for the continuing student education of the pregnant school girl, married or unmarried, and for those marrying prematurely.[1] Many have accepted a new role as consultants to educators on sex content in the curriculum and teaching methods, helping individual teachers with sexual problems interfering with teaching, and combating extremist community groups fighting against all sex education. Through his professional experience with unwed mothers, the social worker is in a unique position to know the personal sufferings and social costs resulting from the casualties of sexual ignorance in any community. The social worker is especially aware of the need for abortions, family planning, and marriage and premarital counseling; he is acquainted with venereal disease problems. He is also experienced in transmitting knowledge of community problems to policy-makers or organizations, citizen groups, students, other professionals, and politicians who exert influence upon policy outcome. Sex education in elementary and high schools is increasingly viewed as the most effective way to reach children; and Sex Information and Education Centers (such as those in New Orleans) can be equally effective in working with adults.

The late 1960s and early 1970s were characterized by considerable and near-violent infighting among communities and school districts over the issue of sex education and the directions it was taking.[2] The wishes of each community should be decisive in sex education programs. Teachers and social workers are no more expert on morality than anyone else. Schools, if they must transmit moral values, must transmit those of the community to the degree they can be identified. The expertise of the social worker is just one input into policymaking, and it must rely upon its influence on others to affect final policy outcome. In a democracy, "experts are on tap, never on top."

The consequences of rapid change, always threatening to security and the status quo, can very seldom be predicted or even comfortably accommodated. The other side of man is characterized by a thirst for change and innovation, a need to explore and learn the new—an unending quest. New knowledge generated by sexual research results in new technology that alters human values and presses for realization of different life styles. The erotic revolution incites some to think of utopias and others of distopias.[3] These different persuasions, if acted upon, can create conflicting goals in educational policy. The resolution of value conflicts in a majoritarian, pluralistic democracy depends upon how relevant the issue is, or can become, and the resources that can give a person or organization power leverage to compel others to change.[4] How does one humanly resolve the conflict between those who view current levels of change in sex education policy as violative of their value system, because the change is coming too fast, or too slowly? How does one rank and weigh differing priorities? Many of these questions have set clients and consumers of education and its related services, and professionals in educational institutions to glaring at each other across a gap. If this gap is to be bridged, what amount and type of two-way traffic can the bridge support? The institution of the school will probably survive and grow only if it maintains a good supporting constituency, including students and parents.[5]

The current policy dilemmas can be understood by looking at the historical trends that characterize both sexuality and sex education over time. Neither sexuality nor sex education advanced in isolation from the main social and technological forces of civilization, but were required to act and react to them, both affected by and affecting each other.

Sex Behavioral Changes

After sexual evolution made copulation a social as well as a biological act, some means to control sexual behavior became necessary to group survival. Procreative and non-procreative sexuality fell to normative control which has sometimes been slow to change. Prohibitions and taboos regarding sex behavior became structural and enforced by group norms and became entrenched in the culture and finally rigidified into criminal law. Each generation passed on to the following one its sexual code with little questioning of its true relevance or unnecessary repressions.

The fourth evolutionary[6] change in sexuality now current resulted in a confluence of two cultural subrevolutions: one is the normative and the other is the technological. The normative relates to the resexualization of the female body and the technological to the increasing feasibility of conception control, separating procreative and non-procreative heterosexuality. The resexualization of the female body began with the decrease in the force of religion, the decline of Victorianism, and a beginning tolerance for the subject of sexuality both verbally and in written form.[7] Coupled with these changes were those inspired by the feminist movement (today called the Women's Liberation Movement), which began in the late 1800s and was an effort to gain equality socially, sexually, and politically.[8] The technological revolution in conception control began several hundred years ago with the introduction of the condom and later, a wide range of chemical and mechanical devices that subsequently gained acceptance. Today full conception control, which separates sexuality from procreation, is physically available for most persons though not necessarily psychologically acceptable. Thus man has used knowledge transmitted by the educational institution to acquire the means to divorce sexuality from procreation, and he is now using the educational process to teach the alternatives that exist for him when faced with sexuality free from pregnancy fears.

A Brief History of Sex Education

Sex education has always been a questionable policy in schools. In the late eighteenth century the middle class in Europe and America was engrossed in the "century of the child" and the "child-saving" movement,[9] wherein social services were used as a way to control adolescent behavior. Emphasis was placed upon the economic costs to society of sexual ignorance and only secondarily upon the personal costs to the young female. Thus early pro-sex educationists placed stress on the economic cost of illegitimacy and venereal disease and on the alleged personal effects of masturbation and precocious sexual development. The psychoanalytic movement had impressed upon many parents the fact that sexual development begins at an early age and that adult mental pathology can be traced to children's sexual ignorance and misunderstanding. Early research had revealed considerable sex ignorance in school children,[10] and this was believed responsible for numerous sociosexual problems. Middle-class "salvation"-oriented groups began pressing for formal sex instruction in preference to chance revelation, natural development, or lower-class family crudeness.

The industrial revolution stimulated the decline of the rural agrarian family closeness, as family members migrated for urban employment, and the family socialization process regarding sex norms began to lose some of its impact upon offspring.[11] Further impetus came from the realization that society had imposed upon police and other public order guardians the duty of protecting morality and women, rather than educating each citizen in the essential matters regarding sexuality so that he could protect himself or herself. Thus it was felt that primarily from one's knowledge of the *dangers* of various aspects of sexuality one could develop a sense of responsibility, rather than from continued emphasis on more laws, policemen, and prisons. Teaching began to emphasize the development of inner controls instead of reliance on externally imposed force and compulsion. In the decade of 1890–1900 the medical profession began publishing crude research indicating the relationship of sexual ignorance to various diseases, mental problems, and marital difficulties, and they lent their prestige to freeing the topic of sex for more open discussion. The medical approach, or disease model, stressed the "negative" aspects of sexual behavior in terms of the physical and mental pathology it generated, an approach that characterized sex education until approximately 1930.[12]

While some question arose over the propriety of sex education for children in the early years, no significant conflict occurred over who was to teach the subject. At the turn of the century mothers were viewed as having the most natural opportunity to receive and respond to questions of sexual matters from their children. A middle-class bias was reflected in encouraging mothers to consult their family doctor or clergyman for advice on their children's sexual problems. Despite constant fear of censorship, books for both children and parents began appearing at the turn of the century which dealt in rather harsh moralistic terms with sexual issues. Much of the sex-education literature published from 1850 to 1900 was influenced by the writings of the educator Basedow, a pupil of Rousseau, who, in his book *Elementarwerk* (1770), transmitted via pictures a theory of sex education for children from the age of ten years.

As early as 1802, doctors began questioning the reliance upon parents, particularly of the lower class, as teachers of sexuality, many of whom suffered sexual ignorance and mistaken notions that were in turn visited upon their children. In the decade of 1880–1890 one brave physician, Thomas Beddos, began to deliver lectures to students in the public school system.[13] By 1900, school authorities and doctors were agreed that parents were both morally and intellectually incapable of transmitting "proper" sex education to their children. The decision to place sex education in schools appears to have been made by those in power over educational policy—i.e., teachers, doctors, middle-class parents, and civic-minded women's groups. At that time, schools were considered necessary to build upon and supplement the sex education that supposedly took place in the home. In an effort to teach sexuality in as depersonalized a way as possible, botany was chosen as the best discipline for its transmission, because it could be taught without embarrassment to the teacher. In general, the same historical forces that gave rise to educational institutions were operative in changing our concepts of sexuality and its norms. Some of the traditional family functions, such as the protective, economic and educational, slowly shifted to the state and its schools; family members became more independent of each other; "adolescence" became a study in itself; and, more slowly, love and marriage began to lose their economic compulsion.

By 1890 the sex education problem was viewed as serious enough for concerned middle-class citizens and professionals to set up organized groups to press their interests. The progress of this can be seen in the following brief chronology:

1890—Establishment of the National League for the Protection of the Family. Here religionists and moralists took the first initiative to make taboos and restrictions more effective through sex education in schools.

1895—Establishment of the American Purity Alliance. This group lectured students in various schools on the horrors of venereal diseases.

1902–1904—First international institute held in Europe on problems of sex education. In 1904 Dr. Prince Morrow made first policy statement to control venereal disease through sex education for the New York County Medical Society.

1905—Establishment of Society for Social and Moral Prophylaxis, which in 1914 became the American Social Hygiene Association, currently the American Social Health Association. This organization publishes various types of data and teaching resources on sexual problems for use in schools.

There were many separate plans, policy proposals, and programs, many separate movements, and hundreds of books and pamphlets dealing with sex education during the period 1900–1940—this being the historical period that witnessed a substantial acceptance of sex education in public schools by both parents and professionals.

By 1948 even the conservative National Conference on the Education of Teachers endorsed sex education in teacher college curricula. By 1960 it was safe for the White House Conference on Children to encourage sex education in elementary and high schools.

A seventy-year period (1900–1970) can be isolated to cover the rise of sex education and radical changes in concepts and norms of sexual behavior. This period represented an historic shift from a sex values system based on a fear and force psychology, emphasizing the economic costs of deviant sexuality (i.e., venereal disease, illegitimacy, mental illness, and moral decay) to a value system in which full human sexuality is viewed as a right, a pleasure, an area into which society and government may not intercede (except for public welfare interests) and where sexuality is taught as a creative and recreative function, a vital life form to be utilized by each individual. In an age of affluence and abundance, of diversity in life styles, of new freedoms, it appears to some that we can afford a sex education that emphasizes the responsibilities of sexual behavior as well as its freedoms. It is this latter concept, as developed within educational policy, that brings us to today's sex educational problem.

The Current Policy Plight

Sex education in the public schools experienced a slow but steady rise in acceptance from approximately 1930 to 1960. It was generally accepted and approved by communities and school systems, although various school systems across the land varied in content taught and the age at which students were introduced to the subject. By the middle 1960s, symptoms of discontent began to appear. In 1962 a group of professionals formed the Sex Information and Education Council of the United States (SIECUS). This organization was concerned with making human sexuality a respectable "health entity" worth researching and teaching[14] and was very effective in bringing the sex education problem to national attention. Coupled with this was a H.E.W. educational grant in 1967 of a million dollars for sex education projects in the U.S. with government endorsement. In addition, the decade of 1960s saw an elevation of "feeling," "emotion," and body sensation, the rise of sensitivity training to recreate feeling, a less technocratic–materialistic image of man, and the decline of science and rationality.[15] The liberalization of man as a feeling and sexual being as it was reflected in the new sex education emphasis, engendered opposition from various conservative groups. Such groups began printing anti-sex education literature and organizing citizen and parent groups to protest against such programs in the schools.[16] These approaches were fairly effective and in 1969, thirty-four states experienced critical attacks upon sex education content in the public schools, and several declared a moratorium on sex education. It was at the historical point when sex education lost much of its "thou shalt not" orientation and moved toward a view that sexuality is a joyful and meaningful experience that organized opposition began to develop.

Pro and Con

Advocates for sex education cite the following factors:[17]

1. Parents do not talk to their children about sexuality, or if parents do discuss it, the information comes too late or is in error. Parents tend to indoctrinate rather than educate.
2. Students want sex education in their schools, and they are being given some participatory role in school policy formation.
3. Sex education may reduce mental illness, emotional maladjustment, excessive guilt, and perversion.
4. Sex education will reduce venereal disease, illegitimacy, unwanted pregnancies, promiscuity, and mental breakdown with a sexual etiology.
5. Sex education received during their school years helps adults use their sexuality in "mature and responsible ways."

Those in opposition to current sex education in public schools cite the following reasons in support of their position:[18]

1. Sex educational efforts in the past cannot be proven to have accomplished their goals. No evidence is available to indicate that sexual behavior is influenced one way or the other by sexual education. For example, people are not promiscuous because they lack sex education. Sex information in these circumstances is harmless and irrelevant. People are promiscuous when unloved, bored, or incapable of loving. Classroom information would not make them loved or capable of loving, unloved or un-neurotic. Likewise, girls and women seldom conceive because of ignorance of conception, but due to a lack of access to contraceptives. In short, sexual conduct has little to do with ignorance but a great deal to do with emotions not affected by cognitive information.
2. Sex, within the law, is still a matter of the private domain into which public institutions have no right to intrude. Private experience and one's private parts should not be made public.
3. Teachers must make moral judgements when moral questions arise in class. To do this is to take sides and to suggest views and practices to students that may be opposed by their parents and that cannot be justified by science. Schools must transmit community moral

values despite their impossibility of assessment, not those of the teacher-experts, unless they coincide.

Conservative arguments that the teaching of sexuality in schools is part of a communistic plot to corrupt the nation, or that sex education incites children to sexual crimes are so absurd that they will not be graced with counter-arguments.

One need only look at the change in sexual conduct over the years, sex educational history, and the current pro and con on sex education to realize exactly what sex education policy is today. It is an amalgam of local values, few facts, sex taboos, yesterday's repressions, clichés and contemporary opportunisms. Sex education policy appears serendipitous and seriocomic. Much of social policy is this way because it is based on the outcome of conflicting interests, not agreed-upon facts, so that professionals have had a difficult time influencing policy outcomes.[19] No one can define what "the good sexual life is." American opinion can be dichotomized into two political groupings, one of which fears "sexual democracy" and the other, continued "sexual fascism." We seem to have polarized into a two-party sex system. Both of the groups seem to be arguing for the same policy goals, but through different means. Both agree that there is no one chosen human sexual pattern for all that can be taught; but one group states that, if this is so, the family and peer group should influence; the other, that the school should serve this role.

Some combination of these different means to a common end is desirable. Parents and students, policy participants, and segments of every school's constituency are demanding more and more control over the operation of their schools. School administrators and school social workers with their expertise have not kept the public informed of new changes, knowledge, and ideas. Such communication gaps result in growth-debilitating backlash. Efforts by the school social worker to learn to function more effectively with various school administrations[20] must be matched by an equal concern for the social worker's role in community education and sex education for adults.[21] If, as the adage states, in every crisis both danger and opportunity exist, the present sex education controversy may be the springboard to move into a new era in which full and diverse self-enhancement, of which sexuality is a vital part, may become a living reality for youth and adults.[22]

Sex education policy for tomorrow must address itself to questions such as: Who should teach it? How should it be taught? At what age should it be taught? In view of social–class and cultural differences in sexual behavior, what should be taught? What groups of lay citizens, students, and professionals should be involved in establishing sex education policy? But even more fundamental and unanswered questions underlie these. They are those that have confronted educational institutions throughout history. How we answer them will shape future policy in this country: What is human sexuality for? Sex education for what?

NOTES

[1] F. Mauney, M. Fox, and M. Vines, "Tenth-Grade Girls and Early Marriage: A School Agency Project," *Social Casework*, February 1966, pp. 98–104. M. Howard, "Comprehensive Service Programs for School-Age Pregnant Girls," *Children*, September 1968, pp. 193–97.

[2] "Sex Education Splitting Many Communities Across U.S." *New York Times*, 14 September 1969, pp. 1 and 77. "Sex Education," *Medical World News*, Vol. 10, no. 40 (October 1969), pp. 25–30. On September 18, 1969 the first National Convention on the Crisis in Education was called to organize opposition to sex education and sensitivity training. Mary Breasted, "Saving Sex for the Back Seat," *Village Voice*, 18 September 1969.

[3] J. Poland and S. Sloan, *Sex Marchers* (Los Angeles, California: Elysium, 1968). C. Winick, *The New People: Desexualization in American Life* (New York: Pegasus, 1968).

[4] K. Gergen, "Assessing the Leverage Points in the Process of Policy Formation," in R. Bauer and K. Gergen, *The Study of Policy Formation,* (New York: Free Press, 1968), pp. 181–203.

[5] F. Rourke, *Bureaucracy, Politics and Public Policy* (Boston: Little, Brown and Company, 1969), pp. 89–117.

[6] For an excellent brief history of the changes in human sexuality over time, see J. Bernard, "The Fourth Revolution," *Journal of Social Issues* 22 (1966), pp. 76–88.

[7] W. Young, *Eros Denied—Sex in Western Society* (New York: Grove, 1964), particularly chapters 7–9 and 22–23.

[8] E. Brecher, *The Sex Researchers* (Boston: Little, Brown and Company, 1969), pp. 142–198.

[9] A. Platt, "The Rise of the Child-Saving Movement: A Study in Social Policy and Correctional Reform," *Annals* 381 (1969), 21–38.

[10] G. Hall, "Contents of Children's Minds on Entering School" *Pedagogical Record*, June 1891.

[11] H. Wilensky and C. Lebeaux, *Industrial Society and Social Welfare* (New York: Free Press, 1965), pp. 67–81.

[12] Brecher, *op. cit.,* pp. 50–61. See also T. Szasz, *The Myth of Mental Illness*, 1st ed. (New York: Hoeber, 1961).

[13] H. Ellis, *Studies in the Psychology of Sex* (New York: Random House, 1937), Part 3, pp. 33–94. This is a good history of early sex education efforts.

[14] Sex Information and Education Council of the United States, Inc., *Sex Education* (New York: SIECUS, 1968).

[15] T. Roszak, *The Making of a Counter Culture* (New York: Anchor, 1969), pp. 1–84.

[16] E. Dunbar, "Sex in School" *Look Magazine* 9 September 1969, pp. 15–18. *Bulletin of the John Birch Society* January 1969.

[17] J. McCary, *Human Sexuality* (New York, Von Nostrand, 1967), pp. 1–18. SIECUS, *op. cit.*

[18] E. Haag, "Why Sex Education at All?" *Current* no. 12 (November 1969), pp. 31–35.

[19] C. Levy, "The Social Worker as Agent of Policy Change" *Social Casework* 51 (1970), pp. 102–108.

[20] E. Litwak and H. Meyer, "The Administrative Style of the School and Organizational Tasks," in F. Cox, ed., *Strategies of Community Organization* (Itasca, Ill.: Peacock Publishers, 1970), pp. 78–91.

[21] E. Middlewood, "Sex Education in the Community," in C. Broderick and J. Bernard, eds., *The Individual, Sex and Society* (Baltimore: Johns Hopkins University Press, 1969), pp. 83–99. One model social work program for adults is the Community Sex Information and Education Service, Inc., P.O. Box 4246, New Orleans, La. 70118.

[22] G. Leonard, *Education and Ecstasy* (New York: Delacorte, 1968).

SUGGESTED READINGS

Breasted, M. *OH! Sex Education.* New York: Praeger, 1970.

Broderick, C., and Berhard, J. *The Individual, Sex and Society.* Baltimore: Johns Hopkins University Press, 1969.

Gagnon, J., and Simon, W. "They're Going to Learn It in the Street Anyway." *Psychology Today* 3 (1969) no. 2, pp. 46–7.

Lindblom, C. *The Policy Making Process.* Englewood Cliffs, N.J.: Prentice-Hall, 1968.

Powers, G., and Baskin, W. *Sex Education: Issues and Directions.* New York: Philosophical Library, 1969.

26

Sex and Social Policy

LESTER A. KIRKENDALL

The play "Green Pastures" portrays the untutored Negro's concept of God and Heaven. One scene shows "De Lawd" returning to Earth to appraise the results of His creation. He is severely disappointed for He finds a roistering, dissolute mankind living in a way quite contrary to His commandments. "De Lawd" becomes very dissatisfied with His handiwork, and resolves to sweep clean the face of the Earth and start over. As part of this decision He seeks out Noah and asks him to build the Ark.

He tells Noah, "Dey's gonter be a flood. De levees is gonter bust an' everythin' dat's fastened down is comin' loose, but it ain't gonter float long, cause I'm gonter make a storm dat'll sink everythin' from a hencoop to a barn."

This description of the Flood's devastation is both legendary and modern. It vividly describes the current social turmoil which is a consequence of our remarkable and extensive scientific and technologic developments.

When we think of mechanical and technical advances and the changes directly associated with them, it is easy to believe that "everythin' dat's fastened down is comin' loose." The evidence is all about us. High-powered cars dart along broad but crowded transcontinental freeways and alter our concepts of transportation; a worldwide network of airways brings highly diverse cultures into close association; automatic processes are producing factories with fewer workers; miraculous medical advances which lengthen life are changing the proportions of the age groups in the population; the harnessing of atomic power is beginning to alter our practices in the use of energy; and the awesome power of thermonuclear weapons is threatening the existence of civilization.

These developments produce great changes with far-reaching consequences, and affect us tangibly in many ways.

But these developments, and others, strike still deeper and affect us in subtle ways not so easily perceived. Our patterns of human behavior, our characteristic ideas and concepts are undergoing important changes also. Certain cause-and-effect relationships which are less obvious than the material changes just noted are producing them.

Specifically, some very profound alterations are now taking place in sexual standards and practices, and in attitudes toward sex and sexual behavior. These, too, are the consequence of powerful social, technologic, and scientific forces which operate outside the awareness of most persons. They include such developments as methods for controlling conception and disease; the exceedingly rapid growth of the world's population; the movements and interchange of people across racial, cultural, and ethnic barriers; the lengthening life span; shifting sex roles; attitudes growing out of the emphasis on scientific inquiry; commercialization of sex; and the welter of confusing and contradictory opinions which have arisen about sexual patterns. There are still others.

The Challenge

Patterns of sexual behavior are changing, and there is an increasing freedom in associations between the sexes. How can we accommodate to these changes and how should we cope with them in terms of the social problems they raise? If we fail to accept this responsibility for the clarification of values and the development of standards, conditions will become worse—not better.

The challenge is even broader. It has become that of understanding how to use sex as a positive, fulfilling force in living. At the North American Conference on Church and Family held in 1961 the cochairman, Dr. Evelyn Duvall, declared: "The Twentieth Century has seen a basic shift from sex-denial to sex-affirmation throughout our culture."[1] By affirmation was meant a greater readiness and more openness in the recognition of and use of sex in various phases of life. How can this affirming attitude be used constructively, rather than destructively?

The discussion which follows examines the various forces which are altering sexual attitudes and standards. Its purpose is to be realistic and logical about the situation which exists. No particular sexual pattern is suggested or advocated, though a suggestion is made as to the bases upon which our sexual standards should rest. Thought and re-education are needed to evolve a sexual standard which will fit modern conditions.

The Waning Power of Fear-Evoking Deterrents

The motivating power of the fear-evoking deterrents which have long been used to establish and control sexual behavior has very greatly declined. Threats of dire consequences formerly supported a standard of sexual abstinence outside marriage—the threats of conception, infection, and detection—but these have been almost wiped out by advances in the fields of (a) contraception, which markedly diminishes the likelihood of pregnancy, (b) prophylaxis and medication, which makes venereal diseases less dreaded, and (c) the automobile and urban living which make isolation and anonymity possible and public opinion less oppressive.

Nor is this all. Not only have these threats declined in their power to control; with further scientific developments they are destined to decline still further. This is, of course, the thrust of all scientific endeavor—to reduce threats, to make the uncontrolled controllable, and make the unknown known.

Technical developments indicate that conception can be prevented if desired. Whether these methods are used effectively is another matter, but control is apparently now possible. And with modern methods of detection and treatment, venereal diseases are not the bugaboo they formerly were. Statistics citing increases in venereal diseases only prove the failure of fear as a deterrent.

As for the fear that others will know and disapprove of sexual associations, what of this?

Adolescent children in the United States are now accorded great freedom from parental control and direction. In urban centers particularly, they can easily develop associations with persons who are complete strangers to their parents. Good roads and the automobile have released them from adult supervision whether they live in city or country. Many young people either have cars of their own or have access to automobiles. They are able to find privacy and to escape easily into anonymity.

There is also the tacit rule that couples in parked cars shall not be disturbed. Residents of local communities know the locations of the *lovers' lanes* or parking spots in that community and simply avoid or ignore them. Thus it becomes possible to engage in sexual relations with the almost practical certainty that it will never be known, unless the couple becomes careless or promiscuous and so introduces unnecessary risks.

The chaperone as an active and forceful supervisor is a thing of the past. Chaperones at adolescent social events, usually selected by the youths themselves, are there more because of tradition than because they serve a meaningful purpose. They are ordinarily expected to sit at one side, engage in bored conversation with each other, and discreetly overlook what may be going on about them.

Criticism of couples engaging in premarital intercourse or experiencing a premarital pregnancy is much less severe now than formerly. Disapproval is certain to be voiced, but the general practice is to help the couple organize their situation and get on with the business of living.

With the decline in power of these fear-evoking deterrents, what conditions do we face? One theologian puts it this way, "To use the language of formal ethics, a 'prudential' sex standard will no longer work, if the ideal is premarital continence and marital monopoly. And when people have stuck to ideals out of the fear of what will happen when they cheat, they are helpless when that crutch is gone. Fear as a motive is a crutch, a sign of weakness and not of strength."[2]

A more profound and probing effort than has ever been made before to find a meaningful basis for sexual standards is in order.

A Sexual Economy of Abundance

The shift from attitudes favoring sex-denial to those which tolerate sexual expression has been accelerated by certain social–health developments which have freed sex from some of the restrictions and restraints which formerly surrounded it. It may be said that we have entered upon a sexual "economy of abundance"—a circumstance which generates a different approach to the consideration of sexual ethics.

We are all familiar with the economy of abundance resulting from technical efficiency in the production of material goods. Our agricultural and industrial systems are producing foods and other commodities in such an embarrassing plenty that the distributive machinery of our economic system has been unable to keep up. As a result we have been forced to re-examine our traditional attitudes toward production and consumption, work and play, thrift and savings, the importance of maximum productivity, the significance of leisure, and toward the economic system itself. Virtues, important in an economy of scarcity, seem to get us into more trouble in an economy which produces material goods in abundance.[3] The same seems true when we consider the "economy of abundance" in sex.

The clearest illustration is associated with population increase. For centuries and centuries the human race eked out a bare existence, so far as maintaining its numbers was concerned. The life span was short and wars, famine, pestilence, disease, and other disasters kept the total population at a level which did little more than insure the survival of the race.

It has been estimated that in 1830 the population of the world was about one billion. Then medical advances began to lengthen the life span. More infants reached adulthood, and adults lived longer. Industrial developments and a growing agricultural know–how made it possible to feed more and more of these people. By 1930 the world population had reached two billion. It reached about three billion in 1960, and there is the prospect of seven and one-half billion in the year 2000.

This problem of a burgeoning population concerns the people of the

United States, as well as those of India, China, and the "underdeveloped" countries. In the first place, the people in the overpopulated countries are exerting tremendous pressures on the more sparsely populated sections, and on those resource-wealthy parts of the world which might help support their exploding populations. Second, even without immigration, the population of the United States itself is rising rapidly. According to one study: "The population of the U.S. may double in the last half of this century, just as it did in the first half. According to our medium projections, the number of inhabitants will reach 300 million shortly before the end of the century and 312 million by 2000, as compared to 157 million in 1950. Looking a little less far into the future, it seems fairly certain that our population will surpass the 200 million mark by 1980 unless atomic war occurs."[4] Surely an economy of abundance so far as reproduction is concerned!

Yet, for centuries the dogma has been taught that the only laudable and often the only ethical purpose of sex is for procreation. This characterizes most Roman Catholic teaching even now, and at one time or another has been part of the teaching on sex of many Protestant denominations. Other purposes of sex in marriage have been proposed, but . . . "usually, however, procreation is listed as the first purpose of marriage."[5]

Thus, fundamentally, our sexual standards which have evolved over the centuries in a very complex fashion have rested on the proposition that the natural and only proper use of sex is for reproduction. For centuries this approach to sexual morality was needed to insure the survival of the race. Attitudes disapproving contraception, masturbation, homosexuality, sterilization, and other sexual practices arose because these uses of sex were obviously negating or interfering with the use of sex for reproduction.

What now happens to these sexual restrictions and prohibitions when confronted with overpopulation and the "standing-room only" signs now being hung out by the population experts? Certainly sex standards can no longer rest logically upon the assumption that the entire creative capacity of human sexuality is needed for population growth. If they were to rest on this assumption, this would suggest a very limited use of sex—a restriction which few people are likely to respect.

Much current religious teaching has rejected the concept that sexual expression should be governed and restricted by the procreative intent, yet the attitudes associated with this concept still underlie much of the teaching about sex and sexual practices. Neither do discussions of sexual ethics deal with this issue forthrightly. It is most difficult to reconcile centuries of restrictive teaching and thinking about sex with rapidly changing social conditions, and a surplus of people in the world.

Improved health practices also favor a sexual economy of abundant results. Better nutrition, fewer debilitating childhood diseases, and quicker, more complete recoveries from illnesses have made a more vigorous, robust, and energetic people, more able and ready to engage in sexual activities if they wish, whatever their stage of life. One interesting reflection of this development is the increasing frequency with which concern is expressed for adequate sexual functioning in old age.[6] It could be said that these improved practices have added years to our life and life to our years.

These same advances possibly add to the potential abundance in yet another way. Puberty, i.e., sexual maturity, seems to be coming earlier and the climacteric later. This lengthens the portion of the total life span available for sexual participation.

The increased leisure time now available to many persons also gives them more time and opportunity to participate in sexual activities for the sake of pleasure if they wish to use sex that way. This is reflected in the more related and open attitudes currently being exhibited. Martha Wolfenstein, in her study of the changing attitudes toward moral behavior as they relate to child-rearing practices, has noted that in various areas of discipline and child care the emphasis has changed from denial, exertion of rigorous control, and performance of duty, to approving enjoyment and pleasure as an acceptable end. Miss Wolfenstein refers to this as a "fun morality."[7] Unquestionably the same movement which she discerned in child-rearing practices extends to sexual attitudes and practices as well.[8]

Leisure is unoccupied time which has been released through the shortening of the work day or work week, but for this discussion leisure can come through still another kind of "released time." Parents, and mothers in particular, now devote fewer years to child rearing than when, in order simply to replace themselves, a couple had to produce five or six children. Under the latter circumstances the burdens of child rearing resulted in worn-out women who not only had no zest for sex, but who were afraid of it. With smaller families women are through with child rearing earlier, and in middle age are free again to devote themselves to their husbands and the satisfactions of life in general, including the physical.

Another important factor in gaining the added leisure and freedom from burdens of child bearing, as noted, has been the development of effective contraceptives. Man has reached the time when he is able to decide at will how many children he will have or whether he will have children at all. This fact alone has powerful social and psychological implications for the use of sex within and outside of marriage.

So just as the flood of material goods has irrevocably forced us to reappraise our traditional attitudes toward work, savings, production, play, and leisure, now the flood of population, better health, longer years, reservoirs of energy, and leisure time are forcing us to reappraise our sexual standards. Can, or should, a sexual morality geared to the use of sex for reproductive purposes only, stand? This is the question.

Cultural Intermingling

A third social force with marked impact upon conventional patterns of sexual behavior is the intermingling of people from all parts of the world. This holds for persons of all races, all nationalities, and all the world's religions. Ideas, practices, and concepts which formerly were strange fascinating tidbits from an anthropologist's case-book now crop up right in one's own community. Thousands of American young men and women have visited other cultures and have come in contact with other patterns of male-female relations, family life, and sexual expression. Travellers from other lands visit the United States with equal freedom. The ease and rapidity with which people move to other parts of the world, and the world coverage by mass media, has made hundreds of thousands of Americans acquainted with other cultural patterns for handling sex, and as many people in other lands have heard about ours. In this shrunken globe the social and sexual patterns of one culture are being challenged over and over again as they are placed in proximity to differing social–sexual patterns of another culture.

An interesting illustration of this occurred in one of the writer's family living classes sometime ago when an exchange student from Argentina and another from Iceland discussed the dating and sexual practices and standards in their two countries. The Argentinian, a boy with a Spanish–Catholic background, described a society in which much care is taken to prevent unmarried young men and women from having free, unchaperoned associations. As a result there is very little if any premarital intercourse involving dating partners. However, he told the class, in his section of the country it is common for boys at age fifteen to sixteen to find their way to a prostitute for their initial sexual experience. A boy who was not aggressive enough to make the arrangements himself might be helped by his father, an uncle, or an older brother. This practice is opposed by the church but nevertheless is a part of the local culture.

In Iceland, in contrast, there is considerable sexual freedom and permissiveness by American concepts. Young people of high school ages, the student said, are permitted to come and go pretty much as they please. Many boys and girls carry keys to their own homes. A boy or a girl might invite a member of the other sex to his home and his own bedroom after a party—a generally accepted practice about which the parents ordinarily are not consulted. This reference to this kind of freedom excited the curiosity of the American students who envisioned all kinds of promiscuity and indulgence. One student asked if the illegitimacy rate was high. He responded by saying that he knew of two or three girls who had become premaritally pregnant. He then added that "this became a lot worse, though, after American service men were stationed in Iceland."

This cultural cross–cutting creates a growing tendency to question all cultural patterns, both one's own and those of others (a tendency in keeping with our emphasis on the "scientific attitude"). It gives rise to reluctance to accept answers based upon provincial custom, arbitrary authority, or abstract references to *good* and *bad,* or *right* and *wrong.*

Standards based upon the doctrines of a particular religious sect may be meaningful and persuasive within that sect. Allegiance to them depends upon staunch loyalty to that group, and rejection of ideas and practices followed by other groups. Maintenance of such an exclusive loyalty, however, demands isolation and immobility and these are rapidly becoming impossibilities.

So, more and more, the need becomes more obvious to find some approach to standards which will cut across cultural differences yet at the same time will take them into account. Cross-cultural communication and understanding is becoming imperative. Attempts to limit these considerations to males or females alone, to one particular culture or to one specific religious sect, have become completely outmoded.

Evolving Sex Roles

Still another factor of tremendous importance which is altering our conventional patterns is the changing relationship between men and women. This change is most obvious for the women, and draws more attention than does the change in the masculine role. Modern women have much greater freedom in choosing their own patterns of living than a century ago. As they compete freely with men, they are coming to demand a *satisfaction* in the realm of sex which parallels the freedom and satisfaction of men. This includes both the marital and the premarital relationships. For example, unmarried girls, either individually or in groups, often have apartments of their own, and may invite friends of either sex for unchaperoned visits and activities. From this it is an easy step for women to ask for the freedom in sexual participation that is accorded to men.

Thus with industrialization, urban living, education for women, and equal rights for all individuals regardless of sex, conventional sex roles in good part have gone the way of the fear-evoking deterrents.

These shifting roles extend to the marriage relationship, of course, and the issues arising from them are sharpened by our changing concepts of the purpose of marriage itself. The view that a wife should be subservient to her husband has been giving way to an equalization arrangement. The idea that procreation is the major purpose of marriage and necessary for its fulfillment has shifted to concern for personality satisfactions of the partners.

Along with these changes have come revised concepts concerning the nature of sex. As Frank says,

> Today . . . women are beginning to find that marriage conceived in terms of conjugal rights and duties may be morally justified and legally sanctioned, but . . . it does not respect their integrity and makes demands upon them that are often humiliating and degrading. . . . The age–old conception of marriage as conferring a right upon the husband to demand sexual compliance by the wife has been so widely and strongly held by men that many are unable to understand what a woman means when she objects to performing her conjugal duties, as the law and the church expound them and have told her husband that he has a right to demand.[9]

Scientific Inquiry

One important consequence of the scientific approach is to teach us to question what is not clear. The concern for gathering facts, to determine cause and effect, to know both immediate and long–range consequences, to think rationally on all issues, and to understand the principles which operate in any particular situation—these are part and parcel of the scientific method. Children are told to ask questions, curiosity is encouraged, and a probing mind is a virtue—but not when it comes to sex! In this area we still try desperately to exclude the scientific method.

But even in matters of sex the scientific approach is beginning to have some influence. For example, refraining from masturbation, at the turn of the century, was definitely a moral issue. Its disapproval by religious authorities was supported by medical authorities. Any use of masturbation was said to lead to dire physical and psychologic consequences, too serious to contemplate.

As research demonstrated the almost universal practice of masturbation,[10] however, and as clinical investigation failed to uncover the terrible consequences which were supposed to result, the pressure against it relaxed. Today's literature on masturbation reflects relatively little of the severe moral disapproval formerly so prominent. In fact, some reputable professional people[11] have suggested that masturbation has positive psychologic consequences. And so a taboo and a bugaboo give way to scientific inquiry.

Extramarital sex relations were formerly regarded as an adequate cause for the termination of the marriage relationship, and it was common opinion that no marriage could withstand the consequences of extramarital sexual experience on the part of one of the partners.

Again research has revealed a greater prevalence of extramarital sexual experience than might have been expected,[12] and clinical data have demonstrated that some marriages do stand up under its impact. In fact, as with masturbation,[13] statements can be found to the effect that extramarital sexual experience can even be handled in such a manner that a strengthening of the marriage relationship may result. Thus Dr. Frank[14] writes,

". . . some extra-marital sex relations, considered as immoral, may be, and often are, ethically desirable and humanly fulfilling."

The trend in regard to sex standards has been under scrutiny. Dr. Ira Reiss[15] has distinguished not one standard, but four, each of which has certain adherents. These standards are (a) chastity before marriage, (b) the double standard, (c) sexual permissiveness when affection exists, and (d) sexual permissiveness without affection. Reiss, after his study, feels that (a) and (b) are declining in strength, that (d) will never have many adherents, and that (c) is probably the coming sex standard.

The writer[16] demonstrated that the consequences of and attitudes toward premarital sexual involvement vary with the degree of affectional attachment. Effects and outcomes of premarital intercourse are determined by such factors as ability to communicate, motivations, and capacity to provide protective measures and assume responsibility for the outcomes.

Dr. Alfred C. Kinsey and his investigators have probed the sex lives of hundreds of American men and women, and turned up data on such matters as masturbation, homosexuality, premarital and extramarital relations, and other phases of sex conduct which were highly disturbing to many people.

Coupled with research is a marked freedom to treat sexual subjects openly in the popular literature and other media for mass communication. No one can doubt the growth of this freedom.

Whether one likes any of this or not does not change the consequences. The trend is to examine sexual behavior scientifically. Even more severely tabooed aspects of sexual behavior are coming under scrutiny and being discussed openly. Many studies are in progress on homosexuality, premarital sexual patterns, illegitimacy, sexual offenses and sexual offenders, and sexual promiscuity. They all suggest the impossibility of keeping sex a taboo subject, and of enforcing social standards from positions being undermined by facts derived through scientific inquiry.

Contradicting and Conflicting Opinions

To further confuse the situation, we find relatively little agreement as to what sexual attitudes or standards should exist, and the place and importance of sex in our society. Authorities and ordinary folk do not always agree. Among the many contradictory and opposing opinions, practices, and attitudes the following may be listed:[17]

1. Our own society in general stands firmly for premarital chastity, sexual sobriety, and a minimum of premarital sexual experimentation; *but*
   a. Adults use sex as a lure in an effort to promote business enterprises, in such a way to threaten the conventional standards continuously.
   b. Anthropologic studies show ours to be one of the most restrictive in this respect among various cultures studied.[18]
   c. Some of the religious teachings which support these standards are now being challenged or reinterpreted, while cultural changes are producing conflict at the same time.
   d. Virgin boys report that adults do not support them in maintenance of their chastity and that in their peer group they feel quite defensive concerning their lack of experience. Most adults have no knowledge of the sexual pattern which the youth are following unless it is brought to open attention by some misadventure.[19]
2. Sex is regarded as a *delicate* subject—one from which serious damage may result if it is not handled with great wisdom; *yet* books, plays, magazines, and mass media treat sex very openly and stress mainly the enticing, exciting aspects of it. One might well conclude if one escapes exposure, no other problem is involved.
3. Men and women are supposed to be understanding and mutually respectful of one another; *but* "the double standard" of sexual conduct permits emotional and sexual expressions to members of one sex which are denied to members of the other.[20] On the other hand some data indicate certain male-female differences which may suggest a need for some differentiation in standards. Some of these differences may be inherent; others are deeply embedded in our culture.
4. We have tended to regard cultures with more sexual freedom as less civilized and less advanced than our own; *but* the multiplication of contacts through visitors and informational media makes it clear that we could, and should, learn much from these cultures.

5. We feel that the sexual function, for the protection of individuals and the social structure, should be exercised in the context of love; *yet* some evidence indicates that the negative consequences of premarital experimentation are least in the more permissive cultures.

6. Parents, teachers, and religious leaders often teach that premarital intercourse will very likely cause guilt and distrust, or interfere with marital adjustments; *but*

   a. Some studies indicate that couples, especially engaged pairs, experiencing premarital intercourse state that it strengthens their relationships.[21]

   b. Some research findings indicate that premarital intercourse may be related if not conducive to more effective sexual adjustments in marriage.

   c. Some counselors, therapists, and philosophers see positive values in such experiences, and parents may be advised to be more lenient and accepting toward premarital intercourse.

7. The importance of sex education has long been emphasized, *yet* what is done clearly falls far short of what is needed.

8. Adolescence is often regarded as a period of marked sexual urgency which almost demands expression; *yet* there is good evidence that the sex drive is mainly psychologic in nature,[22] and therefore amenable to education.

9. Youths want help in building an understanding of sex and in coping with their sexual problems, *but* adults are quite ineffective in providing this help, nor is there evidence that they are becoming more effective.

Issues Needing Attention

The action of the forces which have just been discussed has had certain consequences. Certainly this century has seen a widespread disregard for the ideal of strict confinement of all sexual activities to the marital relationship. What people give lip service to and what they actually do are two different things. The chasm between profession and practice was clearly revealed by the studies made by Dr. Alfred Kinsey and his associates. Far from being discredited, the general validity of the Kinsey studies is continually being documented and supported by the studies of others.

This, then, seems to be the point at which we have arrived:

a. Powerful technologic forces have eroded the basis for the conventional attitudes and positions which have been held toward sex. These forces give no indication of dissipating their power; rather their power will probably increase.

b. There is a definite breaking away from the conventional standards, and a freedom in sexual practices and in discussions in public media which did not exist a few decades ago.

c. There are some important issues which now need resolution.

These issues may be cast in the form of questions.

Within what value framework shall judgments about sexual behavior for all age levels of the population be made? If a more positive approach is needed, what shall it be?

Does sexual experimentation in childhood and adolescence serve some desirable and legitimate developmental function? When might it be helpful? when harmful?

Should there be differential standards of sex behavior to take into account social class differences, age, and maturity?

Shall engaged couples be accorded sexual expressions denied those who are experiencing less intense emotional involvements?

If the double standard is to be resolved, should the new standard be nearer the present male or the present female standard?

Should our standards continue to disapprove all individual and interpersonal premarital and nonmarital sexual expression? If some expression is condoned, what kind shall it be, and under what circumstances should it occur?

Does some childhood and adolescent sexual functioning have a significance which we have failed to recognize?

How deeply should we seek to embed sexual behavior in a context of love?

How should sex be treated in advertising and in mass media?

Should we accept the orderly dissemination of contraceptive information to all groups in the population instead of permitting it to be spread through underground channels as now occurs? Should we proceed further with removing the stigma of illegitimacy from unmarried mothers and children born out of wedlock?

Should we hold to the belief that increasing freedom in the use of sex is a threat to civilization and that its free use should be restricted in every way possible? Under what circumstances does sexual denial have important values for the individual and for society?

Should all literature or art which might appeal to prurient interests be banned from circulation? Does such literature afford a kind of sublimation or diversion which is important for some people?

In view of the wide chasm between youth and adults, how can sexual values be discussed and passed from one generation to another?

We need to be thinking openly and objectively about issues such as these. There are, however, powerful forces which work both for and against an attempt to deal with them in an orderly, rational fashion. These forces may be looked upon as being liabilities and assets.

Liabilities and Assets

There is abundant evidence that a redirection of thought and a keener awareness of the problems of managing the sexual impulse are needed. There are certain liabilities which hamper efforts to do this. If we are to accomplish a redirection, it is important to recognize these liabilities and the problems they have created.

1. An unreasoning and irrational fear of sex.

This long-standing fear has been much reinforced in the past half-century by the powerful influence of Freudian psychology. Freud believed that the individual is constantly threatened by powerful impulses, or instincts, seeking to break through conventional social restraints and attain satisfaction at whatever cost. The sexual impulse is one of these fearful powers always striving for expression, always endangering social relationships.

Strong drives toward satisfaction of the sexual impulse exist—this cannot be denied. Yet there are other strong impulses with which we can deal with relative objectivity and which we regard as subject to direction. The marked suspicion with which sex is regarded and our inability to deal straightforwardly with our sexual feelings and needs have made it much more difficult to direct the sexual impulse. We have many difficulties in our social policies and our attitudes toward sex which might otherwise have been avoided.

2. The sexual problem is regarded as a problem of youth, rather than of adults.

Adults are prone to view childhood and adolescence as periods in which sex education is important, periods during which sexual mistakes may be made and problems may arise. Book after book, pamphlet after pamphlet, and innumerable articles have been written to tell teachers, parents, and religious leaders how to inform children and youth about sex; how to build attitudes in youth, and safeguard them against mistakes.

These materials are important and help meet a real need in the early years of life. Certainly one of the tasks facing children and youth is learning about sex, its purpose and manifestations, and fitting it satisfactorily and meaningfully into their lives. They need all the help they can get.

But when thinking and educational efforts stop here, they fall far short of recognizing the attitudes and problems of adulthood on sex education. The problem of youth is to incorporate sex satisfactorily into patterns of personal living. That so many fail so badly is the consequence of the failure of adults to live up to their responsibility, and suggests that adults, rather than youth, are the ones most direly in need of sex education.

Sexwise, adults need to work toward two highly important objectives.

First, they must create the tone—the atmosphere in which these perplexing problems can be considered frankly and openly. They must cut across sex lines and generation groupings to discuss sex matters with the same facility and freedom that they discuss economic or health problems. This will require reading and study, and a conscious and conscientious effort by adults to free themselves from deep-seated inhibitions and preconceived ideas.

Secondly, they should see sex in relation to other aspects of life. Sex has been so isolated and torn out of the context of total living that it is extremely difficult to have a balanced view of it.

The reasons are obvious, for example, for suggesting that in our preoccupation with sexual morality we have failed to recognize as moral issues those problems involved in the management of our hostile and aggressive impulses. If we could gain a broader perspective, we might recognize that the harm arising from the unethical expression of our aggressive impulses far exceeds the harm resulting from the mismanagement of the sexual impulse. Few thinking persons would deny that mankind is more likely to be done in by unbridled aggressions and hostilities than by unbridled sexuality. Yet we occupy our time and attention with sex as a moral issue and do not recognize that hostility and aggression are even more serious moral problems.

This leads us to such inconsistencies as fighting all-out battles against sexual pornography, while permitting the pornography of violence, brutality, and death to flood our homes and schools through mass media and over the airways. No reputable business person would dare sell phallic symbols to or stock *Lady Chatterley's Lover* for adolescents. Yet a tank or a submachine gun is commonly regarded as a suitable Christmas gift for children (a symbol of the Prince of Peace!), or an amusement parlor will install a dime slot machine which allows the user to test his skill at dropping an atomic bomb on a city.

These illogical positions are the result of our tearing sex out of context and of our persistent attempts to ignore and deny it as an integral part of our nature.

Once these objectives have been accomplished, the next task is that of social policy setting, the establishment of values, and the formation of attitudes. We are in great need of wise and courageous thinking concerning matters of sex—and the need is rapidly becoming greater.

3. Adult attitudes toward sex have been so repressive that still other undesirable consequences have resulted.

As an example, parents and other adults tend to react fearfully and with marked hostility and agitation when some sexual offense occurs. Their exaggerated reaction produces far more damage in the offended person than the sexual aspects of the action ever could. Thus, in any situation in which the genital organs are exhibited publicly, reactions are usually highly agitated and reflect much more disturbance than were only the upper half of the torso exposed. The damage to children who may have witnessed the exposure results more from the agitated and disturbed reactions of the adults around them than from the exposure per se.

These attitudes of fear and rejection toward sex have made objective discussion of sex problems extremely difficult. Proposals for a re-examination of our policies and attitudes toward sex meet with immediate suspicion and resistance. Changes in our legal and social attitudes toward the treatment of homosexuality, treatment of sexual offenders, poronography, sex education in the schools, and many other items are denied or distorted. Laws against abortion have remained on the statute books relatively unchanged for 150 years despite marked changes which affect the need for and the application of such laws.[23]

There are still other inconsistencies. We have created feelings and fears which are applied only to sex, and not to other aspects of life. We fear that any open acknowledgment of pleasure attached to sex may lead to unrestrained indulgences. Yet we study ways to make foods tasty and tables attractive and to stimulate gustatory appetites, and do not expect that gluttony will be the consequence.

Time is spent debating whether children should see the fully nude bodies of the parents, yet no one is concerned when children see their bare feet. Again it is the fear that the sight of genitals will set loose some sexual demon within the children.

With respect to humor, sex is made so serious or so sacred (as it should be at times), that we cannot enjoy any humor or feel any lightness toward it (as we should be able to at times). We do have our "dirty" jokes, but why must they be "dirty" jokes if they are genuinely witty? Many of them are pointless and humorless, told only because they touch upon sex. But the same kind of a pointless joke in regard to eating or physical exercise would simply be forgotten and not told and retold.

As a result of these adult attitudes, youth and adults are widely separated from each other ideologically and sociologically in matters of sex. One study found that both boys and girls rated "petting" and "sex" as more difficult to discuss with parents than any other of 36 topics.[24] With the existence of such a chasm the adults may criticize youth, but if they do, their very remoteness often means that what they say has no effect. The same circumstances, as still another study indicates, make it impossible for them to extend support and appreciation to youth on their sexual conduct even when it is within approved patterns.[25]

There are certain forces which if they can be utilized should be assets in any effort to work toward a sounder and more rational concept of sexuality.

1. A Slowly Increasing Objectivity Concerning Sex. The increasing scientific interest in sex and the growing volume of research has contributed to a greater degree of freedom for discussion. The freedom can hardly be said to have been paralleled by an equivalent degree of objectivity, but it does at least provide a situation in which frankness and straightforwardness become more possible.

2. A Deeper Understanding of the Nature and Needs of Man. This is a consequence of the development of psychologic insights into the nature of human nature, the character of sex, and the potential outcomes of various courses of action. There is much yet to learn on these matters but the growing body of knowledge should provide an increasingly firm and sound basis upon which to erect social policy.

3. An Awareness of the Inevitability of Change. The extent to which mechanical and technologic developments have produced obvious material changes has already been mentioned. These alterations have produced strong and repeated emphases on the inevitability of change. Experiences with social dislocations and recognition that new approaches are inevitable have helped somewhat to prepare people for changes in the field of morals and sexual behavior.

Resolving the Confusion

Confusion and uncertainty have been a spur to analysis and re-evaluation in this field. Interested groups and individuals are studying, testing, and probing in an effort to provide direction and to enlighten the general public concerning the nature of the problems being faced.

The range of suggested solutions is wide. Some battle staunchly to hold to the traditional theologic position. No ground is given, and scientific findings produce no change in views. Thus, a recent publication, *Sex and the Church,* by the Missouri Synod of the Lutheran Church comments that "America is experiencing a moral breakdown which is doing deep damage to its children." The availability of contraceptives, lack of proper home guidance, the impact of two world wars, and the present imbalance between science and religion are cited as some of the factors contributing to this breakdown. To combat this trend, the writers hope for a return to traditional religious concepts: "Modern man needs desperately to regain the real meaning and purpose of sex in its religious and moral context as related to the divine institution of marriage. More than that, he needs to rediscover the meaning of life itself under God. This discovery cannot be fully made until God's Law breaks down indifference and irresponsibility, and the Holy Spirit through the Gospel gives repentance and faith and creates a new spiritual life. Christian character can be found only at the foot of the cross."

Others counsel a thorough revision in the direction of greater freedom in sexual practices. "All the realistic evidence points to the desirability not only of fully educating children about sex, but of making contraceptive and prophylactic information and equipment completely available to all persons who reach the age of possible fertility. . . . It is only because we keep rigidly reciting to ourselves the moral ditty about the catastrophic nature of premarital coitus that we cannot even clearly see, let alone do anything constructive about, our completely unnecessary, utterly idiotic premarital sexual morality."

Church leaders are concerned and their interest in re-examining the religious teaching and positions in matters of sex is a significant development. One outcome of this concern was the convening of the week-long North American Conference on Church and Family in May, 1961. Called by the Canadian Council of Churches and the National Council of Churches of Christ in the U.S.A., this conference brought together some 550 Protestant church leaders from the two countries. Meeting with them was a group of sociologic, medical, and psychologic specialists with research and service experiences in the field of marriage and sexual behavior.

The delegates reviewed the latest research findings[26] in regard to divorce, mixed marriages, remarriages, early marriages, teenage sex behavior, premarital pregnancies and forced marriages, masturbation, homosexuality, infidelity, and sterilization. They heard specialists say that it was no longer possible to frighten young people into conforming to conventional sexual standards. The day is past, they were told, when threats of negative consequences would hold young people (or people of any age for that matter) in line.

In the meantime, evidence is mounting to indicate that the motivating force in the matter of sexual behavior is not the overwhelming power of the sex drive or a mere matter of intellectual decision. The individual who feels he is successful, achieving, accepted, and appreciated—in short the person who has the sense of "going somewhere"—has no great difficulty in managing his sexual impulses in a socially acceptable way. The promiscuous person, the individual who is using sex exploitatively, is very likely seeking satisfactions through sex that he could not find through other more acceptable ways. Many of these individuals come from backgrounds filled with conflict, rejection, and failure.

A study[27] was made in 1943–44 at the San Francisco Psychiatric clinic of 287 promiscuous and 78 potentially promiscuous girls. These girls represented typical pickups and prostitutes. The purpose was to determine the kinds of families, the types of personalities, and other pertinent factors common to this group of girls.

The following paragraphs are taken from the report:

> Family disorganization was characteristic in the case histories. Approximately 40 percent of the patients' parents were married and living together, although among these many had had marital difficulties, including separations followed by reconciliations. Among 60 percent of the patients, parents were separated, divorced, or deceased. In many of these broken homes the parents had remarried one or more times. In a few instances the patients had no knowledge of their fathers, and illegitimacy of the patients was known or suspected. To this story of broken homes there was the sequel of placement in boarding schools, foster homes, or in the homes of relatives for varying periods of time. . . .

> Contrary to popular belief, no evidence was revealed to indicate that this problem is produced by above average sex drive. In fact, *the majority of habitually promiscuous patients used promiscuity in an attempt to meet other problems rather than in an attempt to secure sexual satisfaction.* . . .

A later investigation made by the Psychiatric Service of the San Francisco City Clinic scrutinized male promiscuity. A total of 255 men were included in this study.[28]

In discussing the motivation for habitual promiscuity in men the investigators say:

> Promiscuity . . . was revealed to be a problem in interpersonal relationships. The degree of [sexual] satisfaction experienced by the promiscuous men was greater than that experienced by the promiscuous women; however, it appeared that in many cases, as with the women, promiscuity was engaged in in an attempt to solve other problems. In nearly all cases this behavior appeared to be the result of conflicts, inadequacies, or disorganization within the personality. Incapacity for sustained love relationships or impairment of that capacity was revealed by almost every patient. Active hostility toward women was present in varying degrees among some of the men. . . .

> . . . no evidence could be secured that promiscuity was the result of greater than average sex drive. With the exception of two patients the men did not themselves offer this explanation, and in those two cases it appeared that this explanation was a rationalization offered to cover up difficulties in relationship to women and sexual conflicts. Neither clinical data nor Rorschach studies revealed greater than average sensuality.

Dr. Harold Greenwald, a psychiatrist, looked into the backgrounds and personality characteristics of call girls.[29] He noted in particular their impaired capacity to establish satisfactory interpersonal relationships. His subjects "felt the need of relationships so deeply that they frequently put up with a great deal of mistreatment and brutality rather than break them up."

This does not say that all persons who have been spared trials and tribulations of this nature will be sexually chaste and abstemious. But it does say that sexual control and direction would be a much simpler matter could children be reared in loving, stable homes, and in communities in which they found meaningful places as individuals of worth.

The American Social Health Association has conducted studies[30] of teen-age sex behavior designed to find the correlates of sexual behavior. One of these researchers, Dr. Martin Loeb, suggested three conclusions:

First, teen-agers who trust themselves and their ability to contribute to others and who have learned to rely on others socially and emotionally at least likely to be involved in irresponsible sexual activity. . . .

Second, teen-agers who have learned to be comfortable in their appropriate sex roles (boys who like being boys and wish to be men, and girls who like being girls and wish to be women) are least likely to be involved in activities leading to indiscriminate sexuality. . . .

Third, both boys and girls have a need to discuss serious problems with adults who they feel can be helpful—that is to say, trusted.

Clearly Loeb's conclusions have implications for social policy concerning sex. They suggest the need for quite a different approach from negative threats and imposition of irrational fears as a way of setting standards and ordering behavior. They would seem to support the framework which the writer used in his study of premarital intercourse as a possible beginning at the level of values, for values are apparently at the heart of any change. This framework is built about the idea that the essence of moral behavior rests in the kind of interpersonal relationships which men establish among themselves.

This point of view may be summarized as follows: Whenever a decision or choice is to be made concerning behavior, the moral decision will be the one which works toward the creation of trust, confidence, and integrity in relationships. It should increase the capacity of individuals to cooperate, and enhance the sense of self-respect in the individual. Acts which create distrust, suspicion, and misunderstanding, which build barriers and destroy integrity, are immoral. They decrease the individual's sense of self-respect, and rather than producing a capacity to work together they separate people and break down the capacity for communication.

This concept may be set up in chart form (see below).

There are two important provisos to this principle. One is that it is never, or practically never, enough to look upon a decision as involving only two persons. No two individuals can isolate themselves so completely that their decisions will have no meaning for the rest of society. This implies that we must seek interpersonal relationships which in the long run, rather than the short run, will make it possible for all persons, regardless of race, age, or sex, to work together in understanding and harmony. It may be easy for two individuals or a small group to build a sense of unity or cohesion but through a process which would seem to frustrate the long-run objective of establishing an ever-broadening sociality. Morally this is not defensible.

The second proviso is that an individual or a group must at times stand for principles which counter common practice because to espouse them promises in the long run to further out-reach and to dissolve barriers. Standing for principle may be at the expense of short–term relationships with one's social groups, friends, or relatives. Acting upon this proviso calls for courage and self-governorship.

This approach to moral judgment rests upon the fundamental assumption that man by nature is a social being. His basic satisfaction as an individual, in fact his very survival both as a person and as a species, depends upon the realization of a satisfying sociality. Unless this is realized, the pleasures and satisfactions resulting from the exercise of any particular capacity or appetite become meaningless. Without this sociality his personal potentialities cannot be realized and his individual satisfactions are lost.

It therefore follows that our first concern should be for helping man realize and experience his need and capacity for sociality. Upon this basis our code of moral conduct must rest. Morally our central concern must be for the development of effective interpersonal relationships. The crucial, overriding moral issue is not whether there should or should not be a certain pattern of sexual behavior. The issue is: *How may we use all of our capacities—intellectual, special talents, dexterity, physical prowess, sex, whatever—in the service of improved interpersonal relationships among all persons?*

BASIS FOR MORAL JUDGMENTS

Those actions, decisions, and attitudes are:

Right—Moral   Wrong—Immoral

which produce

Right—Moral	Wrong—Immoral
1. Increased capacity to trust people	1. Increased distrust of people
2. Greater integrity in relationship	2. Deceit and duplicity in relationships

3. Dissolution of barriers separating

4. Cooperative attitudes

5. Enhanced self-respect
6. General attitudes of faith and confidence in people
7. Fulfillment of individual potentialities and a zest for living

3. Barriers between persons and groups

4. Resistant, uncooperative attitudes

5. Diminished self-respect
6. Exploitative behavior toward others
7. Thwarted and dwarfed individual capacities and disillusionment

NOTES

[1] Evelyn M. Duvall and S. M. Duvall, *Sex Ways—In Fact and Faith* (New York: Association Press, 1961).

[2] Joseph Fletcher, "A Moral Philosophy of Sex," in *Sex and Religion Today,* Simon Doniger, ed. (New York: Association Press, 1953).

[3] David Riesman, Nathan Glazer, and Reuel Denney, *The Lonely Crowd* (New York: Doubleday & Company, 1955), Chap. 2.

[4] R. Freedman, *Family Planning, Sterility and Population Growth.*

[5] Oscar E. Feucht, *Sex and the Church* (St. Louis: Concordia Publishing House, 1961).

[6] I. Rubin "Sex Over 65," in Hugo Beigel, ed., *Advances in Sex Research* (New York: Harper & Row, 1963).

[7] Martha Wolfenstein, "The Emergence of Fun Morality," *Mass Leisure,* Eric Larrabee and Rolf Meyersohn, eds. (New York: The Free Press, 1960), pp. 86–96.

[8] Nelson Foote, "Sex as Play," *Social Problems* 1 (1964): 159.

[9] Lawrence K. Frank, *The Conduct of Sex* (New York: William Morrow, 1961), pp. 145–46.

[10] A. C. Kinsey, W. B. Pomeroy, and C. E. Martin *Sexual Behavior in the Human Male,* (Philadelphia: W. B. Saunders Company, 1948).

[11] A. C. Kinsey, W. B. Pomeroy, C. E. Martin, and P. H. Gebhard, *Sexual Behavior in the Human Female* (Philadelphia: W. B. Saunders Company, 1953).

[12] L. A. Kirkendall, *Sex Education as Human Relations* (Sweet Springs, Mo.: Roxbury Press, 1950).

[13] Walter Stokes, "Modern view on masturbation," *Sexology* 9 (April 1961), 2–5. See also Wardell B. Pomeroy, "Masturbation," Evelyn M. Duvall and Sylvanus Duvall, *op. cit.,* Chap. 10.

[14] Ibid. Dr. Frank in his writing makes a distinction between morals (rigid social code) and ethics.

[15] Ira Reiss, *Premarital Sex Standards in America* (New York: The Free Press, 1960).

[16] Lester A. Kirkendall, *Premarital Intercourse and Interpersonal Relationships* (New York: Julian Press, 1961).

[17] Adapted from Arthur E. Gravatt and L. A. Kirkendall, "Teen-Agers' Sex Attitudes and Behavior," in Evelyn M. Duvall and S. M. Duvall, eds., *op. cit.*

[18] G. P. Murdock, *Social Structure* (New York: The Macmillan Company, 1959).

[19] Irving B. Tebor, "Selected Attributes, Interpersonal Relationships and Aspects of Psychosexual Behavior of One Hundred College Freshman Virgin Men" (Ph.D. diss., Oregon State College, 1958).

[20] I. L. Reiss, "The double standard in premarital intercourse: a neglected concept," *Social Forces* 34 (1956), 224.

[21] E. W. Burgees and P. William, *Engagement and Marriage* (Philadelphia: Lippincott, 1953).

[22] Lester A. Kirkendall, "Sex Drive," in Albert Ellis and Albert Arbarbnel, eds., *The Encyclopedia of Sexual Behavior* (New York, Hawthorn Books, 1961), Vol. 2, pp. 939–48.

[23] Alan F. Guttmacher, "Abortions—Medical and Social Review," Evelyn M. Duvall and S. M. Duvall, eds., *op. cit.*

[24] Marvin C. Dubbé, "What teenagers can't tell parents and why," *Family Life Coordinator* 4 (1956), 3.

[25] Robert A. Harper, "Marriage counseling and the mores: a critique," *Marriage and Family Living* 21 (1959), 13.

[26] The research data on these subjects was summarized in Evelyn M. Duvall and S. M. Duvall, eds., *op. cit.* The proceedings of the conference are in *Foundations for Christian Family Policy*. This book can be ordered from the National Council of Churches, 475 Riverside Drive, New York, N.Y. 10027.

[27] Benno Safier, M.D., et al., *A Psychiatric Approach to the Treatment of Promiscuity* (New York: American Social Hygiene Association, 1949).

[28] Ernest G. Lion, et al., *An Experiment in the Psychiatric Treatment of Promiscuous Girls* (San Francisco, Calif.: City and County of San Francisco Department of Public Health 1945).

[29] H. Greenwald, *The Call Girl* (New York: Ballantine Books, 1958).

[30] M. B. Loeb, *Social Role and Sexual Identity in Adolescent Males* (New York: National Association of Social Workers, 1959).

SUGGESTED READINGS

Etzioni, A. "Toward a Theory of Societal Guidance," In *Societal Guidance*. Edited by S. Heidt and A. Etzioni. New York: Crowell 1969, pp. 7–32.

Gagnon, J. and Simon, W. "Prospects for Change in American Sexual Patterns." *Medical Aspects of Human Sexuality*. January 1970, pp. 100–117.

Lisewood, R. "Variety: The Spice of Marital Sex." *Medical Aspects of Human Sexuality* 3 (1969) no. 11, pp. 105–12.

Rogers, C. "Interpersonal Relationships: U.S.A. 2000." *Journal of Applied Behavioral Science* 4 (1968): 265–280.

Roy, R., and D., "Is Monogamy Outdated?" *The Humanist,* April 1970, pp. 19–26.

Specht, H. "Casework Practice and Social Policy Formation." *Social Work* 13 (1968): 42–53.

Epilogue

The Fable of the Restored Left Arm

Virginia M. Satir

Once upon a time thousands of years ago, a man was standing on a cliff, high above some jagged rocks below. It happened, as he was standing there, that another man passed by very close to him and accidentally bumped him.

Automatically, the first man's left arm swung out, knocking over the cliff the second man, who somersaulted and made loud and discordant symphony-like sounds as he went over. This had never been heard or seen before.

Some other people, who happened to be near enough to see, became excited with the movement and the sound and began emulating the first man. The rocks below were soon covered with the broken bodies of the people thrown over.

Other people saw this and said there was something wrong with what was going on, so a big investigation was held. All the experts came. It was a very short investigation because *it* was so obvious what the trouble was—THE LEFT ARM.

This required immediate action. A law was soon passed, forbidding anyone to expose his or her Left Arm, or to use it if necessary on any occasion except one hour on his or her birthday, and then only completely in private. Anyone caught exposing or using the Left Arm could be deported, beheaded, or imprisoned. The fact that there were millions of people whose Left Arms had never gotten them into any trouble made no difference. LEFT ARMS WERE DANGEROUS. Every care must be taken to avoid this danger.

This was going to be very hard because Left Arms are very handy to have around, especially if you want to lift anything. But people tried hard. After all, who wants to be deported, imprisoned, or beheaded? They covered their Left Arms very carefully. Only right arms could show. The fact that every left side of a person now had a peculiar hump was obvious to everyone, which, indeed, made them look very ugly. However, no one mentioned the hump or the ugliness except in very low whispers here and there; mostly it was indicated only in looks.

People did try. They walked sideways past each other, so the hump would not show so much. This helped a little.

They got busy building elaborate structures in their homes to hide from one another. After all, it was important to keep the Left Arm clean.

Of course, all of this was extremely difficult, especially at the beginning. People were always having the urge to straighten out their arms. It was very uncomfortable. Many, many persons lost their lives in these early days because they would not control themselves. Some few did manage. They used various means, one of which was to go about only when there were no other people. This was worrisome and not very reliable because one never knew who was going to be popping out of some doorway. People said that people were not friendly any more. They seemed suspicious of one another.

Things eased a little in the succeeding generations. They bound babies' Left Arms tightly to their bodies as soon as they were born. This way maybe babies would not know what they were missing, but they heard about it anyway from the whispers in the alleys from adults who did know.

What adults really wanted to do was to cut off the offending Left Arm, at birth but they could not quite bring themselves to do this. It seemed so inhuman. However, with some children, by the time they were twelve, the binding had worked so well that the Left Arm just fell off naturally. That was good. It left the hump, but it removed the temptation.

Most of the Left Arms, however, remained very small and shrivelled. (It takes a long time for the body to mutate such a big change.) No one knew for sure but there were stories that fingernails were growing on the Left Arms, and "they" said some would measure twenty feet if uncurled. "They" said that the weight of the fingernails was what made the hand so heavy, which was why the body was off balance. There were many other stories about the ugliness of the Left Arm. It was scary to think about. All the worst dreams were about Left Arms. Children were constantly warned about Left Arms from the cradle on up.

Of course, the backs of all people did become very crooked. One of their arms was used so much more. Everything one did had to be done by one hand. When the people played the game of "Catch the Greased Pig," which was *the* national game, it truly was a great accomplishment. There were very few winners. In fact, there was only one. They made a statute for him. This kept hope alive.

Back pains became very frequent, and of course there were many operations, but somehow that did not seem to help much. (The hump was considered normal, so no one ever thought of connecting that to back trouble.) Backs just kept getting more and more crooked, left arms smaller and smaller, and left sides humpier and humpier.

The research of that day, of course, corroborated what was going on.

One day, an especially daring man in his late 50s, who had had many questions, decided to take *a horrible risk*. He could see that society was falling apart. Something had to be done. He worked out a very secret plan to bring together a few trusted friends in a cave he had found far below the earth's surface, where he was sure to be safe.

After much humiliation, embarrassment, and anxiety, they opened up the dreaded subject of Left Arms. Then they began to look at them, and then TOUCH them. As this happened, the Left Arms had the experience of moving. Then the people noticed that they had strange reactions in the rest of their body which made them think that maybe there was a connection between their Left Arms and the rest of their body. Later on they even wondered about their Left Arms and friendliness.

Through many trials and tribulations, the small group met and experimented. They came up with the unmistakable conclusion that they *must* for survival's sake, change the law on Left Arms and restore the Left Arm to its rightful place. It was clear now that not only survival, but health and progress of the world depended upon making this change. This would be a big and dangerous job. Many feared that they would not live long enough to see it accomplished.

There were little breakthroughs here and there—enough to keep up hope. Now only a few of their number had found their way to jails.

Gradually new people who were considered trustworthy were added to the group. The news of what was going on leaked out and travelled swiftly through the underground. The movement had begun.

Many years later, one of "them," was elected governor, and to everyone's surprise, another was elected president. Lots of people thought that fraud was involved, but luckily, they lived in a democracy and people had voted by secret ballot.

After the elections, bigger and bigger changes came until one day it was possible for everyone to show their Left Arms openly, talk about them, and even admire them. There were even contests about who had the loveliest one.

People found out how easy it was to lift things with two arms, rather than one. Back troubles began disappearing. Eyesight got better because people did not have to walk sidewards anymore. You see, from so much sideways moving, the eyes had become very narrow and vision had become very distorted.

When people could see openly, the human body without the hump and the crooked back was truly beautiful.

People would often be heard to say afterwards, "Can you imagine that a long time ago in the dark ages, people thought Left Arms were dangerous!"

I don't think we are yet as far along as our fable, but we are going in that direction.

About the Editors

LeRoy G. Schultz received his B.S. and M.S.W. from Washington University. He is now Associate Professor of Social Work at the School of Social Work, West Virginia University where he is Chairman of the Social Policy and Services sequence. He formerly taught at the School of Social Work, University of Missouri. From 1957–1966 he was Assistant Director, Probation and Parole Division, St. Louis Circuit Courts and a member of the Governor's Citizens Committee on Delinquency and Crime, State of Missouri. He is a frequent contributor to legal, criminological and correctional journals and has been Editor of *Social Welfare in Appalachia* since 1969. He is presently a member of the Publications Committee, Council on Social Work Education.

Harvey L. Gochros is Professor of Social Work and Chairman of the Practice Sequence at the School of Social Work, West Virginia University, a Visiting Professor of Social Work at the University of Hawaii, and an Instructor in Continuing Education at Case Western Reserve University School of Applied Social Sciences. He was formerly Chief of Psychiatric Social Work at the Department of Psychiatry, University of Missouri at Columbia and was on the faculty of the School of Social Work and the Department of Community Health and Medical Practice at the University of Missouri. Dr. Gochros has been a family and marital counselor with social agencies in Denver, St. Paul, and New York City. He has conducted numerous classes for graduate students and workshops for practitioners on social work approaches to sexual problems. His articles on behavior modification and on social work education and practice with sexual problems have been published in several professional journals. He received his doctorate in social welfare from Columbia University.